P9-AOZ-486

SOUTH AFRICA
SOCIOLOGICAL PERSPECTIVES

SOUTH AFRICA:
SOCIOLOGICAL PERSPECTIVES

EDITED BY

HERIBERT ADAM

LONDON
OXFORD UNIVERSITY PRESS
NEW YORK   TORONTO   CAPE TOWN

1971

Oxford University Press, Ely House, London W. 1

GLASGOW NEW YORK TORONTO MELBOURNE WELLINGTON
CAPE TOWN SALISBURY IBADAN NAIROBI DAR ES SALAAM LUSAKA ADDIS ABABA
BOMBAY CALCUTTA MADRAS KARACHI LAHORE DACCA
KUALA LUMPUR SINGAPORE HONG KONG TOKYO

ISBN 0 19 215191 6

© Oxford University Press 1971

Printed in Great Britain by
Richard Clay (The Chaucer Press) Ltd
Bungay, Suffolk

CONTENTS

INTRODUCTION

There is no paucity of publications on South Africa. Most of them, however, amount to little more than a polemical denouncement of the Apartheid system. Instead of socio-economic analyses, confessions are offered as to how unprejudiced the authors are. Indignation about injustice or ironic comments by an enlightened liberalism over supposed paradoxes of an illiberal unenlightenment characterize these declamatory writings. The term 'tragedy' is the preferred category to come to grips with a conflict which is frequently viewed as a kind of natural destiny, taking its predetermined course. It seems doubtful whether such a perspective of unpolitical moralism is adequate for understanding an historical development, in which the South African race system represents neither a perverse exception nor the mere stupidity of late colonialists.

White South Africans (as well as Africans if they had the choice) act according to their perceived interests. For a sociological study, therefore, it appears appropriate to analyse the changing interest structures rather than to condemn their manifestations. Such an undertaking attempts to depart from mere expressions of moral disgust and tries instead to anchor racialism as well as protest against it into the structural conditions of the specific South African set-up. Its aim is thus to ground subjective responses and their institutionalized forms within the objective social forces which have given rise to them. Only such an analytical perspective can avoid the trap of wishful thinking and unrealistic assessments of power relations.

This effort to be 'objective' neither entails nor implies an emotional detachment on the part of the authors concerned. Far from being uncommitted to change, or detached from the experience of injustice, all the contributors to this volume share an essentially critical orientation towards Apartheid, although in various degrees and for different reasons. Within this framework they represent a variety of political outlooks, but have one quality in common: namely, professional expertise in the areas on which they write. With a few exceptions, all fifteen authors have widely published previously and gained international reputations in their respective research areas. They all have extensive personal experience of the South African situation, and some continue to teach in the country. Thirteen of the articles were specifically written for this volume and appear here for the first time; two contributions are reprints.

The words in the title 'Sociological Perspectives', despite the suggestion of disciplinary demarcation, aim at an approach which transcends traditional divisions in the social sciences. It rejects the compartmentalization of knowledge along narrowly defined disciplines in favour of an approach which includes all relevant perspectives in the investigation of complex social phenomena. Only six of the fifteen contributors can be termed professional sociologists; the others include two political scientists, two psychologists, two anthropologists, an economist, an historian, and a law professor. In utilizing this teamwork approach to a controversial topic, with representatives from several different disciplines, it is hoped that a more accurate analysis may be achieved than is possible through the efforts of one individual social scientist working within the confines of a singular theoretical perspective.

The selection of the topics aimed at a comprehensive coverage of most of the major social phenomena in the country in terms of their history, present functioning, and likely future development. Care has been taken by most contributors to discuss South African problems not in isolation as mere case studies, but within a comparative framework, thus deriving hypotheses on the basis of historical insights as well as familiarity with similar phenomena elsewhere. Such an approach sets the alleged uniqueness of the South African conflict in its proper perspective. The most important criterion for the selection of the topics was their theoretical and practical relevance for potential change. Instead of focusing on such ephemeral issues as tribal rituals, which have been the traditional concern of many anthropologists in South Africa, essays related to the position of the urban African under white domination or the rise of political movements were considered more worth while. Inevitably, however, many important themes (particularly in the realm of political economy) could not be dealt with in detail due to limitations of space.

Despite its emphasis on what are considered relevant issues, this collection is likely to be criticized from two opposing standpoints: on the one hand that it is not impartial enough, and on the other that it is mere academic theorizing and of little help in actually instrumenting change in Southern Africa. Indeed, this study was never intended to be a handbook for the politician. It does not offer suggestions or advice as to how desired goals might be efficiently achieved. What it presents is the effort of many scholars to analyse the complex dynamic of the South African social system in operation. Such an endeavour constitutes an indispensable prerequisite for any realistic policy of social change. If this collection functions as a reality principle in this respect, then critical theory has aided practice far more than mere indignation can ever hope to achieve.

The first three articles present an overall picture of South African developments from an historical perspective (Ngubane), a comparison with similar phenomena in other societies (Andreski), and a description of the three major types of racial segregation (van den Berghe). A brief outline of research done on race relations in South Africa (Mann) is followed by a recent survey on the white power-elite (Adam). Two articles analyse African nationalism (Carter, Meer). Problems of the urban African and his acculturation are investigated in the contributions by Hellmann and Mayer. Two studies deal with educational questions (Adam, Dickie-Clark). One author scrutinizes the legal system of control (Mathews). The socio-cultural background of Afrikaner nationalism is dealt with in articles by Ford and Doxey, the latter focusing in particular on the labour market. A more theoretical contribution concludes the volume: Danziger describes the changing legitimation of white power.

I am indebted to colleagues who contributed by writing articles specifically for this collection. I am also grateful for permission to reprint two pieces. Special mention must be made of the diligent proof-reading and suggestions offered by Sylvia Hale. Finally, I should like to thank the staff of the Political Science, Sociology and Anthropology Department of Simon Fraser University, especially Bonnie Braaten, who typed the manuscript with great care.

H. ADAM

CONTRIBUTORS

HERIBERT ADAM, a former associate of the Frankfurt Institute for Social Research, has done fieldwork in South Africa and taught at the University of Natal. He is at present Chairman of the Political Science, Sociology and Anthropology Department at Simon Fraser University in Vancouver, Canada. His publications include *Modernizing Racial Domination* (1971).

KOGILA ADAM teaches Sociology at Vancouver City College. During 1966 and 1967 she taught at the University College for Indians in Durban, South Africa.

STANISLAV ANDRESKI has taught at Rhodes, in Chile, and in Nigeria, and now heads the Department of Sociology at the University of Reading in England. *The African Predicament* is his latest book (1968). His earlier publications include *The Elements of Comparative Sociology* (1964), *Military Organization and Society* (1954), and *Parasitism and Subversion* (1966).

GWENDOLEN M. CARTER is Director of the Program of African Studies at Northwestern University. Her best-known publication is *The Politics of Inequality: South Africa since 1948* (1958).

KURT DANZIGER was Head of the Psychology Department at the University of Cape Town before coming to York University in Toronto. He has published numerous articles in professional journals.

H. F. DICKIE-CLARK is Head of the Sociology Department at the University of Natal in Durban, South Africa, and has published a study: *The Marginal Situation* (1966).

G. V. DOXEY teaches Economics at York University in Toronto and has published *The Industrial Colour Bar in South Africa* (1961).

RICHARD B. FORD is Associate Professor of History at Clark University in Worcester, Massachusetts. He has recently worked on an African curriculum for American high schools.

ELLEN HELLMANN is a South African anthropologist who is known for her studies of urban Africans and has edited the *Handbook on Race Relations in South Africa* (1949).

J. W. MANN is Head of the Psychology Department at the University of the Witwatersrand in Johannesburg. Most of his publications deal with race relations and other theoretical questions in social psychology.

A. S. MATHEWS is Head of the Law Department at the University of Natal in Durban. He has published (together with R. C. Albino) on the S.A. Detention Laws.

PHILIP MAYER is Head of the Anthropology Department at the University of Durham. His book, *Townsmen or Tribesmen* (1961), has become the classical study of acculturation and traditionalism in South Africa.

FATIMA MEER teaches Sociology at the University of Natal in Durban. She has published *Portrait of Indian South Africans* (1969) and *Apprenticeship of a Mahatma* (1970).

JORDAN K. NGUBANE, a journalist, was active in South Africa's Liberal Party before he went into exile. He has become widely known through his unorthodox book *An African Explains Apartheid* (1963). He was visiting lecturer at Howard University during the 1969–70 academic year.

PIERRE L. VAN DEN BERGHE is Professor of Sociology at the University of Washington in Seattle. His books on Africa include *Caneville* (1964), *South Africa: A Study in Conflict* (1965), *Africa: Social Problems of Change and Conflict* (1965), *Race and Racism* (1967), and *Race and Ethnicity* (1970).

I

JORDAN K. NGUBANE

SOUTH AFRICA'S RACE CRISIS: A CONFLICT OF MINDS

I

Most white South Africans elect to regard their country's colour crisis as a racial clash. This has obvious, interlocking advantages. It emotionalizes discussions of a problem which, in the best of situations, does not readily lend itself to objective treatment. This in turn often creates deadlocks which surrender the initiative to influence events to the advocates of Apartheid. The emphasis on race projects Apartheid as the unique solution to a unique problem. In this setting the search for alternatives becomes largely an irrelevant exercise.

In the present contribution, the race crisis is viewed as a conflict of minds; as a clash between two irreconcilable outlooks which, in important essentials, belong more or less to the same stream of civilization. One current in this stream works for the continuous extension of the area of liberty for the person while the other seeks to narrow it. The dominant current in the African community is the subject of this discussion.

In the three centuries of contact with the white man, the black South African evolved a syncretic culture with its own ideal of fulfilment and norms of thought, behaviour, and action. It also had its own political traditions and institutions. Over the generations it acquired an identity of its own—to which we shall come later. Apartheid seeks to destroy this identity. This will to destroy, and the African's resistance to it, constitute the core of South Africa's race problem. While colour and economic and political injustice feature prominently in the resulting clash, they are largely the visible forms in which the conflict of minds expresses itself.

The African's cultural pattern has its roots partly in the history of South Africa during the last three hundred years and partly in the philosophy by which he understood life and reality.

Jan van Riebeeck landed at the Cape of Good Hope in 1652 to establish a victualling station for ships of the Dutch East India Company plying between Europe and the East. He brought along with him a group of settlers. Contrary to popular belief he did not find the Cape uninhabited. There lived around it an African people whom he christened the Hottentots from the way he understood them to speak. These Africans were cattle farmers and roamed the Cape flats grazing their herds. The arrival of the white man among them started a chain of reactions which continues to this day to influence the relations between black and white.

In the Europe from which the settlers came, the prevailing notions of citizenship, justice, and morality were very much unlike those of the Hottentot. Most Europeans of that era still seriously associated governmental power with absolutism. The blood of martyrs killed in the Inquisition had hardly dried in the market-places of some Western countries, and the tragedies resulting from this blot on Christian civilization were almost living experiences to some of the settlers. Predestination taught that certain people were created for particular destinies in life, and hence the fact that the white man had technological superiority or that the man of colour was a slave meant simply that the Christian God had created the white man for a higher destiny and the African for a lower one. Although this God was virtue infinitized, he was also harsh, uncompromising, and jealous; to fear and emulate him was life's highest purpose.

In the Cape environment the settlers formed a minority group vulnerable to dangers initially from the Africans, which over time fostered an emphasis on the value of group consciousness as a guarantee of survival.

From the eighteenth century onwards, increasing numbers of settlers crossed the boundaries of the Company's area of jurisdiction and established themselves largely as farming groups. During the Napoleonic Wars some of these communities declared their independence from Holland and proclaimed their own short-lived republics. In the interior, the Afrikaners—who called themselves first the Trekboers and later the Boers—

developed a ruggedness and love of independence which are among their chief virtues. Yet this isolation from contact with the mainstream of civilization also had the effect of retarding spiritual development and stunting intellectual growth. They were cut off from the humanistic and other influences which liberalized attitudes in Europe, particularly with regard to coloured peoples. This closure is spectacularly revealed in the events following the emancipation of the slaves and the Great Trek from the Cape in 1837. In the newly established Afrikaner republics, the indigenous Africans were openly discriminated against and denied any recognition as citizens.

The factors listed above enhanced the value of the group at the expense of the individual; promoting a pattern of thought, belief, and behaviour which saw the truth, reality, men, and events from the perspective only of the survival of the group. Apartheid is the political expression of this *morality of survival*.

II

After the expiration of their contracts at the Cape, the majority of settlers did not return to Europe, but remained to establish themselves as farmers. Immigrants came in to swell their numbers, and this marked an important turning-point in the relations between black and white. The free farmers needed more land, and this forced them to push increasing numbers of Hottentots from their pastures. There were not enough labourers to work the farms; the slaves from the Far East were inadequate for the needs of an expanding economy; and hence they looked towards indigenous African labour. The Hottentots led a largely nomadic life as herdsmen, and partly as a result, their social and political institutions were less developed than those of Africans in the interior such as the Nguni and the Sotho. They could offer little resistance to the encroachment of the whites. At first they showed little enthusiasm for giving up their nomadic life to work in white homes or on the farms. But as their herds were reduced by wars with the white man, by trade, and by disease, impoverishment set in. By the end of the seventeenth century they had already started entering the white areas in search of jobs.

The Hottentot who left his people to sell his labour for a cash wage in the white areas started a cultural and economic revolution which is one of the main keys to the understanding of South Africa's race problem. He exposed himself to a new and different life. In the white man's world he acquired strange habits of thinking and living. The influence of European food, hygiene, clothes, speech, sex life, and general mode of behaviour all combined to transform him into a new type of African. He experienced a new sense of freedom and responsibility. He became aware of his potential for being better in a new direction. He appreciated his individuality in an altogether different way. He discovered that he could determine his personal destiny without the help of the tribal group. Life produced new challenges wherever he turned.

When he returned to his people, it was as a stranger. He found their customs and taboos narrow and limiting. They frustrated the free development of his newly awakened personality. He realized that he could not make the best possible use of his life within the fixed horizons of the tribe. For its part, the tribe often regarded him with suspicion. He was either the corrupting influence from the white side or the agent of the white man in its midst.

In time economic and social pressures combined to force him out of the tribe. He could not go and live among the white people or be swallowed up by them; he was a pagan, illiterate, with a different colour and language and culture. The whites feared that if they integrated him into their life he would in time dilute their blood, corrupt their culture, and finally destroy them as an ethnic group along with their achievements. Only a few Hottentots intermarried with the whites. Repudiated thus by his tribe on the one hand and the white people on the other, he gradually settled down in shanty-towns on the periphery of white towns and villages. There, he started creating for himself a new social world somewhere between the two racio-cultural blocs which always had the potential to crush him if they wanted to. Survival for him in this setting lay in a realistic and non-violent balancing of his relations with both sides.

To become an efficient worker he had to adopt at least some of the ways of the white man, and he blended these with what he had brought along from the tribe. A syncretic culture emerged which was distinctly his. This pattern, crude and simple as it was, was the creation of his mind; the unique product of his environment and experience, and he could enlarge his personality freely within it. It was based on realistic adaptations to the demands of having to survive between the suspicion of the tribe and the contempt of the white man. The fact that it had its roots in the worlds of the tribe and the whites transformed him into a new person in history: the New African. For his culture to survive there had to be permanent contact with its sources of inspiration. The tribe could not be destroyed for he derived his physical being from it. Conversely, the white man had to belong permanently to South Africa if the shanty-towns were to survive and with them the new culture. If he pulled out, the tribe could descend on the shanty-towns, set them on fire, and kill their inhabitants. From this circumstance was to develop part of the New African's commitment to non-racialism.

For his part, the white man wanted the African at a convenient distance from his home or town. The black servants could enter the white areas by day to work, and return to the shanty-towns when the sun set. The two worlds would keep apart and develop along separate lines.

The whites did not have a very high opinion of the culture of the shanty-towns. The type of person it was producing, in the absence of schools and other organized civilizing agencies, was often a confused and sometimes dangerous mixture of un-reconciled cultural ingredients. He was, however, better than the tribesman in that he did a better job when he worked. The whites referred contemptuously to the shanty-town communities as *die oorlamse volk*—the handy people. The Nguni lingual group (Zulu and Xhosa) Africanized the adjective into *amahumusha*. This was the name by which the early urban workers came to be known by the tribe.

A culture born of economic necessity naturally saw in materialistic fulfilment life's highest purpose. To grow and enrich itself it had to borrow freely and blend whatever it procured. Eclecticism came to be another of its distinguishing features. In order to borrow successfully, the people from whom the borrowing was done could not be enemies; they had to be made to want to give wherever possible. Besides, they had the

B

guns. Rejection of the paramountcy of the group and emphasis on the importance of the individual characterized the new cultural pattern. Thus, from the very beginning of things, the imperatives of cultural, economic, and physical survival dictated that the earliest workers should be individualistic, materialistic, eclectic, and free of race consciousness.

At first the urban workers in every African community were always a minority while the majority belonged to the tribe. If they were not a numerical minority *vis-à-vis* the white man, they were certainly a military and economic one. This position of weakness between the two powerful blocs enjoined on them the need to develop a deep-rooted tradition of realism.

III

Movement into the interior brought the white man into contact with the Xhosa, Sotho, and Zulu sections of the African people. This produced results which, in important essentials, were similar to those noted among the Hottentots. There were first the wars, and then the peace and the economic pressures which produced the Nguni–Sotho version of the culture of the shanty-towns.

But before we get to this, let us follow a process which took place in the rural areas of the Western Cape and which complemented the urban revolution in the life of the Hottentots. Here, a ferment had begun from about the middle of the eighteenth century producing changes which corresponded to what was happening in the shanty-towns. Christianity had been introduced by the whites to the Hottentots. It taught that the individual's life could be modelled according to an objective ideal; that it could be perfected if that was desired. To do this successfully, the person's first loyalty had to be to Christ. The individual had an almost unlimited potential for being better, for achieving. These teachings awakened startling evaluations in the self-perception of the tribesman. If he was the breath of God and the shaper of his personal destiny, why did he have to suffer so much? If final fulfilment could be in perfection and eternal bliss, in something he could attain without the help of the tribe and its taboos, what need had he to bother about conforming to its dictates?

The tribe as a whole frowned heavily on these revolutionary teachings, and some of the missionaries were compelled to establish reserves where the converts could lead Christian lives away from their pagan brothers. In these, as had happened in the urban areas, the Africans were not integrated in the life of the whites. The missionary was a teacher and not a social equal. The converts accepted the Word and the new life that came with it, but they could not, at the same time, abandon all of the cultural traditions they had brought along from the tribe. As had happened in the shanty-towns, they set about evolving a cultural pattern based on borrowings from both the tribal and white sides. This is dealt with at length below, in the examination of its evolution among the Nguni–Sotho Africans.

IV

The Nguni and Sotho Africans were cattle-breeders and tillers of the soil. They had established kingdoms and set up stable governments before the white man reached them. Their way of life was based on what we shall, for lack of a better description, call the *Sudic* evaluation of the human personality. The word 'Sudic' describes the black- or brown-skinned peoples with kinky hair of Sub-Sahara and embraces present or partial or past commitment to an ancient cultural pattern which seems to have thrived somewhere between the Niger and the Nile about a thousand or more years before Christ. Basil Davidson has said of the 'Sudic' people:

These were pioneering peoples. They tilled where none had tilled before. They mined where there was none to show them how. They discovered a valuable pharmacopoeia. They were skilful in terraced irrigation and the conservation of soil on steep hillsides. They built new and complex social systems. They transformed whatever they could borrow from other and technologically more advanced social systems to the north, added and adapted and experienced and invented until in the course of time they acquired a range of technique and mastery of art, a philosophy and attitude and temperament and religion that were unique to themselves, and make the 'negroness', the negritude, that they have today.

The word 'Sudic' is derived from *sudd*, the Arabic for the

vegetable matter which is said to have drifted from the marsh-lands where the Nile had some of its sources. The root-word has been chosen for its associations. The early 'Sudic' people seem to have emerged into history from somewhere in this region. Their Zulu-speaking descendants believed that creation began in the marshlands of the north. The first human being, then a spirit-form, was incarnated within a cleft reed in a prehistoric marshland and emerged from it in his present physical form. That part of Africa—Sub-Sahara—which is inhabited by the des-cendants of the ancient 'Sudics' will be referred to as the *Sudant*.

This nomenclature has obvious advantages. It is a convenient description of the dark-skinned peoples of Sub-Sahara taken broadly—and only broadly—as an entity. It distinguishes them from the Arab African. Their past, present, or partial commit-ment to the 'Sudic Ideal'—their philosophy and religion—developed in them feelings and responses which often suggest derivation from a common tradition. The 'Sudics' and their descendants evolved parallel or identical customs, laws, and social or political institutions which mark them out as people who, at some time in history, might have embraced a pattern of culture with many things in common. One might speak of 'the Sudant' in the same way as one speaks of the Orient and the Occident.

In time some of the 'Sudic' people or their descendants migrated from their homelands and scattered towards the west, the east, and the south of the continent. Many of them preserved, with varying degrees of success, some traditions or modifications of the philosophy which had given meaning to their ancestors' lives. This philosophy developed in the wanderers a dynamic of discovery and integration, a spirit of adventure and daring, an ability to synthesize experiences and ideas, and a will to survive which saw them through the diaspora, slavery, and colonial rule to the moment of rebirth into freedom.

We do not as yet know as much about these remarkable ancestors of the so-called 'Negro' as we should. But tradition, particularly in Southern Africa, suggests that the 'Sudic Ideal' was characterized largely by its evaluation of the individual. It regarded him as the incarnation of an immortal spirit-form; an ancestral spirit clothed in flesh and therefore sacred. The spirit-form was the individualization of a consciousness which activated creation. The person was the equal of his neighbour because ultimately both were spirit-forms. The individual was the central figure in creation.

To the Zulu, whose understanding of the 'Sudic Ideal' has been followed in this discussion, evil did not have an extraneous source, such as the Satan of Christianity, from which it issued to corrupt the person. It was one of the qualities of being, a product of the individual mind. Fulfilment for the person was in making the best possible use of his life as a member of a corporate society: the community of the living and the 'dead'.

Since the consciousness lived, it was continually in motion, fulfilling itself in an infinity of ways through all its individualizations—from the tiniest grain of sand through the person to the galactic system. The countless movements of creation were but variations of the single cosmic motion, for an infinite consciousness which was a cosmic unity could have only one movement, even though it might appear to send its individualizations revolving in different directions. All the movements conformed to a single pattern of rhythm and produced what the Negro poet Aimé Césaire calls 'the harmony of creation'. When the trunk of a tree was shaken, the branches and leaves seemed to move in different directions. But these movements were responses by the individual parts of the tree to the same force. In this order of unity there could be no relationship of 'otherness' between the whole and its parts or between one individualization and another. Identification of the person with his neighbour was the highest virtue.

The Zulu lawgivers down the ages believed that the person and the family had creative potentials which were unique to them. The person produced the idea by which he changed his environment, and the family produced him. These reformers concentrated on making the family a strong, well-organized, and efficient microcosm whose primary functions were to produce the individual, to equip him for the task of making the best possible use of his life, and to protect him and help him move towards his moment of fulfilment.

In this person-centred order, the government was recognized as an organic and dynamic tool evolved to serve the ends of the community, the family, and the person. It derived its value from the security of the citizen, the efficacy of the family, and the strength of the state. It grew or stagnated in response to the demands and capabilities of the person and the family.

Unlike the person and the family, the government did not have a soul. Political power could not be concentrated in it. It lay in families and flowed from these peripheral sources to the centre. This is the rock on which communism has bruised its nose in many parts of Africa. An ancient principle of government stated: *Inkosi yinkosi ngabantu*. Legally and literally this meant, 'The king rules by the will of the people.' No matter how benevolent the government, it was not an end in itself. If it imposed its oppressive rule over the citizen his right to revolt was recognized. Zulu history has a whole galaxy of gifted rebels. But as tyrants, ancient and modern, have never regarded tolerance as a political virtue, some Zulu rebels were murdered and others forced to flee their country. When the great Shaka arrogated absolute power to himself and attempted to set himself up as master of all the Zulus, they murdered him.

A synthesis of ideas took place when the missionaries preached among the Nguni–Sotho Africans which altered the relationship between the West and black South Africa. From a situation of tutor and taught, with time the two became somewhat uneasy co-partners in a deepening appreciation of the worth of the individual. The pagan humanism of the 'Sudic Ideal' combined with humanistic influences in Christianity to produce an enlargement of the personality and a depth of tolerance in the African community which worked for the continuous extension of the area of freedom for the person. The marriage of the two humanisms aligned the African's syncretic culture with that tradition in the West which regarded the individual as a sacred end in himself and which sought to widen the area of liberty for him. It was not a coincidence that the syncretic culture assumed the character of a liberating influence or that it identified itself with Western humanistic influences.

Defeat on the battlefield weakened the African's commitment to the 'Sudic Ideal'. He became aware of a greater power than the ancestral spirit, which did not want him to sacrifice beasts to it. In any case a refugee could not have had many of them. It merely wanted his soul reformed. The white missionaries called it God. Some Africans liked it.

Where the tribe was already battling for survival against the armed might and initiative of the white man, emphasis on freedom for the individual, on his unconditional loyalty to God and not to his king and country, and on the uselessness of the earthly group for purposes of salvation, all threatened the discipline and the unity of the community. The tribe knew of only one corrective for treason. Numbers of early Christians were murdered to stem the tide of 'cultural treachery'. Very many others fled—as the Inanda community did in the land of the Zulus—from their ancestral homes to settle in mission stations or reserves where, as in the shanty-towns, they began creating for themselves the world after their design and evolved a syncretic culture based, like the urban pattern, on borrowings from both sides of the colour line.

Among the Nguni–Sotho Africans the mission culture always differed from its shanty-town counterpart in two major respects. Content was given to it by a set of clearly defined moral and theological ideals and not economic urges. Secondly, the tribe had never really taken up arms against *amahumusha*. At worst it had despised and dismissed them as the degenerates who crawled on their bellies, as the saying went, to lick the spittle of the white man. On the other hand, it had actually killed numbers of converts and had forced many of them to turn their backs permanently on it. This repudiation was final and irrevocable. The break between the tribe and the converts was complete.

The religious refugees had been forced to throw themselves into the hands of the white man—the missionary—for protection. In that situation race had had to lose all its meaning for them. Like *amahumusha* the converts realized that non-racialism was one of their guarantees of survival.

The tribe was disturbed by these splits. The emergence of *amahumusha* and the converts was a revolt in its ranks. Both the townward trend and the acceptance of Christianity constituted a challenge which weakened it. It replied by giving the rebels distinguishing labels which would make them readily identifiable as enemies. It had already called the townsmen *amahumusha* and had evolved patterns of behaviour which put them in their place. It referred to the converts as *amakholwa* (the believers) and reserved to itself the title of *abantu basemakhaya* (the people who belong to where the homes are).

Contact with the white man thus split the African people into three groups, each one of which had outlooks and attitudes which distinguished it from the others. The tribesman, working against the background of defeat and no cultural benefits from the white side, preferred an heroic stance and hoped, to a greater or lesser degree, for an ultimate appointment on the battlefield which would push the white man into the sea and restore to the Africans their land and freedom. History has in some ways modified the angularity of this approach. The modern heroicist insists on asserting African initiatives as the dominant influence in South African national life.

The mission African laboured for a society made up of like-minded and like-spirited equals in a state where race was no longer a factor of political significance. He had a passionate hatred for violence and relied heavily on peaceful methods, diplomacy, and appeals to morality and reason in his campaigns to reform South African society.

The segment descended from the early urban workers was concerned with the colour bar not so much as a moral evil, as the mission people were, than as the factor behind the Pass Laws, low wages, and poor working and living conditions for the black man. Its preference for realism in a community with a schistose mind made its behaviour-patterns curiously unpredictable. In the days when the idealistic moderates from the mission stations dominated African politics, the urban proletariat was all for non-violence, constitutional methods, and collaboration across the colour line. When the idealists changed their tune and plumped for passive resistance, the urban locations distinguished themselves and sent thousands of volunteers to jail, in addition to supporting their families. In the early 1960s the heroic Pan-Africanists called for 'positive action' against race oppression. Sharpeville occurred, to be avenged by the emergence of Poqo (the terroristic offshoot of the Pan-Africanists), which was murderously anti-white. Poqo made its most spectacular demonstration of strength in the urban area of Paarl, in the Cape.

A warning must be given against reading too much into the unpredictability. The urban African is exposed to the harshest operations of the race laws. As a result he is more sensitive to challenges against them. If the idealists promise relief, he rallies to their banner. If they fail and the heroicists offer something better, he chooses to go with them.

The unpredictability of the urban mind sometimes produced ugly situations. In January 1949 the predominantly Zulu-speaking Africans of Durban suddenly and without warning rose against the Indian community in the city and murdered men, women, and children and burned down hundreds of their homes. There certainly was a lot of ill-feeling between the African workers and traders on the one hand and their Indian opposites. The African workers did not like Indian competition for jobs. The African traders said the Indian traders used unfair means in driving the African out of business. An unplanned incident in the centre of the city caused what should, in normal circumstances, have been a free-for-all fight and not much more. The heroic tribesmen, employed in large numbers as stevedores at the Point, heard of the clash between the Africans and the Indians and decided their hour to strike had come. They sallied by night into Indian suburbs and left behind death and destruction. The initial reaction of the townsmen ranged from active support to indifference. My house at Inanda was nearly burned down by angry Africans when I protested against what was being done to the Indian minority.

The differences in cultural backgrounds constituted a threat and a challenge to the New African. If allowed to find their own forms of political expression they would generate conflicts and tensions which would permanently incapacitate the community for a successful revolt against white supremacy.

In summary, the developments traced above and the problems and dangers faced produced norms of thinking and behaviour in the New African which we shall call the *morality of fulfilment*.

South Africa's race problem may be seen also as a conflict between two moralities: that of fulfilment, which is historically committed to freedom, and that of survival, which upholds the supremacy of the white skin. The group-consciousness and intolerance of the latter morality single it out as belonging primarily to that side in the West which attached maximum importance to the group and sought to narrow down the area of freedom for the person.

The policy of Apartheid, promoted by this morality, is trying to reverse the historical processes set in motion by the coming of the European to South Africa. Inherent in this process are the awakening of the Africans into a new economic destiny, the rise of the Coloured or mixed community produced from the purely physical encounter between black and white, and the emergence of a syncretic culture which, while African in origin, is Western in orientation. These changes cannot be reversed without grave danger to the polity as a whole, but the morality underlying Apartheid is too concerned with considerations of Afrikaner survival and dominance for the real implications of this fact to be grasped. Until very recently the Afrikaner experience did not have a real tradition of liberal thinking on the race question. For a long time it gave the impression that it thrived on punishing a person for being the child of his parents. It used the noun 'humanist' as a swearword and on the specific issue of race relations between black and white it worked for limiting the African's freedom and for reducing, wherever possible, his potential to be a better person.

V

Industrialization became the epochal magnet which drew large numbers of people into the towns in search of employment. Coming from widely different backgrounds *amahumusha*, *amakholwa*, and *abantu basemakhaya* did not find it easy to live together in the urban shanty-towns—Nancefield and Sophiatown in Johannesburg and Korsten in Port Elizabeth were some of the most famous. The townsman already knew the ways of the white people, but neither the converts nor the tribesmen liked him, although for different reasons. The former hated his materialistic outlook while the latter thought him a cheat who had sold his soul to the uglier side of the whites.

Economic factors, the race laws, the location system, and the police made no distinction between one cultural or lingual group and the other. The people involved were all black and were treated alike. This turned out to be a blessing in disguise. It worked against each group seeking its own forms of political expression and in that way adding to the differences which already split the African community.

Police pressure, economic exploitation, and the race laws created the need for meaningful political unity. This was during the second half of the last century. At the time the African did not have a force in his community which would be strong enough to override the lingual and cultural differences and move all sides towards political co-operation. The Church entered this situation and moved events towards cultural unity. It invited the converts from all lingual and cultural groups to worship together. It pioneered in the establishment of schools and admitted into them children with all sorts of backgrounds, broke down their prejudices, and gave them a uniform outlook on life. The end-product was a citizen who was no longer handicapped by lingual or tribal loyalties and prejudices. Fulfilment for him came to be, first, in identifying himself with those Africans outside his own lingual group who had evolved their equivalents of his new cultural pattern and, secondly, in achieving according to norms and criteria which had universal acceptance. He was made to feel that he was heir not only to his own people's attainments but also to a richly variegated past which was made up of the achievements of the various African peoples taken as an historical unity because of their experience of contact with the white man. His people's history became a part of the history of a larger African family. The link with the Hottentot was woven into the historical experience of the Xhosas, Zulus, and Basotho. The chain of continuity from 1652 was preserved by the similar challenges faced and identical responses. In short, the product of the schools in the towns ceased to be narrowly Zulu, Xhosa, or Sotho; he was proud to know himself as the African.

The resulting widening of horizons sharpened the desire for a more satisfying form of political collaboration. The need for co-ordinated political responses had been stimulated by fears that some of the whites were thinking of a united front against the African. The suspicion of white intentions had been so great, particularly when the white-led churches became a unifying influence, that some of the nationally-minded Africans broke away from them to form what is today known as the Separatist Movement; that is, churches not led by the whites.

The generation which emerged from the mission and town schools grew up with a new sense of nationhood. This brought *amahumusha* and *amakholwa* together. They gradually merged their cultural experiences to produce a synthesis which blended the traditions of the shanty-towns and the mission stations. New borrowings were made from the white side and, to a larger extent, the tribal. The final pattern which emerged had almost no parallel in English-speaking 'Sudic' Africa. Characteristically, the tribe called it *isidolobha*, the culture of the towns (from Dutch: *dorp* = town).

The new cultural pattern was unique in a number of ways, but one aspect deserves special attention here: while the cultures of the tribe, the shanty-towns, and the mission stations each produced a mind orientated in a single direction, the urban synthesis gave the African a composite or schistose mind which would, in one mood, think on the heroic plane and, in others, on the idealistic or realistic. If need arose, it could combine all three approaches.

Today, one does not need to have come from the tribe to be heroic in outlook or to hail from the mission station or the urban areas to be idealistic or realistic respectively. *Isidolobha's* schistose nature enables one to see events from one perspective or the other. Robert Mangaliso Sobukwe, the once jailed leader of the Pan-Africanist Congress, comes from a largely proletarian and peasant background but is the principal spokesman of contemporary heroicism.

The schistose mind has its strong and weak points. It militates against collective group reaction, almost in any crisis. That forced Poqo to kill probably more Africans than it did whites. The murdered Africans were unyielding opponents of terrorism or racism or violence. The new mind can be said to have a built-in objectivity which is one of the glimmers of hope in a situation of deepening tragedy.

At the same time the schistose mind is a distinct handicap in a crisis involving moral, ethnic, and political issues. It does not move swiftly enough to the point of agreement and co-ordinated action. Some of the defeats the morality of fulfilment has suffered can be explained on this score. But then, the African is not in bad company in this regard. Democracy thrashes issues out before a decision.

VI

One of the most important turning-points in the history of the African's syncretic culture was the decision by the whites, during the first decade of the present century, to establish the Union of South Africa. The leaders of the New African saw in this a challenge to *isidolobha*, the morality of fulfilment, and African unity. They viewed Union as an attempt by the whites to gang up against the man of colour. They feared that the whites would establish a closed ethnic state in which the white skin would be the key to opportunity. In such a society the white man would be the permanent master and the African the slave for ever, and an irremovable ceiling would be established beyond which the African would not be allowed to make better use of his life. The leaders regarded this as reflecting the moral and spiritual retardation from the days of isolation and slavery; they put their heads together and called a conference of representative Africans— including the tribal chiefs.

This gathering met in Bloemfontein in 1912 and occupies a place of its own in the annals of the New African. It was an attempt on the part of the leaders of the New African to reconcile the three moods of their people for the purpose of translating cultural unity into co-ordinated political action. The New African asserted his initiatives successfully in the conference and established himself as the unquestioned leader of the community. The conference, which was dominated by the townsmen and mission personalities, avoided a racial reaction to the race provocation behind Union. They elected to regard the colour conflict as a clash of irreconcilable values.

The delegates frowned heavily on violence and chose to use diplomatic and other peaceful pressures to appeal to the conscience of the whites or to split them. They sought to align progressive humanity with their side against the white supremacists. Above all, they defined the type of society which would accord best with the morality of fulfilment. They wanted South Africa to be an open, non-racial state in which the person would be free and able to make the best possible use of his life regardless of race or colour. As was to be expected, the delegates preferred peaceful methods to buy the time they needed to consolidate political unity and awaken the world to the dangers of racism. The African National Congress was established at this conference.

The decision to buy time is of particular significance. In the first fifty years after Union it did not affect the relations between black and white very deeply. But by the early 1960s it had scored some victories. It had enabled the African community to internationalize the colour crisis, brought about the diplomatic isolation of the Apartheid regime, and, internally, divided the white community on the race issue. These gains are poor consolation against Apartheid's excesses of violence in Sharpeville and elsewhere, the hanging of political prisoners, the people exiled or thrown into jail or who lost their freedom in other ways, and the Draconian laws which have since made South Africa a typical police state in everything but name—in so far as the African is concerned.

If the developments just referred to represent a catastrophic defeat at present for the morality of fulfilment, indications are not lacking which point to future situations of conflict. One of the common factors in the nationalism of the African and the Afrikaner today is the ground both have covered in moving towards the extreme right. Oppressive legislation provokes increasingly militant reactions from the African and makes heroic policies more attractive. This has forced both sides into a disturbingly vicious circle in which the intransigence of the one goads the other into taking up positions of corresponding extremism. The present lull is but a phase in a process which moves in predictable cycles.

The African's immediate reaction to Sharpeville has been to retreat from the political fight for the present in order to lick his wounds in his locations and reserves. The Government has seized on his defeat to execute some of its programmes of re-tribalization. Some people fear that one day the African will decide to come to terms with the inevitable and accept Apartheid. His repudiation of the whites, which would follow, would isolate the few liberal-minded whites and leave the race problem defined purely in terms of black and white. In that setting the white liberal is likely to find himself forced to fight with the Apartheid side to defend himself, his family, and the white skin. This is precisely one of the goals of the Apartheid regime.

While the prospect of a straightforward colour clash must not be ruled out, a distinction should always be made between adjusting to political realities and a cultural revolution. Re-tribalization seems probable. If it comes, the re-tribalized African might develop an exaggerated loyalty to his language group and possibly narrow his political horizons. If he does that, dangerous tensions and conflicts will develop in his own community. But this is not the point aimed at. Whether he liked it or not, he would move to fulfilment in the Bantustans within the framework of *isidolobha*. There is now no such thing as tribal culture in South Africa. Whatever passes for it represents the last remains of a way of life which lost its meaning under the impacts of conquest, education, and industrialization. The last three factors, incidentally, produced *isidolobha*. Their growth and strength reinforce it. There seems no possibility that the advocates of Apartheid might one day decide to do without them.

For the morality of survival to persuade the re-tribalized African to abandon *isidolobha*, it would have to bring about a cultural revolution; to offer him something more attractive and tangible than the semi-freedom the Transkei enjoys. Unfortunately for it, it lacks the moral and spiritual resources which would embolden it to give real freedom and economic independence to the Bantustans.

Real freedom would, among other things, produce sovereign independent African states with direct access to the sea. The possible transportation of arms over the territory of these maritime countries would threaten to alter the present balance of racial forces in South Africa. One finds it extremely difficult to imagine how any advocate of Apartheid would, in all his senses, encourage this sort of thing.

One's doubts here are reinforced by Apartheid's performance. In the twenty years that it has been in power, not one sovereign independent Bantustan has been established. The much-publicized Transkei is not much more than a South African colony with limited powers of local government. Its capital, Umtata, has separate residential areas for black and white. Pretoria controls the police and the courts of the land.

Britain and France have, during the last twenty years, freed millions of Africans, very many of whom admit that they were less advanced educationally and economically than the black

South African when they got their independence. Pretoria itself boasts that the Africans of the Republic are more advanced, as a group, than all 'Sudic' communities on the continent. In spite of this the Government cannot trust them with independence. All this reduces Apartheid's promises on the Bantustans to a gigantic and tragic bluff.

The point being emphasized is that while re-tribalization might succeed, the attempt to deculturate the New African in independent Bantustans might produce unexpected results. Apartheid's inability to give the African a satisfying form of fulfilment will continue to force him to recognize Free Africa and that section of mankind which opposes racism as together constituting the world to which he belongs and within which he can feel wanted. This and Apartheid's attitude to the man of colour seem certain to produce a new synthesis of political experiences in the 'independent' Bantustans. Just as cultural unity led to political unity last century, so is *isidolobha* almost certain to produce some form of political collaboration among the free peoples of the former High Commission Territories (which are now Botswana, Lesotho, and Swaziland) and the 'independent' citizens of the Transkei and other possible Bantustans. The main stimulus which will move events in this direction is, of course, the fact that Apartheid constitutes a standing affront to every person of African descent. Already, there is talk in some of the former High Commission Territories of a confederation of the independent black states of South Africa. Such a union would not be the sort of thing Pretoria would like on the Republic's borders.

One must guard against being too optimistic about the capacity of the African states to alter the course of events in South Africa. The former High Commission Territories are too badly placed geographically and economically to want a collision with South Africa in conditions where she could destroy them as viable states. Some of the Bantustans are in a better position here. They would have access to the sea and direct communication with the rest of the world. For some time to come, however, not even these will be ready for a show-down with Apartheid.

The point made is that new situations of conflict are developing and that these might be dangerous if Maoist China does not abandon her dreams of leading the non-white peoples of the world. There is no real external reason why she should be in a hurry to give up her aspirations on this plane. The newly freed non-white peoples of the world are largely underdeveloped and poor. In their haste to lead better lives they will encounter inevitable frustrations. They will then resist with difficulty, unless the United Nations is reformed to make it an effective force for peace, the temptation to allow race to be one of the main issues dividing mankind towards the end of the century. Apartheid's humiliation of the African would then be a valuable weapon in Maoist China's hands for dividing the West and the Sudant.

VII

If the situation described so far leaves the reader pessimistic about the possibility of changing the course of events in South Africa it is to be hoped, at least, that it emphasizes the complexity of that country's race question. The deadlock in the United Nations on the Apartheid issue underlines the same difficulty. Strange as it may sound, some members of the South African Government are beginning to show signs of being frustrated by their inability to honour their pledged word on the Bantustans, for example. The present Prime Minister's so-called outward-looking policy and his expressed enthusiasm for meeting African heads of state are carefully calculated expressions of this frustration. They certainly do not represent an attempt to re-examine the foundations on which the morality of survival is based. The Apartheid regime would not survive if it did that in the atmosphere which exists in South Africa. Their significance lies in the challenge to Free World and Free African statesmanship which they constitute. Black and white in South Africa need to be pushed towards an arrangement which will enable them to cool their tempers and in that way pave the road to a purposeful and constructive dialogue which could in the end produce agreement across the colour line on final goals.

With the dialogue as the starting-point, certain possibilities open up for an altogether new approach to Apartheid. But the scope of the present contribution precludes the discussion of

C

these possibilities. Let it suffice to mention two obvious advantages of the dialogue. The final goal of a negotiated political settlement could encourage the Western powers to renew their support for efforts to solve the race problem and make South Africa, because of her skill and achievements, an influence working for interstate collaboration, peace, and stability on the continent.

The other point to consider is the motivating urge which gives form and direction to the African's agitations for reform. In Southern Africa, the 'Sudic' African is working ultimately towards a new synthesis of experiences; towards something which will ensure that no person is punished for being the child of his parents: a social order in which the individual will be free and able to make the best possible use of his life. The white contribution to the synthesis would be as valuable as his. He wants to merge these for the purpose of creating an order of society to which black and white will feel they belong and within which they will feel wanted and secure.

There is evidence of history to establish his bona fides. Over the last hundred and fifty years or so he has been consciously welding into a unity the historical and cultural experiences of his various lingual groups. An aspect of this achievement of which he is proudest is that he produced *isidolobha* without any African group losing its language or other cultural attainments.

On this plane he regards his skill and experience as richer than anything the Afrikaner can produce. In a more or less similar position of weakness, the latter insisted on the Afrikanerization of the German, the French, etc. The New African does not wish to swallow up the white community and destroy its identity. This identity gives it virility and enhances its ability to achieve. A non-racial, virile, and achieving South Africa could, in the foreseeable future, fill on the continent the role played by America in the western hemisphere.

Even if there was no historical evidence to prove the African's earnestness of purpose, the white man is in too strong an economic, political, and cultural position to lose much by merely talking to the New African on how best they might live together as equal citizens in the land of their birth.

Sceptics might argue that it was easy for the New African to unite his people. There was their land and freedom to regain;

there was, also, race humiliation. Granted. But in the era of
turbulence which stretched from the middle of the eighteenth
century to the first half of the nineteenth, the 'Sudic' Africans
fought each other with savage brutality and, in the process,
generated hatreds which were deeper than the attitudes which
prevail between black and white at the moment. The poverty
of the African and the white man's skill in creating wealth
provide limitless scope for collaboration across the colour line.
This is why all over Free Africa white men find themselves
wanted. But, by insisting on a closed ethnic state, citizenship in
which is determined by race, Apartheid reverses this process; it
polarizes attitudes in racial directions, isolates the whites in a
predominantly black continent, and gives the African a vested
interest in the expulsion of the white man from Southern Africa.
China's development of portable nuclear weapons would ultimately transform this into a conflict very much like the war in
South Vietnam. Already there are Africans who are thinking of
an agreement with China on the manufacture of portable
nuclear arms which would establish a balance of terror in
Southern Africa as the first prerequisite for the expulsion of the
whites. Awareness of this prospect, among other dangers, must
have prompted President Kaunda to lead an anti-Apartheid
mission to Western capitals in October 1970. If past failures are
any guide, diplomatic pressures alone are unlikely to produce
the desired results. There is need not only for clarity on final
goals but also for a philosophy and technique for deracialization.

Let it be said in conclusion that, complicated as the race
question is, it remains a human problem. Its complexity suggests that continued efforts to bring the two sides to the conference table hold out some hope of a solution—perhaps the only
hope.

2

STANISLAV ANDRESKI

REFLECTIONS ON THE SOUTH AFRICAN SOCIAL ORDER FROM A COMPARATIVE VIEWPOINT

No other country has so often been censured at the U.N. nor is so unanimously condemned by people of most varied faiths and loyalties—ranging from Christian theologians and traditional liberals to communists and conservatives. Such a unanimity might be regarded as an encouraging proof of a worldwide improvement in moral standards, were it not for the fact that many of the condemnators are guilty of cruel oppression and large-scale massacres. Once we begin to doubt whether it is really the enormity of the suffering wreaked upon its victim that singles out Apartheid from other instances of subjection, we must face the question of how the South African social order compares in this respect with other systems of exploitation.

To start with a strictly economic criterion of the standard of living of the burdened classes, it is clear that South Africa is far from being the worst country in the world. Though very poor in comparison with the affluence of their Europoid masters, the majority of Bantu South Africans eat better and are better housed and clad than the ordinary inhabitants of the independent African states with the possible exceptions of Ghana and the Ivory Coast. It goes without saying that this comparison refers only to the condition of the common people, as South Africa has no proper equivalents to the African elites and inter- mediate layers. In comparison with the German or Swedish car-owning workers, the Bantu live very miserably indeed, but in comparison with the Bolivian, Algerian, or Pakistani peasants, or the slum-dwellers of Cairo or Calcutta, they are well-off. True, it might be said that such comparisons are irrelevant, and that what really matters is not the absolute standard but the relative deprivation, as it is the latter that makes people suffer. Personally, I do not accept this argument; I think that by the yardstick of the least suffering of the smallest number—which may be easier to apply than Bentham's criterion of the greatest happiness of the greatest number—a system which condemns the smaller proportion of its subjects to starvation and disease ought to be preferred. By this criterion South Africa is far from being the place of the greatest suffering—ranking in this respect considerably above India, Pakistan, or Egypt—although it is greatly inferior to the North Atlantic welfare states, or even to the more prosperous African states like Ghana or the Ivory Coast, where the ordinary people may not be better off materially than the South African Bantu, but are much less bullied and not at all humiliated.

If we take severity of repression as our next criterion, we also find that it is not in South Africa that we see the most massive recourse to bloodshed, imprisonment, and torture. There can, of course, be no doubt that the subject races live in South Africa under a harsh yoke, but it must not be imagined that in Santo Domingo, Ethiopia, or Iran a peasant or a pauper gets a less rough and contemptuous treatment from his masters.

It is not the ill-treatment of the poor (which is common enough in other parts of the world) that distinguishes South Africa, but the forcing down into the proletariat of people who in virtue of their wealth and education might aspire to more freedom and a higher status; although even in this respect we have many examples of persecutions of minorities—wealthier and better educated than the majority—ranging from the Jews in central and eastern Europe and the Armenians in the Ottoman Empire to the Chinese in Indonesia and the Indians in newly independent Kenya.

No doubt it is the efficiency of the machinery of coercion that enables it to avoid the bloodier methods of repression. The shootings at Sharpeville were unquestionably a deplorable affair, but with their tens of victims they were a mere child's

play in comparison with the Colombian '*violencia*'—a combination of a peasant uprising with banditry and vendetta—
which has been raging for two decades and has claimed more
than half a million victims. The Indonesian soldiers and Muslim
militants have exterminated at least twice as many communists
in a few days. Smaller massacres, involving nevertheless tens of
thousands, took place in Guatemala, Zanzibar, and Rwanda,
while something not far removed from genocide has gone on
recently in Nigeria and the Sudan. Even the maintenance of the
traditional Amharic domination over Galla and Somali peoples
of Ethiopia has required within an equivalent time-span much
more killing than the enforcement of Apartheid has done.
Almost needless to say, facts such as these do not prove that the
South African system is good, but they must be taken into
account to see its demerits in a correct perspective.

We must deplore the existence of political prisoners but we
should also bear in mind that on this score, too, South Africa's
record is not as bad as that of many other countries. Though
reliable figures are difficult to find, it seems exceedingly likely
that there are more political prisoners in South Korea or Cuba
than in South Africa, while the inmates of the penal colonies in
China outnumber the entire South African population. In
Stalin's days the Soviet forced-labour camps used to contain
nearly twenty million people; and even today, after fifteen
years of improvement, there are good reasons to believe that
proportionately to the population (not to speak of absolute
numbers) more people are imprisoned in Russia than in South
Africa.

Such comparisons, to repeat, cannot exonerate Apartheid but
they do raise two important questions. The first is: why is the
suppression so efficient that it needs to resort to killing and jailing on a much smaller scale than is the case in many other
states? The second question is, why does the South African
variant of oppression draw upon itself a wider opprobrium than
do others which involve more killing, maiming, and jailing?
Let us leave the first question for later on, and begin with the
second.

The argument that Apartheid is not too bad is often countered by saying that it degrades people in a particularly pernicious way by denying their humanity. That it exposes the sub-

ject races to humiliations is beyond doubt, but it is debatable whether these humiliations are more severe than those endured by the burdened classes in many other parts of the world. It does not seem that a peon on a Nicaraguan or Paraguayan hacienda is addressed more politely or generally treated with more consideration than is his South African counterpart; while, despite their equality in law, the majority of the Hindu pariahs live in a much greater physical and moral degradation than any sector of the South African population. Despised castes exist also in Japan and many parts of Africa; in Senegal the custom of caste endogamy operates throughout the society. Nor is it true that South Africa is the only place where injustice is becoming more extreme, first because Apartheid is no novelty, and what has been occurring recently is simply its codification; and, secondly, because in almost all so-called developing countries the living standards are deteriorating (owing primarily to the population explosion) and, in consequence of the increasingly bitter struggle for existence, the treatment meted out to the poor is becoming steadily worse.

A more convincing argument for singling out South Africa is that whereas in other countries inequality and degradation stem from the 'blind' action of economic forces and from unintended consequences of old customs, in South Africa they result from a deliberate policy backed by the full force of the law. Though correct in some respects, this argument can be criticized as being unduly formalistic, because everywhere there is a close correspondence between the real (as opposed to the nominal) activity of the state and the nature of the society; and there cannot be many cases of massive injustice without the connivance (if not active support) of the government. On balance it undoubtedly makes a difference whether the official organs are trying to attenuate or to bolster up the inequality, but professions of good intentions need bear no relation to the effective policies. It could even be argued that by being enshrined in the law, exploitation is made more tolerable because it is at least free from a mockery of broken promises and from pain caused by unfulfilled expectations. Furthermore, lawless oppression permits excesses—such as murder or rape—which a legally circumscribed discrimination may avoid.

There are no convincing reasons why a legally enforced

discrimination must always be more pernicious than unlegalized forms of exploitation; and on balance I feel that the most important criterion is how in reality people are treated. The Marxists are perfectly right to insist that equality *de jure* is often accompanied by extreme inequality *de facto*; and there is no reason why this should not apply to racial discrimination.

It is even possible to discern certain advantages in legally regulated as opposed to unregulated exploitation. Take, for instance, the taboo on marriage and sexual relations across the race barriers—enshrined in the so-called Immorality Act— which has certain positive aspects, despite its well-known nefarious effects upon the situation of people of mixed or uncertain parentage and upon human freedom in general. Under the circumstances of great inequality of power and wealth the said taboo protects the women of the burdened races from sexual exploitation by their masters, of the kind to which domestic servants were exposed even in puritan Victorian England, and which remains commonplace in most poor countries of Latin America.

Despite the hilarious motifs in the peeping-Tom methods of detection, the Immorality Act is ruthlessly enforced regardless of the status and influence of the culprits; with the consequence that a number of highly respectable or even important people (including some dignitaries of the ruling party) have been sentenced to imprisonment. However, the mere fact that the deterrent of ostracism and professional ruin was regarded as in need of reinforcement by the threat of years in jail proves that the temptation must be strong and widespread. Indeed, the pink masters' habit of leaving their small children in the care of brown nannies cannot fail to build up a conditioned reflex linking dark skin with expectations of emotional and bodily satisfactions; particularly as the brown nannies very often show more warmth and joy than the pink mothers do. The obligation to forget such indulgences and to repress the longings for the prototype of the source of infantile pleasures, for the sake of adult respectability and of the honour of the race, sets into action the well-known Freudian process of reaction formation, which rules out indifference and turns the desire into hate and contempt. This mental mechanism largely accounts for the miscellaneous obsessional and delusional myths and rituals of

Apartheid which (in contrast to sheer economic exploitation and the monopolizing of power) cannot be regarded as rational methods of forestalling a vengeance, or of satisfying the normal desires for wealth and for having somebody to look down upon. The fears of pollution and the obsessional concern for the 'purity' of the race in fact strongly resemble the celibate priest's preoccupation with sex.

In assessing the relative merits (or demerits) of a system we must take into account the direction of the migration—on the justifiable assumption that it flows towards a more satisfactory environment on the whole—and in this respect we find that the net current runs into rather than out of South Africa; which is not simply the result of restrictions on leaving the country. The exiles are few and recruited (apart from the Europoid intellectuals) almost entirely among the educated Africans and Indians on whom the system bears hardest, whereas a considerable number of unskilled workers from independent African states come to the Republic in search of work, while very few South African labourers ever try to leave. This, of course, does not prove that the South African system is good, but simply that (despite its injustice) it is more efficient at producing wealth than the countries further north, and that most people prefer food to equal rights if they have to choose; and consequently that mass misery may be an even greater evil than racial discrimination. Naturally, it is best to have both prosperity and justice, particularly as on the whole social harmony fosters economic progress while strife impedes it—but only very few countries in the world have the good luck to enjoy such a happy combination. So, the worldwide hostility towards Apartheid cannot be due to revulsion against the magnitude of the suffering inflicted upon its victims, because by this criterion many other states, which are left in perfect peace at the U.N., deserve at least as much condemnation.

The true explanation of the worldwide unanimity against Apartheid has little to do with internal injustice—which, to repeat, is common enough among the signatories of the Charter of Human Rights—but stems from the incompatibility of the South African system of stratification with the requirements of polite intercourse between the governments and elites of the world.

When a foreign businessman, diplomat, or tourist arrives in Paraguay or Haiti he may be sorry for the beggars, the starving peasants, the flogged prisoners, or the emaciated labourers; but all their calamities in no way affect his own position: he stops at a good hotel and is treated with deference appropriate to his station in life. In contrast, a dark-skinned visitor to South Africa will be classified as belonging to the lowest layer of the society, regardless of how elevated might be his position in his own country. Even if he were the President of Indonesia or the King of Arabia or the Emperor of Ethiopia, he would be treated by all the common pink South Africans as a person of low status.

The uniqueness of the South African system of stratification consists of allocating status according to criteria which are not merely internal but also worldwide, and distinguish entire nations as well as the South African castes. This amounts to a refusal to recognize the status of the leaders of most other nations; and the pink South Africans insist on grading the top people from dark-skinned nations as equivalent to their own underdogs. No wonder, then, that the dark-skinned elites throughout the world feel deeply offended, and use every opportunity for publicly condemning the pink rulers of South Africa.

So long as throughout most of the world the dark-skinned races remained under the tutelage of lighter-skinned rulers, the South African stratification corresponded to the global grading —and there was no trouble. Decolonization, however, put an end to this concordance, while the shrinking of the world in terms of transportation and growing trade have multiplied contacts and, therefore, the occasions for clashes between the South African code of behaviour and the attitudes required for polite relations between top people from different parts of the world. Because the very existence of the international organizations depends on such relations, they cannot digest Apartheid, find it more noxious than other forms of oppression, and never tire of casting yet another anathema, while mass deportations, exterminations, and pogroms in other parts of the world never call forth their censure.

If the South African castes were distinguished by purely internal criteria which could not be applied to foreigners— being called, say, delphins, goblins, and gnomes—then the treatment meted out to the underdogs would elicit no wider wave of indignation than the massacres of the Ibos by the Hausas or the deliberate spreading of smallpox among the Indians of Brazil. As it is at present, the South African system constitutes a standing insult to the dark-skinned elites throughout the world; and can continue to exist only so long as the tropical states remain plunged in poverty and disorder.[1]*

The question of why South African society developed into its present form is even more interesting than the one which I have just attempted to answer. However, having treated it at greater length than would be possible here in *The Elements [Uses] of Comparative Sociology*,[2] and, by way of contrast, in *Parasitism and Subversion: The Case of Latin America*,[3] I shall only mention that I have advanced there an explanation in terms of the following main factors:

1. The low status of women in Spanish and Portuguese dependencies fostered massive concubinage which led to a mixing of races, whereas the opposite was the case in South Africa.
2. The more authoritarian organization of the Catholic Church —contrasting with the more democratic government of the Calvinist assemblies—enabled it to give a greater weight to its missionary interests and to override more easily the segregationist inclinations of the settlers.
3. The contrast in physical traits was much less striking between the Spaniards or the Portuguese and the Amerindians than between the Dutch or the English and the Bantu.
4. In Brazil and Central America the Africans arrived as uprooted and reshuffled slaves, whereas the Bantu faced the European conquerors as organized tribes or even nations, and most of them retain roots in the traditional social structures to this very day.

In the chapters on South Africa and on anti-semitism in *The Elements [Uses] of Comparative Sociology* I have also argued that, contrary to a common preconception, discrimination against ethnic, racial, or religious categories is to a larger extent due to selfishness than to prejudice in the sense of mistaken judgement; and can be understood only in the light of the principle of

---

* Notes and references are to be found at the end of each chapter.

omnipresence of struggle in social life discussed in the intro-
ductory chapter of my *Military Organization and Society*.[4] Unable
to repeat all the relevant points from these publications, I have
to confine myself to a few additional remarks on the influence
of the status of women upon race relations, which constitute
a continuation of the discussion of this topic presented at the end
of Chapter 19 of *The Elements [Uses] of Comparative Sociology*, and
in the section on 'The Sexual Roots of Anti-Social Behaviour'
in *Parasitism and Subversion: The Case of Latin America*.

In the books just mentioned I have examined the consequences of polygamy versus monogamy upon social mobility and
the extent of exploitation and strife as well as upon the segregation of races, without taking the active role of women into
account. One can, however, look at this matter from a slightly
different (and complementary) angle. In a steeply stratified
society, where the masters can do with their servants what they
like, there are ample opportunities for sexual exploitation.
Consequently, since in no society can the women attain a truly
dominant position, and since few women like to share their
husbands, the women of the privileged layer have an obvious
interest in curtailing the freedom of their husbands to use their
female underlings for pleasure. Now, there is only one way in
which they can achieve this goal without undermining, or at
least severely curtailing, their husbands' power over the subordinate layer, on which their own privileges and wealth rest;
and this is by putting a taboo of sexual untouchability between
their own and the subordinate class—which is easier if the
barrier of stratification coincides with ethnic, religious, or racial
differences. True, such a taboo also curtails the sexual opportunities of high-born women, but (even if it is not true that by
and large women are less inclined to infidelity than men) in
patriarchal societies women have little freedom anyway; and so
the only thing they can achieve is to curtail their husbands'.

Steeply stratified societies often permit sexual intercourse or
even marriage between high-born men and humble women,
but as a rule severely punish such relations when the gap in
status is of the opposite kind. So, if the initial position of women
is sufficiently high to give them some powers of persuasion and
some means of exercising pressure (as was the case among the
Boers as well as among the English settlers) they will try to

impose analogous restrictions on their husbands' freedom with the females of the subordinate class. By doing this they are not only eliminating undercutting rivals, compelled to render similar (if not better) services for a much lesser material and immaterial reward, but are also safeguarding their children's position by forestalling competition for paternal care, wealth, and status from the offspring of concubinage.

So the women of the master race have a vested interest in the colour bar; and it is a well-known aspect of colonial history that the relations between the ruling nation and their subjects invariably took a turn for the worse with the arrival of European women, made possible by steam navigation and improvements in comfort and medicine.

Before concluding these reflections let us cast a brief glance at the question raised but left untouched earlier: namely, why is the South African system so well able to perpetuate itself? To say 'because it is so efficient' amounts only to an additional description rather than an explanation, as it merely obliges us to rephrase the question and ask: why is the system then so efficient?

One of the reasons is the absence of corruption (in the limited sense of bribery and embezzlement of public funds) which stands in striking contrast to what goes on in Latin America, the rest of Africa, and in fact most of the world. Indeed South Africa is the only country in the world (apart from Rhodesia which is its *de facto* extension) where extreme inequality in wealth and power does not entail widespread corruption; for all the other countries likewise free from the latter flaw are democratic welfare states without a similar gap between the rich and the poor.

Apart from the influence of Protestantism, the orderliness and the relative absence of bribery, which characterize the workings of the organs of government, stem from the persistence of the traditionalist and patriarchal family pattern among the Boers (who have supplied the entire administrative and political personnel) and the rarity of concubinage and illegitimacy, in contrast to Latin American customs; and, as suggested earlier, family patterns have much to do with the relative rigidity of the barrier between the ruling layer and the subject races.

Their insulation from their subjects helps the ruling race to preserve the traditions of Protestant puritanism, which would no doubt disappear in a process of intermingling of cultures and genes. Coupled with the appropriation of more than half of the wealth by the privileged one-fifth, this barrier also ensures that all the individuals with access to power are well paid and have no links of kinship or friendship with the sufferers from the system; so that neither kindness nor gifts are likely to tempt them from a rigid enforcement of the law. Furthermore, as the most needy candidates for public employment are excluded by virtue of their race, there is no pressure for extending the size of the civil service beyond the capacity of the treasury to re-munerate them well—so that South Africa has no counterparts to the human type in prominence in all the poor countries: the bureaucrat who cannot live decently without indulging in peculation. Moreover, the segregation between the rulers and the ruled impedes the formation of 'pipelines' of confidential relations through which bribes might flow. In consequence the Indian merchants find it much more difficult to obtain con-cessions through bribery than did the Jews in eastern Europe before Hitler.

Perhaps more important than any of the factors just men-tioned is the fact that the presence of a clearly defined and strikingly visible boundary between the master and the subject races stimulates among the former the spirit of solidarity—a kind of embattled warriors' *esprit de corps*—which deters them from making profit at the price of even a minor disloyalty to their camp and its leaders. Though no longer as free as they were two decades ago, the members of the privileged race willingly accept the infringements of their constitutional rights which they regard as necessary for their collective survival—just as most nations do in war. The police have to watch only a very small minority among them: mostly intellectuals who have taken to heart the ideals of the French Revolution or have fallen under the spell of Marxism. The most unusual practice of confining the opponents to their domicile or a few miles' radius could not work without a widespread readiness to denounce the evaders to the police. The recalcitrants of other races, who could easily conceal themselves in a crowd of sympathizers, are kept well-guarded behind bars.

Like Sparta (to which it presents a number of analogies) the

South African system rests upon coercion and the sheer habits of obedience, without the benefit of an effective religious or ideological prop which would inculcate into the minds of the burdened races that it is their duty to obey. Why, then, does a revolution not break out? The reason is that a successful revolution requires a split among the rulers and a minimum of unity among the ruled, unless it ensues from a defeat in war. Now, whereas the pink South Africans are well-organized and united, their subjects continue to be divided by ethnic and tribal affiliations and by the disorganizing effects of detribalization, although through their experience at work, and despite the deliberate limitation of education, the South African Bantu have become in many ways more Europeanized than any other African population.

Apart from efficient administration, the extremely unequal distribution of income (permitting an intensive private accumulation of capital) constitutes one of the chief factors of the economic growth which is without a parallel in Africa apart from the Ivory Coast. The restricted purchasing power, due to low wages of the majority, could lead to an excess of saving and a slump, but this has not happened and is unlikely to happen because the privileged race, who appropriate more than a half of the aggregate income, forms a much larger part of the population than did the capitalists in Europe and America in the thirties.

One final reflection: how does the fate of the South African Bantu compare with that of the American Negroes? On the material plane, of course, the latter enjoy fabulous affluence in comparison with the ordinary people anywhere in Africa; and the United States Government is trying to help them, while the masters of South Africa are busy making the yoke heavier. Psychologically, however, the American Negroes give the impression of suffering more. The first part of the explanation is that most of the South African Bantu can fall back upon their tribal and clan solidarity which has by no means entirely disappeared, and which has no equivalent among the 'atomized' Negroes. Secondly, a rigidly prescribed role creates fewer chances of disappointment and degrading rejection than a more fluid situation. One cannot be rebuffed if one does not even try to join; and it is precisely in order to avoid humiliations occasioned by unsuccessful attempts to integrate that the prophets of Black Power preach voluntary withdrawal from the American nation.

Though the South African Bantu have been reduced to serfdom, they have been spared the trauma of slavery, and the psychological burden of a partial descent from the rejected progeny of the hated master race. There can be little doubt that belonging to a conquered nation is mentally healthier than being a member of a despised minority caste; particularly as the purely numerical relation between the masters and the subjects roughly determines the average exposure to hostile contacts—the frequency of ill-treatment per head, so to speak. A member of a downtrodden minority has above him a larger number of people who can snub or bully him than a member of a downtrodden majority; and is, therefore, exposed to a much greater chance of unpleasant encounters.

REFERENCES

1. Recoiling from the crudity of racialism, most writers on Africa have fallen into the opposite prejudice of inverted racialism, according to which the Africans can do no wrong. To fill the gap I have tried to give a realistic analysis of the new states in *The African Predicament: A Study in the Pathology of Modernization*, Michael Joseph, London, 1968; Atherton Press, New York, 1969.

2. ANDRESKI, S., *The Elements [Uses] of Comparative Sociology*, Weidenfeld & Nicolson, London, 1964; University of California Press, Berkeley, 1965, Chs. 19, 20, and 21.

3. ANDRESKI, S., *Parasitism and Subversion: The Case of Latin America*, Weidenfeld & Nicolson, London, 1966; Pantheon Books, New York, 1967.

4. ANDRESKI, S., *Military Organization and Society*, 2nd edn., Routledge & Kegan Paul, London, and University of California Press, Berkeley, 1968. Ch. 1.

The books listed above are not cited in support of the views expressed in the present chapter but merely to indicate where I have treated some closely related problems which could not be discussed within its limits.

3

PIERRE L. VAN DEN BERGHE

RACIAL SEGREGATION IN SOUTH AFRICA: DEGREES AND KINDS*

No other state in world history has devoted as large a proportion of its energies and resources in imposing racial segregation as South Africa has done since 1948. While Apartheid has been the object of an abundant literature, one of its important aspects has not received much attention, namely the degree of physical distance achieved by measures of segregation. We can distinguish three main degrees of segregation:

(1) *Micro-segregation*, i.e. segregation in public and private facilities (such as waiting-rooms, railway carriages, post-office counters, washrooms, etc.) located in areas inhabited by members of several 'racial' groups;

(2) *Meso-segregation*, i.e. the physical separation resulting from the existence of racially homogeneous residential ghettos within multiracial urban areas;

(3) *Macro-segregation*, i.e. the segregation of racial groups in discrete territorial units, such as the 'Native Reserves' of South Africa, now being restyled as 'Bantustans'.

The above distinction, however, is not only one of degree but also of kind. Each form of segregation fulfils different purposes from the viewpoint of the ruling albinocracy, and entails different consequences for South African society as a whole. Let us first examine the 'gains' of the white group from the various forms of segregation, then analyse the internal contradictions

* Reprinted from *Cahiers d'Études Africaines*, VI, *23*, 1966.

inherent in macro-segregation, and finally turn to the differential economic effects of the three types of racial separation.

It is often said that the Apartheid policies of the present Afrikaner Nationalist Government constitute simply a more systematic and intensified version of traditional practices of racial discrimination and segregation. This statement is true in the sense that large-scale implementation of all three kinds of segregation extends at least as far back as the nineteenth century. In recent years, however, the Nationalist Government has increasingly stressed macro-segregation. There are two apparent reasons why this should be the case. First, if one accepts the Government's premises that interracial contact promotes conflict and that Apartheid is the only salvation for the albinocracy, then it follows that maximization of physical distance between racial groups is desirable. Second, macro-segregation in the form of the 'Bantustan' policy can be presented, for purposes of international apologetics, as an attempt at equitable partition between separate but equal nations within a happy commonwealth. Indeed, a favourite argument of the apostles of Apartheid is that their policy substitutes vertical, non-hierarchical barriers between ethnic groups for a horizontal, discriminatory colour bar.

Beyond these obvious considerations, this shift of emphasis in the implementation of Apartheid from micro- to macro-segregation is motivated by more basic factors. To be sure, micro-segregation is still as rigidly enforced as ever before, but not with the same order of priority. Micro-segregation with grossly unequal facilities is a constant symbol of the racial status hierarchy, and is a source of emotional gratification, economic advantages, and other practical conveniences for the white group. Substantial as the gains accruing from micro-segregation for the whites are, however, this aspect of Apartheid is a 'luxury', in the sense that it contributes little to the maintenance of white supremacy and that it further exacerbates the non-white masses. (The Portuguese, for example, still maintain their rule in Angola and Mozambique without any resort to legal micro-segregation, thus claiming to be free of racial prejudice; similarly, the white-settler regime of Rhodesia has gone some way towards the elimination of micro-segregation without in any way jeopardizing its power monopoly.) The preservation of micro-segregation in South Africa serves mostly to indulge the albin-ocracy's phobia of racial pollution, but micro-segregation is definitely not a cornerstone of the socio-political order.

Meso-segregation, i.e. the maintenance of racial ghettoes, arose in the nineteenth century as a way of making the non-white helotry as invisible as possible to the *Herrenvolk*, and of preserving the latter from the moral and physical contami-nation of congested, unhygienic slums. The presence of many domestic servants living on their employers' premises, how-ever, made most 'white' sections of town *de facto* interracial. In addition, there were a number of racially mixed residential areas in Cape Town, Durban, Johannesburg, and many smaller cities.

When the Nationalists came to power in 1948, they proceeded to make meso-segregation as impermeable as possible through the policy of 'group areas'. Tens of thousands of people were expropriated, expelled from their domiciles, and 'relocated' according to their pigmentation. Even the number of non-white domestic servants allowed to live with their white employers was sharply reduced, a distinct departure from earlier practices. The enforcement of meso-segregation involves many hardships for non-whites, threatens much of the Indian and Coloured middle class with economic ruin, and entails considerable profits for many thousands of whites. But, beyond these side effects, the complete ghettoization of South African cities is ostensibly being promoted as a cornerstone in the maintenance of the *status quo*.

The presence of millions of non-whites in cities is deplored by the Government, but reluctantly accepted as an economic necessity. Given the latter, the Government endeavours to en-force a new style of rigid meso-segregation, in great part for reasons of internal security. With mounting unrest among Africans, military and police control becomes increasingly crucial. The older non-white shanty-towns with their maze of narrow, tortuous alleys were often located close to white resi-dential or business districts; they are now systematically being razed as a major military hazard. They are being replaced with 'model townships' with unobstructed, rectilinear fields of fire, and wide streets for the passage of police vans and armoured cars. The new ghettos are typically situated several miles from the white towns, with a buffer zone in between; they are sprinkled with strategically located police stations, and often enclosed by barbed wire.

Macro-segregation, because of its many practical and ideological implications, is perhaps the most interesting aspect of Nationalist racial policy, and hence deserves closer attention. Total territorial separation is the avowed ideal which Apartheid seeks to achieve for all racial groups. Ideally, the Government would like to cram the eleven million Africans into the impoverished, eroded, and entirely rural 'Native Reserves' which constitute 13 per cent of the nation's territory. The rest of the country would then acquire a pristine white purity. While the Government realizes that this aim is Utopian, it is nevertheless implementing an elaborate scheme, the so-called 'Bantustan' policy, to keep as large a percentage of Africans as possible in these rural slums. Africans deemed to be 'redundant' in the 'white' areas are constantly being 'endorsed out' of them and sent to their 'Bantu homelands'. The Bantustans have several obvious security advantages: they are relatively isolated, dispersed, ethnically homogeneous, distant from the 'white' cities, and devoid of any urban concentrations of more than a few thousand people; and communication within and between them is difficult.

In its basic conception, the 'Bantustan' policy of the South African Government is not new. Interpretations of its 'real' intention vary, but the limits of actual variability in implementation which the Government is prepared to tolerate can be determined with a fair degree of precision. In 'minimum' form, the Bantustans are a revamping of the 'Native Reserve' along the following main lines:

(1) Geographical segregation of as many Africans as possible from non-Africans and of specific African ethnic groups from each other.

(2) Pretoria-sponsored cultural revivalism, and the elaboration of pseudo-traditional authority structures.

(3) An extension of the sphere of local autonomy under the authority of Government-appointed chiefs, which, in effect, amounts to a shift from 'direct' to 'indirect' rule.[1]

Leo Kuper gives a vivid description of the 'minimum' Bantustan scheme as it is at present being implemented:

Here the power of the White man is displayed in a comic opera of equality with the Black man, indeed of homage to his tribal essence. Here backward tribal reserves are in a state of Messianic transformation to satellite bucolic Ruritanias. . . . The policy is to retribalize Africans and to fragment them into separate tribal entities, self-policed, introspectively detached from each other and from the White man's world, and self-perpetuated by the insemination of tribal ardor.[2]

In this sense, the Bantustan concept amounts to the transformation of the South African colonial empire from an internal one as analysed by Leo Marquard,[3] to an external one: the 'Native Reserves' are being restyled into semi-autonomous puppet states or protectorates under a quasi-traditional aristocracy.

At the other end of the 'tolerable' spectrum from the Government's viewpoint is the 'maximum' notion of Bantustans as 'separate Black States'. While this alternative is clearly distasteful to the Government, it was being envisaged, as early as 1961, as a possible line of retreat in response to external and internal pressures. Thus, Prime Minister Verwoerd said in reaction to this possibility: 'This is not what we would have preferred to see. This is a form of fragmentation which we would rather not have had if it was within our control to avoid it.'[4] Even under nominal political 'sovereignty' the Nationalist Government counts on the ethnic division, small size, and utter economic dependence of the Bantustans to maintain them in a colonial relationship. Developments in the High Commission Territories in the near future may provide reasonably good predictors of the possible political behaviour of the independent Bantustans, and thus indirectly influence Nationalist policies.

The basic question concerning the future of the Bantustans and indeed of the Republic as a whole then becomes: Will the Government be able to contain the Bantustan scheme within these fairly narrow limits? My argument is that it will not, in part because of international pressures, in part because of mounting conflicts in the 'white' areas of the Republic, and lastly because of the dialectic unleashed by contradictions within the Bantustan scheme itself. We shall focus here on this last point.

There are four major aspects to the contradictions evident

in the Bantustan policy; all of these are, to a large degree, un-anticipated consequences of that policy, and threaten to make its implementation in the Transkei the opening of Pandora's box from the Government's point of view.

The first aspect concerns the use of the magic word 'independence'. In 1951, Verwoerd was careful to emphasize:

> Now a Senator wants to know whether the series of self-governing Native areas would be sovereign. The answer is obvious. . . . It stands to reason that White South Africa must remain their guardian. . . . We cannot mean that we intend by that to cut large slices out of South Africa and turn them into independent States.[5]

Later, he ostensibly reversed his stand by stating eventual 'independence' as a possibility. The lack of a time-table, or indeed of an even approximate definition of the term, made the statement vacuous, particularly in conjunction with Verwoerd's 1963 statement: 'We want to make South Africa White. . . . Keeping it White can only mean one thing, namely White domination, not leadership, not guidance, but control, supremacy.'[6] However, the magic word has been spoken, partly, no doubt, as a carrot to the collaborationist African chiefs, and perhaps also on the assumption that the statement would be taken at face value by some leaders of Western powers on the non-intervention of which the future of Apartheid hinges to a considerable degree.

It seems likely that the independence pronouncement, however vague, will exacerbate, or even create, rather than mollify, opposition. There are already signs that this is happening in two opposite ways. The strategy of many African chiefs who have decided to further their power and pursue their interests within the Bantustan framework is to exert whatever pressure they can against the Government in terms of the avowed goal of 'independence'. The most cautious form of 'subversion from within' involves little danger to its advocates since it is couched in government rhetoric and ostensibly follows government logic. The sheer use of the term 'independence' represents a retreat, if only a verbal one, on the part of the Government, and it is in the nature of tightly oppressive regimes that concessions easily lead to an escalation of demands, as already shown by several tremors of protest among Transkeian chiefs.

The rhetoric of independence has also opened up a new avenue of opposition to Government policy. Unlikely as this may have seemed until 1961, the Government is now under attack from the right, both from the rural, platteland elements within its own party, and from the United Party. The latter in particular claims to accept the independence pronouncements at face value, and takes the Government to task for partitioning the Republic and creating hostile black states in its midst. Thus, de Villiers Graaff proclaimed:

We would scrap the Bantustan plan. We shall retain South Africa as one integral unit with fifteen million people. We shall not fragment it into a group of States, some of which may become, and indeed are likely to become, hostile to White South Africa. We reject the idea of one man one vote, and we shall retain White leadership all over South Africa and not only in parts, as Dr. Verwoerd would have us do.[7]

Consequently, the Government faces an interesting dilemma. On the one hand if it refuses to transfer sovereignty to the Bantustans, the latter will be exposed more and more clearly as elaborate shams, and this may even precipitate a revolt of the puppet chiefs. On the other hand, should the Government take definite steps towards granting political independence to the Transkei and other future Bantustans, it must face the danger of losing the support of its reactionary Afrikaner electorate.

The second contradiction in the Bantustan scheme is somewhat related to the first. It concerns the extension of universal adult franchise to Africans of the Xhosa and Sotho groups who live in the Transkei or whose theoretical 'homeland' is supposed to be located therein. The Government may have assumed that the cathartic effect of casting a ballot would reduce the hostility of Africans, and that this franchise would meet demands for 'one man one vote'. It is clear, however, that few Africans are satisfied with virtually meaningless voting rights which entitle some ethnic groups to elect a minority of members in a Legislative Assembly which is itself subject to Pretoria's veto and the jurisdiction of which is restricted to only *some* of the people living in 3·2 per cent of the Republic's territory. If anything, it seems probable that the exercise of an ineffective franchise heightens the level of discontent. What can be more frustrating than to be allowed to express one's hostility to Apartheid, only to witness the forcible establishment, during a state of emergency, of a 'self-government' led by appointed chiefs whose position was overwhelmingly defeated at the polls?

In this respect, the Transkei scheme is fundamentally different from a Fascist-type regime where ritualistic plebiscites, propaganda, mass rallies, and the like are used to create the illusion of consensus. In the Transkei, Africans have been allowed to express their strong opposition to Apartheid at the polls, only to see their views disregarded and overridden. This use of the franchise seems to maximize discontent, in that it reflects the Government's contempt for African opinion. Implicitly, the latter is regarded as so inconsequential as not even to be worthy of a concerted propaganda effort to 'sell' Apartheid.[8]

The third and perhaps most interesting contradiction in the Bantustan scheme concerns the stand on the racial issue taken respectively by the collaborators and those in opposition. Ironically, the opponents of Apartheid, as represented by Victor Poto, take what is ostensibly a 'pro-white' position. They protest against the plan to make the Transkei an exclusively black state, and favour 'multiracialism' with equal opportunities and rights to all including whites. Conversely, the collaborating chiefs, under the leadership of Kaiser Matanzima, express their uneasy agreement with Apartheid by raising the thinly veiled spectre of anti-whiteism.

Since Apartheid is the product of white racism, it is not surprising that it calls forth black counter-racism. The latter is, of course, repressed by the South African Government when it takes a militant nationalist form as in the Pan-African Congress. However, black racism can also be couched in Apartheid phraseology and take the form of extolling narrow ethnic nationalism, and giving vent to xenophobia. Indeed, there is no safer way for an African to express his hostility to whites than to make use of the official hate ideology. The Government keeps warning Africans of outside 'hyenas' and 'jackals' who come to exploit or deceive them; it tells them what noble savages they are so long as they do not let themselves be spoiled by Western culture, etc.

Thus Apartheid and the Bantustan concept can easily become

latent platforms for a surreptitious and insidious variety of ethnic particularism and anti-whiteism. Such is Mbeki's interpretation of the Transkeian Chief Minister's motives: 'A cold, haughty man who nurses an enmity towards Whites and wishes to escape their oppressive presence, Matanzima has chosen to try to do this by using Apartheid. . . .'[9]

The fourth contradiction inherent in the Bantustans is the most basic of all and indeed underlies the other three. Both the practicability of the Bantustans and their acceptability to sufficient numbers of Africans hinge on a massive redistribution of wealth and power at the expense of the albinocracy.[10] More specifically, the economic viability of partition in South Africa depends on the manifold enlargement of the African (and indeed other non-white) areas, on the large-scale subsidization of subsistence agriculture by the money sector of the economy, and, consequently, on drastic land and income redistribution. Politically, if the partitioned areas are to retain any federal association, the basis of such association must clearly be an effective sharing of power between the constituent racial groups in the joint government rather than the Bantustan blueprint of a white colonial state dominating a half-dozen or more labour reservoirs administered by puppet chiefs.

It is obvious, however, that these necessary conditions to any viable partition scheme are precisely those which the Nationalist Government desperately seeks to avert through its Bantustan scheme. The latter is apparently based on the assumption or the hope that Africans and the outside world are mistaking the 'comic opera' of equality and the shadow of economic development for the real things. The Bantustan scheme is thus in part an ineffective attempt to mollify internal and external opposition at minimal cost to the ruling caste, and in part a blueprint for the improvement of the state's repressive apparatus.

All four paradoxes or contradictions in Bantustan policy which we have briefly examined raise doubt as to the Government's ability to control Apartheid's latest litter of feral children.

In summary, Apartheid aims to introduce between racial groups the greatest degree of physical separation consistent with economic imperatives in a highly industrialized society. Macrosegregation is deemed by the Government to offer the greatest chance of continued white supremacy, but, where white industry, mining, and agriculture require non-white labour, lesser degrees of segregation are acceptable.

The last aspect of our analysis concerns the differential economic consequences of micro-, meso-, and macro-segregation. Many analysts of the South African scene have observed that Apartheid involves a great economic cost and interferes with economic development. Apartheid certainly conflicts with principles of economic 'rationality' and Government policies often assign priority to political as opposed to economic aims. Directly and indirectly, the economic cost of Apartheid is no less for being difficult to assess with any degree of precision. The three degrees of segregation, however, have different effects and entail different economic costs.

Micro-segregation is certainly the least costly of the three. Segregated non-white facilities are either vastly inferior to the white ones or altogether non-existent. To avoid any suggestion of a 'separate but equal' doctrine, a law was passed (the Reservation of Separate Amenities Act) providing for segregated *and* unequal facilities. True duplication of public conveniences is highly exceptional, and segregation often means nothing more than the exclusion of non-whites from many places. Thus microsegregation frequently involves a saving over what it would cost to provide adequate facilities for the entire population, and there is little or no economic incentive for the white group to abolish it.

With the introduction of the new style of meso-segregation, the Government is deliberately paying an economic price for the maintenance of white supremacy. Much of that price, however, is not paid by the Government, but by the Africans who have to finance many of the amenities in their streamlined ghettos, and bear the cost of transport to and from the 'white' areas where they work. In addition, white employers of non-white labour suffer indirectly from the lower labour efficiency resulting from employee fatigue and time wasted in transit. Consequently, while the total economic cost of ghettoization is quite high, the direct price paid by the Government and the bulk of the white electorate which votes for the Nationalists is relatively low.

Macro-segregation is potentially the most expensive for the Government. The sums required to subsidize economic develop-

RACIAL SEGREGATION: DEGREES AND KINDS   47

ment in the Bantustans in order to raise the standards of living above starvation would run into hundreds of millions of dollars. But, here again, the Government only spends a small fraction of the necessary sum on the development of the 'Bantu homelands'.[11] What the Bantustan policy does, in effect, achieve economically is to perpetuate the sharp distinction within the South African economy between a high-production money sector and a *sub*-subsistence one. The productive potential of the one-third of the African population which is kept in or even forced back into the Reserves is thus vastly under-utilized. In the same way as South Africa combines politically the properties of a quasi-democracy for the *Herrenvolk* and a colonial tyranny for the Africans, economically the country is, at once a booming industrial nation and one of the most destitute of the 'underdeveloped' countries.

From the above analysis, it seems that all three levels of segregation on which the policy of Apartheid rests are doomed to economic and political failure for a combination of reasons. Micro-segregation serves little purpose in the preservation of the *status quo*, but also involves a minimum of cost to the Government. Its major function is to provide a bigoted albinocracy with some psychological and material 'fringe benefits' of oppression.

Meso-segregation is considerably costlier but on it rests the political control of the highly explosive urban areas. From the viewpoint of the maintenance of white supremacy, meso-segregation is thus essential. Only through the compartmentalization of racial groups into streamlined ghettos can the dominant white minority hope to combat open insurgency. On the other hand, the implementation of meso-segregation with the entire repressive machinery of 'reference books', 'influx control', 'job reservation', 'population registration', and 'group areas' is directly responsible for the overwhelming majority of acts of protest and revolt against Apartheid. Thus the ghettoization of urban life brings with it the hypertrophy of the police and military apparatus. Not only is the militarization of an ever-growing proportion of the white population expensive, but its effectiveness is limited by at least two factors. First, the open and unrestrained use of military violence, given the climate of world opinion, threatens the Government with outside intervention. Second, as the whites monopolize all key positions in government, industry, transport, communications, etc., the simultaneous mobilization of the albinocracy on any sizeable scale would bring about considerable disruption of civilian activities, not to mention the problem of the protection of dependants.

In the foregoing analysis, I have tried to show that the continued enforcement of meso- and macro-segregation is essential to the preservation of white supremacy. However, Apartheid also generates conflicts and contradictions the control of which involves an ever-rising cost in economic, human, and military resources. Micro- and meso-segregation in urban areas create an undercurrent of revolt precariously held in check by a growing police and army apparatus, and the Bantustan scheme unwittingly threatens to destroy the entire edifice of white supremacy.

REFERENCES

1. For a recent analysis of the role of African chiefs in the Transkei see W. D. Hammond-Tooke, 'Chieftainship in Transkeian Political Development', *Journal of Modern African Studies*, Dec. 1964, *2*, 513–29.
2. KUPER, LEO, *An African Bourgeoisie*, Yale University Press, New Haven, and London, 1965, 22–3.
3. MARQUARD, LEO, *South Africa's Colonial Policy*, Johannesburg, 1957.
4. Quoted in Brian Bunting, *The Rise of the South African Reich*, Penguin, Harmondsworth and Baltimore, 1964, 310.
5. Quoted in Pierre L. van den Berghe, *South Africa: A Study in Conflict*, Wesleyan University Press, Middletown, Conn., 1965, 118.
6. Ibid.
7. *African Digest*, Vol. 12, *3*, Dec. 1964, 81.
8. This is but one of the several ways in which South Africa differs from a Fascist-type regime. See van den Berghe, op. cit., for a more extensive treatment of this point. Bunting on the other hand stresses, and indeed overstresses, the similarities of South Africa with Nazi Germany. See Bunting, op. cit. The Southern United States constitutes a closer parallel to South Africa than does Nazi Germany, Fascist Italy, or Franco's Spain.
9. MBEKI, GOVAN A. M., *South Africa: the Peasants' Revolt*, Penguin, Harmondsworth and Baltimore, 1964, 137.

10. Although the vast majority of African leaders have rejected the partition of South Africa on any terms, there have been a few dissenting voices. E.g., Jordan Ngubane has advocated an ethnic confederation accompanied by drastic land reform. Cf. his book *An African Explains Apartheid*, Pall Mall, London, and Praeger, New York, 1963, 220–32.

11. Only a small fraction of the conservative 1956 estimate of £104 million recommended by the Tomlinson Commission for a ten-year period has so far been expended. On the other hand, defence expenditures aimed primarily at the repression of internal unrest have climbed from £40 million a year in 1960–1 to £104 million in 1963–4.

4

J. W. MANN

ATTITUDES TOWARDS ETHNIC GROUPS*

I SCIENTIFIC INQUIRY

Science is supposed to get better and better as time goes on; and it is probably true that the scientific study of race attitudes has become more and more rigorous over the years. If rigour has truly increased in social science, it follows that some of the earlier South African work on race attitudes will not quite come up to the standards now prevailing.

It does not follow, however, that the studies done in South Africa are particularly backward compared to studies done elsewhere at the same time. The South African research gives the impression of really being part of the general current of race-attitude research running through the English-speaking world of social science; and of having preoccupations, standards, and techniques that are largely indistinguishable from those met with nowadays in other countries where English is widely spoken. A glance at the list of references at the end of this chapter will show, in fact, that a substantial proportion of the studies have made their appearance in American journals. Also it is relevant to note that some of the studies have not been done by South Africans but by visitors to South Africa. Harvard alone, for instance, provided Allport, Pettigrew, and van den Berghe.

Since South Africans and others have managed to investigate race attitudes in South Africa (and, as the list of references shows, their investigations have been numerous over the last three decades and are still being vigorously conducted), and since furthermore the investigations have to all appearances kept in step with international standards, a pertinent question

* See Note on p. 72.

is easily answered with a yes. The question is whether it is possible to study race attitudes in South Africa with adequate freedom in collecting data and with acceptable objectivity and strictness.

Two considerations give weight to the question. On the one hand, South Africa is, from a coldly scientific point of view, very nearly the perfect laboratory in its potential for the study of race attitudes. Several ethnic groups co-exist, the major ones distinguished in race-attitude studies usually being the white (English-speaking, Afrikaans-speaking, and Jewish) and the non-white (African, Coloured, and Indian). Ways of life differ, sometimes sharply, from group to group. The tongues in use are many and can differ as much as English does from Xhosa or Xhosa from Gujarati. There is plenty of variety in skin colour and other physical features of high visibility. Intergroup strains are perennial and occasionally violent.

On the other hand, any attempt to turn the country into a laboratory might meet with resistance from people who submit that dabbling in racial matters is likely to stir up passions or draw attention to conditions they think best left unpublicized. Pressures might come from others who would like the scientist to convert the laboratory into a munitions factory to supply one or other group with arms for defence or attack in interracial strife.

On the whole, though, the total strength of the resistance and the pressures does not seem enough to keep the laboratory from being used simply as a laboratory. Social scientists, after all, have good scientific reasons for spending a fair amount of time in this laboratory. Elsewhere[49] I have mentioned five of the reasons. Briefly, they are that race attitudes are vital elements in the social order of a country like South Africa; that they are influential in guiding daily conduct, as well as being widespread; that they show extremes of intensity that other attitudes may not reveal; that marked distortions of behaviour are sometimes involved in them; and that they are easy to elicit. No doubt several other reasons could be added to this list. One was advanced by MacCrone,[30] who pointed out in the introduction to his book that race attitudes are not only of personal significance but also raise basic principles of Western civilization.

The studies I shall consider below all reveal scientific aspirations in matters of technique and the preservation of objectivity. Most of them were carried out by psychologists, although specialists in sociology and education have made notable contributions. By and large, the studies show what attitudes are standing against social change or helping it along. Several studies look beneath the attitudes for deep-lying forces pulling against change or pressing towards it. Some try to record changes in attitudes and society that have already taken place or are taking place. A few deal with a specific way of deliberately changing attitudes and imply that thereby society itself can be changed.

2. MAJOR ISSUES

The big issues in the South African work are also the big issues in the work done elsewhere. From the five issues I have selected for discussion, it will be seen that many social scientists have not been content with surveys of surface trends but have tried to seek out basic principles and grapple with the factors beneath race attitudes. It may even be wondered whether the drive to get to the heart of things has not been too impatient. Certainly, as I shall point out in a subsequent section, there has been a dearth of large-scale surveys using representative samples; and it is just such broad surveys that show how race comes to terms with race and how much race relations change.

Ethnocentrism

The issue here is whether most of the people in a group put their own group above other groups. MacCrone[30] was the pioneer in studying this issue. His chief instruments were a scale of 'attitude towards the Native' and a social-distance scale. He was careful to work out the reliabilities of his measures, which he also tried to validate. Not all who have succeeded him have cared to establish levels of reliability and validity for their measures, let alone improve on the levels he obtained. His own measure of attitude towards Africans, after more than thirty years, still seems to scale in the same way as it originally did, although nowadays student raters show greater variety in their attitudes than his raters did.[52]

For his subjects he chose 632 white university students. He classified them as belonging to the English-speaking, Afrikaans-speaking, and Jewish ethnic groups. According to his measure of social distance, each one of the three ethnic groups fell short of maximum tolerance for itself. Nevertheless, each group extended more tolerance towards itself than towards any other group.

More recent studies have disclosed similar trends. After studying 627 white students of the University of Natal in 1956, Pettigrew[56] prepared a table which shows that from 89 to 93 per cent of the students were willing to marry ethnic congeners, while at most 66 per cent were willing to marry ethnic outsiders. So vehemently was the Indian group spurned that a fifth of the non-Jewish students chose the response 'I wish someone would kill all of them.' Like Pettigrew, van den Berghe[61] used a measure of social distance. He also drew upon students of the University of Natal for subjects; but his 383 subjects were both white and non-white and included student nurses and technical-college students as well as university students. His results indicate that the group least rejected by his mainly English-speaking white subjects was the English group; the group least rejected by his Indian subjects was the Indian group; and the group least rejected by his African subjects was the 'City African' group.

Crijns[10] confined his subjects to 113 Africans who were either graduates or students of a university. The social-distance scale applied to them revealed that their tolerance was greater for various African groups than for other groups. A social-distance scale was again the measure when Lever[25] in 1959 took a 10 per cent random sample of the high-school pupils in each of 44 Johannesburg schools for whites. Although unable to draw subjects from every one of the 52 high schools that were actually in Johannesburg, Lever did manage to sample every Afrikaans-medium high school. He found that his Afrikaans-speaking subjects (none of whom were Jewish) put the Afrikaans-speaking group well above any other group in the hierarchy of preferences.

Clearly there is ample evidence of ethnocentrism in the various studies of social distance. Studies of other kinds add to the

E

evidence. Kuper,[21] for example, asked African teachers to rate six ethnic groups on various qualities. His finding was that on the average the teachers gave the Zulu group the highest rating. This is ethnocentrism once again, because the teachers themselves were mainly Zulu.

Generalization

If a person dislikes one non-membership group, is he likely to dislike the others too? The question is important because a positive answer suggests that the dislike may stem from something inside the individual rather than from the specific qualities of the various non-membership groups themselves. Originally, MacCrone[30] had made a search for common factors in the social distance put by members of white groups between themselves and members of groups different from their own; and Pettigrew[56] later did the same. Their findings agree closely. It seems that attitude towards non-membership groups does evince generalization; but that there is also a special kind of generalization covering white non-membership groups only. The impression fostered by the findings is that if an Afrikaner, say, dislikes the Indians he is likely to dislike all other non-Afrikaner groups as well; but his dislike of the non-Afrikaner white groups will be of a different, and milder, kind compared with his dislike of the non-white groups.

Personality

One basic factor lying beneath generalization may be a particular pattern or dynamic system of personality traits. In his earlier work, MacCrone[30] had expressed a strong interest in the psychodynamics of prejudice, paying especial attention to psychoanalytic theorizing, as in his discussion of unconscious elements in aversion from the colour black. He came to envisage a 'Calvinistic–Puritanical' personality, which in many ways resembled what is widely known today as the authoritarian personality.[38] Some of his empirical work on race attitudes centred about questions of personality. In this book, he reported no link between the attitude towards Africans and fair-mindedness.[30] His later work leaned heavily on factor analysis. Among other things, it suggested that such traits as aggressiveness and assertiveness lie beneath the intolerant–tolerant outlook of whites;[33] that racial aggressiveness shown by whites has a relatively heavy dependence upon extrapunitiveness;[35] and that two kinds of toughness are essential features of the Calvinistic–Puritanical personality.[38]

A factor analysis he carried out with Starfield[40] indicated that white hypersensitiveness is slightly associated with anti-African attitudes. To account for some of his factor analyses, he resorted once again to interpretation of the psychoanalytic kind, picturing for example the ethnoerotist, whom he described in Freudian terms as having submissive and neurotically compulsive tendencies.[36]

Pettigrew[56] was another to look for the personality underneath the attitude. Drawing upon the researches into the authoritarian personality, he used an F scale to find, as expected, that authoritarian features of personality in whites go with remoteness from people outside the membership group, particularly non-whites. With improved scales, Orpen[53] was later able to confirm the link between authoritarianism and ethnocentrism in whites.

Sociocultural factors

Attitudes being complex things, scientists do not really expect a single basic factor like personality to run below the surface. This is so even when their interests are temporarily concentrated on one factor only. There is indeed convincing evidence that, however important the personality factor is, it is not enough to explain everything about attitudes. Using the same subjects from whom he obtained data about ethnocentrism and generalization, Pettigrew[55] made another investigation which implied that personality by itself does not explain the high level of intolerance he uncovered. Turning to sociocultural factors for a fuller understanding, he found that anti-African attitudes were stronger in those born on the African continent than in those born elsewhere, although the former were no more authoritarian in personality than the latter. Presumably, being born in Africa brings about a particularly thorough exposure to the local culture and its anti-African norms. If sociocultural factors

are so important, the prospects of personal attitude change
become coloured with a certain shade of optimism. After all,
even with a personality that is stubbornly resistant to change
there is still hope of achieving desirable race attitudes by changing social settings.

An obvious sociocultural factor to link with race attitudes is
ethnic-group membership. In study after study, the Afrikaans-
speaking group stands out as the white group to put the widest
social gap between itself and the Africans.[30, 34, 56, 25, 28, 61] There
may also be a difference between each of the two other main
white groups in remoteness from Africans. The Jews are less
remote than the English-speaking, according to tendencies
detected by MacCrone,[30, 34] Lever and Wagner,[28] and Pettigrew.[56] The last-mentioned, however, subjected his data to
statistical testing and concluded that the difference was not
significant. Statistical tests of significance have regrettably not
been reported for some intriguing evidence that goes to show
that whites are more intolerant than non-whites.[61, 31]

Other matters of society and culture that have been looked
into are sex and parental attributes. Different observers seem to
have encountered different aspects of the sex factor. Calculations of variance convinced MacCrone[30] that sex was a relatively minor factor in white intolerance; and inspection of the
tables presented by him shows that sex differences are slight,
with the males usually exceeding the females in intolerance.
Again, tables presented by van den Berghe[61] disclose slight
differences between male and female whites in remoteness from
non-whites, with one sex not consistently more remote than
another. On the other hand, white women keep their distance
from non-whites more markedly than white men do, according
to a statistically significant difference reported by Pettigrew.[56]
Furthermore, in white English-medium schools, girls are significantly closer to Coloureds and Indians than boys, according
to Lever,[25] who, however, uncovered no other sex difference.
Perhaps, as Lever hints, the various studies agree so little with
one another because they do not sample the whole white population in a representative enough way. At any rate, when a sex
difference in attitude has been claimed, it has been traced to
influences of a sociocultural rather than of a genetic kind. Thus,
females have been supposed, as carriers of culture, to reflect

cultural norms better than males;[56] or have been said to face stronger taboos against crossing colour lines.[61]

As for parental attributes, the evidence is also rather mixed. A factor sometimes thought important is paternal occupation, which has been taken as an index of socio-economic status.[34, 25] MacCrone[34] concluded that race matters more than class. In his results, paternal occupation did not emerge as strikingly related to intolerance towards non-whites, except when urban paternal occupations were compared with rural. Pettigrew[56] did, however, find that having a father who does manual work conduced more towards aversion from non-whites than having a father in a non-manual job; and his result is statistically significant. Lever[25] looked for statistically significant differences but did not always find them. Those he found in examining social distance from Africans put children of men in one occupational category closer to Africans than children whose fathers were in some other category socio-economically below it. Educational level of the father is another factor that does not yield entirely straightforward evidence; but it was true of pupils in Johannesburg English-medium provincial high schools that social remoteness from non-whites generally widened as paternal education dropped.[27] Attempts to link paternal occupation and education to general social distance were made by van den Berghe;[61] but in doing so he did not take specific notice of social distance from non-whites. The factor of parental origin has also been examined for the bearing it might have on intolerance. Having parents born in England did not make English-speaking whites noticeably less intolerant towards Africans than having parents born in South Africa.[31, 37]

Awareness and Identification of Race

All race attitudes are acquired. So states a law on race attitudes. It is probably the firmest law; and it may even be the only one, if absolute and unqualified sway is to be the test of a law. Anyone interested in changing attitudes should be encouraged by it because what is acquired may well be more plastic than what is inborn, and what is not inborn need never make an appearance.

The awareness that races differ from one another must be a

vital stage in the acquisition of race attitudes, for without such awareness one race cannot be preferred to another. The onset of awareness engaged the attention of Gregor and McPherson,[18] who asked South African infants aged between 3 and 7 to choose between dolls, one chocolate-brown and the other with a fair complexion. Thirty of the infants were white and 139 were from the Venda tribe. Gregor and McPherson found the same tendencies as investigators had in the United States. Race awareness seems to begin early, because when asked to point out which doll looked like a white child only four of the Venda and only two of the whites could not do so. Apparently, race preferences also begin early. A majority of the whites preferred the white doll. It was the white doll again that was fancied when the Venda three-year-olds were told to choose. Five-sixths of them chose it.

However, the latter type of finding becomes suspect in the light of a critical and very thorough study by Meij.[50] A modified doll-test was applied to 425 Tswana children aged 3 to 7. By means of a detailed analysis, Meij confirmed the existence of race awareness in most three-year-olds. Nevertheless, Meij felt that it would be going beyond the evidence to claim clear support for the existence of race preferences in most of the children. No doubt some of the racially aware were showing race preferences; but choosing among dolls reveals attitudes to dolls and not necessarily attitudes to races.

Signs of early race awareness were detected again when Melamed[51] presented specially-prepared pictures to white children. There were twenty-five subjects in each of the age-groups 6, 8, and 10. Besides being on the whole able to apply an ethnic label to a picture of a brown-skinned person, the children revealed marked physiognomic dislikes. A dark skin and thick lips were the most rejected facial features.

Although the focus is upon children when research is into the beginnings of race awareness and preferences, adults have a use in kindred research. Assuming that the ability to distinguish one race from another develops with time, it is conceivable that the development is uneven, so that notwithstanding entry into adulthood some distinctions are better made than others. A race is recognized more accurately by its own adult members than by adult members of other races. So Pettigrew, Allport, and Barnett[57] found when they presented a racial miscellany of photographs through a stereoscope to whites and non-whites in Natal. The only exception to their finding was provided by the relatively inaccurate African subjects; and even they were at their best in identifying Africans.

3. STUDIES OF RACE-ATTITUDE CHANGE

It is a truism that what is to be changed has to be known properly before it can be changed efficiently and successfully. Acceptance of the truism may explain why little has been done on attitude change in South Africa, although the nature of the attitudes themselves has been thoroughly probed, as the data in the section above affirm.

One way of studying change is to go back into history. The grounds for doing this may have an extra firmness when changes in South Africa are at issue. Comparing his experience of race attitudes in both America and South Africa, Allport[1] felt that the forces of history and tradition were more strikingly evident in the latter land. To observe the workings of historical forces over the years, the social scientist has to abandon his accustomed techniques of quantification and depend instead on documents and personal evaluation. Nevertheless both Mac-Crone[30] and Crijns[10] have made the necessary methodological departures with apparent profit. MacCrone's research in particular demonstrates how closely changes in the attitudes of whites have followed changes in society and how extensively race attitudes have already changed in South Africa.

For a time after white settlement began in the seventeenth century, groups were distinguished more by religion than by race or skin colour.[30] Nevertheless even at the very beginning there was an undercurrent of racial superiority in the attitude of whites, according to Crijns.[10] However, it was only in frontier days towards the end of the eighteenth century and the beginning of the nineteenth that race attitudes like those displayed today were noticeable, although white colour prejudice was not yet as rigid as it has become since.[30] MacCrone[39] holds that, despite the passing away of frontier conditions, attitudes embodying them are still adhered to by contemporary white South

Africans and in fact have been recently re-animated in the Afrikaners.

In addition to his historical studies, MacCrone[34] undertook a quantitative investigation of contemporary race-attitude change. He questioned white university students at two-yearly intervals from 1934 to 1944. The Afrikaans-speaking students showed scant modification in anti-African attitudes over the years; but there was a trend for both English-speaking and Jewish groups to become more tolerant as time went on. Similar trends emerged when, some years after Pettigrew's work, students at the University of Natal were again used as subjects.[22] Although the students were as authoritarian and as conformist as Pettigrew[55] had originally found them, this time the anti-African attitudes of those students who were not Afrikaans-speaking were weaker than they were originally.

Of course, trends such as these are solid evidence of only one kind of change. They cannot really be used to demonstrate that particular Jewish students, for example, become more tolerant as they grew older or that the whole of South African Jewry leaned more and more towards tolerance. They can merely show that students are not what they used to be; that in one year the Jewish student population had attitudes of one kind and in another year it had somewhat different attitudes (assuming that MacCrone's Jewish students were representative of that population, which they may or may not have been—the evidence is unclear). It is perfectly possible that attitudes remained stable in most Jewish individuals and in the whole Jewish group; but that the kind of Jewish student who went to university changed with the years. For a satisfactory demonstration of attitude change, either representative samples would have to be drawn regularly from a particular population, or a longitudinal study would have to be made of the changes taking place in particular individuals over time. As far as I can discover, no longitudinal study of race attitude change has yet been undertaken in South Africa.

Although there are problems enough in accurately identifying the changes that happened in past centuries and are happening today, some social scientists have looked beyond the passive recording of change to the question of how fully change can be brought about by their active intervention. An air of almost surprised optimism is sometimes the result.[26] The efforts of the Army Education Services, as recounted by Malherbe,[42] were conspicuously successful. At least this is what Malherbe maintains; disappointingly he does not offer a quantitative assessment of the success. Short courses used to be run for servicemen, who were encouraged by the course captain to discuss social issues freely after factual and undogmatic lectures. Discussions about Africans that began with emotional utterances and the bandying about of stereotypes might after a few days become subdued and orientated towards facts. Questionnaires completed anonymously at the end of a course suggested that many a prejudice had given way during the discussions. Malherbe cannot tell how permanent the changes were. At all events, it is his conviction that attitudes are modified by approaching them in a roundabout way while steering clear of moralizing. 'They must be stalked.'

Recently, Lever[24, 26] has been able to reduce the social remoteness of whites from Africans and Coloureds quite easily. He conducted two experiments, each involving over two hundred university students as subjects. He exposed some students to a short and apparently factual lecture on race and intelligence. Willingness to have social contacts with Africans and Coloureds was clearly encouraged by the lecture. How long a lecture-induced change lasts in the South African setting can still only be guessed at and awaits further experimentation.

4. METHODS AND SUBJECTS

Several of the puzzles about race attitudes remain puzzles not because nothing has been done to solve them but because the solutions rest on solving certain additional problems of procedure. I have already suggested that some research on sex differences and attitude change is inconclusive because the methods of the research have had shortcomings. I intend now to glance at a selection of the methodological difficulties that stand in the way of firm conclusions about race attitudes.

A difficulty that is rarely encountered nowadays is posed by unquantified research. The investigator practising this type of research does not express his observations numerically but offers his general impressions instead. It is a very doubt-provoking way of investigation because race prompts bias so easily that even the scientist may not be completely detached. Evidence consisting solely of the investigator's impressions is harder to weigh for prejudice than evidence mainly in the form of tallies and measurements. There are times, naturally, when the scientist can scarcely do otherwise than purvey unquantified evidence. In historical probings of attitudes, for example, the only evidence may be the impressions of a deceased diarist. However, studies of contemporary race attitudes that hinge on the investigator's own impressions are also sometimes undertaken. An example of an early study of this kind is one by Brown.[9] He felt that there was rather less African race consciousness in 1935 than might have been expected, although he anticipated that it would increase and believed that African intellectuals were already critical of the social system. Recently, van den Berghe[62] produced an unquantified assessment of interracial attitudes in a Natal rural town. One of his impressions was that Afrikaner whites have been attracting strong feelings of hostility from the majority of the Africans.

A cardinal difficulty in race-attitude studies, and one that stands out clearly when data are numerical, is representativeness. If the subjects whose attitudes are measured do not represent a larger group to which they belong, the attitude is tightly circumscribed as there can be no presumption that what holds true for the small group of subjects holds true also for the larger group from which it is drawn. If, furthermore, the group of subjects is a very small one, the findings have a very limited application indeed.

Of the studies I have already dealt with, the one by Lever[25] is exceptional in deliberately seeking representativeness through random selection of subjects from a larger population. Equally exceptional is a survey of which a sketchy account has been published by Hudson, Jacobs, and Biesheuvel.[19] In 1964, they interviewed every hundredth voter on the voting lists of a dozen Transvaal constituencies. They found that almost three-quarters of the respondents (who were all white) believed the colour issue to be the greatest problem facing South Africa today, and that about two-fifths felt that some form of white dominance offers the best solution to 'the native problem'. Two decades earlier, as Malherbe[41, 42] reports, the Army Education Services tried to make the whites they chose for questioning representative of the entire South African army and air force. Although strict randomization was not achieved, a rough kind of representativeness was; and the total of subjects—about 7,000—is alone enough to make the study important. From the results it is evident that regularly a little over two-fifths of the subjects gave gradualistic answers. These subjects favoured the extension of rights and opportunities to Africans, provided it were done slowly.

Representative or not, the subjects of the South African race-attitude studies are time and again drawn from the white population. More often than not, they are students. Perhaps social scientists have been inclined to take the easy way out of investigatory difficulties. Doubtless research is made easier by choosing subjects who are readily available, who talk one of the two official languages, who do not pose difficulties of illiteracy, and who do not have an unfamiliar style of life. It is eased also if there is no call to cope with subjects who burn with anti-white hostility or hide their views from a questioner because he is white. The principal investigators, it must be remembered, have all been white. In passing, I think it worth observing that the investigators who have been based at a university have usually been based at an English-medium one: except for a few studies, like the unpublished dissertations discussed by Lever,[25] the Afrikaans-medium universities have not shown an interest in the scientific exploration of ethnic attitudes.

Of course, there may be a case for concentrating upon white attitudes. Whites control the country; and while they do their attitudes probably carry inordinate weight. Nevertheless, the constant use of white subjects hardly makes for a balanced view of ethnic attitudes. This is not to say that non-whites have been totally neglected. I have already mentioned several studies in which non-whites have figured; and there are a number of others which have been devoted partly or entirely to non-white attitudes.

Educated African subjects have provided evidence of hostile feelings towards Afrikaners,[32] or whites in general;[10] and have been less disposed than uneducated Africans to admire whites.[15] African workers have preferred African supervisors to white;[58]

and African clerks have not been as likely to think their efficiency dependent upon respectfulness towards white supervisors as their white supervisors have.[60] Urban Africans in Durban have shown a marked distaste for Indians.[43] In giving stereotypes, African subjects have demonstrated that there is a negligible correlation between the labels they apply to their own group and the labels applied to it by subjects from other ethnic groups.[29]

As for Coloureds, subjects rated as able to pass as white have shown no stronger pro-white orientations than relatively un-passable Coloureds who match them.[44] Again, a sample of Coloureds from a Durban residential area in which three different races are stirred together has shown signs of avoiding both whites and Indians living near by.[59] The superior–inferiority dimension in Indian attitudes towards whites has emerged from an experiment involving Indian university students. Led to believe that they were competing with whites, the Indians on the whole have expected defeat in certain contests like those involving social polish but not in others like those involving inner qualities.[46] Indians, Coloureds, and Africans have been lumped together for comparison with whites in an inquiry into the attitudes of students of political science. From the comparison, it has appeared that the proportion approving marriage between whites and non-whites is higher among the non-whites than among the whites.[7]

These findings notwithstanding, the race attitudes of the non-whites, who after all constitute the vast majority of the population, have not had the attention they deserve. At least part of the neglect is traceable to a backwardness in developing appropriate measuring techniques. Present-day attitude research is almost invariably research into verbal behaviour. Ways by which researchers can elicit verbalizations about different races from non-whites who may be illiterate or into whose languages questionnaires cannot easily be translated are fortunately being developed. Biesheuvel has devised not only a questionnaire technique for measuring the attitudes of educated Africans[2, 5] but also methods of interviewing and holding group discussions with uneducated Africans whose attitudes are sought.[3, 4] His techniques are readily adapted to inquiries into attitudes towards ethnic groups. Moreover, De Ridder[14] has given examples of how a thematic apperception test for Africans can be used to delve into race consciousness. Although some of these methods may force the investigator to work harder at collecting and interpreting data than he would have to if he were merely passing out questionnaires and scoring them, they hardly entitle him to be defeatist about gauging non-white attitudes.

5. SOME NEGLECTED ISSUES

As their techniques improve, researchers should not only get better answers to the familiar questions about race attitudes but also be given the confidence to ask seldom-asked questions. The technically difficult problem of tying up ethnic attitudes directly with sudden race riots is an instance of an issue that so far has attracted little research. It is an important issue because racial explosions show how powerful are the pressures towards social change. The violent anti-Indian aggression of African mobs in Durban during 1949 produced general comments from social scientists[20, 63] but no specific attitude research. If the aim is to predict and prevent riots, the research should focus upon the course that attitudes take before a riot detonates. None the less, attitudes after the fury has subsided merit some attention too. Attitudes implicit in the reactions of whites and Africans to a railway disaster have been traced by Page and Fernandez.[54] In 1965, a train derailment at Effingham Road killed eighty-nine Africans; and the first white to come on the scene was put to death by a mob of enraged African survivors. Page and Fernandez began to collect data straight after the fatal events. Data of value can also be collected after much milder outbreaks. This was shown when the mutilation of an exhibition commemorating victims of the Warsaw Ghetto prompted Lever[23] to sound the reactions and anti-Jewish feelings of sixty students in the vicinity of the exhibition.

Another neglected issue pertains to the ethnic group. It is not only that at least one South African ethnic minority, the small Chinese group, has been ignored in race-attitude research; but also that ethnicity in general has been meagrely dealt with. The easy option is the one all too often preferred. Someone, for example, is categorized simply as an African, on the evidence

goes to a school for Africans, or has a brown skin, or
that he is an African. The fact is that there are different
s and kinds of belonging to an ethnic group. Instead of
ining the attitudes of only 'Africans' or 'whites' or
'Indians', the scientist could go about things in a more detailed
fashion. In deciding exactly what his subjects are, he might find
out how salient ethnicity is to them; how enthusiastically they
cling to membership of the group they call their own or crave
membership of another; how completely their fellow-members
regard them as belonging to the group; how fully they share the
culture and norms of the group; and what sub-groups they belong in. In part, the last-mentioned point was raised by Doob[16]
when he complained that the specific tribal affiliations of African
subjects are often ignored. The complaint can be extended
to embrace all the major ethnic groups, since, just as Africans
fall into distinct sub-groups, so, too, do Indians and Coloureds;
and even a group like the English-speaking whites can be
broken down not only into the parts showing the English or
South African parental origins distinguished by MacCrone[31, 37]
but also into parts showing parental origins ascribable to different countries all over the world.

The part played by values has also been neglected. They are
supposed to lie at a deeper level than attitudes. Presumably,
success in changing the values underneath ethnic attitudes
would count for more in terms of permanence and inclusiveness
than mere success in changing some surface attitudes. A try at
finding a link between ethnic intolerance and moral values has
already been made by Lever.[25] From his provincial school
subjects he chose the 100 most and the 100 least ethnocentric
subjects. One of his findings was that there was a significant
tendency for the most ethnocentric to frown especially hard
upon disturbances in church. What has not been explored yet
is the bearing on ethnic attitudes of values that sharply distinguish whites from non-whites. An example of a value dimension
that separates whites from non-whites is self–society orientation. Non-whites, and Africans in particular, are strongly
orientated towards society and service to the community, in
contrast to whites, who cherish personal and private satisfactions.
This is a conclusion that in whole or part can be extracted from
value studies initiated by Gillespie and Allport[17] and carried on

by Danziger[11, 12, 13] and others.[6, 8, 45] Of course, self–society orientation might have nothing to do with race attitudes; but, given the existence of markedly different values in different ethnic groups, a worthwhile search could be made for certain basic values that dictate particular race attitudes and at the same time are more characteristic of one ethnic group than another.

It would not do to ignore the understanding of the attitude itself that could come from inspecting the attitude that is specifically ethnic. Most of those who have looked closely and scientifically at South African race attitudes seem to have been more interested in understanding race relations than in understanding attitudes. It is true that to all appearances the measured attitude nicely indicates how relations between races are faring and how better or worse they are becoming. This is all the more reason, however, to ask what an attitude is supposed to be. Social scientists are by no means always clear and in agreement about the nature of this nebulous and unobservable thing. Race-attitude research stands or falls by the soundness of the attitude concept, so it is in the interests of those who conduct such research to use their work to clarify the attitude and its essential accompaniments as well as to clarify race relations.

The actual target of the race attitude provides a specific example of a general attitudinal factor that clamours for clarification. A subject may be asked how willing he is to dance with an African or what emotions are aroused in him by the South African whites. Exactly what do the words 'an African' or 'the South African whites' signify? It is not as though the questioner has a living African or a crowd of whites standing in front of the subject whose reactions he wants to observe. Instead, he is trying to find out the subject's reactions to an abstract concept of a generalized individual or of a whole group. Race-attitude research deals more with attitudes to abstractions than with attitudes to races. The abstraction moreover may not refer realistically to the stimulus in overt racial encounters. Nobody will encounter all living white South Africans all at once or even necessarily encounter a person recognized as typical of white South Africans. Penetrating research into abstractions, words, and concepts will surely be needed as long as they seem to be the initial targets of most attitudes. There have already been attempts to disentangle reactions to an abstractly conceived individual from reactions to an abstractly conceived group;[47, 48] and, although not markedly successful, they at least go tentatively along the path that leads to some of the much-needed research.

Altogether, with an abundance of problems and natural facilities, as well as a sufficiency of techniques and interested social scientists, race attitudes in South Africa have the potential to attract a still more searching regard in the next few decades than they have done in the last thirty years.

REFERENCES

1. ALLPORT, G. W., 'Gordon W. Allport', in E. G. Boring and G. Lindzey (eds.), *A History of Psychology in Autobiography*, Appleton-Century-Crofts, New York, 1967, 5, 1–25.

2. BIESHEUVEL, S., 'A Technique for Measuring Attitudes of Educated Africans', *Proceedings of the South African Psychological Association* (Johannesburg), 1953, No. 4, 13–20.

3. BIESHEUVEL, S., 'The Measurement of African Attitudes towards European Ethical Concepts, Customs, Laws and Administration of Justice', *Journal of the National Institute for Personnel Research* (Johannesburg), 1955, 6, 5–17.

4. BIESHEUVEL, S., 'Methodology in the Study of Attitudes of Africans', *Journal of Social Psychology*, 1958, 47, 169–84.

5. BIESHEUVEL, S., 'Further Studies on the Measurement of Attitudes towards Western Ethical Concepts', *Journal of the National Institute for Personnel Research* (Johannesburg), 1959, 7, 141–55.

6. BLOOM, L., 'Self Concepts and Social Status in South Africa: A Preliminary Cross-cultural Analysis', *Journal of Social Psychology*, 1960, 51, 103–12.

7. BLOOM, L., DE CRESPIGNY, A. R. C., and SPENCE, J. E., 'An Interdisciplinary Study of Social, Moral, and Political Attitudes of White and Non-White South African University Students', *Journal of Social Psychology*, 1961, 54, 3–12.

8. BOTHA, E., 'Some Value Differences among Adults and Children in South Africa', *Journal of Social Psychology*, 1964, 63, 241–8.

9. BROWN, W. O., 'Race Consciousness among South African Natives', *American Journal of Sociology*, 1935, 40, 569–81.

10. CRIJNS, A. G. J., *Race Relations and Race Attitudes in South Africa*, Janssen, Nijmegen, 1960.

11. DANZIGER, K., 'Self-Interpretations of Group Differences in Values, Natal, South Africa', *Journal of Social Psychology*, 1958, *47*, 317–25.

12. DANZIGER, K., 'Value Differences among South African Students', *Journal of Abnormal and Social Psychology*, 1958, *57*, 339–46.

13. DANZIGER, K., 'The Psychological Future of an Oppressed Group', *Social Forces*, 1963, *42*, 31–40.

14. DE RIDDER, J. C., *The Personality of the Urban African in South Africa*, Routledge & Kegan Paul, London, 1961.

15. DOOB, L. W., *Becoming More Civilized*, Yale University Press, New Haven, 1960.

16. DOOB, L. W., 'Psychology', in R. A. Lystad (ed.), *The African World*, Praeger, New York, 1965, 373–415.

17. GILLESPIE, J. M., and ALLPORT, G. W., *Youth's Outlook on the Future*, Doubleday, New York, 1955.

18. GREGOR, A. J., and MCPHERSON, D. A., 'Racial Preference and Ego Identity among White and Bantu Children in the Republic of South Africa', *Genetic Psychology Monographs*, 1966, *73*, 217–53.

19. HUDSON, W., JACOBS, G. F., and BIESHEUVEL, S., *Anatomy of South Africa*, Purnell, Cape Town, 1966.

20. KIRKWOOD, K., 'Failure of a Report', *Race Relations* (Johannesburg), 1949, *16*, 87–106.

21. KUPER, L., *An African Bourgeoisie*, Yale University Press, New Haven and London, 1965.

22. LENT, R. H., HOLTZMAN, W., and MOSELY, E. C., 'Sociocultural Factors and Personality in Intergroup Attitudes', paper read at April meeting of Eastern Sociological Society, 1967.

23. LEVER, H., 'The Defacement of a Ghetto Exhibition', *Jewish Journal of Sociology*, 1964, *6*, 213–19.

24. LEVER, H., 'An Experimental Modification of Social Distance in South Africa', *Human Relations*, 1965, *18*, 149–54.

25. LEVER, H., 'A Comparative Study of Social Distance among Various Groups in the White High School Population of Johannesburg', unpublished doctoral thesis, University of the Witwatersrand, Johannesburg, 1966.

26. LEVER, H., 'Reducing Social Distances in South Africa', *Sociology and Social Research*, 1967, *51*, 494–502.

27. LEVER, H., and WAGNER, O. J. M., 'Father's Education as a Factor Affecting Social Distance', *Journal for Social Research* (Pretoria), 1965, *14*, 21–30.

F

28. LEVER, H., and WAGNER, O. J. M., 'Ethnic Preferences of Jewish Youth in Johannesburg', *Jewish Journal of Sociology*, 1967, *9*, 34–47.

29. MACCRONE, I. D., 'A Quantitative Study of Stereotypes', *South African Journal of Science* (Johannesburg), 1937, *33*, 1104–11.

30. MACCRONE, I. D., *Race Attitudes in South Africa*, Oxford University Press, London, 1937.

31. MACCRONE, I. D., 'A Comparative Study of European and Non-European Differences in Race Preferences', *South African Journal of Science* (Johannesburg), 1938, *35*, 412–16.

32. MACCRONE, I. D., 'Reaction to Domination in a Colour-Caste Society: A Preliminary Study of the Race Attitudes of a Dominated Group', *Journal of Social Psychology*, 1947, *26*, 69–98.

33. MACCRONE, I. D., 'Race Attitudes and Personality Traits', *South African Journal of Science* (Johannesburg), 1949, *46*, 117.

34. MACCRONE, I. D., 'Race Attitudes: An Analysis and Interpretation', in E. Hellmann (ed.), *Handbook on Race Relations in South Africa*, Oxford University Press, London, 1949, 669–705.

35. MACCRONE, I. D., 'Some Factorial Determinants Affecting the Racial Anxiety Aggression Syndrome in European Subjects', *Proceedings of the South African Psychological Association* (Johannesburg), 1951, No. 2, 16.

36. MACCRONE, I. D., 'Ethnocentric Ideology and Ethnocentrism', *Proceedings of the South African Psychological Association* (Johannesburg), 1953, No. 4, 21–4.

37. MACCRONE, I. D., 'Parental Origins and Popular Prejudices', *Proceedings of the South African Psychological Association* (Johannesburg), 1954, No. 5, 10–12.

38. MACCRONE, I. D., 'Factorial Concomitants of Ethnocentrism', *Proceedings of the South African Psychological Association* (Johannesburg), 1955, No. 6, 8–10.

39. MACCRONE, I. D., 'The Frontier Tradition and Race Attitudes in South Africa', *Race Relations Journal* (Johannesburg), 1961, *28*, 19–30.

40. MACCRONE, I. D., and STARFIELD, A., 'A Comparative Study in Multiple-Factor Analysis of "Neurotic" Tendency', *Psychometrika*, 1949, *14*, 1–20.

41. MALHERBE, E. G. (attributed to), *What the Soldier Thinks*, General Staff Headquarters, Pretoria, 1945.

42. MALHERBE, E. G., *Race Attitudes and Education*, South African Institute of Race Relations, Johannesburg, 1946.

43. MANN, J. W., 'Attitudes to Other Racial Groups', in W. C. Hallenback (ed.), *The Baumannville Community*, Institute for Social Research, University of Natal, Durban, 1955, 182–96.

44. MANN, J. W., 'Group Relations and the Marginal Personality', *Human Relations*, 1958, *11*, 77–92.

45. MANN, J. W., 'Race-linked Values in South Africa', *Journal of Social Psychology*, 1962, *58*, 31–41.

46. MANN, J. W., 'Rivals of Different Rank', *Journal of Social Psychology*, 1963, *61*, 11–27.

47. MANN, J. W., 'Inconsistent Thinking about Group and Individual', *Journal of Social Psychology*, 1967, *71*, 235–45.

48. MANN, J. W., 'Inconsistent Impressions in Assessing Individual before Group', *Psychologia Africana* (Johannesburg), 1967, *11*, 143–50.

49. MANN, J. W., *Race Attitudes Today*, Institute for the Study of Man in Africa, Johannesburg, 1967.

50. MEIJ, L. R., 'The Clark Dolls Test as a Measure of Children's Racial Attitudes: A South African Study', *Journal for Social Research* (Pretoria), 1966, *15*, 25–40.

51. MELAMED, L., 'The Use of Facial Features in Racial Recognition', unpublished Honours dissertation, Department of Psychology, University of the Witwatersrand, Johannesburg, 1967.

52. MELAMED, L., 'A Re-examination of MacCrone's Race Attitude Scale', *Psychological Scene* (Johannesburg), 1967, *1*, 19–20.

53. ORPEN, C. E. N., 'Ethnocentrism and Authoritarianism in the White Population of South Africa', unpublished M.A. thesis, University of Cape Town, 1966.

54. PAGE, H. W., and FERNANDEZ, J. W., 'Reactions to Disaster: Two Studies in South Africa', to be published in a forthcoming volume edited by G. C. Kinloch.

55. PETTIGREW, T. F., 'Personality and Sociocultural Factors in Intergroup Attitudes: A Cross-National Comparison', *Journal of Conflict Resolution*, 1958, *2*, 29–42.

56. PETTIGREW, T. F., 'Social Distance Attitudes of South African Students', *Social Forces*, 1960, *38*, 246–53.

57. PETTIGREW, T. F., ALLPORT, G. W., and BARNETT, E. O., 'Binocular Resolution and Perception of Race in South Africa', *British Journal of Psychology*, 1958, *49*, 265–78.

58. READER, D. H., 'African and Afro-European Research: A Summary of Previously Unpublished Findings in the National Institute for Personnel Research', *Psychologia Africana* (Johannesburg), 1963, *10*, 1–18.

59. RUSSELL, M. A., 'A Study of a South African Interracial Neighbourhood', Institute for Social Research, University of Natal, Durban, 1961.

60. SHERWOOD, R., 'The Bantu Clerk: A Study of Role Expectation', *Journal of Social Psychology*, 1958, *47*, 285–316.

61. VAN DEN BERGHE, P. L., 'Race Attitudes in Durban, South Africa', *Journal of Social Psychology*, 1962, *57*, 55–72.
62. VAN DEN BERGHE, P. L., *Caneville: the Social Structure of a South African Town*, Wesleyan University Press, Middletown, Conn., 1964.
63. WEBB, M., 'The Riots and After', *Race Relations* (Johannesburg), 1949, *16*, 85–96.

Note: This chapter was completed in September 1967. Attempting to be brief, I decided not to discuss certain theses and dissertations (from universities like Rhodes, University of Cape Town, and Stellenbosch) and such valuable studies as BRETT, C. A., *African Attitudes*, South African Institute of Race Relations, Johannesburg, 1963, and HERMAN, S. N., *The Reaction of Jews to Anti-Semitism*, Witwatersrand University Press, Johannesburg, 1945.

5

HERIBERT ADAM

THE SOUTH AFRICAN POWER-ELITE: A SURVEY OF IDEOLOGICAL COMMITMENT*

(a) Purposes and Methods of the Survey

If one accepts the assumption that in the foreseeable future it is unlikely that any change in South African policy will result from the initiatives of the governed within the country, or from economic or military measures outside, then the character and possibility of changes within the ruling group itself gain particular significance as a determinant of future conditions. A ruling group is seldom a monolithic block, and internal differences of opinion, tensions, and contradictions might signal important sources of change. A careful survey of the white power-elite could reveal underlying attitudes which are not always evident in the official declarations on the race policy. A knowledge of the motives of those responsible for the realization of 'separate development' can shed important light on the policy itself and the sincerity of its expressed promise of 'equality'. The life chances of the majority of the population and the treatment which they can expect to get are directly and entirely dependent on the prejudices and decisions of their rulers. The ruled have no institutionalized power to counteract these decisions in any way.

With these considerations in mind, an empirical survey of selected members of the South African power-elite was under-

* I am thankful to my colleagues D. Barnett, H. F. Dickie-Clark, G. B. Rush, and R. Wyllie, who commented on an earlier draft of this paper.

taken during the first period of Vorster's regime, beginning in the autumn of 1966 and continued into 1967.*

The survey focused on persons who belonged to the decision-making elite within the white group, and who were prominent in implementing the race policy in various fields. It seemed meaningful to distinguish political, administrative, and economic sectors of the white power-elite; this grouping is consistent with the historical development in which the Afrikaans-speaking section evolved as the exclusive political power-group and the English-speaking section as the mainly economic one. Their differences, as revealed in this survey, are compared with subsequent developments, especially the open split within Afrikanerdom which was not evident at the beginning of Vorster's premiership, and hence not directly considered in this survey.

For technical and financial reasons it proved impossible for a single researcher to achieve a fully representative sample in the statistical sense. The aim instead was a more limited insight into *typical* opinions of the three elite groups. While the sampling of the respondents does not allow conclusions about the distribution of opinions *within* the groups, it does afford comparisons of typical clusters of attitudes *among* them.

It is probable that the attitudes of the elite groups do not represent the opinions of the average white South African. The respondents are more likely to have expressed a less dogmatic version of the race policy in view of their upper-class status, their real power, and their better education. Their less threatened position allows professional people to be more tolerant, as has been established in various studies of racial attitudes. Sixty-eight per cent of the respondents held university degrees, and 57 per cent had travelled outside Africa at least once within the last ten years.

A bilingual questionnaire was mailed to parliamentarians and entrepreneurs, and distributed by internal mail or personally among higher civil servants and a small number of businessmen.

* The survey and the journey to South Africa were financed by the Deutsche Forschungsgemeinschaft. My appreciation is due to Dr. E. F. Flohr for the initiative he took in arranging the necessary contacts. Many South Africans aided the research in various ways, and their help is gratefully acknowledged. Although they were familiar with the author's critical view of the race policy of their country, their unshakable conviction that the Apartheid policy speaks favourably for itself if viewed in a scientific way, made the survey possible.

The approached sample responded surprisingly well and returned 349 completed questionnaires. While, according to
expectations, only 40 (25 per cent) of the approached members
of the South African parliament replied, 206 (42 per cent) of
the entrepreneurs and 103 (80 per cent) of the officials responded. This variation seems due mainly to the different mode
of contacting respondents in the three categories, as well as to
reasons relating to the time and interests of the approached
members.

The 206 entrepreneurs represent all branches and sizes of
enterprise, but they are to a greater extent located in Natal than
in the three other provinces. Twenty-two per cent employed, or
were in charge of, less than 50 persons; 42 per cent between 50
and 500; and 26 per cent more than 500 employees. The
majority (80 per cent) employed more non-whites than whites;
44 per cent had a labour force composed of more than three-
quarters non-whites.

The sample of civil servants came mainly from the Departments of Bantu Administration and Bantu Education. In addition, questionnaires were distributed among officials in various
Bantustans, mostly administrative and agricultural advisers and
white members of staff of the three university colleges for
Africans. Their answers reflect the predominant approach of a
technically qualified expert group which is responsible for the
planning and practical implementation of the programme of
'separate development'. They belong to the small number of
whites in South Africa who have professional contact with the
African world beyond the master–servant relationship, and they
play a critical role in the actual formation of policy, as many
political analysts have noted. This is particularly true for a class
of civil servants who are not simply dutiful administrators of
government policies but regard themselves as zealous defenders
of a particular party in power.[1] As a South African sociologist
working on a similar survey of various elite groups has under-
stated it: 'It is generally accepted that the public service is at
present predominantly staffed by people who are at least not
unsympathetically disposed to the convictions and policies of the
ruling party.'[2] Seventy-one per cent of all white South African
officials belong to the Afrikaans-speaking section (as compared
with 58 per cent in the total population), and this percentage is

considerably higher in the upper echelons and certain branches of the public service such as the police (87 per cent) and prison staff (99 per cent Afrikaners).[3]

The still predominantly English-speaking business world, while supporting a *laissez-faire* racialism, tends to oppose increasing State intervention in the labour market, since greater economic integration is in the direct interest of private capital. The same process, however, jeopardizes the privileges of the European, primarily Afrikaner, blue- and white-collar working class and hence the Government, dominated by Afrikaners, attempts to enforce economic segregation. In this conflict between the colour-blind interest in a productive labour force and Afrikaner protectionism of white 'civilized labour', South Africa, it is said, has evolved as 'probably the only country where the big business community is visibly to the left of the Government'.[4] It is this controversy about the pragmatism of racial domination which is the central theme of this survey.

Respondents were asked to express their views on a variety of topics in four areas:

1. Attitudes towards Africans and racism in general.
2. Economic aspects of Apartheid.
3. Chances of Apartheid perpetuation or modification.
4. Inter-white frictions, especially between Afrikaans- and English-speaking sections.

The significance of four variables was tested in relation to these issues: occupational position; ethnic group membership as indicated by home language; level of education; and travel abroad.

Thirteen questions seemed to be the maximum for a mailed questionnaire, if the return quota were not to be jeopardized, and because of this limitation in length, some important issues could not be raised. Among these are the different opinions on the Coloureds and, as already mentioned, the controversies within Afrikanerdom. The main purpose of this study was not to ascertain *why* specific attitudes were held—a task which could only have been attempted through lengthy personal interviews—but to document typical opinions and to analyse their distribution among influential groups. All questions were phrased in the official terminology and the answers precoded in a form appropriate to the internal political debate. For example, a term such as 'International Communism' was used, which has a specific meaning in the domestic South African debate which cannot be readily conveyed by more differentiated categories applied from outside. Other items had to be expressed in similarly vague or ambiguous ways.

The questionnaire was introduced with the following statement: 'Three German scientists are at present undertaking a study tour through South Africa for six months in order to obtain an objective view of recent developments. As part of this scientific research programme, we wish to draw on the experience and opinions of authoritative sources: parliamentarians, administrative experts, and leading economists, so as to provide us with the means of obtaining an overall picture of the country's controversial problems.' Given the concern of many South African whites with outside criticism of their country, many respondents seem to have actually welcomed the opportunity to correct what they viewed as the biased image of the country abroad. Many questionnaires contained pages of additional comments.

The most important results of the survey are presented below; and in the light of these findings, recent trends in white South African policies are analysed in order to ascertain changes and to speculate about future tendencies.

(b) *Attitudes towards Africans*

'Foreigners usually hear the most diverse viewpoints on Bantu characteristics and their specific treatment. Which of the following seven contradictory assertions are, in your opinion, true or false?' Under this introduction seven frequently heard statements were presented to the respondents. These statements all reflect various aspects of the official Apartheid policy, although perhaps seldom so blatantly expressed.

The first statement summarized one of the central ideological tenets of Apartheid, namely, that 'The Bantu should remain Bantu; they ought to develop along their traditional lines and should not be merely uprooted Western imitations.'

The underlying idea that each 'race' group should have the opportunity and obligation to 'keep its identity'—that is, to adhere to group-specific traditions and to be proud of this—ostensibly provides the legitimating rationale for Apartheid. In spite of living under the conditions of an urban proletariat, all Africans are nevertheless expected to revert to traditional tribal definitions and to accept the authority of chiefs in remote rural areas. What some militant blacks in the United States advocate as a means of psychological liberation from the dominant culture is in South Africa prescribed by the dominating minority itself whose interests are served by the cultural splits and political retardations of the majority. An ideologically similar culture-approach thus has diametrically opposed functions in different structural settings.

The state officials vote unanimously* in favour of preserving the difference between urban Western culture and pre-industrial, tribal society. Among the entrepreneurs, a minority pleads for acculturation. One can only speculate about the extent to which the interviewed industrialists are aware of the fact that the productivity of their black employees is dependent on their adaptation to Western industrial norms. When formulated as a statement of fact, however, all interviewed groups nevertheless doubted the complete acculturation of the average urban African. The differences in their responses are now no longer significant.[5] This is evident in the almost unanimous rejection of statement two: 'In his behaviour and set of values the average urban Bantu has adapted himself to such an extent to the way of life of the white people that hardly any actual differences remain.'

To be sure, under conditions where he is officially defined as different and hence severely limited in his life chances, even the most acculturated African can hardly be expected to lead the life of a member of the privileged white group. The power-elite, however, refuses to accept the inevitable trend towards a basic common set of values of all members of an industrialized society. Scepticism prevails even where the successful adaptation process has been officially certified and reached a standard which 99 out of 100 whites never achieve. The 90 per cent agreement on statement three is proof of this: 'Even when a Bantu has a doctorate, Western culture is often a layer of veneer: deep down he remains a Bantu.'

* For the detailed results on the seven tested statements, see Table 1 (p. 80).

The basic equality between members of both groups is virtually rejected, but a critical change, however, has taken place between the ideology dominant in the earlier period and that of the Apartheid programme since Verwoerd. What is now practised is a system of racially defined discrimination and exploitation without, however, justifying it with the traditional ideology of race inferiority. South Africa now displays racialism without racism. The insistence on the biological inferiority of the blacks and the natural superiority of the whites—a central assumption in the Social Darwinist version of racism—is officially considered out of date, even though still implied latently. The underprivileged ought no longer to be regarded as inferior, but solely as different. The tendency towards greater rationality in the implementation of domination is also reflected in the official ideology, which now focuses on cultural and social differences. The idea of inherent inferiority was, after all, based on faith; it was fictitious and easily shattered by examples to the contrary. In contrast, reference to the cultural pluralism of the different population groups has indeed a real basis, especially since ethnocentrism is promoted by the forced separation of Apartheid policy. The results of the imposed separatism no longer need an ideological justification; their mere existence demonstrates their correctness. In the view of our respondents, however, different customs and norms are still reducible to eternal, natural laws and are not explained with reference to social and historical factors, as evidenced in the agreement with statement four: 'The Bantu is not inferior to the white man, but his nature and behaviour are different and will always remain different because this is in accordance with the law of nature.' The differences in response between the three groups are not significant here. This does not apply, however, if one compares the respondents who stayed overseas for some time, with those who had never left Africa: the latter group tends to agree with the statement more frequently.

It is so common in South Africa to view social conditions in biological categories that socio-economic and historical-cultural circumstances are hardly conceived as possible reasons for different patterns of behaviour. As such, sociological explanations are categorically rejected, as the responses to statement five demonstrate: 'Between the white man and the Bantu there

TABLE I

Attitudes towards Africans

	Parl. (40)	Offic. (103)	Entr. (206)	Afrik. (164)	Engl. (167)	Total (349)
	%	%	%	%	%	%
1. Bantu should remain Bantu						
True	88	99	74	96	68	83
Undecided	2	1	6	1	8	4
False	10	—	20	3	24	13
2. Minimal difference between urban Bantu and whites						
True	5	6	9	6	9	7
Undecided	5	1	3	2	4	3
False	90	93	88	92	87	90
3. Doctorate is veneer						
True	88	95	87	94	85	90
Undecided	5	2	3	2	4	3
False	7	3	10	4	11	7
4. Not inferior but different by nature						
True	83	84	72	83	73	77
Undecided	7	7	8	4	10	8
False	10	9	20	13	17	15
5. No difference in abilities but in opportunities						
True	10	14	15	10	18	14
Undecided	12	—	7	4	7	5
False	78	86	78	86	75	81
6. Bantu is a child who needs centuries						
True	63	69	76	69	79	73
Undecided	10	9	9	7	10	9
False	27	22	15	24	11	18
7. Democracy is not practicable						
True	88	91	91	92	89	91
Undecided	2	2	2	1	3	2
False	10	7	7	7	8	7

is no difference in ability—the difference lies in the opportunities provided.' Significant here is the difference between the professional groups, not between the language groups. Another significant difference exists again between those who had been abroad and the more local group, in which 86 per cent (compared with 77 per cent of the former group) reject the statement.

The overt expression of this basic attitude can indeed be called paternalistic.[6] The African is viewed as an immature child, who needs the help and supervision of the ruling father. This relationship, however, is not a generational one; it is timeless, able to be defined only in terms of centuries, as it is phrased in statement six: 'The average Bantu is a child, some hundred years behind the white man in development; basically, however, he is capable of developing to an equal standard—given a few centuries longer.' The relatively high number of rejections of this statement seems to be due to its ambiguous formulation, as some additional comments indicate. Many respondents disagree with the suggestion that the Bantu is basically capable of developing to the same standard, even if one generously grants him 'a few centuries longer'.

From such a perspective it is only logical to conclude that Africans are unable to participate in a political system that is based on the principle of equality of its subjects, even if they possess various levels of political consciousness. At the same time, to be sure, the numerical consequence of such an alternative, which would jeopardize white power, is clearly admitted as illustrated in the overwhelming agreement with statement seven: 'On account of the traditional background of the Bantu as well as the difference in numerical strength between the races in South Africa, all the ideas of modern democracy cannot be put into practice here.' Judging from this last statement, which no longer focuses on vague problems of development but directly on the political constellation, even the existing slight difference between the more 'progressive' English-speaking respondents and their Afrikaner counterparts has disappeared. Only those with overseas experience doubt the statement to a slightly higher extent.

With the change of the traditional white legitimation for separation from outright *baasskap* (direct master–servant relationship on the basis of openly demonstrated superiority) to the emphasis on educational and cultural difference as the rationale for white power, the ideology of white privilege has been adjusted to the changes in the socio-economic structure inside the country as well as the political developments on the international scene. Pragmatic arguments for maintaining law and order in the interest of a booming economy have largely been substituted for the sacred belief in the divine civilizing mission of the whites. There are, however, limits to the rational justification of racial segmentation. As different cultural identities disappear in a common industrialized way of life, racial stratification needs to fall back on its traditional rationalization, at least informally. Only the insistence that inherited, natural, and unchangeable characteristics of human beings are decisive for their behaviour provides the rationale for racial segmentation. Continuing adherence to the traditional stereotypes of racial distinctions has to be understood not merely as a relic of an unenlightened past, a kind of scientific lag, but also as the only lasting and individually satisfying justification of separation in a situation where 'cultural parallelism' has to be imposed by the ruling group for the security of its privileges. Table 2, focusing on the well-known biological rationalizations of racial separa-

TABLE 2

Biologically Determined Race Distinctions

'Concerning physical differences between the white man and the Bantu (apart from the colour of the skin and the texture of the hair) there are, as is well known, various anthropological theories. From a biological point of view, which of the following factors do you consider relevant?'

	Parl. (40)	Offic. (103)	Entr. (206)	Afrik. (164)	Engl. (167)	Total (349)
	%	%	%	%	%	%
Odour						
Difference	75	76	85	79	82	81
Undecided	17	15	9	16	9	12
No difference	8	9	6	5	9	7
Sexual Behaviour						
Difference	58	65	60	60	60	60
Undecided	32	25	19	30	16	22
No difference	10	10	21	10	24	18
Skull Formation and Brain Structure						
Difference	80	74	72	74	70	74
Undecided	18	21	19	21	21	19
No difference	2	5	9	5	9	7
Hereditary Character Predispositions						
Difference	75	80	80	75	83	80
Undecided	15	14	11	15	10	12
No difference	10	6	9	10	7	8

tion, tests their relevancy in the eyes of the power-elite and reveals the superficiality of the new legitimation.

Intentionally, no definition or clarification of relevancy was provided. It was assumed indicative in itself that respondents were prepared to consider brain structure, character disposition, or sexual behaviour in terms of racial differences 'from a biological point of view'.

If, in spite of the overwhelming majority who still think along traditional South African lines, the slight differences among the respondents could be classified into two ideal types according to the four factors tested, the less bigoted type, as could be expected, is the English-speaking entrepreneur with overseas experience and university training, while the other extreme is represented in the Afrikaans-speaking official without university training who has never left South Africa.

When analysing racial attitudes in South Africa in a comparative perspective, an additional and decisive factor has to be taken into account: prejudices have direct survival value for the whites, in contrast to anti-Semitism or anti-coloured feelings in Britain or the United States. The sociocultural basis of officially endorsed stereotypes in a situation in which group conformity guarantees the survival of privilege accounts for the heightened prejudices, and not merely personality components in themselves, as Pettigrew has demonstrated in a cross-cultural comparison of intergroup attitudes.[7] The 'externalizing' personality components, the dispositions for projections, and underlying authoritarianism are probably not higher in South Africa than in any comparable society without Apartheid. On the contrary, statutory legal intolerance now covers so firmly all possible deviance that personal intolerance becomes unfashionable. In contrast to a Klan supporter in the American South or an anti-Semite in Germany, a South African white need not hate his antagonist; he frequently displays benevolent generosity towards his non-white subordinates on the basis of his entrenched power. He can afford increasingly impeccable behaviour in the rare personal contacts. Indeed, respecting the basic human dignity of an African has become an important prerequisite of a streamlined system, short of accumulating explosive incidents, as the members of the South African white power-elite well realize.

(c)   Economic Aspects of Apartheid

When reviewing the major source of change inside the country, almost all liberal writers on South Africa point to the antagonism between an expanding economy and its ideological restrictions. 'Two major elements of the social structure, namely the polity and the economy, pull in opposite directions, thereby creating rapidly mounting strains.'[8] Industrialization and racial obstacles, especially the prohibition of mobility and the absence of a non-racial achievement principle, are viewed as incompatible and leading to further tensions. 'Presumably, there must be some point at which an equilibrium can no longer be maintained between continued economic growth and increasing political rigidity.'[9] Implicit in these analyses is always the assumption that the South African economy is inescapably bound to the pursuit of growing productivity, inferring that 'economic rationality urges the polity forward beyond its ideology'.[10]

In the light of these central notions it would seem highly relevant whether or not the Government succeeds in achieving what Herbert Blumer contends to be the firm subordination of private industry under official Apartheid policy, 'despite apparent disfavour shown by many industrialists to different portions of the programme'.[11] From a theoretical point of view, the example of South Africa could test Blumer's general assertion to the contrary, that in a racially ordered society 'industrial imperatives accommodate themselves to the racial mould and continue to operate effectively within it'. To all intents and purposes South Africa contradicts the assumption that technological advancement automatically brings about political modernization as well. The denial of the achievement principle and other wasteful restrictions in terms of potential productivity does obviously still guarantee a sufficient output in a rapidly expanding economy. Given the existing political constellation, the Apartheid order might well be a prerequisite for private profits which would be substantially lower in a democratically organized non-racial society with powerful unions and other unrestricted forces opposing the easy exploitation of labour divisions along racial lines. On this issue, the domestic white South African discussion centres on the practical question of how the present ratio of black and white in the urban areas can be preserved or even reversed. The steady influx of labour from the rural areas to the industrialized centres has been, as in all developing countries, historically the most decisive change in South Africa, where now roughly one-third of the 15 million Africans live permanently in segregated townships outside the cities. Although 80 per cent of the 3·8 million whites live in cities, they are still outnumbered by non-whites by about 2:1.

Essentially four measures for changing or stabilizing this so-called explosive racial ratio in the urban areas are discussed:

1. *Increased Immigration.* Backed by State support, the country has been able to gain about 35,000 white immigrants annually in recent years. A large proportion were Catholics from southern Europe, who were in addition slightly dark-skinned and therefore frequently considered by Afrikaners to be 'unassimilable'. Consequently, the official immigration policy has come under attack from extreme right-wing Afrikaners. In any event, the magnitude of immigration hardly influences the urban racial ratio. It does, however, provide a source of desperately needed skilled manpower without lifting job reservation on a larger scale.
2. *Mechanization and Automation.* This way of reducing the labour force presupposes a market with high domestic purchasing power, which does not yet exist in South Africa so as to make extensive automation profitable.
3. *Border Industries.* According to this decentralization scheme, labour-intensive factories are established in or moved to areas near the African 'homelands' from where the necessary labour is provided. The Government subsidizes entrepreneurs willing to take over the disadvantage of geographically remote production. Thus far, border industries have proved successful in the vicinity of urban centres, where economically favourable conditions had existed anyway.
4. *Intensified Influx Control.* Industrial expansion based on black labour is supposed to require special Government permission; at the same time, influx regulations are tightened with the intended goal of gradually reducing the ratio of black labour.

Except in the case of immigration, all measures are viewed with significant differences by the industrial groups. On the
G

whole, the entrepreneurs seem to hold a more pessimistic opinion in so far as possibilities of changing the urban racial balance is concerned. A comparison between Afrikaans- and English-speaking businessmen, however, indicates clearly that it is not the professional factor but rather the ideological outlook which accounts for this attitude.

Similar differences can be found in the opinions about the industrial colour bar. Although informally loosened under the pressure of an increased bottleneck of skilled labour, the legal practice of job reservation is still the most decisive race regulation, both for long-term economic expansion and for the

TABLE 3

Attitudes towards Racial Changes in Urban Areas

'Which of the following measures do you regard as the most successful in changing the numerical ratio between white and black people in urban areas?' (Multiple choice possible.)

	Parl. (40)	Offic. (103)	Entr. (206)	Afrik. Entr. (44)	Engl. Entr. (149)	Total (349)
	%	%	%	%	%	%
Increased immigration	70	54	66	52	69	63
Mechanization and automation	70	55	27	41	26	40
Border industries	75	79	51	84	41	62
Influx control	60	51	26	59	16	37
None—change impossible	10	7	17	2	22	12

social structure of the country. On the other hand, the traditional colour bar, particularly white exclusiveness in the upper employment brackets, is seriously threatened by the very boom which the country experienced in the past decade. It is on this question that the sharpest divergence of opinion among the ruling group can be found: while the English-speaking entrepreneurs would like to increase the already expanding supply of sophisticated African labour, traditional Afrikaner ideology, grounded in the competing interests of the white working class, succeeds in defending job reservation. Where Africans were allowed to enter more skilled positions, this had to be compensated for by higher wages to white workers. For the white unions, the introduction of the achievement principle would mean the abolishing of the traditional 'civilized labour policy' to which the Government is obligated, since one of its main power bases lies in the white workers' group. The opposing view, far from advocating integration, favours the pragmatic, less ideological form of economic domination.

TABLE 4

*Attitudes towards Retaining Job Reservation**

	Parl. (40)	Offic. (103)	Entr. (206)	Afrik. Entr. (44)	Engl. Entr. (149)	Total (349)
	%	%	%	%	%	%
Agreement	78	77	29	73	16	49
Undecided	2	4	7	7	7	5
Disagreement	20	19	64	20	77	46
	100	100	100	100	100	100

* The question was: 'Many economic aspects of the policy of separate development are controversial. With which of the following measures do you agree and which do you reject?' The table indicates the responses under the head 'Retaining Job Reservation'.

No other question yields such extreme differences of opinion. Indeed, it is remarkable that in the case of the Afrikaner industrialists, ideological commitment to the official policy proves obviously stronger than business interests. Contrary to the view that economic position alone determines political beliefs, the majority of Afrikaner businessmen appear to sacrifice at least verbally their profit interests for an adherence to official race policy. The fact that half of the Afrikaans-speaking businessmen in our sample were managers of semi-autonomous State-controlled corporations and not private entrepreneurs accounts further for their agreement with job reservation.

In another respect, opinions among South African industrialists differ considerably. While the number of employees has no influence on the attitude towards job reservation, significant differences can be found according to the ratio of non-white employees.

Entrepreneurs with a relatively high proportion of non-white employees reject 'job reservation' more frequently, because their expansion is most hindered by racial restrictions.

TABLE 5

Entrepreneurial Attitudes towards Job Reservation according to Number of Employees and Ratio of Non-White Workers

	Employees			Enterprises over 50 Employees	
	Up to 100 (76)	100–500 (60)	Above 500 (48)	More than 75% non-white (76)	Less than 75% non-white (58)
	%	%	%	%	%
Agreement	30	25	31	15	43
Undecided	7	8	4	9	3
Disagreement	63	67	65	76	54
	100	100	100	100	100

Both factors—the absolute number and the ratio of non-white workers—came out as non-significant differences in a further question on the restrictions placed on the use of additional African labour in the urban areas. Here again, however, the great majority of English-speaking industrialists and one-third of the Afrikaans-speaking entrepreneurs disagree with the proclaimed governmental measures.

A similar constellation of opinions was found in the controversy about private investments in the Bantustans. The opposition party always advocated the view that only private initiative would be able to develop and industrialize the rural Bantustans. The Government anti-capitalist rhetoric branded this policy as a neo-colonial form of exploitation, designed to secure new bases of influence for the English industrialists.

It seems obvious that both parties profit from the existing state of affairs, in which the 260 scattered patches of African areas provide, above all, cheap labour pools. An overcrowded, industrially underdeveloped area with people entirely dependent on white benevolence and tribal chiefdoms operated on behalf of the white rulers is a less dangerous threat to white privileges than an economically developing and therefore politically less controllable society. The debate over private or

State-controlled industrialization of the Bantustans cooled down in 1968 with the admittance of private capital in the reserves through State-controlled agencies such as the Bantu Investment Corporation, which ensures that the pattern of development falls in line with the overall Apartheid policy.

TABLE 6

Attitudes towards Prohibition of Private Investments in Bantustans

	Parl. (40)	Offic. (103)	Entr. (206)	Afrik. Entr. (44)	Engl. Entr. (149)	Total (349)
	%	%	%	%	%	%
Agreement	65	64	46	61	39	53
Undecided	7	5	8	7	7	7
Disagreement	28	31	46	32	54	40
	100	100	100	100	100	100

In attempting to reach some general conclusions about the divergent economic aspects of Apartheid, one has first of all to point to the frequently overrated conflicts between the predominantly 'English' business interests and the political authority. Readiness to make concessions on both sides—but less on the part of the Government, which always proved to have the stronger arm under the specific South African circumstances—has so far prevented the eruption of tensions inherent in the Apartheid contradictions between technological modernization and the means by which its productive potential is restricted. Business concessions to Afrikaner political beliefs seem to stem from a realistic assessment of the necessity of State control over the labour force rather than from ideological agreement with the Apartheid implications. Potential profit restrictions as a consequence of this policy are far outweighed by considerations of internal stability and unlimited access to abundant cheap labour which still guarantees a comparatively high return from investments. The political authority on the other side is no less interested in a continuing economic boom. Only with a booming economy can the danger of internal conflicts be frozen and the external threats of sanctions be refuted.

In this, the interests of government and industry coincide. Ideological differences play a role only within this framework of the common goal: to ensure continued white rule.

(d)   Chances of Apartheid Perpetuation

White South Africans are well aware of the fact that their government defies extensive international condemnation, and domestic public opinion reacts with great sensitivity to the slight gestures of foreign sympathy, be they only the visit of a second-class sports team or the political utterances of a film star. Sanctions in the form of the arms boycott and the military threat by African guerrillas on the northern borders form part of the public debate. Heightened nationalism rather than readiness for concessions has been the white reaction to outside condemnation. Hardly any other institution is more ridiculed than the United Nations. In contrast to the concern with threats from outside, however, latent black political developments within the Republic seem largely underrated in the public consciousness, although they are likely to prove more dangerous for white privileges than the sanctions of financially committed Western countries or pressures from the thus far militarily inferior African states. Indeed, with the communist world powers involved in other conflicts, there seems at present hardly any effective challenge to white South Africa from the outside.

Table 7 indicates, in the local terminology, awareness of various threats to white domination.

There are no significant differences among the subgroups of the sample in this aspect.

According to the long-term Apartheid projections, the eight prospective Bantustans will gain complete national independence sometime in the future. It is envisaged that they will perhaps merge together with other African states to form an economic commonwealth at a later stage. The Africans in the white areas of South Africa would then hold the status of foreign migratory workers under the jurisdiction of their respective homelands. Exclusive political self-government rather than territorial consolidation would be the basis of the future independence of the major tribal entities. In due course the Bantustans would become industrialized and consequently increasingly self-sufficient, not only absorbing the surplus population in the already overcrowded 'homelands', but attracting Africans in the metropolitan areas for possible resettlement as well.

TABLE 7

Threats to South Africa

'Which of the following factors do you consider the greatest threat to South Africa and to the successful realization of the programme of separate development?' (Multiple choice possible.)

	Parl. (40)	Offic. (103)	Entr. (206)	Afrik. (164)	Engl. (169)	Total (349)
	%	%	%	%	%	%
International Communism	65	75	74	75	72	73
Lack of understanding in the West	80	83	85	84	83	84
Pressure from independent African states	23	34	40	29	40	36
Black nationalism within the Republic	15	10	7	9	11	9
Immaturity of the South African electorate	25	11	17	13	20	16
Divergent interests of influential industrial groups in South Africa	27	21	7	20	18	14

Assuming for a moment that all the prerequisites of this programme were indeed to be fulfilled, especially that the white electorate would be willing to pour sufficient capital into these areas so that a comparable minimum standard of living could be achieved, at least two major facts would still remain to give the lie to this policy.

1. The main economic resources of the more advanced industrial state, built largely on the basis of non-white labour,
   would remain in the hands of the whites. Political independence for separated tribal units, on altogether 13 per cent of
   the country's land for 70 per cent of the population, would

hardly mean anything in the face of continuing dependence on the all-powerful white state. A large part of the African population, still living as a necessary labour force in the so-called white areas, would possess no rights in places where they were born and, in fact, had lived and worked for several generations.

2. The political and territorial fragmentation of the country, as envisaged in Apartheid and justified with reference to historical processes, would be the outcome of white coercion and power, not consensus. This would remain so as long as the real opponents of Apartheid were not allowed to raise their voice, were prevented from organizing themselves for effective counter-pressure, and, therefore, were unable to have at least a share in such a far-reaching decision. The majority support which the Apartheid policy now seems to receive within the tribal framework cannot be considered as representative of African opinion since the basic rules for this game are laid down by the ruling group and the alternative of a common non-racial society is excluded from African political activity within Apartheid rules.

These imposed aspects of the Apartheid scheme can be demonstrated in the timeless nature of the programme. No decision has ever been announced about when a Bantustan would be considered ripe for complete independence, not even for the Transkei, the Government's showpiece with the least phony preconditions for real independence. The seriousness of the power-elite's intention was revealed in a question which concretizes the theory by mentioning a vague time-limit for Transkeian independence.

It might, however, be possible that the Government would decide contrary to this unofficial opinion in the near future. This could occur both for external propaganda reasons and as a result of internal pressures to prove the sincerity of announced intentions. Since the former British Protectorates, once considered as test cases for Bantustan independence, function as South Africa's obedient satellites, suspicions in certain circles about the consequences of Transkei's independence have also waned. But while the geographical isolation of Lesotho, Botswana, and Swaziland in the midst of white-settler societies adds

TABLE 8

Independence for the Transkei

'Considering the recent development in the Transkei, do you think that within, say, ten to twenty years the situation there will be mature enough and that it would be sensible to give this territory complete independence, including foreign affairs as well as defence matters?'

	Parl. (40)	Offic. (103)	Entr. (206)	Total (349)
	%	%	%	%
Yes	23	17	15	17
Undecided	10	2	4	4
No	67	81	81	79
	100	100	100	100

to their economic weakness, the maritime location of the Transkei makes her more accessible for arms supplies, and her independence will probably depend on whether this potential threat can be handled.

Alternatives to the present state of Apartheid, the possibility of its total failure, and the collapse of white rule, although seldom admitted, have not disappeared from public debate. Even though the policy alternatives discussed publicly are more or less streamlined versions of 'separate development', they nevertheless could play a role in the modification of the present policy course. Apart from Apartheid, three different blueprints of white policy are frequently mentioned in party debate:

1. A geopolitical partition of the country into two separate white and African states, far exceeding the present territorial design of the Tomlinson Commission;
2. A race federation of semi-autonomous Bantustans which are represented in a central parliament for the whole country— a programme put forward by the United Party;
3. A gradual and partial integration through qualified franchise, as advocated by the Progressive Party;
4. An unrestricted, equal franchise for all people, which has only been advocated by the former Liberal and Communist Parties, but has never gained more than a few thousand white supporters.

TABLE 9

Alternatives to Apartheid

'Should the project of separate development for one reason or the other be discontinued, which of the following alternatives do you then consider as a possible solution?'

	Parl. (40)	Offic. (103)	Entr. (206)	Afrik. (164)	Engl. (169)	Total (349)
	%	%	%	%	%	%
Radical geopolitical separation of races in South Africa	70	64	23	72	11	40
'Race federation'—not independent Bantustans but representation in Parliament by white delegates	15	17	19	12	22	18
Qualified franchise and partial integration of the developed Bantu	2	15	55	10	63	38
Complete integration with general equal franchise	—	1	2	5	3	1
No alternative possible; no answer	13	3	1	1	1	3
	100	100	100	100	100	100

While the Afrikaans-speaking respondents conceive of complete territorial separation as the only alternative to Apartheid, the English tend towards partial integration. This distinct difference would seem to need more careful consideration, especially since it has become prominent among social scientists inside and outside South Africa to think vaguely of total partition as the magical and just formula to resolve the South African racial conflict.

Just partition as a supposedly realistic solution of the country's unsolvable contradictions,[12] or as a logical consequence of the present Apartheid policy,[13] would have to meet some distinct requirements, as Gwendolen Carter *et al.*[14] have pointed out: namely, the territorial separation of urban and economic resources, including the infrastructure of the country, according to the population needs and geographical spread. This settlement would have to be the outcome of extensive discussions and genuine consensus of representative leaders of all concerned groups—a fiction as long as non-white political debate outside the Apartheid framework is restricted and popular leaders are imprisoned or banned. But assuming that all these requirements were fulfilled, even then it remains doubtful whether partition, which in non-industrialized areas like India/Pakistan or Palestine caused wars and continued strains, would ever be applicable in a network of mutual economic dependence in which the historical merits of both antagonists can never be justly sorted out. Generation-long coercion and exploitation on the part of the whites have made Africans believe that only final majority rule can compensate for the colonial past. What might have liberating psychological consequences (but scant material benefits) in political contexts in which minorities have been permanently suppressed by the majority, such as the suggestions of separate Negro and Indian territories in North America, have the contrary effect when recommended to prevent the hitherto suppressed majority from taking over full democratic control from its conquerors. The concept of partition assumes that racial intolerance, once deprived of its material foundation and fear, will last for ever. The very process of sorting out a just partition would, however, presuppose and in itself promote a basic change of white attitudes. If this were to take place racial separation of two territories would be superfluous, especially since the sacrifices demanded of whites by a just partition would be far more substantial than those accompanying the creation of a non-racial society. Compared with the South African reality, these general considerations already demonstrate the dubious character of partition as a realistic alternative.

Similar response patterns to those found on the Apartheid alternatives were received to a question which asked directly about likely future internal trends. As possible developments in the next twenty years, the following were listed:

1. 'On the whole everything continues as it is at the moment.' (*Status quo.*)
2. 'More disciplinary control by the white man and increased legislation will be necessary in order to obtain peace and order.' (Police state.)
3. 'The Europeans will have to make substantial political and

economic concessions to the non-whites—much more than planned in the concept of separate development.' (Concessions.)

4. 'Revolutionary changes as a result of internal unrest and pressure from outside are likely.' (Revolution.)

TABLE 10

Predicted Future Developments

'If, in view of the tendencies in recent years, you should venture a prediction of the internal political development in the next twenty years, which one of the following viewpoints corresponds most to your own?'

	Parl. (40)	Offic. (103)	Entr. (206)	Afrik. (164)	Engl. (169)	Total (349)
	%	%	%	%	%	%
Status quo	53	56	44	62	35	48
Police state	13	14	6	15	3	9
Concessions	27	21	44	17	55	37
Revolution	2	4	3	1	5	3
No answer	5	5	3	5	2	3
	100	100	100	100	100	100

The English-speaking respondents anticipate to a considerable extent the necessity for concessions, while their Afrikaner counterparts believe in the preservation of the *status quo* or, if necessary, even stricter inroads in the civil liberties catalogue. As expected, hardly anyone foresees a revolutionary change of the present power structure. The confidence that white rule can be secured in the long run seems virtually unanimous. Looking realistically at the political and material trends in the rest of Africa since independence as well as the increasingly sophisticated techniques of white domestic power, there seems indeed little challenge for South Africa in the foreseeable future. On the assumption that no major power shifts or ideological reorientations take place in the world scene, the Afrikaner belief in the future perseverance of the racially structured past represents far less wishful thinking than the prediction of change based on dogmatic doctrines.

(e) Changing Ideological Outlook

It is not social change as such that is in question in South Africa but its degree, source, and direction. It is essentially in the realm of white power, in particular within Afrikanerdom, that relevant ideological changes have taken place in recent years. While significant changes in race relations have been successfully arrested for the time being, rapid developments within the privileged group will inevitably bear consequences for the social structure as a whole.

The history of intense mutual aversion and ethnocentric rejection between the two white language groups—even in the face of non-white pressure—need not be recalled here. Recent overtures from both groups since the last great flare-up of mutual aversion in the Republic or Commonwealth debate in 1961 seem one of the major internal developments. This trend reflects the urbanization of the Afrikaner but, above all, a commonly shared economic interest, backed by an increasing state capitalism. Important inequities, nevertheless, persist.

The percentage of English-speaking matriculants in the country is still twice as high as that of the Afrikaans-speaking matriculants (12·9 versus 6·4 per cent). Only 1·5 per cent of the Afrikaans population are university graduates against 3 per cent of the English-speaking group.

What seems more important is that despite the rise of individual Afrikaner capitalists and tycoons and despite an increasing Afrikaner share in urban commerce and industry, the Afrikaner-controlled capital in the total economy stands at 20–30 per cent with great differences in various sectors.[15] Of the total white income, only 45 per cent is earned by Afrikaners. In the upper income strata, the differences are clearer: 3·9 per cent of the Afrikaners earn more than R8000 a year, compared with 13·4 per cent of the English-speaking whites. As has often been mentioned, this relative economic backwardness contrasts with the political power of the Afrikaner who not only staffs the upper governmental positions but can rely on rank-and-file support in the civil service of the country.

How these historical cleavages are mirrored in the perspective of the opinion-makers in both groups seems important. No empirical studies verifying the proclaimed merger of the 'white laager' are as yet available. Although political speeches seem to indicate an increasing identification of the English-speaking section with Afrikaner concepts of race relations, there are no data as to whether this white integration is confined to the political sphere or if it extends to the cultural level of Afrikaner–English relations as well. A rather vague question attempted to gain tentative empirical answers in this realm. It aimed at testing whether the spontaneous feeling of the respondents would lie in diminishing frictions or in continuing differences, although both are not mutually exclusive.

The proportions of respondents who consider the historical differences as irrelevant turned out to be surprisingly high in both ethnic groups. It seems justified, however, to assume that our sample of better-educated and more pragmatic power-group members is on this point hardly representative for the

TABLE 11

Afrikaner–English Frictions

'One often hears the opinion that the historical friction between Afrikaans- and English-speaking South Africans is diminishing. Are you under the impression that this is applicable to the following spheres or that differences still exist?'

	Parl. (40)	Offic. (103)	Entr. (206)	Afrik. (164)	Engl. (167)	Total (349)
	%	%	%	%	%	%
Consciousness as South African Citizens						
Difference	33	21	20	23	22	22
Undecided	2	6	6	5	5	6
No difference	65	73	64	72	73	72
	100	100	100	100	100	100
Political Influence						
Difference	53	53	62	52	71	62
Undecided	20	15	15	16	14	15
No difference	27	37	23	32	15	23
	100	100	100	100	100	100
Cultural Standard						
Difference	33	41	38	40	38	38
Undecided	25	13	17	14	17	17
No difference	42	46	45	46	45	45
	100	100	100	100	100	100
Economic Activity						
Difference	38	32	31	34	30	32
Undecided	22	10	11	11	11	11
No difference	40	58	58	55	59	57
	100	100	100	100	10p	100

general feeling among the average white South Africans, where the old cleavages would seem to persist to a greater extent.

In spite of these reservations, our results do indicate that with the gradual restratification of Afrikaners in economic and professional positions, their tendency towards in-group glorification in opposition to the English out-group also waned and became superfluous. The fifty-year-long collective struggle of a structurally handicapped settler population seems to have come to an end, in the opinion of the majority of those leading group members who were once committed to political and cultural group-patriotism of remarkable intensity. A common white South African nationalism is well on the way to replacing the historical group identities.

In pursuing this line and a more pragmatic race policy, the majority of the Afrikaner power-elite has to reckon, however, with an influential opposition of traditionalists within its own ranks. The vicious in-fights between *verligte* (open-minded) and *verkrampte* (narrow-minded) Nationalists since 1967 have hampered the pace of Afrikaner modernization in external policies as well as in the implementation of the theoretical Apartheid scheme inside the country. The debate centred originally around such ephemeral issues as (1) whether increased immigration of supposedly unassimilable southern Europeans should be encouraged; (2) whether an 'outward policy' of establishing diplomatic relations with black African states and therefore black diplomats in a special suburb of Pretoria could be tolerated; (3) whether Maoris in the New Zealand rugby team should be welcomed and if so, how many; (4) to what extent 'Western liberalism' through imported magazines or proposed television should be tolerated or censored; and finally (5) whether English-speaking Nationalists should rise to prominence in the Nationalist Party or whether only a good Calvinist can be a true political leader, as asserted by Albert Hertzog, the leading traditionalist. In other categories, whether exclusiveness and the solidary isolation of the 'laager' or the non-ideological search for allies can best preserve white power, lies at the heart of the dispute. Given 'the great anonymous masses of rank and file who are Nationalists by instinct, by mystic intuition and not by intellectual rationalizing', as an Afrikaans paper comments,[16] there seems to be little doubt that the appeal to traditionalism could fall on fruitful soil, but that pragmatic *verligte* leadership will continue to hold power as long as it can guarantee 'law and order' and booming economic conditions.

The growing political heterogeneity of Afrikanerdom as a consequence of socio-economic changes and its long political hegemony is not reflected merely in the *verligte–verkrampte* dispute. Afrikanerdom has always had its extreme right-wing ideologists and its few prominent dissenters on the other side, such as Leo Marquard, Uys Krige, Beyers Naudé, Bram Fischer, and, among the younger writers, André Brink and B. Breytenbach. The politically relevant change is the emerging criticism of sacred Afrikaner traditions and beliefs by its own loyal supporters who are not on the fringe of the Volk. For the first time the Afrikaner press criticizes the government for the refusal of passports,[17] the imposition of censorship, as well as the idiosyncrasies of petty Apartheid. Sacred institutions such as the once powerful Broederbond are being questioned. 'Has the bond still a right of existence?' asks Dirk Richard, the editor of *Dagbreek*.[18] His explanation of the waning role of this influential lobby is revealing: 'It no longer acts like a powerful entity from its influential hiding-place, for the same quarrels, differences of opinion and gradual division which Afrikanerdom is experiencing in the open have also penetrated into the Broederbond.'[19] Even though the Afrikaner press is far from giving up its major role as a Government propagandist versus the English press, it indicates at the same time the slow emergence of more sophisticated readers who appreciate the cautious questions by more liberal or at least pragmatic critics. There is the possibility that this trend could lead to the formation of comparatively enlightened political pressure-groups within Afrikanerdom, similar to the foundation of the dissident Christian Institute in the religious sphere.

It is questionable whether the notion of a cohesive Afrikanerdom will continue to have much political meaning beyond the obvious cultural characteristics of this group. In the absence of strongly felt internal or external pressures, the former unifying emotional bond among Afrikaners is certainly giving way to a diluted ethnocentrism and nationalism, to be revived periodically in election campaigns or on memorial days. The growing secularization of Afrikaners in the religious sphere is being paralleled by less emphasis on the ideological basis in the political realm. It is indicative that the National Party in 1970 for the first time since 1948 lost votes in both general and provincial elections. In white South Africa too, traditional political adherence can no longer be presupposed as a kind of inherited group disposition. To be sure, these trends among the ruling group of the country have so far hardly influenced its basic racial policies, but they would seem to be prerequisites for any realistic perception of Afrikaner self-interest. Whether the now more sophisticated white laager can afford the pragmatic concessions necessary to appease its powerful challenger becomes the decisive question for its future fate. Although ideological attempts are made to reconcile white privileges with African aspirations, the overall consciousness of the South African power elite as revealed in this survey appears to point instead to a gross political lag in terms of any realistic assessment of post-colonial conditions. With non-white dependence as a prerequisite for white privileges, the transformation of South Africa into a multi-racial society of equals seems unlikely to take the smooth course of recent Afrikaner-English integration. However, the flexibility of the South African power elite to adapt its system of dominance to changing conditions, to strengthen it economically, and to streamline it politically by concessions towards deracialization, should not be underestimated. Ambivalent progress though it may seem to the advocates of heightened polarization, it could nevertheless prove to be the most decisive factor for future development in the South of Africa.

REFERENCES

1. Many studies emphasize the idealistic and paternalistic dedication of South Africa's domestic colonial officers, devoted to the unsolvable task of 'preparing the natives for self-government fifty years too late', as Douglas Brown states. See *Against the World: A Study of White South African Attitudes*, Collins, London, 1966, 115. It is this group whose attitudes would seem to be the most relevant in the context of this study.

2. VAN DER MERWE, HENDRIK W., 'Race and Politics among the White South African Elite', unpublished paper intended for

H

presentation at the Annual Meeting of the African Studies Association in Montreal, 1969.

3. *Hansard*, cols. 2185–95, 16 June 1966.

4. MACRAE, NORMAN, 'What Will Destroy Apartheid?' *Harper's Magazine*, Mar. 1970, 40.

5. All statements about significant differences in this report are based on greater than the 0·05 level of confidence.

6. Previously Pierre van den Berghe has emphasized this paternalistic approach in contrast to the opinion which ascribes to the South African fascistic features. See van den Berghe (ed.), *Africa: Social Problems of Change and Conflict*, Chandler Publishing Company, San Francisco, 1965, 502; also by the same author, *South Africa: A Study in Conflict*, Wesleyan University Press, Middletown, Conn., 1965.

7. PETTIGREW, THOMAS F., 'Personality and Sociocultural Factors in Intergroup Attitudes,' *Journal of Conflict Resolution*, 1958, 2, 29–42.

8. VAN DEN BERGHE, *South Africa*, op. cit., 274.

9. KUPER, LEO, 'The Political Situation of Non-Whites in South Africa', in W. A. Hance (ed.), *Southern Africa and the United States*, Columbia University Press, New York, 1968, 103.

10. HOROWITZ, RALPH, *The Political Economy of South Africa*, Weidenfeld & Nicolson, London, 1967, 427.

11. BLUMER, HERBERT, 'Industrialisation and Race Relations', in Guy Hunter (ed.), *Industrialisation and Race Relations*, Oxford University Press, London, 1965, 252.

12. TIRYAKIAN, EDWARD A., 'Sociological Realism: Partition for South Africa?', *Social Forces*, *46*, 1967, 2, 208–21.

13. TURK, AUSTIN F., 'The Futures of South Africa', *Social Forces*, 1967, *45*, 402–12.

14. CARTER, G. M., KARIS, T., and STULTZ, N. M., *South Africa's Transkei: The Politics of Domestic Colonialism*, Northwestern University Press, Evanston, 1967, 181.

15. It is assumed that Afrikaner capital now controls 9 per cent of the mining industry, 37 per cent of the iron production, 20 per cent of the coal, and 32 per cent of the asbestos production (*Sunday Times*, 9 April 1967). Other assessments claim the Afrikaner part in commerce is 28 per cent; in the bank sector, 14 per cent; and in secondary industry, 9 per cent (*Newscheck*, 24 Nov. 1968).

16. *Die Vaderland*, 8 Sept. 1969.

17. See *Die Beeld* in the case of the playwright Athol Fugard, 14 June 1970.

18. *Dagbreek en Landstem*, 13 Sept. 1970.

19. Ibid.

6

GWENDOLEN M. CARTER

AFRICAN CONCEPTS OF NATIONALISM IN SOUTH AFRICA*

African nationalism in South Africa is distinctive in its setting, objectives, and, to a lesser degree, tactics. Nowhere else on the continent, with the possible exception of Algeria, has African nationalism confronted so strong a local white power structure, one that since 1948 has been dominated by a powerful national-ism of its own: Afrikaner nationalism. Nowhere else has African nationalism operated within a dynamic industrial and com-mercial structure that exerts a compelling attraction and influ-ence on all the inhabitants of the country. Nowhere else have the political rights of Africans become progressively lessened, rather than extended.

By every canon except international law, South Africa in-corporates a 'colonial situation', no less restrictive in all except economic growth than any colonial system that has existed in Africa. Inevitably, therefore, the expressions of African national-ism in South Africa, like those in colonial Africa, are condi-tioned by the superior power of the white authorities and white community whose policies and actions determine the milieu within which Africans must live. That the latter milieu is more set in its mould and inclined to increasing rigidity under pres-sures for change, rather than responsive adaptation of the type characteristic of colonial countries after World War II, is a natural result of the fact that changes in political, economic, and social relations in South Africa would affect internal, not merely international, relations. Such changes have generally

* Melville J. Herskovits Memorial Lecture delivered under the auspices of the Centre of African Studies, Edinburgh University, 16 March 1965.

been viewed with apprehension by the dominant white group, and particularly by that section of the population, chiefly Afrikaans-speaking, that knew the sting of 'poor white' insecurity in the 1920s. Subsequently trade-union activity and government action combined to overcome the crisis created by unproductive farms and lack of industrial opportunities. None the less, the memories of the past coupled with constant contact with increasingly skilful African and other non-white workers provide a backdrop against which it is not difficult to stir latent sentiments of fear of competition for jobs as well as of the preponderant numbers of non-whites in every urban centre of the Republic.

Organized expressions of African nationalism in South Africa, more like those of West than East Africa, have been largely urban-founded and based, and their leadership drawn from the educated professional middle class. As elsewhere, foreign training and experience (for example, Dr. A. B. Xuma, President-General of the African National Congress for the significant nine-year period from 1940 to 1949, received his medical degree from Edinburgh University), and awareness of American Negro and of Pan-African movements were important stimulants to what was attempted. Indeed the founding of the African National Congress (A.N.C.) in 1912 was the direct result of the experience abroad of four lawyers: Dr. I. P. KaSeme, who had a brilliant career at Columbia University and subsequently at Jesus College, Oxford, and the Inns of Court, and three other African lawyers who had just qualified in England, Alfred Mangena, Richard Msimang, and George D. Montsioa. The first President of the South African Native National Congress, as the A.N.C. was first named, was the Revd. John L. Dube, who had been at college in the United States. More distinctive is the fact that in South Africa, far more than in other countries in Africa, local white residents and both Coloureds and Asians have contributed, both positively and negatively, to the formulation of philosophies, character of tactics, and type of organization of African nationalist movements in South Africa.

No less significant for the course of African nationalism in South Africa is the fact that from the founding of the first formal African political organization, the Native Electoral Association, in 1884, there have been whites who formally or informally have associated themselves with African aspirations. These whites have represented a wide spectrum of political beliefs ranging all the way from traditional conservatives to left-wing Communists. Their numbers were never substantial enough to exert effective influence on the white electorate: even the Progressives with their almost 70,000 votes in the 1961 election could put only one member into the House of Assembly, while the Liberals never won a national election in any except an African constituency, of which there have been none since 1960. None the less, the influence over the years of those whites who have been most sensitive to African needs and aspirations helped to keep the standard-bearer of African nationalism, the African National Congress, from becoming exclusivist in attitude, and kept alive the hope of eventual African participation in a common community.

The most open expressions of African nationalism may be grouped summarily into two broad categories that historically have alternated with each other. The first category includes the efforts animated by what may be called 'South Africanism', a fundamental and lasting objective. This philosophy upheld the goal of common citizenship and made its primary appeal to the white community to promote the changes necessary to achieve this goal. The second category includes the more purely Africanist efforts to stimulate a sense of African self-confidence and self-reliance in seeking both an end to colour discrimination and a positive role in the moulding of South African society.

Before World War II, the efforts to promote 'South Africanism' included at least two distinct types of approaches: the first, a common association with liberal whites, and after 1920 with left-wing whites, in organizations unified by a common purpose; and the second, through appeals to what were thought to be common Western values.

The earliest obvious example of common working together was the Native Electoral Association, organized in 1884, as already noted, by the Cape Independents with the help of John Tengo Jabavu who, in the same year, founded the most famous of African newspapers, *Imvo Zabantsundu* (Native Opinion). Jabavu had acted in 1884 as election agent for James Rose Innes, an Independent who was contesting Victoria East, a frontier constituency between predominantly white and African areas. It is worth remembering that at that time Africans, who, since representative government had been granted the Cape Province in 1853, had possessed the vote on the same terms as Europeans and Coloureds, numbered 47 per cent of all voters in the five border constituencies in the Eastern Cape and over 50 per cent in two of them. Their potential political influence frightened the European members of the Cape Parliament, apart from the Independents, and in 1887 the Parliamentary Legislation Act resulted in striking some 30,000 Africans off the common roll. Even so African voters held the balance of power in seven constituencies between 1896 and 1910. But after Union Africans were never again in a sufficiently strong political position to influence the character of white political organization. It is an interesting reflection on the white fears that progressively reduced and ultimately nullified African political influence in South Africa that it was the temporarily possessed voting strength of the Africans that resulted in this mild type of multi-racial political association. By the time the Liberal Party after 1953 attempted a somewhat similar use of African support in their election campaigns, it was necessarily in all-white or all-African constituencies, and in the former the effect was to promote fear and distaste rather than to increase understanding.

Another major example of association of Africans with liberal whites was in the Joint Council movement started in the late 1920s by J. D. Rheinallt Jones and Howard Pim for common discussion of mutual problems. After the Institute of Race Relations was founded in Johannesburg in 1929 these Councils, which operated in many parts of the country, worked under its aegis. The Joint Councils promoted the old Cape liberalism of the vote belonging to all educated men, and some at least of their white members did not shrink from the prospect of an extension of the African franchise to the place where there could be an African majority. The Africans themselves in these Councils tended to be quieter than their white associates, and later Africanists maintain, perhaps unfairly, that African participation in the Joint Council movement diluted African nationalism in the 1920s and contributed to the obvious weakness of the African National Congress in this period. From the more positive side, the Joint Council movement increased understanding on both sides and might have led to more active politically-inclined working together except for the crisis in African confidence caused by the Hertzog legislation of 1936 that removed the Cape African voters from the common roll.

Another case-study could be of the Industrial and Commercial Union (I.C.U.), whose early successful industrial effort coupled with the colourful leadership of Clements Kadalie of Nyasaland made it the dominant African organization of the 1920s. Because it was not primarily a nationalist or politically inclined organization, though its impact was felt along both lines, the I.C.U. has been deliberately left out of consideration, however, despite its important character, and the rival efforts first of the Communists to exert control and subsequently of the Scottish trade unionist, William G. Ballinger, to direct the organization to constructive efforts.

The second type of approach of organizations promoting 'South Africanism' was to appeal to common Western values. This was the line of the early years of the African National Congress, founded in 1912 out of provincial associations as the African equivalent, however inadequate, of national white political organizations. This 'South Africanism' seeks a South African nation of which Africans are an integral part. It accepts the essential role of white South Africans but asserts also the Africans' own essential contribution to that country. It stands for African values but as part of a broader, national scheme of values, a synthesis or blending through harmonious interaction.

This approach has always been the most broadly appealing and, in this sense, the most significant one throughout the history of African nationalism in South Africa. While it has had different manifestations, and been sharply criticized as 'collaborationist' from time to time, there is little doubt that fulfilment of this aspiration could satisfy all African nationalists, even those who have preached a more exclusive Africanism and have adopted the ultimate and despairing tactic of violence.

Before World War II, the chief ways of putting forward this broad 'South Africanism' appeal were to organize mass meetings and to file petitions against discrimination and in support of common rights. On the eve of South African Union, the National Native Convention protested at the exclusion of Africans from Parliament. A generation later, in December 1935, all African political associations in the country joined together in the All-African National Convention, in a unique demonstration of unanimity, to protest vehemently against the Hertzog–Smuts legislation to remove the Cape Africans from the common voting roll. The United Transkeian General Council in Umtata, the oldest government-approved organization for expression of African opinion, voiced its opposition no less emphatically. In between these efforts, petitions against specific grievances were carried to the British Government (which refused to receive them because South Africa had been granted responsible government and then dominion status), to the Versailles Peace Conference, and to the South African Government itself.

A critical African memorandum drafted early in the 1950s blamed lack of results on the A.N.C. belief 'that changes in the conditions of the people could be brought about by relying on constitutional methods which involved explaining to the authorities the effect of their laws and policies on the African people.'[1] Yet it seemed appropriate to educated middle-class Africans in the period before World War II, particularly in the light of their existing degree of association with whites, to appeal in these terms and by these means to Europeans whom they felt to hold similar values to their own.

Writing in 1922 in the *Guardian* on 'The Race Problem', R. V. Selope Thema, General Secretary of the South African Native National Congress, maintained in a fairly characteristic statement that

this is a human problem, which can only be solved by approaching it in the spirit of humanity. The right to live of every race of mankind is indisputable. This being so, each race of mankind has the right to work out its own destiny and live its own life without let or hindrance. . . . We claim our rights of citizenship first as the aboriginals of this country and second as British subjects; we claim equal opportunities and facilities for improvement; we claim a voice in the government of our country and in the administration of monies which we pay to the Treasury of the State; we claim the equal protection of the law with the other citizens of the state—in short, we claim equal political rights with our fellow subjects.[2]

At the same time, his scepticism that there would be any response to his appeal to common values and to natural rights appears as he added: 'Under democratic institutions it is only the interests of those who have the power of the ballot that are considered and safe-guarded. . . .'

A more official statement of the broad 'South Africanism' concept is presented in *African Claims*, incorporating the 'Atlantic Charter from the Africans' Point of View,' and the Bill of Rights adopted in 1945 at the Annual Conference of the A.N.C.[3] The former reflected the keen interest of Africans in the war aims voiced by President Roosevelt and Prime Minister Churchill, aims that they specifically related to their own needs.

The Bill of Rights began, 'We, the African people of the Union of South Africa, demand the granting of full citizenship rights such as are enjoyed by all Europeans in South Africa.' It proceeded to specify political rights, namely, the right to vote and to be elected to all political offices; the right to equal justice, to 'own, buy, hire or lease and occupy' land and movable property, to engage in all forms of lawful occupations 'on the same terms and conditions as other sections of the population', to free and compulsory education, to be appointed to and hold office in the civil service and to equal treatment in social service; and to freedom of residence, movement, and the Press. The African Bill of Rights is a basic statement of human rights presented in twelve points with elaborations. It was the crowning formulation of the fundamental aims of what may be called the African 'establishment', the moderate, middle-class, professional leadership of the A.N.C. typified by Dr. Xuma.

Interacting with this broad 'South African' approach, which concentrated on appeals to whites for the rights of common citizenship, is the first of the alternative emphases: an assertion in the early 1940s by the newly formed Youth League of 'Africanism' in both its national and its Pan-African senses. Among the best-known figures of the Youth League were the future leaders of both the A.N.C. and the Pan-Africanist Congress, the PAC: Nelson Mandela, Oliver Tambo, and Walter Sisulu on the one side, and Robert Sobukwe and A. P. Mda on the other, with Jordan Ngubane sympathetically associated. They preached a new militancy that asserted the goal of African self-sufficiency in working for their objectives and in the early years of the Youth League they opposed close association with whites and Indians and with Communists. To stir up their African supporters, the Youth League (officially

formed in 1944 as an arm of the chief organ of African nationalism, the African National Congress) preached self-confidence,
self-reliance, and a common sense of African unity inside and
outside South Africa to provide cohesion, a sense of purpose,
and a belief in the possibility of ultimate success for African
aspirations. Confronted with a reduction, indeed almost elimination, of the small political opportunities and influence
possessed up until 1936 (the opposite trend to that which was to
begin operating and accelerate so quickly in British and French
African territories after World War II), the 'Africanist' stimulus
to the broad 'South African' objective took form in a philosophy
to stir African pride, and in specific proposals, outlined in some
detail in the Programme of Action of 1949, to provide alternative means of appealing to the ruling group notably through
self-suffering in the Passive Resistance Campaign of 1952.

A year and a half before the Pan-African Congress in Man-
chester of October 1945, the Manifesto of the Congress Youth
League affirmed its belief 'that the national liberation of
Africans will be achieved by Africans themselves', and its faith
'in the unity of all Africans from the Mediterranean Sea in the
North to the Indian and Atlantic Oceans in the South'. It
declared that 'Africans must speak with one voice'. Moreover,
in a phrase comparable in concept to that of Afrikaner nationalism, the creed of the Youth League began by avowing that there
is a 'divine destiny of nations'.[4]

It was A. M. Lembede who formulated the philosophy of the
movement in broad and stirring terms. 'History is a record of
humanity's striving for complete self-realization,' he wrote, and
each nation has 'its own particular contribution to make towards the general progress and welfare of mankind'. Basically
he called for a combination of old and new. He harked back to
'our great heroes of the past, e.g. Shaka, Moshoeshoe and other
great chiefs' who had fought for African freedom. He also looked
forward to contributions that could be made in the future.
Introducing into the nationalist philosophy an economic concept, he declared that 'the fundamental structure of Bantu
Society is socialistic. . . . Our task is to develop this socialism by
the infusion of new and modern socialistic ideas.' On a more
universal plane, he suggested, perhaps partly out of his Roman
Catholic upbringing, that the past and the present could be

united by retaining and preserving 'the belief in the immortality of our ancestors', but declared also that 'our ethical system today has to be based on Christian morals since there is nothing better anywhere in the world'.[5]

In another article Lembede described what he saw to be the policy of the Congress Youth League.[6] Its seven points, here summarized only briefly, were Pan-African in orientation and hortatory in spirit. Speaking at first of the continent as a whole, he maintained that Africa is a black man's country and Africans are one. The leader of the Africans would come out of their own loins.

As for South Africa, Lembede agreed that co-operation between Africans and other non-Europeans on common problems and issues might be highly desirable, but felt that this occasional co-operation could only take place between Africans as a single unit and other non-Europeans as separate units. Non-European Union, as sought by the Non-European Unity Movement, which had Coloured as well as African members, he found to be 'a fantastic dream which has no foundation in reality'.

Above all, he stressed that 'the divine destiny of the African people is national freedom. . . . Freedom is an indispensable condition for progress and development.' At the same time he warned that 'Africans must aim at balanced progress or advancement'. As for economics, he felt, like most later African leaders, that they were second to politics. 'After national freedom, then, socialism. . . . Our immediate task, however, is not socialism, but national liberation,' an acceptance of the inability of Africans to shape South African society so long as they were politically powerless.

That these concepts were not racially exclusivist but rather aimed at establishing the integrity of the African as an individual and of Africans as a group is made manifestly clear in the Programme of Action.[7] Its fundamental principles, the document states clearly,

are inspired by the desire to achieve national freedom. By national freedom we mean freedom from White domination and the obtainment of political independence. This implies the rejection of the concept of segregation, Apartheid, trusteeship, or White Leadership, which are all in one way or another motivated by the idea of White

Domination or domination of the White over the Blacks. Like all other people, the African people claim the right of self-determination.

The particular right for which they fight, however, is not for separatism but for 'the right of direct representation in all the governing bodies of the country—national, provincial and local. . . .'

Those who formed the Youth League had long been frustrated by the techniques of protest and appeal used by the A.N.C. Now they proposed to employ a new set of weapons: the boycotting of 'all differential political institutions' (the programme which the All-African Convention had recommended since 1943), and on a more positive line 'immediate and active boycott, strikes, civil disobedience, non-cooperation and such other means as may bring about the accomplishment and realization of our aspirations'.

The impact of the Youth League philosophy on the A.N.C. showed itself concretely in the defiance campaign of 1952, in which some 8,000 trained African volunteers deliberately sought arrest to publicize their opposition to what they termed 'unjust laws'. The six laws specified ranged from the universally hated pass laws to the recent and potentially far-reaching provisions of the Suppression of Communism Act. As far as the franchise was concerned, only the Separate Representation of Voters Bill was singled out, the measure through which the Government was attempting to remove the Coloured voters from the common roll in Cape Province as Africans had been removed in 1936.

Opposed to this activist approach, but with what was in essence a 'South Africanism' philosophy, the All-African Convention attempted to lead Africans towards its fundamental and comprehensive objectives through the technique of non-collaboration. These objectives are laid down succinctly in the Ten Point Programme.[8] Its key provisions are the specific right of all adults to the franchise and to be elected to national and local political bodies, and a more general statement claiming 'full equality of rights for all citizens without distinction of race, colour and sex'. In accordance with the latter principle it calls for revision of the land acts, of the civil and criminal codes, of the system of taxation, and of labour legislation and its application to the mines and agriculture. To these specific objectives related to current restrictions on Africans are added the normal freedoms of Western society—freedom of speech, press, meetings and associations, movement and occupation, inviolability of person, house, and privacy—and a claim for 'compulsory, free and uniform education for all children up to the age of 16, with free meals, free books and school equipment for the needy'.

Compared to previous documents drafted by African associations the Ten Point Programme is distinguished by its breadth of range, practicality, and specific interconnection of political, economic, social, and educational rights. That it received less publicity than did the A.N.C. manifesto and actions is chiefly due to the A.A.C.'s approach and federal character. The latter meant that it worked through affiliated organizations, in particular the Cape Teachers Association, not as did the A.N.C. through mass meetings, announcements of intentions, and overt acts. The A.A.C. itself believes its influence has been still more potent than that of the A.N.C. and that its doctrine of non-collaboration has helped to stimulate such spontaneous anti-government actions in rural areas as non-compliance with stock culling and burning of huts of pro-government chiefs.

The A.A.C.'s federation formed part of a still wider federation, the Non-European Unity Movement, that included certain Coloured associations. This type of multiracial non-European working together might have been acceptable to Lembede. After his death, however, the Youth League became temporarily still more Africanist, even to the point of racialism. Then, as the Afrikaner Nationalist Government through the Suppression of Communism Act of 1950 openly threatened all who acted in broad multiracial or non-racial terms, many of the younger as well as older members of the A.N.C. decided to cement their relations with the South African and Natal Indian Congresses, that had already used the techniques of passive resistance in Durban in 1946 to protest at residential segregation, and also to establish links with whites and Communists, of whom they had been suspicious while the multiracial Communist Party was still legal but who now became fellow sufferers from government restrictions. It was not until the Defiance Campaign obviously failed by 1953 in its objective of influencing white opinion, however, that the African National Congress swung fully into its second alternation: a return to formal association with a white organization, this time the left-wing Congress of Democrats, and with other non-white organizations, notably the South African Indian Congress and the largely ineffectual Coloured Peoples' Organization, these four together with the South African Congress of Trade Unions making up the Congress Alliance.

The concept of nationalism animating the Congress Alliance harks back to some degree to the earlier 'South Africanism' but with a more militant tone, both in objectives and in tactics, and with an economic aspect, including nationalization, lacking in earlier formations. Its chief activity was the formulation and publicizing of the Freedom Charter.

The genesis of the Freedom Charter was a simple but potent conception. Searching for a means of maintaining the sense of participation by Africans in seeking their own objectives that had been stimulated by the Defiance Campaign, Z. K. Matthews, the most distinguished of African academics, and his wife Frieda, hit on the idea of urging Africans everywhere to write down their grievances and desires and send them to their local A.N.C. centres. In at least some areas, this plan resulted in hundreds, perhaps thousands, of scribbled statements on odd scraps of paper. These ideas were drafted centrally by representatives of the Congress Alliance into the Freedom Charter, a somewhat curious mixture of nineteenth-century liberal aspirations and twentieth-century socialist aims.

Although subsequently used by the Government in the long drawn out but abortive Treason Trial (for which the arrests were made in December 1956 and the final acquittals not until March 1961), the Freedom Charter was largely free of Communist phraseology. Its theme was 'the freedom of the African people from all discriminatory laws whatsoever' and it envisaged a social welfare state in which 'no one shall go hungry' and 'rest, leisure and recreation shall be the right of all'. On the other hand, the document incorporated no explicit doctrine of social change and proposed no specific programme of action.

The most original feature of the Freedom Charter in terms of the history of African nationalist concepts was the demand for public ownership of mineral wealth, banks, and monopoly industry, and a redivision of the land among those who worked it. The most controversial statement was the opening sentence in the Freedom Charter:[9] 'We, the people of South Africa,

declare for all our country and the world to know—That South
Africa belongs to all who live in it, black and white. . . .'

The Charter was not presented to the A.N.C. in advance of
the Kliptown meeting, at which it was accepted on 25–6 June
1955, and many Africanist-minded members quickly voiced
their dissatisfaction with the document. Although officially
adopted by the A.N.C. early in 1956, opposition continued until
friction reached a breaking-point—and the alternation back to
the Africanists came once more into play.

In a letter sent to the Speaker of the A.N.C. conference held at
Orlando on 1–2 November 1958, the group that subsequently
became the Pan-Africanists took their stand against the opening
phrase in the Freedom Charter:

Seeing that it claims that the land no longer belongs to the African
people, but is auctioned for sale to *all* who live in this country:
In numerous conferences of the A.N.C. we have made it clear that
we are committed to the overthrow of White Domination and the
restoration of the land to its rightful owners.[10]

They maintained too that the Kliptown Charter was 'in irreconcilable conflict' with the 1949 Programme of Action. The
letter ended by stating: 'We are launching out openly, on our
own, as the custodians of the A.N.C. policy as it was formulated
in 1912 and pursued, up to the time of the Congress Alliances.'
In March 1959 the Pan-Africanist Congress was formally
established, with Robert Mangaliso ('wonderful') Sobukwe,
Lecturer in Zulu Studies at the University of Witwatersrand, as
President.

The Youth League had worked within the A.N.C. and had
invigorated and advanced it; the later Africanists finally rejected the A.N.C. and began a rival organization creating a ferment of bitterness that still weakens both, despite the common
bans imposed on them after Sharpeville and efforts both inside
and outside the country to overcome their division. Partly the
break came because of a belief that the A.N.C. was being
dominated by the white Communists of the Congress of Democrats, and by Indians. Partly it was a reflection of the new
situation in Africa itself, where Ghana had become independent
in 1957, the All-African Peoples' Conference had met in Accra,
and the atmosphere was optimistic and stimulating as the

transfer of power approached for so many African countries. The South African setting, in contrast, was far more restrictive than in 1944, with many African leaders still involved in the Treason Trial, severe laws in readiness for outbreaks of dis-affection, and Nationalist controls consolidated.

Despite the differences from the earlier Youth League period the appeals made by Sobukwe echoed aspects of those of Lembede. Sobukwe, too, exhorted, appealed for African self-confidence, and railed against weakness. He said on 30 August 1959, in his State of the Nation Address,

> . . . our task is to exorcise this slave mentality and to impart to the African masses that sense of self-reliance which will make them prefer self-government to the good government preferred by the A.N.C.'s leader. . . . We are calling on our people to assert their personality.[11]

More concretely than Lembede, Sobukwe spelled out his view of Africanism in classic Pan-African terms:

> We aim, politically, at government of the Africans by the Africans, for the Africans, with everybody who owes his only loyalty to Africa and who is prepared to accept the democratic rule of an African majority being regarded as an African. We guarantee no minority rights, because we think in terms of individuals, not groups. . . . [We will go on until] every person who is in Africa will be an African and a man's colour will be as irrelevant as is the shape of his ears.

In this picture of the continent, South Africa was not excep-tional nor apart: 'True democracy can be established in South Africa and on the continent only when White supremacy has been destroyed.'

Where Lembede had spoken of socialism, Sobukwe talked of Africanist Socialist Democracy, comparable in concept to the African socialism of independent African states.

> Africanists reject totalitarianism in any form and accept political democracy as understood in the West. We also reject the economic exploitation of the many for the benefit of the few. . . . [We should borrow the best from both East and West, but] retain and maintain our distinctive personality and refuse to be the satraps or stooges of either power bloc.[12]

Where other Africanists had spoken mainly of the need to appeal to the African masses, Sobukwe stressed their crucial role. 'The illiterate and semi-literate African masses', he maintained, 'constitute the key and centre and content of any struggle for true democracy in South Africa.'[13]

Despite continued differences between the A.N.C. and PAC over the degree and type of association with whites, and particularly left-wing whites, there seems little conflict between their concepts and their long-range aims. At his trial in 1962, the most widely acknowledged younger leader of the A.N.C., Nelson Mandela, spoke of the inspiration coming from traditional African society, and suggested that 'in such a society are contained the seeds of revolutionary democracy in which none will be held in slavery or servitude, and in which poverty, want and insecurity shall be no more'.[14]

The older, middle-class appeal to common liberal standards had been combined with a newer broad-gauged socialism and a sense for traditional African values. Africanism is an integral part of the African view of a future 'South Africanism'.

Despite alternations of emphasis and appeals, despite different structures and leaders, the same basic notion runs through these expressions of African nationalism: the desire that broadens to an insistence on full participation in a common national enterprise. Surprisingly enough there is relatively little racial exclusivism in ultimate objectives to match that of the whites. White domination and racial discrimination are to be overthrown as soon as feasible but the whites are accepted in their individual capacities as long as they prove their 'Africanism' by their dedication to the continent of Africa and their acceptance of the principle of majority rule. Perhaps only the imminence of large-scale bloodshed would make these conditions attractive to South African whites, but in the perspective of their fear of being swamped, decimated, or expelled if African control were established it is worth emphasizing that these broad South African views are rooted in a traditional and stable outlook that has extended as long as have the conscious expressions of African nationalism.

There is, however, one further expression of African nationalism in South Africa that is becoming increasingly racially exclusivist and thus cuts across all the mainstreams of African nationalist thought. This strand is the objective of an autonomous and ultimately independent area or state within which

I

Africans will have full control. This is a notion advanced as a second best from time to time throughout the whole period under review, commonly as a result of frustration. In his Presidential Address to the A.N.C. in 1921 entitled 'The Exclusion of the Bantu', the Revd. Z. R. Mahabane bitterly opposed segregation but agreed that a certain value might result from separation

if due provision had been made for the partition of the land into 'hemispheres' of equal size and like quality for locating the respective races, each race being given the right to manage its own internal affairs, even though the advice of the more developed race might be necessary in connection with the affairs of the less developed race.[15]

In his article on 'The Race Problem' Selope Thema in the next year maintained that the interwoven interests of Europeans and Africans made it virtually impossible to 'segregate the native so as to enable him to develop according to his own lines', a theme already proposed by whites who felt challenged by growing integration. It could be done, he said, only if the principle of self-determination was accepted and

this principle means the division of the country into two parts to be controlled respectively by Europeans and Africans. That is to say, each race will have its own sovereign rights to manage its affairs in its portion of the country without interference from the other.[16]

In his Presidential Address to the All-African Convention in June 1936, protesting at the Cape African removal from the common roll, Dr. D. D. T. Jabavu also sharply defined alternatives: 'segregation and colour bars must go; alternatively we want a separate State of our own where we shall rule ourselves freed from the present hypocritical position'.[17] These are only examples of a theme that appears not infrequently in the context of last resort. It is a comment on the African desire to share the fruits of a flourishing economy to which they contribute essential manpower and skill, on their realism about the difficulties of breaking up so integrated an economic structure, and on their opposition to fragmentation, that this theme is played in so low a key.

The Nationalist Government programme of separate development, however, has raised the issue of territorial separation to a realm of practicality that gives it new importance. In the Transkei, South Africa's first 'Bantustan', the two political parties stand respectively for African exclusivism and for a multiracial or non-racial society in the 'South Africanism' tradition. While Paramount Chief Victor Poto and Knowledge Guzana uphold the latter line, the Chief Minister, Chief Kaiser Matanzima, maintains that 'this country is ours' and is urging the progressive withdrawal of whites from that territory.

Thus the polarization of sentiment, of which moderate Africans have warned for so long, and that is now so obvious in South Africa, is acquiring an African territorial base. It might be the final tragedy of South Africa if the broad view of South Africa as a whole, upheld by African leaders of the variety of persuasions that have been described, should give way to a narrowed, racially based African separatist view, and if intensified white exclusivism should be matched by an equally intense black exclusivism. At that point the latent passions both of rural and urban Africans might be freed from the restraints imposed over long years by organized leadership with effects one hesitates to contemplate.

On the broad issue posed at the start, the not surprising conclusion appears to be that major dangers for race relations result from rigidity, compartmentalization, and lack of outlets for satisfying broadly based aspirations, but that the virtual monopoly of force in white hands remains a powerful deterrent to hostile action. As far as future aims are concerned, however, the effect of increasing racialism may be to replace the constructive objectives voiced by Africans in the past by a virulent self-centred black nationalism that could ultimately lead to disaster.

REFERENCES

1. Memorandum dealing with the Programme of Action adopted at the annual conference of the African National Congress, Dec. 1949, and 'Some Aspects of the Policy of the A.N.C.', typed, c. 1953.
2. SELOPE THEMA, R. V., 'The Race Problem', *Guardian*, 1 Sept. 1922.
3. *African Claims in South Africa*, Congress Series No. 11, A.N.C., Johannesburg, 1945.

4. 'Congress Youth League Manifesto', Provisional Committee of the Congress Youth League, Mar. 1944.

5. LEMBEDE, A. M., 'Some Basic Principles of African Nationalism', *Inyanaso*.

6. LEMBEDE, A. M., 'Policy of the Congress Youth League', *Inkundla Ya Bantu*, May 1946.

7. Programme of Action adopted at the annual conference of the African National Congress, Dec. 1949.

8. TABATA, I. B., *The All-African Convention (The Awakening of the People)*, Johannesburg People's Press, 1950, 79–81.

9. Presented at a meeting of the Congress of the People, Kliptown, June 1955.

10. Letter sent to Mr. Speaker, A.N.C. Conference held at Orlando, 1–2 Nov. 1958, signed by S. T. Ngendane.

11. SOBUKWE, R. M., 'The State of the Nation', Address to Pan-Africanist Congress of South Africa, Orlando, 30 Aug. 1959.

12. SOBUKWE, R. M., Opening Address at the Pan-Africanist Inaugural Convention, 6 April 1959.

13. Ibid.

14. MANDELA, NELSON, Address to Court before Sentence, 7 Nov. 1962, in *We Accuse*, Christian Action pamphlet, London, n.d., 25.

15. MAHABANE, REVD. Z. R., 'The Exclusion of the Bantu', Presidential Address to the African National Congress, 1921, *Selected Speeches of Revd. Z. R. Mahabane*, Program of African Studies, Northwestern University, n.d., 15.

16. SELOPE THEMA, op. cit.

17. JABAVU, D. D. T., *Presidential Address to All-African Convention*, Lovedale Press, Lovedale, South Africa, 1936, 13.

7

FATIMA MEER

AFRICAN NATIONALISM—
SOME INHIBITING FACTORS

Background

The South African social structure is not legitimated through
popular consensus. The State is propped up by a massive
system of coercion, leaning heavily on police power and dispens-
ing with the rule of law when expedient. Territorial and social
separation of component ethnic groups vitiates the development
of a common South African society and splinters the people into
a number of antagonistic groups. The situation suggests an
ideal launching-pad for social disintegration. Sociologists have
described the system as in a state of deep conflict, and international politicians have declared it to be a threat not only to
its own internal peace but to world peace. That conflict has
been brewing for over half a century and during that time
accumulating laws have increased the political and economic
impotence of non-whites. Yet the expected and often proph-
esied conflagration has not occurred.

This is strange, considering that African political consciousness has had a much longer history in South Africa, the African
National Congress having been established in 1912, and that
African rates of industrialization, urbanization, and westernization, with the consequent sharpening of power aspirations,
have been higher in the Republic than elsewhere on the continent.

The question arises, why is it that Africans, who constitute
about 80 per cent of the population and who contribute almost
70 per cent of the country's labour force, have failed to utilize
their power to force the change necessary to improve their
conditions?

The most obvious answer lies in the nature of the South African State, in the fact that it has through its highly restricted electorate appropriated all the power it needs and that it uses this power to hold in abeyance any indigenous counter-power. Compelling as this answer is, it is not complete. The awe-inspiring strength of the State is possible only because of the complementary weakness of its subjects, and both factors are in turn the products of the peculiar South African social structure.

That social structure has made it possible for the State, in the first place, to dispense with the need for popular consensus to legitimize its power, and secondly, to entrench itself in complete and indefinite control over the people. It has simultaneously made it impossible for Africans to develop a sustained nationalism capable of wielding the type of power to match that of the State. The power of the South African State, however, does not rest on sheer brute force. Its expression has grown subtle over the years, and it is the introduction of this second element which contributes to its present strength. The South African Government, through a mixture of persuasion and overt force, has cast a spell over the people, so that they appear today to be co-operating in their own indefinite subjugation. In complete control of practically every medium of mass communication, with even the independent English dailies, with some notable exceptions, avoiding news coverage which might meet governmental disapproval, the State appears to have succeeded in making the average non-white believe that he is happier in South Africa than most non-whites in other parts of the world, and that his existing economic security is far more valuable to him than any dreams of freedom, which in any event turn sour on awakening as in the rest of Africa.

Even the threat of emergent opposition from the non-white middle class, the traditional reservoir of leaders, appears to have been obviated by deflecting the aspirations of its members into channels of new opportunities. A few may now achieve such prestigious occupations as those of inspectors of their ethnic schools, matrons, and in the future even superintendents of their own hospitals, and in their 'group areas' they may administer their own civic affairs. In Verulam, on the Natal north coast, the entire city council is Indian, and for the first time in their history Indians run the affairs of a whole town, determining and collecting local revenues and planning all amenities. They constitute themselves into a licensing board and deliberate at hearings which were previously conducted by whites alone. They see this as real power, and competition for leadership is high. In the Transkei, the impossible seems to have happened and freedom appears to have been offered on a platter. Without the sacrifices, blood, and tears predicted by 'agitators', an African prime minister heads an African parliament and in co-operation with African legislators plans the life of the people. Where before there was no access to the higher echelons of government, now Indian councillors sit with a high-ranking minister around a common table and personally discuss problems and exchange social graces.

The Afrikaner, only a stone's throw from his rural traditions, manipulates his official role with an emotionalism which is usually foreign to bureaucracy and displays a capacity to become involved with his subject which was absent in his English-speaking predecessor. This may have its adverse effects, but it also makes for informal easy relations and in turn undermines potential non-white militancy. While the prestige of non-white 'dignitaries of state' in their own communities may be questionable, there is little doubt about their usefulness since they often provide the only obvious channel through which officialdom may be approached to ease the petty rigours of Apartheid in particular instances.

Balancing the rewards available to the intellectual and professional are the threats of awful punishment for non-compliance and criticism. It is hardly surprising that vested interests, no matter how dubious, are treasured, that co-operation is high and opposition virtually non-existent. It is not even easy for non-whites, particularly Africans, with talent and training to risk a search for alternative opportunities in other countries, for the State invariably will allow only a one-way ticket which precludes re-entry to one's place of birth and familiar surroundings.

Force, however, remains a spectre rather than a physical reality for most South Africans, both white and non-white. Its use is sporadic, pinpointed, and secret. Banishments, deportations, house arrests, interrogations, imprisonments, continue all the while. The Press on the whole ignores such events, and apart from the closest relatives, most people are unaware of them.

Observers have often made the error of regarding Apartheid as an invention of the Nationalist Party imposed on the country in the last twenty years. They have been misled into believing that it is a new and alien graft being transposed from the outside and therefore doomed to failure. In fact, Apartheid is the only custom South Africans, both white and non-white, have ever known, hence the facility with which the present government has entrenched every new law. There may be those who draw academic distinctions between the concept of Apartheid and of the segregation that preceded it. To non-whites the difference is basically linguistic. Where United Party-type racialism was ambiguous and hypocritical, and United Party administration therefore enigmatic, Nationalistic Apartheid is clear-cut and has the courage, albeit dubious, of its convictions. The whites set out to establish white domination in South Africa, which they rationalized as trusteeship. Afrikaners believe that they are continuing that role of trusteeship more effectively and justly than preceding governments, and there are non-whites who would agree with this. It would be difficult to establish that the status of non-whites in South Africa had deteriorated since the advent of the Nationalists. On the other hand the stronger impression exists that the economic status of the average non-white has improved alongside that of the average white person, though there has been no lessening in the gap between them.

There are those who turn nostalgically to the South African liberal tradition traced to the Cape and who would believe that the present South African social structure is rooted in something other than Apartheid. In fact the Cape liberal tradition itself always operated for and never against white interests.

The liberal protest was largely a protest against the institutionalization of racial laws rather than against racialism itself, which it accepted as a convention. Liberal organizations have promoted segregated schools, parishes, theatricals, and socials even when not pressurized by law to do so and when free to integrate. Jews and Englishmen have run exclusive clubs from which non-whites have been debarred, and it is highly doubtful whether a single Church, Catholic and Anglican included, would dare to integrate all its activities if laws against social integration were suddenly dropped.

While non-whites resent racial discrimination and its assault to their dignity they are able to understand white ethnocentricism, being ethnocentric themselves. There is very little social inter-action between component non-white groups. Coloureds are conscious of colour differences among themselves, Africans of tribal differences, and Indians of language and religious differ-ences. Apartheid encourages and reinforces such conventions, the origins of which precede South African racialism. It is the presence of these reactionary factors built into the component cultural systems, rather than imposed on them from the out-side, which prevents the emergence of a well-knit non-white united front against Apartheid.

Underlying everything, and supporting the whole structure more firmly than any other single factor, is the migratory labour system through which the State not only props up a high standard of white living, and thereby ensures the support of its electorate, but simultaneously emasculates the mass so that it is incapable of presenting any real threat. The African worker has no real roots and no single loyalty. He lives between the reserve or Bantu homeland and the town, often between two women and two families. In that situation aggression which should grow outwards and become rationally locked in conflict with its true source of provocation and seek a logical solution there, is deflected inwards and irrationally dissipated in the neighbour-hood and family. Racialism and its exploitative principle are deeply hated, but the aggression this gives rise to does not accumulate into a volcano which will erupt sometime in the future. Steam is constantly let out and tensions released through Africans' aggression directed against themselves. The violence that Africans commit against themselves through house-breaking, assault, homicide, and even suicide, is far in excess of any violence which flows outward to other groups.

It is against a background of such complexity that one views any real opposition to South African racialism. Pitted against the promise of freedom and equality, is the reality of a function-ing social system, based on an economy which could be sounder but, in terms of the habits and expectations of South Africans, is sound enough.

Although the thrust towards African nationalism is usually traced to the founding of the premier African political body, the

African National Congress, it never really got off the ground until 1950. Within a decade, to all practical purposes, the Government had snuffed it out of existence and replaced it with its antithesis, the Bantu Authorities Act, with the specific aim of strengthening tribalism and reacting against nationalism, which it declared to be alien and foreign to the people.[1]

First-Generation African Leaders

The first generation of urban African leaders, particularly those prominent on the executive of the African National Congress up to the end of World War II, were incapable of developing African Nationalism for a number of reasons, prominent among which were their involvement with the Western and Christian ways of life, their alienation from the masses, and their continued vestiges of tribal loyalties.

The leaders were in the main mission-educated and mission-sponsored Christians who had gained impressive degrees abroad and who were greatly influenced by, and had infinite faith in, Christian democracy. They emerged at a time when Africans at the Cape had the vote, when an African had been actually elected on to the Cape Provincial Council, and when their contact with Christian liberals, many of whom were powerful in Parliament, was such as to make them believe that the process of evolution was working in their favour, that their problem was fundamentally one of appealing to the Christian and liberal conscience inherent in white men and of raising the living standards of Africans to accord with Western values. They expected equality to follow as a matter of course once Africans attained required standards of education and civilization. Enlisting the sympathy of whites and educating blacks were hence enshrined as fundamental goals in the first constitution of the African National Congress.

This being their prognosis, their great patience with the Government and liberal advisers was not surprising. They responded to such extreme provocations as the 1913 Land Act, which deprived Africans of land rights over 90 per cent of the South African soil, and the 1936 Franchise Act, which deprived them of their voting rights in the Cape, with great equanimity, resorting to respectfully worded petitions and politely conducted deputations rather than to overt hostility. The shooting of nine African miners and injuring of 1,200 in 1946 on the Rand, following a strike for a rise in the average wage of two shillings and threepence a day for African miners, caused their most anguished reaction when they accused the Government of Fascism and Nazism, thereby shocking one of the most publicized South African liberals, J. H. Hofmeyr. Apart from this injudicious outburst, however, the African National Congress co-operated fully with the Government and its leaders and sat on the Government-constituted Native Representative Council despite the rejection of that Council as a dummy organization by an influential body of African opinion which called for its boycott.[2]

The political consciousness of the first generation of African leaders had been roused by the same factor of hurt to personal dignity which had caused the young Gandhi in 1894 to abandon his return to India and found the Natal Indian Congress. The Indian lawyer had been boxed on the ears for daring to sit with whites on a train; the African attorney, founder of the African National Congress, I. Pixley KaSeme, revolted against being told he could not walk on the pavement because he was black. Both in their colonial vanquished states had blamed their vanquishing on the folkways of their people. Both had sought emancipation from their apparently inferior culture and thereby inferior status through the only means they believed was available to them, that of assuming white culture and becoming 'white men'. They had absorbed the post-Industrial Revolution values of the West which declared men to be free and equal and according to which the life chances of a person were determined by personal achievement, and not irrevocable ascription. Both had rejected their own pre-industrial social systems in which every social position in the family, tribe, or caste was ascribed and invested with sacred sanctions. With the characteristic zeal of new converts, they had integrated the new way of life, seeking to do so at its very source in England and America, where their apparent acceptance in those societies unrestrained by racial barriers had made them believe that they had in fact become white men and had escaped the stigma of their 'race' and their inferior cultures.

Now in South Africa had come the shocking realization that

Western and Christian concepts of achievement were rigidly circumscribed by race. Where Gandhi, however, was quick to draw a distinction between white values and white men, African leaders continued to see an inevitable link between the two and thereby confounded and compromised their cause. Gandhi distinguished white values from their source and, regarding them as universal rather than peculiarly Christian or Western, promoted them far more convincingly than white racialists or British imperialists could ever have done. At the same time, by discarding the superficial features of white civilization, he regained his lost pride in the folkways of his people and on the basis of this evoked the necessary national ethos which paved the way to Indian self-determination.

By contrast African leaders continued to feel a sense of shame in their heritage, and since their people were caught up in this heritage, their feeling of shame extended to them as well.[3] In a sense they were as fearful of the African masses as the whites, and, influenced by their liberal friends, became easily allied with white interests, rationalizing these as the interests of Christian civilization and hence as worthy of preservation at all costs. So it was relatively easy for African leaders at the All African Convention in 1936 to move that though whites might be entitled to adult suffrage, non-whites required 'a reasonable measure of education and material contribution to the economic welfare of the country'[4] to be so entitled.

The old leaders had failed to generate African nationalism also because they themselves had never really escaped tribalism. The African National Congress as founded in 1912 was essentially a club of chiefs and intellectuals, and an insecure club at that, since the interests of the two were in conflict. The stated interest of the intellectuals was African nationalism and hence anti-tribalism. The power of the chiefs depended on preserving tribal ethnocentricism, and to that extent in strengthening tribal separateness. While the chiefs never appeared in the forefront and did not feature in deputations and petitions, they had a marked effect in vitiating the desired unity, to the extent where even the intellectuals could not see themselves apart from their respective tribes. This was not very remarkable, bearing in mind that these intellectuals had not experienced any appreciable measure of intertribal contact and that they had left as young men to study abroad in universities dispersed over America and Britain and on their return had rejoined their tribes, there being no other non-tribal society into which they could have become absorbed.

New Leaders and the Rise of African Nationalism

The post-World War II leaders, by contrast, had trained in South African universities, where they had learnt to disregard tribal barriers, and more had had experience in mixing with other South African students. They felt above all acutely embarrassed by the dependence of their leaders on sources outside themselves for leadership and guidance. A strong reaction set in against foreign ideologies, and these were held to be unsuited to the African cause. The role of liberals was seen as that of alleviating tensions and preventing conflict, but always at the expense of African interests. Incapable of curbing the brute force of the State, liberals were said to curb the brute force of the people and thereby indirectly to help white domination. The old idea that the liberal and Christian conscience would finally redeem Africans was dismissed as totally unrealistic, since Christianity itself was seen as subservient to the interests of white domination. This was expressed by rank-and-file leaders in such statements as: 'The English people preached that bloodshed is a sin before God. As a result of that the heroes of this country surrendered. The African people handed over this country to the Europeans because they had been preached about salvation and hell.'[5] 'You must know a European is a killer. You must know that the Europeans got us by means of the Church, using the Bible.'[6]

At the time that the new leadership emerged as a youth wing of the A.N.C., the President General, Dr. Xuma, had broadened the frontiers of co-operation and had worked with Communists[7] and Indians. A number of influential A.N.C. leaders in contact with African workers had been members of the Communist Party as well, and Indians had shown sympathy with the African cause financially and otherwise. The Indian and Pakistani Governments had brought the problem of South African racialism to the United Nations, and Dr. Xuma had received great support from these delegations when he himself had followed local Indian leaders to the world body. In 1946 he had expressed support for the Indian passive-resistance movement in South Africa at a conference, and a branch from Germiston had joined it in a show of African solidarity. The emergent leaders interpreted these liaisons as further demonstrations of the African's lack of confidence in himself and stressed a 'go it alone' policy, which was understandable in view of the prevailing opinion that Africans were incapable of any kind of independent action.

The first flames of African nationalism were sparked off by the new generation of leaders in the post-World War II period. Drawing distinctions between themselves and whites, they rejected the notion that whites were the custodians of good and saw them rather as custodians of evil. The white man, according to them, regarded as absolute values power, success, and fame, and lived by these. Opposed to the foreign creeds of Communism and Nazism, they declared 'man is neither an economic animal nor beast of prey but body, mind and spirit and history a record of humanity's striving for complete realization'.[8] They interpreted freedom as harmony through co-operative unity, through bringing parts together as a whole. This was their reaction against the South African creed of separatism and the reduction of the African into an expedient abstraction. They saw themselves as the antithesis of their rulers and held that whereas they moved towards unity and harmony, their rulers were moving towards destruction. 'The white man regards the universe as a gigantic machine hurtling through time and space to its final destruction. Africans see the universe as one composite whole, an organic entity, progressively driving towards greater harmony and unity.'[9]

The less sophisticated leaders expressed their attitudes in such terms as: 'The mad white men, they cannot live without eating the blood of the black men.'[10] 'The Boers are bad people. They do not want people to live in peace. They are not God's people, they belong to Satan.'[11] 'There is no Satan and Hell other than Europeans.'[12] 'Before the whites came into this country, people were free. There was no sickness, no killing of others, no arresting of people for passes.'[13] 'The white people in South Africa have done nothing to the Africans, but have done bad.'[14]

Where the older leaders had rejected their past, the new

returned to it using the clarion call 'Mayebuye Africa' ('Africa Return'). This return was necessary, for it accorded them an opportunity to come to terms with themselves and to end their state of alienation from their forebears. The present and the future, they declared, were rooted in the past and so they returned to the legacies of their ancestors. Mass meetings resounded with such statements as: 'Today we remember those leaders who met their deaths while they were fighting for equality. We remember Hintsa, Makana, Tshaka, Dingaan, Masabalala who died fighting for freedom. We continue where they left and we shall continue until freedom is achieved,'[15] 'The bones of Hintsa, Moshesh and others are moving in their graves because Africans are not free,'[16] and 'I am sent here by Shaka and Moshesh. The time has come to fight for our children.'[17]

Assuming power in 1949, the new leaders provided Africans with a militant programme of action in which the role of the mass[18] was vital. They called for a boycott of all elections to governmental bodies and advocated the use of strike, civil disobedience, and non-co-operation. The programme was identical to that developed by Gandhi and used by South African Indians, but the African nationalists declared that it was different and in fact a counter-measure to Mahatma Gandhi's 'self-pitying, arms-folding and passive reaction to oppressive policies'.[19]

Despite the insistence on a 'go it alone' policy, the new leaders' very first call to action reflected the influence of other groups. Its form, a one-day national stoppage of work, was the Gandhian *hartal*, and in its organization both Indians and Communists featured prominently, the latter so prominently as to be in almost complete control of it. This produced an open conflict and caused the A.N.C. leaders to declare that since the workers were Africans and oppressed as Africans 'it is clear that the exotic plant of communism cannot flourish on African soil'.[20]

But in compromising with the 'democrats'[21] they subjected themselves in a sense to the same influences which had negated the efforts of the first-generation leaders, the influence of Western liberalism, though that influence now appeared in the guise of Communism and Gandhiism. African nationalism became confused with racialism and African leaders were prematurely pushed by non-African democrats into making a choice between the rational, liberal nationalism which had emerged in France,

England, and America in the eighteenth century and which had developed into international humanism, and the parochial nationalism based on the idea that each group has its own permanently distinct historical tradition, which the world had combined to destroy as Fascism and Nazism with their implied racialism. The new-generation leaders were never given an opportunity to work out their own intermediate nationalism, and through it to reach out to the other groups as indeed the French, Americans, and English had done. The democratic minority, no more prepared to tolerate African nationalism than white racialists, for reasons among which survival predominated, drew hard and fast categories and thoroughly discredited African nationalism as Herrenvolkism. There was a premature insistence on international, interracial co-operation —a superficial sharing of platforms and a disproportionate representation of non-African democrats on bodies which planned essentially African political action. This was demanded at a stage when Africans, still divided into tribes and into at least three major language groups, had yet to be united, and at a stage when many real and very large chasms existed between the life chances of Africans and those of the other 'races' to whom Africans were expected to extend equality in the future.

It was inevitable that this superficial unity would not last and equally inevitable that the desire for African domination which had moved the new leaders in the first instance, would rise again. In 1959 African unity came to an end when a powerful wing splintered off from the A.N.C. to constitute itself into the Pan-African Congress, with the policy of Africa for Africans. The breach was precipitated by the Congress of the People which followed the Defiance Campaign. That Congress had seen participation from the widest range of democrats yet, bringing in the support of the new left-wing white-organized Congress of Democrats, the trade unions (South African Council of Trade Unions), and the South African Coloured Peoples' Organization. For the first time 3,000 South African delegates of all races had met and resolved on the kind of society they wished to live in, but the Freedom Charter which ensued became suspect in the eyes of many Africans who saw it as an unAfrican, Communist-inspired document.

Of all the democratic elements, that of the South African left had perhaps pushed the hardest against African domination and had inveighed most blatantly against its aspirations. Thus it experienced vehement African opposition from time to time.

The relations between the A.N.C. and the left had a long history of ambivalence. The Congress could not overlook the Communist Party's great contribution in proletarianizing the movement against racialism. Up to the end of World War II, the left had provided the only effective channel to the African mass. The African National Congress's own access to African workers was mainly through those of its members who were simultaneously, and often first, members of the Communist Party, having been attracted to it by its practical programme in trade unionism and the establishing of night schools for African workers. But the Party was essentially white—white-led and white-controlled. Its ideology, too, was seen as white. Hence, though Africans could easily identify with its class theory, they could not reconcile themselves to its white domination. Above all, the Communist Party threatened the leadership of the African bourgeoisie. The incongruous position existed where some white Communists drawn from the higher echelons of white society and enjoying a far higher economic standard than the top A.N.C. leaders considered themselves closer to the pro-letariat and attempted to alienate the top A.N.C. leaders from the rank-and-file ones. Distinctions were drawn between African capitalists, peasants, and workers, and it was suggested that the former two were not as reliable as the last since 'the peasant did not see much further than his own piece of land' (this in South Africa where the African peasant very rarely possesses land) and the 'capitalist or bureaucrat is mostly worried about his profit'.[22]

There were accusations that Communist propaganda levelled against the A.N.C. undermined its unity, and that white Communists, often completely out of touch with non-white realists, sabotaged the efforts of non-white leaders. In the early 1930s, James Thaele, President of the Cape Western A.N.C., had accused Communists of interfering in his territory, saying, 'If you have any smashing to be done, leave it to the Communist Party, and when it is done, they won't be there to rebuild it.'[23] At about the same time, the national executive of the A.N.C. had become disrupted by resignations because the national

K

President, J. T. Gumede, was a member of the Communist Party. In 1944 there had been serious recriminations between the then President of Congress, Dr. Xuma, and the left, following the anti-pass campaign which they had launched jointly and which had not come up to expectations. A serious situation had developed in Port Elizabeth in 1952 when, in the absence of the Eastern Cape leader, Dr. Njongwe, who had been busy at the time touring the country recruiting volunteers for the Defiance Campaign, two new leaders, allegedly influenced by left-wingers, had called for an indefinite strike.

The Indian Congress, too, had its grievance. The Communist Party had opposed its 1946 Passive Resistance Campaign and forbade its executive members from participating in it. Even members of the Indian Congress who had held official positions in the Communist Party had refrained from joining the campaign. That campaign in retrospect proved to be about the most vitalizing factor in sharpening non-white political consciousness.

There had been occasions, too, when prominent white left-wingers who had dominated the field with ideas, had been found wanting when posed with actual physical confrontation such as an arrest following a political demonstration. Such incidents had a very disillusioning effect on non-whites, who began to feel that, like the liberals of the past, the loyalties of members of the left when put to the test were restricted to whites.[24] The unimpeachable integrity of particular whites like S. P. Bunting, Bram Fischer, Harold Strachan, and Roley Arenstein was clouded by such general prejudices.

In the main, however, the African hostility against the left, whether articulated or not, was based on the same factor which had alienated the new post-World War II leaders from the Christian liberals. The left militated against African nationalism in militating against African domination. It prevented the emergence of a suitable and popularly acceptable African ideology by imposing on the A.N.C. its own interpretation of the South African conflict, not as a conflict between black and white, but as a conflict between capital and labour in which the race issue was being used to confuse the fundamental issue.[25]

This was an orientation which the African worker could not logically accept. The idea of an affinity between him and the white workers appeared absurd and far-fetched. It was evident to him that the high standard of living of white workers was dependent on the exploitation of non-white workers, and that white workers would therefore oppose African advancement. Thus, whereas the violence the African suffered at the hand of the capitalist was impersonal and far too complex to be easily appreciated, that which he suffered at the hand of the white worker was personal, direct, and punctuated with considerable brute force. White workers had on numerous occasions blatantly opposed the interests of the blacks to the extent of taking the law into their own hands and discharging the duties of the police in suppressing strikes and using firearms to disrupt their meetings. In 1919 they had assisted the police in routing a pass demonstration.[26] In 1920, they had scabbed on 40,000 African miners on strike on the Rand and had helped the police force them down the shafts. In the same year they had co-operated in suppressing a threatened strike in Port Elizabeth when twenty Africans had been killed.[27] In 1922 they had wreaked revenge against their fellow non-white workers when the Chamber of Mines had proposed lowering the colour bar, killing seven Africans and wounding thirty-six.[28] In 1922 they had shot wantonly at an A.N.C. meeting at Potchefstroom. One African had died, six had been injured.

When, at the beginning of the nineteenth century, the Voortrekker had turned his back on the Cape and rode on, he had done so, not because of conflict with capitalists, but because of the failure of the Government to protect him from blacks who competed against him for land and cattle. Later his descendants, turned peasant and proletarian in the wake of industrialization, had preferred idleness to 'Kaffir work' and thereby to identification with fellow African workers.[29] Possessed with political power, they wielded it to establish the dictatorship of the white proletariat in South Africa, not against capitalists, but against non-white workers. Fearing that capital in pursuit of imperialist profits would compromise their interests, they had formed their own political party, the Afrikaner Nationalist Party, and when in 1922 the capitalist government of General Smuts in pursuit of profit dared to compromise the security of white workers by lowering the colour bar against blacks in the mining industry, they staged the most protracted strike the country has seen. Ably assisted by the Communist and Labour Parties they had sung the Red Flag and ushered in the revolution of white workers under the banner 'Workers of the world unite and fight for a white South Africa'. Two years later, supported by the Communist and Labour Parties, they had established their own government under the aegis of the Afrikaner Nationalist Party. White workers stipulated, then, that so long as power was vested in their hands, racialism would never be allowed to subside, since it secured for them a higher standard of living than could ever be hoped for if South Africa became a people's democracy.

Whatever the ideological and other differences between Communists and Congressmen, their interdependence and conflict became inevitable from the time that the former shifted their task to liberating the non-white workers. In the early 1930s, the conservative African newspaper, *Imvo*, had printed:

Why grumble when violent forms of protest have ultimately to be resorted to, and the aid of Communists solicited? We do not love Communists as such, but a White man would never hesitate to snatch a nigger's hand that saves him from drowning. Neither would a Black man hesitate to call in a Communist, or any other hated and despised person for that matter, who helps him to discard the yoke of bondage.[30]

The Communists, for their part, while suspicious of African bourgeois interests, realized the power of their prestige and sought to exploit it. They knew full well that their own top white leaders could not adequately reach the mass and move it into revolt. They realized, too, that while they might dismiss bourgeois non-white leaders as a liability to the movement, non-whites aspired to be bourgeois themselves, and the presence of their bourgeois leaders confirmed the validity of their aspirations. The Youth League, too, was aware of this aspect of the African psyche, and though disdainful of the old leaders they sought to displace, had known full well that their own success among the people depended largely on their ability to attract a bourgeois head and hence had canvassed for a president general from among such ranks. Luthuli, the last President of the new militant Congress, was himself a conservative, who had remained a member of the hated Native Representative Council until it was finally dissolved by the Government. He was also a chief, and as such a government official. Thus at the time of his election to the presidentship of Congress he had occupied what appeared to many to be two contradictory roles.

The Africans and the non-African democrats had come together on the basis of a shared and common enemy and a common weapon, the non-white mass. Differences in motivation and goals had remained and the component sections of this union had known all along that there would come a parting of the ways, but had hoped that that parting would not be until the common enemy, white domination, had been destroyed. The rise of the Pan-Africanists threatened that hope, but before the new contender could be adequately faced the Government applied strong measures to destroy all opposition by the mass arrest of leaders and organizers, the treason trial, the banning of the A.N.C. and PAC, and the crippling of other democratic organizations through the banning of their leaders.

The nature of the short-lived militancy of the A.N.C. still remains to be analysed. Some insight into this may be gained by a tentative analysis of its three fundamental components: the mass, which remains blurred and which evades any conclusive evaluation; the leadership, which, though subtle and complex, is relatively less difficult to observe; and the weapons or techniques used to gain power.

The Mass, the Leaders, and the Weapons

Members of the African mass are often pictured in labour gangs rhythmically breaking the crust of a road or off-loading cargo at a dock, or as domestic servants. Such representations reveal little beyond their cultivated good humour. Periodically the mass is represented in a riot when the façade of good humour is dropped, and the docker, the domestic, and the road-maker combine and with crude implements of battle picked up from the rubble and dirt unleash what appears to be an unprovoked, insane outburst of savage violence.

Despite such symptoms of deep frustration, non-white political thinking, in the twenty years before extra-parliamentary political parties were made illegal, varied considerably in its assessment of the sensitivity of the mass to its conditions of exploitation and its preparedness to make a first great thrust for liberation. There were those who considered the mass to be ready and awaiting its leaders. There were others who pleaded for greater organization, and others still, who believed that the mass was unripe for any conclusive action. These three viewpoints were expressed by members of the 'Congress Movement' in their speeches and writings, and some typical statements are as follows:

1. *The Mass is Ready for Action and is to Some Extent Ahead of its Leaders*

The peasants are crying out for land, freedom and better life. It is the duty of the National Liberation Movement to assist them.[31]

Women are waiting for Congress lead. Their spirit is high, their anger deep.[32]

The feelings of the oppressed people have never been so bitter. . . . The grave plight of the people compels them to resist to death the stinking policies of the gangsters that rule our country. It is the profound desire, the determination and the urge of the overwhelming majority of the country to destroy for ever the shackles of oppression that condemn them to servitude and slavery.[33]

2. *There is Need for Greater Organization*

We can only succeed if we are able to unite our people completely and mobilize them effectively.[34]

Every non-European in South Africa each day experiences an incident which makes him fully aware of the savage rule under which he lives. But we also know that until the isolated grievances and the spontaneous outburst is canalized into an organized realization of the possibilities of sweeping away the unjust system, the powers that be will continue to have things their own way. . . .

There is a world of difference between a mere awareness of oppression and an organized expression of opposition to it, not only among the leaders, but also among the people.[35]

3. *The Mass is not Ready for a Confrontation*

Headlong collision is not to be yet. Advanced elements must build up the force. Tactics must be used to build a wide basis of leadership and a highly conscious people who will be ready when the time comes.[36]

A revolutionary offensive at this stage is probably out of the question although we cannot be dogmatic even about that. The headlong collision is not to be yet and the strategy for the advanced element now is to work for the rapid build up of the forces of the democratic camp. There must be no reckless militant sounding calls to action which are not attuned to the reactions and state of militancy of the people. We must beware of calls to action which do not lead all the people into action but serve only to cut the militant vanguard off from the masses.[37]

The people are as yet ill prepared and equipped ideologically and organizationally to meet the onslaught of fascism. They are fumbling for a strategy and have not as yet evolved effective tactics and many are immobilized by ineffective leaders and by illusions of legal and constitutional forms of struggle.[38]

The note of caution was stressed even more positively by the non-white political wing opposed to Congress: the Non-European Unity Movement, a Trotskyite organization, particularly strong in the Cape, which rejected the militancy of the African National Congress and its allies as sheer opportunism. It considered the consciousness of the mass to be too latent to validate any effective response and dismissed all attempts to use the mass in a political confrontation as adventurous and opportunistic.

To such criticism the impatient answer was:

There are those who believe that a revolutionary upsurge will inevitably arise, they do not believe it may arise soon. They have no profound notion about establishing political power among the people. They believe that people must first be educated and when the mass has been won over then political power established. South Africa is littered all over with dry fire wood which will soon be kindled into a conflagration. We have only to see the militancy to realize that it will not be long for these sparks to become a prairie fire.[39]

The left, which varied in its views from glorifying the proletariat and investing it with wisdom, insight, and motivation which it found lacking in its bourgeois leaders, to questioning the readiness of the mass and advising caution, put the situation thus:

Without organizational work, designed to give us close and personal contact with the people, political understanding by itself will go wrong, sometimes one way, sometimes another. We have seen both wrong directions in recent months—the over optimism which ignores the real difficulties and the extent of intimidation and the weaknesses of organization, and presses boldly on to completely unreal objectives. And also the undue pessimism, which exaggerates the difficulties, underestimates the political consciousness and the courage of the ordinary people, and hesitates and retreats when the stage is set for advance.[40]

There appeared to be equally good reasons for both optimism and pessimism in assessing the readiness of the mass for a final confrontation with the Government. While African leaders since Union had by and large confined themselves to wordy negotiations or non-violent militancy, the patience of the mass had already run out on some fifty occasions when they had resorted to far greater militancy than the leaders would ever have dared, and displayed greater discipline and sacrifice than could have been expected of them. Dozens of spontaneous pass campaigns, and as many strikes and bus boycotts, had taken place, and on dozens of occasions people incensed by police raids, high taxes, and ejections to literally nowhere, had broken out in desperate violence. In addition to these reactions there were those of the women who had protested against passes and beer-halls and suffered imprisonment.[41] When such demonstrations were not violent, as in strikes, protests against passes, and bus boycotts, the leaders had pursued the masses, rather than lead them. Thus the night-soil boys' strike in 1918 had been followed by an A.N.C. call for a national strike,[42] and the Alexander bus boycott in 1945 had prompted the organizations to set up a bus service committee. Even in implementing the final non-violent blow against Apartheid, the hoped-for indefinite stay away from work, as the bargaining-point for change, the mass on one occasion had demonstrated greater readiness than the leaders. In 1960, following the declaration of emergency and internment of practically the entire membership of the resistance movement, the African labour force of Cape Town had struck spontaneously for almost two weeks.[43]

Yet this picture of a mass ready for the final plunge to liberate itself is deceptive. It is observed by abstracting the motifs of rebellion scattered through a tapestry, which otherwise speaks of reasonable peace and quiet. While spontaneous uprisings are clear indications of deep sores, they are certainly no indication of a people's intelligent, rational, and conscious awareness of the causes of these sores. They are rather the symptoms of mass psychosis, and like the psychotic who is unable to see the root of his passion beyond the immediate trifle which provoked it, so, too, is the vision of the mass shallow and blurred.[44]

From the mass one turns to the leaders of the African National Congress, and here one has to rely mainly on available speeches and writings to gain some insight into their attitude. The new leaders who came into power in 1950 were not completely free of old influences, and their two national Presidents, Dr. J. S. Moroka and Chief A. J. Luthuli, were drawn from the old guard. Another old-guard leader who continued to exercise great influence was Professor Z. K. Matthews. Advisedly or otherwise, these 'giants' from the past restrained the militancy of the youth, and their complete involvement with the new movement was questionable. Matthews left for America to take up an academic post on the eve of the Defiance Campaign in 1952 and could not be present at the Congress of the People (which he had mooted) in 1953 because he had then just been appointed as Principal of a non-white college. Luthuli, though leading the Defiance Campaign as the second President of the A.N.C., never deliberately violated 'unjust laws', and thereby he personally avoided an act of offence against the Government. His first and only act of overt defiance occurred in 1960 when he publicly tore up his pass. Dr. Moroka, the first President of the new A.N.C., withdrew from the campaign, following his arrest after a few months of heading it. He publicly dissociated himself from other arrested leaders by organizing a separate defence for himself and pleaded that he had cancelled a call for an indefinite strike at the Cape in keeping with his stand for racial harmony.[45]

The post-1960 involvement in sabotage of some of the second-generation leaders suggests that there was within the organization a capacity for greater militancy. It must, however, also be borne in mind that so long as the A.N.C. continued to be legal, its leaders faithfully kept to the letter of passive resistance and meticulously avoided violence. This is reflected in an analysis of some two hundred speeches made by 129 national and branch leaders between 1952 and the end of 1956. The speeches were specially selected by the prosecution for their content of violence and treason against the State. Only 11 per cent of the speeches are suggestive of overt violence. The Special Branch, often not very literate and not always reliable, reported the following examples of violent statements:

I will take my stick and tell him to come closer. I will hit him with a stick. We will show the Boers. We will fill sugar bags with their brain.[46]

Those who want freedom are those who are prepared to support a violent rebellion and militant action. Smuts and Hertzog took up arms and fought for their people. That is the only way to be prepared in South Africa, to prepare the people for a violent rebellion. We are in a better position to fight against the forces of reaction than the Afrikaner people were when they fought the British imperialists. I say we have ten million people against two million whites.[47]

If the instructions are given to the volunteers to kill they must kill.[48]

Unless there is blood flowing the Europeans will sit on our necks.[49]

We know that what we are going to do is foul, but we are going to kill these people. They have killed us. They want to kill us. Now we will kill them.[50]

Twenty per cent of the speeches reported could be categorized as anti-white and hence racialist, thus:

The Europeans in this country have robbed us of all our rights. The white now wants to use our people as tools. Europeans are lice. They are parasites busy sucking our blood by means of work for unequal pay.[51]

Before the whites came to this country, people were free. There was no sickness, no killing of others, no arresting of people for passes. A person who opposes us must leave. If the white man says he can't stay with a native, he must just quit.[52]

How many dirty Europeans we find in the market, bitten by lice, but they will never ask their pass? How many non-Europeans are being raped by Europeans? How many of them?[53]

Teachers tell the children that the white person is an enemy. Tell a child that a Boer is your enemy because they tell their children that a kaffir is a kaffir.[54]

The climate of South Africa does not suit the skin of the whites therefore they must go away. How can you expect these people of

Europe to be of any good to us while they were thrown out of Europe because they were gangsters?[55]

We are tired of white supremacy. The whites think they are God. We cannot be booted about by other people in our own country. We are tired of being blood-sucked by the Europeans.[56]

How can drunkards govern the country? Boys of eighteen years of age are driving flying squads and chase us about whereas they should still be at school.[57]

We will not be afraid to tell our children that Chaka was murdered by Europeans and that Europeans are illegal immigrants to this country, who came to rob us of our country as far back as 1652. They should also be taught that our enemy in this our own country is the white man however good he may be and that their treachery is inexcusable and unforgivable.[58]

The greatest single category of speeches, 25 per cent, expressed a martyr-like passive-resistance demeanour, and suffering became identified with martyrdom and salvation.

Won't it be good, my mothers and fathers, when the blood of the youth of African people is spilling for a good cause?[59]

We the oppressed people are prepared to sacrifice with our bodies or blood if freedom should be achieved in that manner.[60]

Are you prepared to die? Freedom is only obtained through death.[61]

Be ready for your death. The manure of the tree of freedom is sweat and blood.[62]

You must be prepared to die for your freedom. It won't matter much as you already are daily dying from hunger and disease and being shot by the police.[63]

The Zulu chief said: 'If we go backwards we die, if we go forward we also die, so we have to go forward.'[64]

We want to tell Strydom and Verwoerd that we are prepared to die about these women's passes.[65]

Whether you die in jail or are shot on the streets for the sake of your people, you will go to heaven.[66]

Suffering not only constituted the means but reached a stage where it became the end in itself. Hence, when penalties for overt opposition to the Government became too high and leaders questioned the wisdom of exposing followers, the suffering of leaders on behalf of their people became the end of the whole resistance movement. Such martyrdom testified to the righteousness of the people's cause, and they drew a not inconsiderable degree of consolation from the notion that since their cause was just, it had the support of the world and ultimately of the force of right over might and over wrong. Hence the leaders made such statements as:

We know the truth, the future is ours.[67] . . . We appeal to you to become the apostles . . . to do this noble and holy job of delivering the people of Africa into the kingdom of heaven on earth. . . . When we are forced to clash between the forces of liberation and fascism, the forces of liberation will triumph.[68] . . . You cannot bring a stop to the march of the people.[69] . . . I know as I know that the sun will rise in the east tomorrow, that a major clash will come and all the forces of reaction will collapse against the forces of liberation. The writing is on the wall when we will crush the forces of reaction.[70] . . . Those who are going to liberate Africa are not unborn children but the present leaders. The day when we will stand and say 'We want freedom' we will get it.[71] . . . Israelites also suffered when they were led by Moses.[72] . . . The Government is digging a grave for us, but they will fall into it themselves like Hitler.[73] . . . History is on our side, science is on our side, the whole world is with us.[74]

One wonders if leaders so given to the cult of suffering and so depending on Messianic statements could have wielded violence even if weapons of violence were available to them. The fact that the post-1960 sabotage movement failed so miserably and was crushed so quickly, tends to suggest that they could not have. Many have assumed that the A.N.C. used the weapon of passive resistance because it had no other. It may be suggested that it also chose that weapon because temperamentally it was more attuned to non-violence than violence. One bears in mind that when on occasion the masses ran ahead of them and resorted to violence, the leaders far from taking advantage of the situation actually condemned and curbed it. There were many gloomy predictions on the eve of the Defiance Campaign that it would fail because of the Africans' inability to submit to the discipline of passive resistance. Such predictions were undoubtedly based on the stereotype of the African as a brutal savage, and by the picture conjured up by current history textbooks which describe the massacre of innocent Voortrekker families by vast hordes of bloodthirsty 'Kaffirs'. In fact, African history since Union is a remarkable testimony of the absence of violence in the face of the most dire provocation. The facts suggest that far from being wild and violent, Africans are singularly unaggressive. The violence unleashed by white workers on the Rand in 1922, leaving within days 153 dead and 534 wounded, is far in excess of any spontaneous outburst of violence on the part of Africans since Union.[75] The white man has always lived in terms of his military tradition, and white workers during that strike easily formed themselves into military commandos. Africans by contrast had disbanded their impis in the last century, and no urban African leader would have dreamed of organizing African workers as warriors during any single political campaign or strike.

The more militant African leaders appeared never to project themselves beyond the role of revolutionaries into that of governmental dignitaries manipulating State power. This is partly exemplified by the fact that they did not give much thought to the future shape of the South African structure—whether it would continue to be capitalistic or whether it would assume some other form. The Freedom Charter for the first time set out a blueprint for the future, but it was alleged that the authors of the Charter were leftist whites and not Africans.

The A.N.C. in its militant phase used the weapon of passive resistance. What were the chances of success of this weapon in the South African situation? Indians had already used the weapon on a number of occasions in South Africa. On the first two occasions they had been led by Gandhi himself, the originator of the weapon and a very remarkable leader of men. Passive resistance had a tremendous effect in awakening Indian political consciousness and in developing Indian nationalism. It had, however, practically no effect in increasing Indian rights in South Africa or in gaining for them any power. Indians themselves had tended to put down this failure to their numerical minority and had come to believe that it would work in South Africa as it had in India, if it was wielded by the mass, that is essentially by Africans.

Passive resistance presupposes that the mass, without any arms but through an assertion of sheer will, can discharge sufficient power to displace a government, or change an existing social system. In other words, in passive resistance, the mass is transformed into the weapon and the whole struggle hinges on sharpening mass consciousness and mass solidarity. This approach was evident in the thinking of A.N.C. leaders and is reflected in such statements as:

> Our potential is the mass of the people chaffing against the yoke of oppression, people waiting for a lead. . . . The only sure road to freedom is through uncompromising and determined mass struggle. . . . We are going to take it with our bare hands, we are fighting them with our fists against their guns and atomic bombs, yet they are still afraid. We must have solidarity to face the Dutchmen with our bare hands.[76]

If change could have been brought about through sheer mass pressure in South Africa, the A.N.C. might well have succeeded, for despite such severe handicaps as a shoestring budget and the virtual absence of such essential media of communication as the press and the radio, its impact on the African population was impressive. However, the weapon of an unarmed mass, no matter how well organized and disciplined, is insufficient in itself in a contest for real power. Mass pressure may provide the final push for dislodging a government or changing a policy only if other forces, mainly economic, have already undermined existing reaction. The mass succeeded in India because of the presence of these forces. It failed in South Africa because of their absence.

Passive resistance is doomed to failure when the stakes are equally crucial to both sides, and the governing party believes that to yield is to lose all. In South Africa to yield to mass pressure is at least to abandon the vantage-point of white economic domination and at most to be subjected to African domination. The whole system of present-day Apartheid has been carefully structured law by law in the last fifty years, not by Afrikaners alone, but by whites generally. The Act of Union, based on segregation, was as much an English as it was an Afrikaner design and had the complicity of Britain. Natal, a predominantly English-speaking colony, and largely settled by Britons, had prior to Union taken effective steps to disenfranchise Africans and Indians.

The South African Government, regardless of the party in

power and whether led by Smuts and Hofmeyr or Verwoerd and Vorster, has never been prepared to tolerate the action of the mass, and its steps to suppress it have always been quick and decisive. Hence in 1918, during the leadership of Smuts, when the A.N.C. called for a strike in order to exact a general rise in African wages, its leaders were for the first time arrested and African meetings banned. A year later two hundred African leaders and pickets involved in an anti-pass demonstration in Johannesburg were sentenced to imprisonment. Sharpeville in 1960 stands out as the greatest atrocity committed by a South African government, yet Sharpeville was preceded by a number of similar incidents, perpetrated by the reputedly benign and internationally more acceptable government of General Smuts: for example the repeated opening of fire on passively resisting Africans in 1920 at Port Elizabeth and in 1946 on the Rand, and the massacre at Bullhoek in 1920 of 163 members of a small community which had resisted forcible ejection from the piece of common ground which had constituted their only home.

African leaders and the African mass in their organized and rational bid for equality ruled out violence altogether. Passive resistance, despite their numerical majority, gained no more for them than it did for South African Indians. It roused their political consciousness but failed to launch them on the road to self-determination. Passive resistance became an end in itself rather than a means to an end. A.N.C. meetings after a while ceased to function primarily as points of contact and channels of communication, but became converted into things in themselves, into cults. Thus, particularly after overt acts of defiance became difficult and well-nigh impossible, meetings constituted the whole form of resistance. Meetings generated group solidarity. People returned to them to become reconfirmed in their faith, in themselves, in their leaders, and in the power of the mass. The meetings developed their own ritual and their own mystical symbols, and for those who habitually attended them they provided a means for a regeneration of the spirit, which had become dulled by oppression. Strong anti-Apartheid, anti-government speeches purged the self of any compromises that might have been made, the singing of liberatory songs strengthened anti-Apartheid values and gave protection against future weakening.

The Use of Violence

In 1961 Africans made their last attempt to oppose the Government legally when the All African Conference, essentially replacing the banned A.N.C., called a one-day stay at home. The Government responded by calling out the army. Nelson Mandela[77] declared, 'If peaceful protests like these are to be put down by mobilization of the army and the police then the people might be forced to use other methods of struggle.'[78] Within months of the statement, it was clear that there was an underground movement of banned organizations and that these, deprived of the weapon of the mass, were resorting to violence. The Umkhonto Wesizwe (Spear of the Nation) attracted recruits from the Congress alliance, and from the underground Communist Party which had been in existence since at least 1955.[79] Where the A.N.C. had remained a racialist organization, its alleged sabotage wing, uncontrolled by public opinion, became thoroughly multiracial and in the underground the distinction between Communist and African nationalist became blurred and unimportant.[80] Poqo, the reputed sabotage wing of PAC, was wholly African, and the National Liberation Committee consisted mainly of whites who had belonged to the Liberal Party. Poqo was terroristic; the other two organizations attempted, and on the whole succeeded in directing violence against inanimate installations of industry and communication.

But even the saboteurs approached their task with the temperament of martyrs, rather than that of terrorists, with the attitude of sacrifice and die rather than that of destroy and run. The end result of the short-lived episode of violence was more self-violence than violence to the enemy. In 1962 and 1963, Poqo killed seven whites and one African chief who, it alleged, collaborated with the Government. It lost five of its own lives in the skirmishes, suffered 3,246 arrests, and 124 of its members were found guilty of murder.[81] Some twenty-five attempts at sabotage were reported. The Government was alerted to the extent that its budget for defence soared from $61·6 million in 1960 to $168 million in 1962–3. Two munitions factories costing £10 million went up,[82] and the Minister of Defence, J. J. Fouché, gave among other reasons the following for increased precautions: 'You must not think we are arming against an external army. We are not. We are arming to shoot down the black masses.'[83]

It is rumoured that the South African saboteurs received financial and technical assistance from external sources—from African and Communist countries. The results indicate that if there was such support, it must have been very niggardly indeed. Against the power and the expertise of the State the performance of the saboteurs was pathetic. Those who went underground were those who had operated above ground. They were men trained to use words and in a sheer contest of reason they would have outdone the average parliamentarian. That was why they had to be banned. But with weapons of modern violence they were hopeless. As non-whites they had been excluded by law from all acquaintance with such weapons. Their school curriculum, too, had been sorely lacking in such disciplines as chemistry and physics. There was bungling of formulas for explosives.[84] Reports of trials of persons now suffering severe penalties make sad reading. The so-called cell meetings appear in evidence to have been no more than haphazard encounters on street corners, badly arranged car rides, or careless academic discussions in flats. There was far more talking than doing, and the doing often proceeded with gross carelessness so that explosives would be transported in broken-down cars.

There appeared, too, to have been very little *esprit de corps* in the underground. This was understandable. The underground was new, inexperienced, and desperate. Recruits were gathered almost indiscriminately, and when one of them was detained for questioning, the network was usually easily prised open. Even seasoned campaigners, prepared to stand by their code, grew embittered when they found that the party to which they had given their allegiance would not or could not even give adequate assistance to their families, while they faced severe penalties. When political activity had been legal, political prisoners had enjoyed the status of martyrs, the community had rallied around them, and publicly organized funds had cared for their families. Persons working underground retained the same expectations for their sacrifices. Thus many became disillusioned and embittered and, in that state, susceptible to becoming witnesses against their fellows.[85]

L

The thrust for African liberation did not succeed because Africans, both in terms of temperament and resources, were incapable of using violence. It failed, too, because Africans lacked sufficient motivation to make it succeed. In 1922 white workers had succeeded in establishing their dictatorship not only because they had possessed both physical and political power, but also because of their stronger motivations. White workers had known power and when threatened with its deprivation had fought desperately to preserve it. Non-white workers in 1950 had never experienced power and could not value it to the same extent as whites. Where non-whites were chasing unfamiliar dreams, whites in 1922 had fought to maintain what they had. Hence they fought not because they had nothing to lose but their chains, but because they had everything to lose— they could be enslaved, reduced to 'kaffirs'.

In retrospect, then, it may be suggested that African nationalism failed because under white Nationalist Party rule the centuries-old South African custom of Apartheid or segregation, internalized by whites and non-whites, has been effectively strengthened by converting it into law and imposing unbearable sanctions against those who would violate it. The structure, however, is not wholly supported by force. Revolution, though dependent on the populace, is not a popular cause. The security of a familiar system, even if limiting, is invariably preferred to the risks of change. It is easier to come to terms with misfortune than to attempt to annihilate it with dubious resources. It may well be, too, that the heavy penalties, which according to prevailing opinion make dissent futile and foolhardy, relieve both leaders and led from the trying demands of conscience. The Government, not as immune to world opinion as would be believed, also uses attractive measures, designed to delude both non-whites and international critics. The power aspirations of the small middle class are appeased by offering it new, albeit restricted, opportunities for achievement. Fundamentally it preserves the structure through a highly sophisticated administrative technique which carefully mixes personal benevolence with the impersonal and hence 'impartial' mystique of the law, which transcends mere human considerations. The non-white victim is beginning to believe that he has the sympathy and support of minor and senior officials, including the prime minister, and that both black and white are equally victims of South African custom and the laws of Apartheid. This myth has the probable effect of improving 'race relations' while retaining the deprived status of non-whites.

Thus, while many factors have combined to support and secure white domination, African Nationalism in contrast has encountered stringent opposition not only from white racialists but also from 'democrats': Christian liberals in the first half of the century, and leftists and Gandhian Indians since World War II. While it is evident that the post-World War II African movement would not have succeeded at the rate it did without the support of these 'democrats', it is also evident that in accepting that support, African leaders exposed themselves to the powerful influence of a value system which recognized two extreme nationalisms, liberal nationalism of which it approved, and the chauvinistic nationalism of the Nazis and Fascists which it identified with racialism and vehemently opposed. Liberal nationalism, in the South African context, meant multi-national-ism, or at least non-white nationalism, for African nationalism was groupism based on race. The nationalism of the post-World War II leaders was hence quickly smothered and African leadership and initiative modified and even under-mined by non-African influences. The Pan-Africanists attempt-ed belatedly to retrieve this situation, but even if the Govern-ment had not intervened to destroy all African opposition, the indications are that the Africanism of that organization, too, would have been weakened by the support it began to attract from members of the white Liberal Party.

The chances are that, with the passing of the Improper Inter-ference Bill, Africans will no longer come under such white influences, and African nationalism of the future will develop as an independent force. Whether that force will have the power to change the South African structure remains questionable, for it is probable that if it does not have the support of local 'democrats' it may not attract support from international 'democrats', from which it has up to now drawn considerable strength, both from the West and the East. International politics have never been as important as now to the destiny of any country, and their importance in resolving national problems is increasing. So it is unlikely, no matter what its nature, that

future African nationalism will on its own effect African liberation. International liberalism, consolidated after the shock of
Nazism and Fascism, is now showing dangerous signs of dis-
enchantment with the Africans and Asians whose liberation it
enthusiastically supported. The racial conflict, isolated in South
Africa in the last twenty years, threatens to take on global proportions and even to replace the present conflict between
Communists and capitalists. White South Africans' fear of black
domination appears to be spreading to the white world, to
America, Europe, and Russia, which in the global context are
themselves outnumbered by the black people. The weak reaction against the usurpation of power by the minority whites
in Rhodesia and the almost foregone conclusion that the South
African Government will make permanent its rule in South-
West Africa, suggest that former supporters of African liberation are now beginning to favour white domination in the
southern tip of Africa.

The chance of African liberation in South Africa through
Western liberalism grows dim, and as the conflict between
China and Russia progresses, liberation through outside
Communist support also fades. If the present conflict between
Communism and capitalism is indeed shifting to a world
conflict between black and white racialism, then the prospects
are that the present *status quo* will continue indefinitely in South
Africa, and will only be changed with a change in the balance
of power between black and white nations.

REFERENCES

1. This is reflected in the preamble to the Bantu Authorities Bill
    1951. See G. M. Carter, T. Karis, and N. M. Stultz, *South Africa's
    Transkei*, Northwestern University Press, 1967, 53.
2. BENSON, MARY, *The African Patriots*, Faber & Faber, London,
    1963, 135.
3. The supercilious attitude that African intellectual leaders showed
    towards the masses is expressed in the following statement: 'The
    teacher is often the best educated, and indeed the only educated
    person in our native areas and locations, surrounded by an
    ignorant population. . . . most young men and women in our

villages are not edifying companions for teachers.' D. D. T. Jabavu, *The Native Teacher out of School: the Black Problem*, Lovedale Book Department, Lovedale, South Africa, 1920, 72, as quoted in L. Kuper, *An African Bourgeoisie*, Yale University Press, New Haven and London, 1965, 73.

4. MOLTENO, Q.C., DONALD B., *The Betrayal of Native Representation*, South African Institute of Race Relations, Johannesburg, 1949, 8.

5. Indictment, *High Treason, Regina v. Adams and Others*, II, Schedule C, Government Printer, Pretoria, 1956, 34. This is the indictment to the famous 1956 Treason Trial when 156 persons, mainly Africans but including all races, were tried for treason and finally found not guilty and discharged.

6. Ibid., 130.

7. The term as used here refers to members of the South African Communist Party. The Communist Party in South Africa worked for a socialist programme and was not affiliated to any particular brand of Communism operative in Europe.

8. BENSON, MARY, op. cit., 111.

9. BENSON, MARY, op. cit., 111.

10. Indictment, *Regina v. Adams and Others*, op. cit., 22.

11. Ibid., 31.

12. Ibid., 34.

13. Ibid., 139.

14. Ibid. 22.

15. Ibid., 134.

16. Ibid., 12.

17. Ibid., 160.

18. The word 'mass' is used here in the context of the underprivileged, primarily the non-whites. Since all non-whites in South Africa suffer deprivation when compared with whites, in its widest context it includes all non-whites regardless of economic status. Non-whites, however, make a distinction between leaders and followers. The mass necessarily implies those who follow and thereby give leaders power.

19. Oliver Tambo, a prominent African National Congress leader, wrote:

Mahatma believed in the effectiveness of what he called the 'soul force' in passive resistance. According to him, the suffering experienced in passive resistance inspired a change of heart in the rulers. The African National Congress (A.N.C.), on the other hand, expressly rejected any concepts and methods of struggle that took the form of a self-pitying, arms-folding and passive reaction to oppressive policies. It felt that nothing short of aggressive pressure from the masses of the people would bring about any change in the political situation in South Africa. As a counter measure to Mahatma Gandhi's passive resistance, the African National Congress launched in 1952 the Campaign for the Defiance of Unjust Laws, or the Defiance Campaign.

Oliver Tambo, 'Passive Resistance in South Africa', in John A. Davis and James K. Baker (eds.), *Southern Africa in Transition*, Praeger, New York, 1966. Tambo has clearly misunderstood Gandhian passive resistance and is wrong in thinking that there was any difference between the Indian and African approach in using it. Whereas the philosophical content of Satyagraha remained crucial to Gandhi, the Indian masses in India and South Africa rarely understood that content or subscribed to it.

20. BENSON, MARY, op. cit., 163.

21. 'Democrat' means here all those who opposed racial domination in South Africa whether they were Communists, liberals, or anything else.

22. Indictment, *Regina* v. *Adams and Others*, op. cit., 98.

23. BENSON, MARY, op. cit., 71.

24. Bartholomew Hlapane, State witness in the trial of M. D. Naidoo, claiming to be a Communist and member of the central committee, and asserting contact between the Communist Party, the African National Congress, and its alleged sabotage wing, the Umkhonto Wesizwe, declared his abhorrence of white Communists in particular, stating that while A.N.C. leaders were incarcerated for life, leading Communists with notable exceptions had avoided such durance vile by cowardly desertion and flight. He also accused them of encouraging others to go to jail and die for the cause and promising support to families of victims and then not carrying out their promise. He further alleged that white Communists pocketed the money which came from overseas for such support. See the Judgement by Justice J. Harcourt (the trial judge) of the Natal Provincial Division of the Supreme Court of South Africa, 30 Nov. 1966.

25. The capitalist exploitation is basic, and it is important that we always remember that. It is sometimes said that it is the 'racialist policies' of the Government which are basic. This is incorrect. For proper understanding it is necessary to go beyond the racialist policies to the economic system underlying them.

Indictment, *Regina* v. *Adams and Others*, op. cit., III, 119.

26. BENSON, MARY, op. cit., 46.

27. BENSON, MARY, op. cit., 50–1.

28. BENSON, MARY, op. cit., 52.

29. HOROWITZ, RALPH, *The Political Economy of South Africa*, Weidenfeld & Nicolson, London, 1967, 35.
30. BENSON, MARY, op. cit., 71.
31. Indictment, *Regina* v. *Adams and Others*, op. cit., III, Schedule D.
32. Ibid., 62.
33. Ibid., 105.
34. Ibid., 130.
35. Ibid., 2.
36. Ibid., 87.
37. Ibid., 73.
38. Ibid., 56.
39. Ibid., 171.
40. Ibid., 9.
41. BENSON, MARY, op. cit., 217; Kuper, L., op. cit., 16–20.
42. BENSON, MARY, op. cit., 42.
43. Ibid., 271.
44. KUPER, L., op. cit., ch. II, for a deeper insight into this problem.
45. BENSON, MARY, op. cit., 191.
46. Indictment, *Regina* v. *Adams and Others*, op. cit., 18.
47. Ibid., 19.
48. Ibid. 37.
49. Ibid., 18.
50. Ibid., 68.
51. Ibid., 112.
52. Ibid., 139.
53. Ibid., 153.
54. Ibid., 22.
55. Ibid., 41.
56. Ibid., 62.
57. Ibid., 65.
58. Ibid., 93.
59. Ibid., 12.
60. Ibid., 12.
61. Ibid., 18.
62. Ibid., 22.
63. Ibid., 28.
64. Ibid., 142.
65. Ibid., 162.
66. Ibid., 12.
67. Ibid., 21.
68. Ibid., 32.
69. Ibid., 19.
70. Ibid., 19.

71. Ibid., 29.
72. Ibid., 62.
73. Ibid., 32.
74. Ibid., 35.
75. Horowitz, op. cit., 97–9.
76. Indictment, *Regina* v. *Adams and Others*, op. cit., II, 91.
77. Nelson Mandela would most probably have succeeded Albert Luthuli as President of the A.N.C. He is at present serving a life sentence for conspiring to plan sabotage.
78. DAVIS and BAKER, op. cit., 258.
79. This emerges from the judgement by Justice J. Harcourt (see ref. 24 above) in the trial of M. D. Naidoo, sentenced to five years' imprisonment for being a member of an unlawful organization, to wit, the Communist Party, and of 'defeating or obstructing the course of justice by assisting named persons to escape from the Republic and thereby to avoid legal proceedings pending against them'.
80. The evidence of Govan Mbeki in the trial of M. D. Naidoo suggests this; loc. cit., 2766.
81. *The Star*, Johannesburg, 6 April 1963, as reported in Davis and Baker, op. cit., 263.
82. DAVIS and BAKER, op. cit., 267.
83. DAVIS and BAKER, op. cit., 259.
84. Exhibit A2 in the M. D. Naidoo case contained a list of chemicals for ignition in which potassium chloride had been inserted for potassium chlorate.
85. Loc. cit., 2804–5. Jack Govender, father of five children and a conventional Hindu, witness in the case of the State against M. D. Naidoo, had joined the Communist Party in 1942, the Natal Indian Congress in 1945, and the underground Communist Party in 1955. He had suffered detention under the Emergency Act of 1960 and was a banned person. In terms of his banning order he was excluded from the harbour area. This caused him to lose his job in the shipbuilding yard where he had worked for over ten years. He was subsequently detained for ninety-seven days for police questioning, placed under house arrest, and finally convicted and sentenced to a year's imprisonment for refusing to testify against his fellows. He estreated bail and escaped to Bechuanaland. During his above-ground political activities, the Natal Indian Congress had shouldered the responsibility of maintaining his family and paying the instalments on his house, his sole asset. In his new predicament, however, he had, according to his evidence, found no support, despite prior

promise of such support, and in Bechuanaland he was made to feel that he was living on the charity of others. The final show-down came when he was beaten up by other escaped 'comrades'. So he gave himself up to the South African police and became a State witness.

8

ELLEN HELLMANN

SOCIAL CHANGE AMONG URBAN AFRICANS

Nowhere in South Africa has traditional Bantu culture remained unaffected by the predominant Western culture, particularly by the introduction of a Western economic system with its far-reaching implications. But it is in the towns, which in South Africa are entirely Western in origin and structure, that the impact has been at its maximum. Although towns have served as the hothouses of change, the response of Africans to the urban environment has not been uniform. Numerous factors in different combinations determine the extent of urban commitment and the degree of acculturation, two processes which usually but not invariably coincide. The main factors, obviously interrelated, are length of urban residence, standard of education, occupation, type of accommodation (compound, hostel, or family dwelling), the possession of land rights in a Bantu area, and the cultural orientation of the home of origin, which affects the values the immigrant brings into the town.

The rapid expansion of towns in South Africa has taken place within the past half-century. In 1921 the total urban population had not quite reached the two million mark; in 1960, the year of the last census, it had increased almost fourfold and was close to 7½ million. Urban Africans numbered 658,000 in 1921 and by 1960 had increased more than fivefold to 3,471,233, rising from 14 to 31·8 per cent of the total African population. In the twenty-four years between 1936 and 1960, the urban African population increased by 2·2 million. It is, therefore, obvious that the majority of adult Africans* will be first-generation

* 1,041,391 (30 per cent) urban Africans were under fifteen years and 1,346,943 (39 per cent) were under twenty years of age. *Population Census, 1960, No. 5*, Bureau of Census and Statistics, Pretoria, 1963.

immigrants who grew up in the rural areas, have experienced both environments, and have interpersonal relationships in both areas. Second-generation townspeople, who are generally assumed to be completely town-centred and to have all their important personal ties located in the town where they were born and bred, form, as yet, a numerically small group: in East London 14 per cent[1] and in Soweto* 15 per cent.[2]

These urban-born form part of the major section of the urban African population which consists of people living in separate townships under conditions of family life. The remainder are migrant workers, some of them voluntary migrants who have no desire to settle permanently in the towns or to have their families join them, and the others involuntary migrants—the would-be townsmen—who are prevented by influx control and other legislation from remaining there permanently and having their wives join them. The number of male migrants from the Bantu areas (i.e., excluding the 'white' farming areas) is estimated at approximately half a million. This figure does not include workers from countries other than the Republic, who in 1964 were likewise estimated to number half a million, of whom some 300,000 were employed on the mines.[3] It is not known what are the proportions of voluntary and involuntary migrants.

The only intensive research among migrant workers has been carried out by Mayer in East London. He found that between one-third and one-half of the total male working force (estimated to number some 15,000)[4] consisted of rurally committed migrants who came to town only because of the need to earn money but did not wish to settle permanently or have their families live there. Mayer gives a detailed account of these Red Xhosa who, as distinct from the School Xhosa, make only the minimal adjustment to town life necessary to enable them to hold a job. They reject town values, which can be largely equated with Western values, do not take part in sport or other recreations offered in the town, are extremely frugal in their spending habits and do not adopt the prevalent higher standard of clothes and food, wear a distinctive emblem to emphasize their continuing 'Redness', do not belong to a Christian Church,

* Soweto is the name given by the Johannesburg City Council to the large African dormitory township, 26 square miles in extent, which it administers.

and form small tight-knit groups of persons from their home area in the country with whom they spend their leisure, drinking together and worshipping the ancestral spirits together. They lead what Mayer calls an encapsulated existence, living in a closed network of social relations which extend from their rural homes. 'To the question *why* Red and School migrants organize their lives in these different manners, it seems almost impossible to find an effective answer,' says Mayer in his concluding chapter. 'The School Xhosa long ago agreed that certain institutions of another group or groups—notably Christianity and formal education—were to be shared by themselves: the Red Xhosa refused. Thus, in the long run, the different potentialities for urbanization shown by these two categories of Xhosa today can be said to have a basis in the different reactions of an earlier generation to a particular conquest situation, over a hundred years ago.'[5]

Neither this sharp dichotomy between conservative tribalists and the more westernized people nor the relatively high proportion of traditionalists found in East London has been reported in other towns. Judging by the available material, less exact and more impressionistic than Mayer's, it seems likely that elsewhere the traditionalists form a considerably smaller proportion of the total urban African population and that both migrants and other sections of urban Africans constitute a continuum shading gradually from the strongly traditional to the markedly Western-orientated, with many varieties of patterns of behaviour and differing combinations of components drawn from both cultures.

While in the early stages of industrialization migrant male workers formed the majority of the urban African population, today people living under conditions of family life predominate. This is reflected in the steadily increasing proportion women form of the total: 19 per cent in 1921, 36 per cent in 1936, 41 per cent in 1960. This trend is, however, likely to be halted by the operation of the present laws which have the effect of limiting entry into the towns to men who are permitted to remain there only while they work for a specified employer in a specified occupation and of excluding the entry of women altogether. In the Western Cape, where the Government is attempting to reduce the employment of African workers by 5 per cent per year and to substitute Coloured workers, the process is likely to be reversed.

Johannesburg is the largest town in South Africa, with the largest African population. Excluding 120,344 living mainly under family conditions in the peri-urban areas to the immediate north and south of Johannesburg and 15,345 workers on the gold-mines living in compounds, the number of Africans in 1967 was 637,726. 504,307 live in townships in family conditions, and the remainder, 133,419 (85,388 men and 48,031 women),[6] live in municipal hostels or compounds or are accommodated on their employers' premises, the latter consisting in the main of domestic servants. The 'single' earners hence form some 22 per cent of the total Johannesburg African population. In Pretoria, where there are 236,000 Africans, the 'single' earners (of whom 51 per cent were married) likewise constituted 22 per cent of the total.[7] This does not, however, indicate what the average throughout the Republic is. It is certainly considerably higher in the Western Cape. Moreover, it must be pointed out that the male and female 'single' earners differ greatly in respect both of urban commitment and westernization. A large number of the male workers are employed as unskilled municipal labourers largely in the cleansing department, as labourers on brickfields and in timber yards, as cleaners in flats and in domestic service, all occupations which carry a low social status and are avoided by men who have qualified for urban domicile, and certainly by the urban-bred. It is because there is a shortage of labour in these occupations that migrant workers are permitted to enter the towns on conditional employment. Domestic service by women is not disparaged to the same extent. Provided she works in one of the upper income group white suburbs, a female domestic worker can earn mention as a 'socialite' in the social columns of the African Press. Personal service is one of the main occupational outlets for the women of the townships, for both immigrant mothers and urban-bred daughters. It is also, because it introduces women so intimately into the mechanics of Western households, a potent agent of acculturation.

The first point that must be made in turning now to Africans living under family conditions is that in towns their incorporation into a money economy is complete. Every requirement has to be bought—something which still astonishes some of the more recent and unsophisticated immigrants. Without a cash income, which for the majority means securing employment, a family cannot live. This seems too obvious to be worth stating. But from this basic precondition of urban living flow a number of consequential changes which have altered the traditional division of labour, affected family relationships, and brought about significant changes in attitudes and values. In place of the leisure men enjoyed in traditional society, they are expected to become the wage-earners for their families, to adopt work patterns which involve learning new skills, accepting a new concept of the division of time into a work and leisure schedule with its associated insistence on regularity and punctuality, and submitting to an alien authority structure. All this is so basic— and commonplace—that this whole process barely merits mention. The fact that this is so is a measure of the rapidity with which a people, originating from a subsistence economy where the family was a self-sufficient unit and good relations with kin and neighbours were the best form of insurance against want, has adapted to a modern industrial economy. The paramount importance of money, the independence of the nuclear family as a unit living on its own, and the dependence of the worker on his own efforts to secure and retain a job and to obtain promotion, the stress on competition rather than co-operation, have engendered a spirit of individualism which appears to be becoming as characteristic of African township life as it is of the white community.

The main changes occurring in the social structure are the weakening of the traditional extended kinship system, the disintegration of the patriarchal homestead, and the emergence of the nuclear family as an independent unit. Many factors contribute to this development: shortage of land in the Bantu areas and a rising standard of wants diminish the economic viability of the traditional large homestead; townward migration, primarily to find work, cannot take place on the basis of the movement of an extended family; housing in the urban areas is designed for the nuclear family. Above all, as has been pointed out in other studies,[8] there is a 'fit' between the needs of industrialization and the features of the modern nuclear family which, in its relative independence, permits mobility unhampered by the claims of kin. Whether, given the choice which an acute and chronic housing shortage has precluded, groups of relatives would have chosen to live under one roof or as neighbours, is an open question. In view, however, of the marked differences in education, standard of living, and status found today even among siblings, it seems unlikely that this choice would in fact have been made.

Apart from a comprehensive investigation in East London of 105 multi-member households of the urban-born and bred carried out by Pauw, there is very little information on the composition and structure of urban families. A number of sample surveys relating primarily to patterns of expenditure have been carried out. These, together with statistics provided by local authorities, show that the household has shrunk in size, varying on average from 5 to 6 persons. A 1962 sample survey in Johannesburg, giving an average of 5·6 people per household, found that only 6 per cent of the sample (an average of 0·33 persons per household) were not members of the nuclear family. None of these surveys, however, included in its terms of reference an analysis of the children in the household nor differentiated between those of the husband and wife in the household and other children. In East London Pauw found many variations in the composition of the households, the average size of which was 5·8 persons. Only one-third of the sample households consisted of mother, father, and children (with between them an additional 17 other relatives), while 45 of the 105 families had between them 101 grandchildren, the majority the children of unmarried daughters.[9] As the incidence of illegitimacy ranges from 26 to 60 per cent of all live births in different towns, it is clear that a number of children in a large number of households must in fact be grandchildren and that many of the families regarded as nuclear are three-generational. In the past household membership was extremely fluid: children were sent to the country to stay with relatives either because the mother took up employment or to protect them from what many parents regarded as the contaminating influences of the town, wives went home to give birth, rural relatives came on lengthy visits. Influx control has sharply curtailed this fluidity.*

* The Bantu (Urban Areas) Consolidation Act 25 of 1945 as subsequently amended provides that no African may remain in a prescribed area (i.e. an urban area) for more than seventy-two hours (the onus of proof resting on him) with-

The dispersion of the kin between town and country and within the town itself, together with the general urban trend for individuals to join groups on a basis of common interests rather than that of kin relationships, has had the effect of weakening bonds with the wider circle of kindred. 'The town-bred', says Wilson, 'suggest that it is only primary and secondary relationships which are of much importance: parents and children, grandparents and grandchildren, siblings and their children visit and co-operate, but second cousins are not of much importance to one unless some bond, other than that of kinship, unites them.'[10] Personal liking and the accident of proximity outweigh formal kinship ties. But kinship still plays a more important part than it does in the white community and ties which have long been dormant are frequently revived at times of distress, especially illness and death. Africans travel great distances and incur expenditure which, on the face of it, is utterly beyond their means, to attend the funerals of even distant relations.

Within the family adaptation to the new conditions of urban living is proceeding slowly and unevenly. The failure to comprehend the nature of the inevitably changed roles of spouses and of parents and children results, in many cases, in considerable friction.

The traditional pattern in a strongly patrilineal society was one of male domination, female subordination, and rigid segregation of conjugal roles. Despite the changed economic role of women—roughly one-third of married women are gainfully employed—their increased responsibilities for home and budget management and for the rearing and education of the children, and the greater interdependence of the members of the smaller

---

out a permit unless he was born there and has lived there continuously, has worked for one employer for ten years or has been lawfully in the area for fifteen years, and in both cases has continued to reside there; the wife, son under eighteen years, or unmarried daughter of such an African may also be in the town provided he or she normally resides with him and has entered the area lawfully. The present-day interpretation of this latter provision is causing considerable hardship. For example, a man qualified to be domiciled in the town in terms of the provisions just set out, who now marries, is permitted to have his wife join him (i.e. enter the area lawfully) only if she comes from a prescribed area. Parents are experiencing great difficulty in securing entry permission for children over sixteen who were brought up by relatives in the country or went to boarding school there unless they have complete documentation—birth and school certificates and housing records—which many of them lack.

urban family, many men maintain their traditional attitudes and patterns of behaviour. In some families women have like-wise retained the attitudes of traditional society, particularly more recent immigrants from the country and women of little or no formal education. In others wives are acutely resentful of their husbands' lack of co-operation and claim the right to greater equality of treatment. In a number of families, notably among the professional and higher-income groups where the spouses both have attained a higher standard of education, patterns of companionship, joint consultation, and shared responsibility are emerging. To the majority of women this represents the ideal to which Africans should aspire—an ideal which they have largely taken over from white society and which many seem to believe is the white norm. Men do not to the same extent accept this democratic pattern as a goal. Even many modern, sophisticated men view the dawning emancipation of women as a threat which will destroy the patriarchal authority they have been conditioned to regard as their right. To what extent male domination in the home is partly a defence mechanism to compensate for the recurrent frustrations and the general lack of status of all African men in a white-dominated society has not been investigated. But the observations of African field-workers indicate that it is a factor which reinforces traditional male attitudes and impedes the accommodation to the new structure of the family—an accommodation which women, to whom it denotes a greater freedom and a relative improvement in status, make more easily.

The same conflicts between traditional patterns and the demands of changed conditions of living manifest themselves in parent–child relationships. In traditional society a whole body of kindred, together with the child's own and its ascendant age-grade, shared in the informal educational process. Respect for seniority was a central principle of the system. Aloof authoritarianism characterized the roles of the father and his kin. 'A father cannot be friends with his child,' says a Zulu proverb. The mother and her kin, particularly her brother, were more indulgent and on terms of an easier familiarity with the child. In recent seminars on family life women stressed the failure of their husbands to co-operate in bringing up the children more than any other aspect of domestic relationships. As in the working

M

class of early industrial Britain, as well as in a number of British working-class families today, it is regarded as 'cissy' (loss of manhood is the township equivalent) for a man to be involved with his children. Here, too, patterns are changing, again chiefly in the upper-educational levels, where warmer, easier, more democratic relations are developing between both parents and children. But the gap between the generations, particularly the gap in knowledge and experience of town-ways, presents a formidable obstacle to understanding. A further grim obstacle is poverty—the average wage of men is in the region of R40 per month—which means that parents are often in the humiliating position of being unable to fulfil even basic needs of their children. Allied with these factors is the traditional pattern subsumed under the Victorian axiom 'Children should be seen but not heard', and what practically amounts to a taboo on discussing sex with one's own children. The upshot is a widespread failure of communication. Many women make immense sacrifices to keep their children at school—'schooling' having become synonymous with 'education'—and yet confront their adolescent children as strangers. In the complex, heterogeneous environment of the towns where a multitude of choices is open to the individual, generally accepted norms of behaviour are as yet only in the process of development, and the home does not know how to give the child the emotional support he needs, it is inevitable that 'loss of parental control' should be the syndrome causing the people continuing and impotent anxiety.

In keeping with the attitude which held that regular sexual satisfaction was the normal requirement of every adult, pre-marital intercourse was a recognized institution in tribal society. But only external intercourse was sanctioned and pre-marital pregnancy was strongly condemned. Various sanctions appear to have ensured that few children were born before marriage. These sanctions no longer operate. Illegitimacy is still in theory frowned upon, but it is of such widespread occurrence that it is accepted as inevitable. In many families a pre-marital pregnancy causes great anguish to the girl and her parents. One symptom of maternal concern is the increasingly insistent demand women's organizations are making for sex instruction to be given in the schools. Illegitimate children are cared for by the family of the mother and are reared on equal terms with the other children, and no social stigma attaches to illegitimate children. The prevalence of illegitimacy is giving rise to matri-focal multi-generation families consisting of unmarried mothers and their children. Pauw found that 11 of the 46 female heads in his sample were unmarried mothers.

Marriage is no longer a contract between two groups of kin, with personal preferences being regarded as a minor considera-tion. The selection of a marriage partner is today determined by individual choice based on mutual attraction and congeniality. But *lobolo*—the traditional transfer of cattle from the family of the bridegroom to the family of the bride which validated the right of the groom's family to the children the bride would bear —is today still paid in the overwhelming majority of marriages, whatever their legal form. The payment of *lobolo* is an indispens-able element in a customary union, that is a marriage contrac-ted according to Bantu law. But *lobolo* is also paid in most marriages contracted by civil or Christian rites, although in towns in the form of money instead of cattle. A 1963 survey in Soweto of 1,514 marriages showed that 36 per cent were custo-mary unions, 52 per cent were Christian or civil marriages with *lobolo*, and 12 per cent were Christian or civil marriages without *lobolo*.[11] Why this element of traditional culture has been so tenaciously retained in marriages under the common law, even though it has lost its basic function of legitimizing the children born of the marriage and securing the co-operation of the two groups of kin involved in the *lobolo* payment in safeguarding the marriage, is not readily explicable. Partly it is due to com-mercialization of the payment which is now related to the educational and occupational status of the bride, although it must be noted that in the most prestigious marriages involving the highest *lobolo* payments the bride's parents spend at least this amount on the trousseau and the wedding reception. The debate which has continued over decades within the African community regarding the merits and demerits of *lobolo*, pro-ponents and opponents equally vehement and women as divided in their opinion as men, shows clearly that the commercial motive is not a sufficient explanation. More recently, and very probably a response provoked by continued official exhorta-tions to the Bantu 'to preserve what is their own' and not to seek to become 'imitation Englishmen', *lobolo* has increasingly been

supported on grounds of cultural pride—'it is our custom.'
Even though they realize that the need to accumulate the
money for *lobolo* often causes lengthy postponement of a marriage sometimes to the point that the relationship breaks up
before marriage, women from all walks of life support it. Their
feeling that their dignity suffers and their worth is diminished
unless *lobolo* is paid appears to have its roots in a society where
the status of women, otherwise uniformly low, was in this way
recognized.

Although monogamy is practically the only form of marriage
in towns—three of 151 marriages in a recent (unpublished)
Soweto survey were polygynous and in no case was more than
one wife present in the town—polygynous attitudes based on
the attitude that a man is entitled to have access to a number of
women persists, and polygyny is being replaced by an informal
system of concubinage and by extra-marital liaisons. There is
much talk in the townships of the extent of marital infidelity, and
the incidence of separations—even if not of legal divorces,
though these, too, are increasing—appears to be high. One of
Pauw's main findings was that the elementary family is the
basic type 'but it shows a strong tendency on the one hand to
lose the father at a relatively early stage and on the other to
develop a multi-generation span'.[12] In his sample of 105 families,
46 had female heads, widows, divorced or deserted women, or
unmarried mothers. In Soweto, on the other hand, the proportion was lower, only 18 per cent of the families having female
heads. In the one township in Johannesburg which is not part
of the large concentration of Soweto, a much older and also
smaller township, 41 per cent of the 660 families had women as
family heads.

I am of the opinion that broken families form a larger proportion than any broad-based survey would reveal because of
the regulations which govern the right to occupy houses in the
townships. Only married men who are qualified to live in the
town and who are permitted to have their wives with them can
become registered occupiers of a house. If this permission is
refused, the inducement for a man to contract a customary
union with one of the many women as anxious to obtain a house
as he is must be great. It is known that this is the reason for
many of the so-called 'shilling-marriages'. It costs 20 cents

(formerly one shilling) to appear before a Bantu Commissioner to complete an affidavit to the effect that a customary union had been contracted elsewhere.* In the past divorced women and widows with children, provided they qualified for urban domicile, could obtain a house. In terms of a directive issued some two years ago by the Department of Bantu Administration and Development, divorcees may not be registered occupiers and must vacate the house on divorce—irrespective of the grounds for the divorce or the order made regarding the custody of the children—and no women at all may in future be placed on the waiting list for houses. Such women are permitted to be sub-tenants of a registered occupier provided they can find one willing to sub-let part of the small standard four-roomed house, a matter which presents considerable difficulty if there are a number of children. There is accordingly a premium on marriage or the appearance of marriage as a means to housing. I am told that in order to appear married, women resort to the expedient of replacing a legal husband who has deserted by a *pro forma* husband who continues to pay the rent in the original husband's name.

That the majority of families consist of parents and children and possibly one or more grandchildren seems beyond doubt. Unlike the situation in the West Indies where the husband is reported to occupy a marginal and hence dispensable position in the family, the African husband is the head of his home. Although, as in working-class Britain, relationships between mother and daughter tend to be close if they live in the same town and there is a greater tendency for the family, if it expands, to have members of the wife's family living with it, the patrilineal principle still obtains. Women, on the whole, do not want to usurp the man's position. They do desire a lightening of the burden they carry by greater sharing and that men would make a larger contribution to household income and spend less on their own personal requirements, particularly on alcohol. They differ on the question of family planning. More men than women desire large families, the related values of fertility and potency being more firmly upheld by men than women. With the advent of the contraceptive pill women are finding it feasible to limit their families without the knowledge of their husbands,

---

* Registration of customary unions is compulsory only in Natal.

and attendances at family planning clinics have increased considerably.

While the family is, as elsewhere, the basic social unit, it is the accelerating development of a great variety of new groupings based on the principle of association and not of kinship which is providing the new social framework for the majority of urban dwellers. Their forms are diverse, their number is legion—'the school of civilization', Wilson calls them. They range from the informal play group of neighbourhood children to alumni associations, from groups of men who regularly drink together at a beer hall to the African Chamber of Commerce. With the exception of a small number of tribal associations which function mainly in the form of mutual aid societies, membership of voluntary associations cuts across tribal affiliations. A small number of associations have developed autonomously in response to the ever-present problems of poverty. Such are the stockfels which consist of a group of people who pay a specified sum of money weekly or monthly into a pool which is given in turn to every member who then becomes the 'owner' of the stockfel and arranges a party from which the profits accrue to him. Many similar pooling arrangements, all different forms of enforced saving without, however, the party associated with the stockfel, exist among small groups of workers, particularly the 'single' workers.

In general the voluntary associations follow Western models. They have come into being to meet new needs, such as those served by a trade union, or to fulfil a need which was traditionally discharged by the family, such as day nurseries for the children of working mothers. The main categories of voluntary associations are, in the first place, the religious, including the strong women's church unions known as *manyanos*; then there are the recreational, including the numerous football, boxing, weight-lifting, and other sports organizations, the cultural, including choirs and drama clubs, the professional, the economic, and the philanthropic. The concepts of community service and of voluntary welfare work unrelated to kindred and friends are gaining ground, particularly among the women, many of whom play prominent roles as office-bearers of welfare societies. As in other communities, the leadership of the major organizations is an interlocking one drawn largely from the middle class. In the past there were political parties striving for equal rights which stressed the demand for the extension of the franchise to Africans as the primary objective in the struggle against discrimination. Since the banning of the African political movements in 1960 subsequent to Sharpeville and its aftermath, no overt political party has been able to exist outside the Transkei.

Status, traditionally ascriptive, is today predominantly an achieved one. As the population of South Africa is racially stratified and individual mobility is confined within the four different racial groups, status is relevant only within that particular racial group. The determinants of status—wealth, education, and occupation—are the same, but the level of achievement required for recognition differs, being highest among whites and lowest among Africans. As, for instance, the average income of whites has been estimated to be ten times that of Africans, and 23·29 per cent of the white as compared with 0·13 per cent of the African population has matriculated or attained a higher educational standard, it is obvious that the determinants of stratification must have different levels.

Within the African community the emergence of at least a twofold class structure into a middle and lower class is clearly discernible, and a consciousness of class differences has developed. Some observers postulate a fourfold stratification: an elite composed of the small group of leading professionals and the few wealthy traders forming an apex distinct from the remainder of the educated and better-off section; and a working class consisting of the semi-skilled and the unskilled workers. So clear-cut a division, which may well take shape in the future, is in my opinion not justified at this stage. It is possible that the division between manual and non-manual workers will also have more implications for status at that time. The wage structure at present bears less relationship to work category than to the circumstances in which Africans entered that category. If, due to the growing shortage of white workers, Africans have replaced whites, the wage tends to be higher than if the occupation was initially one in which Africans were employed. At present, to give one example, workers engaged in transport, especially drivers of heavy lorries, fall into a higher income-group than the majority of white-collar workers and primary school teachers.

The white middle class is the normative reference group for Africans and the degree of westernization is in itself an attribute of status. Education was formerly the main determinant of status. Today, as throughout South Africa, money and possessions tend to outweigh other attributes, although education, particularly a university degree, commands great respect in the African community. Material possessions—house, furniture, clothes, and particularly a higher-price car—are the concrete symbols of 'success' which is another name for status. A distinctive style of life, distinctive patterns of behaviour and standards of value are all, to greater or lesser degree, associated with the emerging middle class. As already indicated, more egalitarian relationships between husband and wife and more democratic family patterns are developing in a number of middle-class families. There is also reason to consider that the incidence of illegitimacy is lower in the middle class. As elsewhere, the life chances of children from more prosperous homes are better and the middle class tends to be self-perpetuating. Marriage is likewise tending to be class-bound. As, however, class differentiation is a recent phenomenon in the African community and because, despite official policies, new occupational opportunities are opening up for Africans in response to the pressures of industrialization, there is scope for relative mobility. Because members of the African middle class are the standard-setters for the community as a whole, the system of stratification reinforces the many other influences promoting a general orientation to Western culture.

While many aspects of culture are interrelated, with the corollary that change in one aspect affects the others, Moore has suggested that certain components of culture are especially autonomous.[13] He cites 'super-empirical components of religious belief' as a possible example. Evidence of the frequent resort to magic and witchcraft and continued observance of rites connected with ancestor worship by many people in the towns lends support to this suggestion. Although according to the 1960 census two-thirds of the total African population belonged to one of the Christian Churches, more than one-half of the respondents in a Soweto sample survey stated that they used the services of what are commonly called witch-doctors (which includes diviners and herbalists, a large number of whom have flourishing practices in Johannesburg and other towns). The proportion is in fact probably higher, as the interviewers reported that informants were reluctant to admit to practising any form of magic because it is regarded as 'non-U'. The use of magic, chiefly in the form of special substances obtained from African medicine-men—herbs, roots, barks, and potions of diverse kinds—which are believed to be able to achieve a desired end through the control of supernatural power is wide-spread and has been adapted to meet every possible contin-gency of life: to win a football match, to pass an examination, to secure an acquittal in a criminal case are some of the in-numerable examples that come to mind. I believe this con-tinued reliance on magic is related to the insecurity of urban existence and the many unpredictable hazards it presents. The extent to which the performance of ancestral rites by Christians is what has been called a 'folklorist survival', comparable to the white community's Easter practices, or the incorporation of the ancestral spirits in Christian worship as mediators between man and the remote Christian God, or a protest against a Christian Church which has failed to match practice with precept, is not known. All three responses are evident.

The other area, closely linked with the magico-religious system, in which traditional practices persist often combined with Western ceremonial, is that of *rites de passage*. At birth, puberty, marriage, and death traditional beliefs often come to the fore. As already discussed, *lobolo* is still paid in civil law marriages. At the coming-out ceremonies of the new-born and at the time of death, the connection with the ancestral spirits is often reaffirmed. Male initiation among circumcision-practising tribes continues to be observed, with the emphasis on the physical operation and not on the educational aspect. In towns boys are not infrequently circumcised in hospitals, sometimes because it is not feasible to send the boy to an initiation school, sometimes because parents want to minimize risks to health.

I have, in the attempt to be relatively brief, necessarily over-generalized and over-simplified complex processes and have made insufficient allowance for individual differences of per-sonality. The juxtaposition of whites and Africans in South Africa, intimately interdependent economically, but politically, educationally, and socially divided by legal and customary barriers, has produced differing responses. But the general direction of cultural development is, I submit, clear. Pauw says, 'The culture of the urban Xhosa of East London is predominantly orientated to Western cultural patterns.'[14] Wilson found that in Langa 'a community has emerged with characteristics very similar to those of urban communities in other countries and radically different from the traditional tribal societies of the Nguni peoples'.[15] I, for myself, do not doubt that the future of South Africa must be envisaged in terms of a dominant Western culture within which there will be sub-cultures sharing the same basic institutions but differing in peripheral cultural traits. While African leaders were free to talk they made their acceptance of Western culture and their demand for the tools which would enable full access to its heritage clear. Significantly, the mystique of negritude and the concept of 'African personality' have made little appeal to the African intellectuals of South Africa. It is also significant, in a world in which linguistic nationalism often acts as an explosive force, that one of the first independent acts of the Transkeian Legislative Assembly was to revert to the system of English-medium instruction in the schools which had obtained until the present government made vernacular-medium teaching obligatory for the first eight years of schooling throughout the Republic.

Had there been any systematic attempt to promote cultural assimilation in the past, the situation might well have been a very different one today. Despite the valiant efforts of the early missionaries and the fine educational institutions they established, educational provision has always fallen far short of the need. Today, more than one hundred years later, even though some two million African children are at school, only 3 per cent proceed beyond the primary schools and less than 1,000 successfully complete high-school education. The refusal of successive governments to recognize the inevitability of permanent African urbanization, their failure to meet the housing and other needs of urban Africans, the active attempts of the present government to discourage Africans from taking root in the towns, culminating in the legislation in 1966 which deprived all urban Africans of any permanent *right* to urban domicile, have engendered a continuing anxiety and insecurity which militate against urban commitment and promote double-rootedness.

The present National Party Government, committed to a policy of separate development which envisages the creation of eight ethnically different self-governing Bantu 'nations', supports its policy on the grounds that the distinction the Republic makes is not one of colour but of ethnic origin, tradition, culture, language, and group solidarity and consciousness. And it is endeavouring to promote this type of national consciousness by means such as the division of urban townships into ethnic areas, vernacular-medium education, resuscitating what had been a languishing system of chieftainship in the rural areas, attempts to reactivate in the towns tribal allegiances which were fast losing their significance, and the prevention of interracial cooperation in social welfare and other spheres. In effect this amounts to an intensification of the continuing and irreconcilable conflict in South Africa between economic development and racial separation. The present government has now added the cultural dimension. Government spokesmen repeatedly and defiantly proclaim that economic development will accommodate itself to the demands of separate development. Meanwhile, South Africa basks in the warm glory of its expanding industries, its growth in national output, its rising *per capita* income. I doubt that even the most fervently held of ideologies can make a whole people voluntarily abstain from pursuing the course of prosperity. And if not, then the economic integration of Africans will continue and with it further assimilation of and adaptation to Western culture.

REFERENCES

1. PAUW, B. A., *The Second Generation*, Oxford University Press, Cape Town, 1963, vi.
2. Unpublished Sample Survey conducted by the Research Section of the Johannesburg Non-European Affairs Department in 1966.
3. LEISTNER, G. M. E., 'Foreign Bantu Workers in South Africa: Their Present Position in the Economy', *South African Journal of Economics* (Johannesburg), Mar. 1967, 42.
4. READER, D. H., *The Black Man's Portion*, Oxford University Press, Cape Town, 1961, 44.
5. MAYER, PHILIP, *Townsmen or Tribesmen*, Oxford University Press, Cape Town, 1961, 293.
6. Figures from Reports prepared by Johannesburg Non-European Affairs Department, 1967.

7. *Income and Expenditure Patterns of Bantu Living under Other than Family Conditions in Pretoria 1965*, Bureau of Market Research, University of South Africa, Pretoria, Report No. 18, 1967, 15 and 17.

8. GOODE, WILLIAM J., *World Revolution and Family Patterns*, Collier–Macmillan, New York, 1963, ch. 1.

9. PAUW, op. cit., Tables 18 and 38.

10. WILSON, MONICA, and MAFEJE, ARCHIE, *Langa*, Oxford University Press, Cape Town, 1965, 74.

11. VERSTER, JOAN, 'The Trend and Pattern of Fertility in Soweto: An Urban African Community', *African Studies*, 1965, *24*, 3–4, calculations based on Table 27.

12. PAUW, op. cit., 149.

13. MOORE, WILBERT E., *Social Change*, Prentice-Hall, New York, 1963, 75.

14. PAUW, op. cit., 194.

15. WILSON and MAFEJE, op. cit., 172.

9

PHILIP MAYER

RELIGION AND SOCIAL CONTROL IN A SOUTH AFRICAN TOWNSHIP

I

This chapter is concerned with 'total' social institutions in an urban setting in South Africa. By 'total' institutions I mean those which seek to control many activities and many aspects of participants' lives, and to impose a total set of values or moral standards. I shall be concerned here with their beneficial influence as agencies of social control in a potentially anomic situation. The material relates to two forms of total organization which I was able to observe operating side by side in the city of East London in the Eastern Cape Province: one embodying a religious (Christian) and the other a tribal value system.

A brief preamble is necessary to outline the general situation of urban Africans in South Africa. The movement of rural-bred Africans into town has proceeded further and faster in this country than in most other African countries thanks to the enormous growth of industry and commerce. But, much though African labour is needed in the towns, Africans are not 'wanted' there in other senses. All the urban areas are officially 'white' areas in the sense that Africans cannot have full citizen rights in them. Moreover the Government is committed to restricting the numbers of Africans in towns. It inherited time-honoured policies of influx control and of encouraging migratory as against settled labour; it has added new schemes for 'border industries' (industrial development near Bantu areas, away from 'white' towns). Its designation of Bantu 'homelands', or Bantustans, where Africans have some political self-expression, has also been linked with measures further reducing Africans' civic rights in the towns. Any one of these measures alone inevitably entails much bureaucratic control. Together—from the viewpoint of African town-dwellers or would-be town-dwellers—they add up to a tight framework of regimentation and compulsion.

In another light, however, the urban African population of South Africa is relatively well off. For those who keep in steady employment there are the benefits of decent, if modest, housing, modern medical services, schools for the children, and an effective municipal administration. Unemployment is not much of a threat, as long as the economy continues expanding and the influx-control regulations continue keeping out rival work-seekers from the country.

It is difficult to guess whether these specifically South African urban conditions generate more or less tension for the town-dwellers than urban conditions in other parts of the continent. The South African system (we may say) probably entails less sheer physical hardship, while it entails more hardship in terms of unjust family separation and restrictions on movement, not to mention insecurity (through denial of freehold) and restriction on social mobility (through job-reservation). Secondly, black poverty is closely confronted by white plenty, in a way that recalls the United States rather than Africa as a whole. Thirdly, the very advanced nature of the urban economy and technology may itself be enough to generate some anxiety in people fresh from a tribal home.

What is certain is that town-dwelling Africans in South Africa express great anxiety about problems of social control. One obvious aspect is the fear of violent crime, causing many town windows to be barred and people to be hesitant about going out at night. But even more pervasive, perhaps, is the fear of the 'traps and temptations' of town life, which have become almost proverbial: one's child or spouse may not necessarily fall into crime, but may nevertheless 'lead a wasted life', 'become aimless', whether by excessive drinking or gambling or smoking dagga (hemp), or by simply failing to hold a job or establish a decent family life. This overall distinction between the respectable and the aimless—those who cope and those who don't—cuts across the nascent class distinctions. It also cuts across the many distinctions of cultural background and moral outlook. This variety of normative systems co-existing and inter-mingling in the city—some tribally derived, some Western-derived—is itself of course one of the sources of anxiety and un-certainty about roles, if not of moral danger.

The burden of this chapter is that normative systems become most effective in town, in the sense of combating 'aimlessness', when they are embodied in a total institution or system, defined by what we shall call the 'totalitarian syndrome'. A person who submits to the tight grip of such a system buys escape from the moral malaise and uncertainty about roles which town life tends to engender through its formlessness, its relatively fast social change, and its confrontation between different and conflicting normative systems. Of course, the totalitarian syndrome carries its own dangers of dysfunction, for the individual and for society. But we are here concerned with its positive or useful functions.

It is a familiar complaint against the Christian Churches in the designated non-white residential quarters, that they seem unable to provide effective moral guidance for the mass of people or even of their nominal adherents. But fieldwork showed that certain sects were notable exceptions: they kept their members under strict social control. This seemed to me to derive from the set of organizational principles which I call the totalitarian syndrome. Such a sect (in fact) constitutes what is practically a face-to-face community within the urban sur-rounding. It does so by becoming a more or less discrete field of interaction: the members are interacting with each other far more than any of them are interacting with non-members, so that in effect a clear line is drawn around the sect membership. Because the sect has found ways and means to perpetuate this situation, it is discharging more than the normal functions of religious associations which may seem superficially comparable. The functions of the sect are more comprehensive and diffuse; the member is required to give much more to the sect than he would normally give to an association; he also receives much more from it. An important element in the syndrome is a moral code which seeks to govern even the minutiae of personal life. It is on this basis that the in-group draws a clear line around itself, and discourages interactions with the out-group. The member feels morally committed to the group standards 'all along the line' and as a result he has very few fields of activity left in which he can comfortably interact with non-members.

In this chapter, I first document the 'community-like' functions of the sectarian body by reference to one particular Christian sect in the city of East London. This sect is then compared with another body in the same city which is not a religious sect, but which also constitutes a discrete field of interactions and exhibits the totalitarian syndrome. This other body is a socio-cultural minority consisting of certain pagan migrants to the city, with strong tribal and rural attachments.

As I have shown elsewhere[1] it is the distinctive achievement of these pagan migrants—as compared with most of the Christian migrants—that they succeed in 'bringing the village into the town', recreating in East London the close network of face-to-face relations and the tight social control which characterize their home communities in the rural reserves.

II

First, a few facts about East London. Individually, most of the African town-dwellers in East London at any given time are migrants from the country; but the pattern of migration, and of having town as the second home, is already an integral part of their folkways, well established for several generations. For many of these Africans town eventually becomes the only home, and there are also numbers of townsmen born, in the second or third generation, for whom it is the only home they will ever have known. Thus, besides urbanization as a current process, we have urbanism as a settled condition.

Like other urban populations the East London Africans have serious problems in the sphere of morality and social control. From what has been said, it will be realized that these are not just the first shock reactions of people being newly exposed to the urbanization process. *Prima facie* the non-white urban locations seem to abound in violent crime, drunkenness, drug addiction, theft, robbery, offences by children out of parental control, and sexual laxity, this last resulting in an extremely high incidence of illegitimate births. There is the dread stereotype of the *tsotsi*— a figure uniquely associated with urban locations—who is described by Africans as a person without any moral controls at all, 'one who has not got the feelings of a human being'.

Africans themselves often lament the immorality of the East London locations, particularly what they see as a lack of respect for parents and seniors. They suggest that the town corrupts children as well as women. Even those parents who are well adjusted to town life themselves may make efforts to send their young children back to the country to be reared by relatives there. Significantly, all this moral disapproval is part of the townsmen's stereotype of themselves, as well as the country people's stereotype of them. Almost all categories of Africans, in and out of town, seem to agree that the urban locations are immoral places, and that born-and-bred townspeople are apt to be the worst in this respect, even if superior to the country-born in skill and sophistication. There is some realization that this hangs together with the anonymity of town. The location is described as a place where 'nobody knows' or 'nobody cares', as against the rural community where (in a favourite phrase) 'we are all one another's policemen'.

This anomie of the urban locations co-exists with a high incidence of Church adherence or organized Christianity. The rural reserves around East London are about evenly divided between Christian and pagan, with perhaps a preponderance of pagans; but in East London itself, with an African population of over 50,000 in 1963, two-thirds or more are found to claim affiliation to some Christian Church.

The majority of these people are old adherents, born into families which had been Christian long before they set foot in town. Missionary effort has been going on in this part of South African for 150 years, and many of the rural communities from which the urban migrants are drawn have consisted for generations either wholly or partly of 'school people'—as they are called; that is, of people who accept in principle the teachings of schools and missions. Theirs is a folk culture with Christianity as one of its elements. By now the clergy and teachers alike are mainly Africans themselves. When the school people migrate to town they find the same denominations there; they simply carry on the old adherence.

It must also be made clear that the majority of these Christians are in recognized denominations, such as Anglican,

N

Methodist, Catholic, and Presbyterian. In this part of South Africa there is not much activity by nativistic or idiosyncratic sects like the Zionist ones which Sundkler has documented for Natal. These are distinguished both by extreme emotionalism and a mixture of Christian with indigenous or idiosyncratic symbolism and ritual, and also by not acknowledging any links with any white Churches. By contrast, I want to emphasize that in speaking of Christian sects in East London I shall mean sects of quite a different type—well established and internationally recognized bodies such as the Seventh Day Adventists, the Jehovah's Witnesses, and the Assemblies of God. These acknowledge origin in and connection with white parent bodies, though they tend to be organized on racial lines, with African clergy for the African congregations. As far as this goes they are no different from the other major denominations in South Africa.

Out of the various sects in East London I have selected for discussion the Assemblies of God—locally known as Bhengu's Church, after its outstanding leader, the Revd. Nicholas Bhengu. This is a branch of the worldwide pentecostal movement, but in keeping with pentecostal ideas the local congregation is fully autonomous. Bhengu's is not only the most flourishing but the best-documented sect of its kind in East London, having been the subject of a recent study by A. A. Dubb.[2]

Almost all of the Africans in East London are drawn from one great ethnic and linguistic group, the Xhosa-speaking peoples, who predominate in the rural hinterland. The one-third in town who are not Christians are what the Xhosa call 'red people'. That is, they are tribally-mixed Xhosa traditionalists, who continue to reject Christianity along with white men's ways in general. This does not prevent them from earning money in town, where they can successfully discharge the role of unskilled worker.

The Red people and the Bhenguists are miles apart in a religious sense, for the Bhenguists are particularly zealous Evangelical Christians while the Red people reject Christianity. Their own religion is the traditional pagan ancestor-cult of the Xhosa, which they practise in town as well as they can, and resume in full when they go back to the reserves.

While many people in East London, both Xhosa and white, openly deplore the fact that the Churches seem to contribute so little in the way of moral control, one Church is frequently singled out as an exception. That is Bhengu's. Bhenguists are described as being decent and law-abiding people. The other category for whom exception is frequently made is the Red people in town—they too are supposed to be decent and well-controlled. Even Christians readily admit the superiority of these pagan ancestor-worshippers in this respect. This consensus is voiced both by location residents and by white employers, in their different ways. To the employers, the Bhenguists and the pagans are the two types who appear as the most regularly honest and reliable workmen. To fellow-citizens in the location, both appear exceptional in their ability to 'control their children' or in having 'proper respect for seniors'. Both are praised for sincerity; the Red people—it is commonly said—whatever their absurdities or other failings by urban standards, are 'straightforward' and 'say what they mean', while the Bhenguists 'practise what they preach' and 'can be trusted'. In this way they are jointly set apart against the common complaint that town is a place 'where no African can trust another'.

This is the convergence which, I suggest, is produced by the operation of similar organizational features on both sides, constituting the totalitarian syndrome, despite the marked differences in religion and professed values.

III

The organizational likenesses will be best appreciated after pointing out various important differences. First, one self-evident difference—Bhengu's Church is an organized religious association defined by religious adherence, membership in a corporate congregation, and acceptance of one charismatic leader. The Red people in town, as such, are not a formal association of any kind, but a sociological category, with no centralizing or corporate organization. They have no leader, meeting-place, or church, and no centralized rituals such as might be addressed to chiefly or national ancestors. (The Xhosa ancestor-cult is a domestic cult, of each family's deceased parents or grandparents.)

Secondly, the Bhengu sect is an innovation dating from a crusade by Mr. Bhengu during the early 1950s, while the Red category stands for conservatism and the tribal past. All Bhenguists are converts admitted individually on the basis of a fairly recent personal experience—a conversion mediated through Mr. Bhengu, which results in being 'saved', often accompanied by healing or some other dramatic testimony. Bhenguists are keen proselytizers. Among the Red people there is no scope for crusading zeal—they are not trying to start anything, but merely to preserve what they regard as their immemorial way of life.

Thirdly, the Bhengu sect, having originated in town, remains primarily of the town; its ideology endorses what we might call urban middle-class values, with emphasis on thrift, neatness, education, working skills, well-equipped homes, and generally raising social status. The Red values and habits are all geared to rural not urban life; Red men regard town as 'just a place by the wayside' and object to it as a permanent home, *inter alia* because their religious rituals, notably animal sacrifice, are so difficult to practise there. Their ideology strongly rejects urban middle-class values; the ancestors (it is believed) require that one should go on living as nearly as possible in the way they lived themselves, and therefore only the bare minimum of conformity to 'Western' ways is tolerated.

Fourthly, the Bhenguist attitude to white people and white civilization is co-operative. The more Western skills are learned the better. Mr. Bhengu himself is highly sophisticated and has travelled widely in Europe and America. The Red attitude to white people is one of reserve and withdrawal; the white man is regarded as a foreigner, perhaps an enemy, with whom the Red man should co-operate only in so far as is strictly necessary, and from whom he should not try to learn anything contrary to the ways of the ancestors.

Finally, the Bhenguist creed is strictly puritanical, notably with regard to drinking, smoking, sex, and worldly amusements such as dancing and the cinema. The Red creed is not: drink and smoking are not only tolerated but positively valued by Red people; sexual pleasure is likewise regarded as a good thing in itself, irrespective of marriage, and only becomes bad if an illegitimate birth threatens established family rights. Red people do not frown on worldly amusements, provided they are of the traditional Red world: thus traditional Red dancing is valued as a good thing, while ballroom dancing, jiving, and the cinema are rejected as bad.

IV

Against this background of differences, there is a shared pattern or syndrome which results in discrete fields of interaction being defined, and in totalitarian control over members. The essence of this pattern is a strong moral command, voiced by the group as a whole, which enjoins each member to have maximum contacts within the group and minimum contacts outside. In rather more detail we might say there are broadly five operative principles:

1. The group believes itself to have a distinctive moral message, which is not shared by the world outside; in fact (as Bryan Wilson has pointed out in his study of English sects) it is a 'protest' against values current in the environment.

2. Hence it expects members to refrain from activities outside, and to limit personal contact with non-members. Too much contact 'outside' might result in the distinctive message being forgotten or distorted. Where it is not practicable to forbid outside contacts, the limitation is on their intimacy or moral content, i.e. one may have to mix with outsiders but one should not admit them to friendship, marriage, or other close personal relations.

3. The group expects members to participate to the maximum in its internal activities, and to have intense relations with fellow members. In this way (as Homans has stressed) the norms of the group are strengthened; the message is kept vivid.

4. Continued observance of rules 1, 2, and 3 is the absolute and perpetual condition of membership. There are no half-measures: the member has a clear-cut choice between conforming and staying in, and deviating and getting out.

5. The moral arbiter is the group itself, the whole group, judging corporately even if some individual is used as a mouthpiece. The moral message is equally vested in all members

and incumbent on all members, and equally shared by them; hence the whole group acknowledges joint moral responsibility for every member, notably the responsibility of watching for deviations and bringing offenders to account.

This, then, is the syndrome seen from the bird's-eye point of view, as it characterizes a group or body as a whole. Seen from the viewpoint of an individual within the body, the syndrome appears as a pair of commands operating in two spheres—the sphere of personal relations and the sphere of activities. In each sphere there is a self-denying ordinance—to avoid activities not sanctioned by the group, and to avoid associates not belonging to the group. Paired with this is the positive injunction—to pursue activities demanded by the group and to associate intensively with other members.

If we consider the sphere of personal relations, it seems clear that the two demands, for minimum participation outside and maximum participation inside, will result in each member forming a network of personal relations entirely *within* the group—bounded by the group; and hence in the group itself constituting a bounded field of interactions.

But in addition it appears both among the Bhenguists and among the Red people in East London, that besides the *total* body constituting a bounded field of interactions, there exist *within* this total body distinct smaller circles, or cells, constituted by close-knit networks of intimate personal relations. In the case of the Red people, as I described elsewhere, these small circles are composed of home-boys, or *amakhaya*, migrants who come from the same local area in the country. They are important *inter alia* because they take first responsibility for the watchdog function; they are the first to notice any signs of deviance in the individual. In my description of the life of Red people in East London I attempted to show how this tendency in network formation is connected with the limitation of activities, the two being interdependent on a theoretical level. I suggested that where there is strict limitation of activities, a few individuals can keep enough ground in common to be able to satisfy mutually all of one another's needs, thus forming a network of personal relations which takes the form of a small closed circle. But where there is not such a limitation of activities, individuals will tend to branch out in various directions, each needing different sets of friends to satisfy his different needs. In that situation the closed circle will not be formed, and the person's network will be of the 'open' type: the persons with whom he associates will not necessarily associate with each other.

I would now like to illustrate the totalitarian syndrome with a brief account of Bhenguist organization and practice.

V

The Bhenguists

The distinctive moral message of the Bhenguists is, of course, their particular brand of evangelical Christianity, with its insistence on being 'saved' through personal conversion and on bearing continual witness through the godly way of life. In its rejection of the normal secular amusements of location people, such as drinking, dancing, and the cinema, this way of life stands out sharply contrasted with that of the community around.

It is true that some other Churches in the locations also forbid secular amusements or drinking, to some extent. The significant difference is that on the whole they are not able to enforce the prohibition, because they lack the face-to-face atmosphere which Bhengu has created through insisting on the twin rules of minimum participation outside the group and maximum participation within. It is this which creates the conditions for totalitarian moral control of the individual, as I shall try to illustrate.

In the early stages of his crusade in East London, Bhengu foreshadowed the rule of minimum participation outside the group by urging converts not to associate with 'unsaved' people.[3] By the time the sect emerged in its present form this had come to be interpreted as ruling out all non-Bhenguists.

Bhenguists are categorically forbidden to join secular associations (e.g. sports clubs such as abound in the location). Being forbidden the normal secular amusements of the location, such as dancing, drinking, cinemas, they are automatically cut off from many personal contacts that would otherwise be made.

Location people are familiar with the exclusiveness of the Bhenguists and often criticize it adversely. A typical comment was: 'The people of Bhengu isolate themselves from others and hardly even greet one who does not belong to their own Church.' As to maximum participation *within* the group, it is an explicit principle of the Bhengu Church that 'members must participate in all Church activities throughout the week, unless they can produce a legitimate reason for not doing so'.[4] Not only Sunday services have to be attended regularly, but week-day prayer meetings, socials, Bible study circles, and so on, which are laid on plentifully. Consistently with this, every member of the congregation is a full member, i.e. no distinction is recognized between full members and mere adherents, as in most other Churches.

These maximum demands contrast with the minimum demand made by many other Churches in the location, e.g. the Anglican Church and its associated body, the Order of Ethiopia. Here the only obligation even upon confirmed adherents is to attend communion three times a year.

In these non-sectarian Churches, ordinary adherents (as distinct from office-bearers or guild members) choose their leisure pursuits as they please; and they choose their leisure-time companions from neighbours, fellow employees, home people, and kinsmen, irrespective of whether they are of the same congregation or not. Contact with co-religionists may be limited to Sunday services. In the choice of 'best friends' the fact of belonging to the same Church is only one factor among many.

It is clear that a Bhenguist, being forbidden to associate with the 'unsaved' and having his leisure time filled up with Church activities, must move for the most part within the limited field of interactions constituted by his sect. Dubb has documented this intensity of relations within the sect, particularly with regard to the small closed circles or cells which are discernible within the total field. In part these are constituted by neighbourhood: Bhenguists tend to form distinct residential clusters within the locations and members of such a cluster have a great deal of contact with one another, to the exclusion of their other neighbours. One informant is quoted as saying, 'At Mbonisela Street where I stay, we [i.e. Bhenguists] are always together in the afternoons and evenings, even if there is no church service for us to go to.'

Bhenguists are taught the duty of watching one another and advising against temptation. It is in the small circle or network of intimates that this can best be done. While the Bhenguist land-lady keeps an eye on her Bhenguist lodgers, they would not dare to smuggle drink into their rooms; while the lodgers keep an eye on the landlady, she would not dare to take a lover. One Bhenguist quoted by Dubb summed up the situation as follows: 'I sincerely say that one cannot do anything in our Church and not be discovered, because the Church members are always eye-ing one another.'

Some time ago, in writing about Red migrants, I said: 'It is by refusing to branch out into new cultural habits that they retain a basis for close-knit networks; while it is by keeping the network close-knit that they inhibit cultural branching out.'[5] I think it is clear that the same circular mechanism applies among the Bhenguists; for example, it is by refusing to drink that one avoids making friends with drinkers, while by keeping to one's closed circle of non-drinking friends one inhibits the possibility of forming the drinking habit.

A point I would like to emphasize here is that the moral code thus enforced upon Bhenguists by their watching brethren is a *totalitarian* code—hence the strength of the system. Even the minutiae of life are scrutinized and morally evaluated. In his preaching, Bhengu dwells a good deal on this world as well as on the next. He exhorts his flock to dress neatly, to save money, to improve their education, to furnish their homes well, and so forth. Few free fields are left in which a member feels he can do as he pleases. Hence no 'open' fields remain in which he could associate freely and comfortably with non-members for specific purposes. He rarely if ever gets away into contexts where he would not be exposed to Bhenguist moral judgements.

Where the moral code is less totalitarian—as in most of the non-sectarian Churches—there are two significant differences. First, the members are left with free fields of activity in which they can associate with anybody else. In such a case the indi-vidual (we might say) is a member of his Church 'for certain purposes', but a member of other associations and other groups for other purposes. Besides adhering to the Church he might, let us say, belong to a sports club and to a set of friends who drink together. From the Church's point of view he may have secret spheres, e.g. keep his drinking or his women concealed from the priest or congregation. This being so he is exposed alternately to a variety of different influences or moral judgements. He can select according to the immediate situation.

In the sectarian Church, like that of Bhengu, the member does not have this choice, being incapsulated within a circle where he hears only one sort of moral judgement and receives only one sort of influence. And he can hardly escape into secret spheres, since all his associates associate with each other.

The second difference entailed by the less totalitarian moral code is that it allows for gradation of moral judgements within the Church congregation itself. Some sins appear less important than others, and—in particular—sins may appear more or less important according to who it is who committed them. In non-sectarian Churches the ordinary members and adherents regard the official moral code of the Church as being strictly binding upon an inner nucleus, consisting of the ministers, office-bearers, and members of the Church guilds. The ordinary members are generally much more tolerant of lapses by those like themselves. In fact it seems correct to say that the ordinary Church adherent or member recognizes at least two moralities: on the one hand the official morality of the Church, binding upon the inner nucleus and receiving lip-service from the rest; on the other hand, the practical morality of ordinary Church adherents—like himself— 'doing what other people do'. It may be tacitly acknowledged that while the Church for example officially forbids drinking, ordinary members drink 'because everyone does it'.

Most Christian congregations in the East London locations are found to consist of a small nucleus of full members, or active members, with a much larger fringe of more doubtful adherents, some of whom are attached to the Church only in name. There will be people who claim this as 'their' Church though they have not even been baptized; people who have been baptized but never confirmed; people who were confirmed but never attend; those who attend but never take communion; and finally the inner circle just mentioned, the office-bearers and members of the Church guilds. It seems that within such a congregation this final sector, the inner nucleus, conforms more or less to the pattern I have been describing for the Bhenguists. Members of the nucleus also tend to form a closed circle, with maximum participation within and minimum participation outside; they also tend to live in one another's eye, to pounce on each other's misdeeds, and to regard the whole official morality of their Church as equally binding on each one of them. But there is a great difference between having this pattern followed by an inner ring—a tiny portion of the whole Church body— and having it followed by the Church body *as a whole*. Only in the latter case, which is the Bhenguist one, does the Church as a whole constitute an effective moral community for all members.

The average non-sectarian Church might be likened to an arrangement of concentric rings, fading outwards like ripples from a stone, with the effectiveness of social control diminishing at every remove from the centre; the outermost rings fade into nothingness as we reach the fringe of half-hearted adherents who hardly know in what sense they 'belong' in the Church at all. The Bhengu type of sect by contrast might be likened to an arrangement of contiguous little circles or cells, like a honey-comb. Each cell—each little network of Bhenguist friends—is as effective as its neighbour, and all together make up a clearly bounded entity. Every member is a full member, and all are subject to the whole totalitarian code.

I would now like to recall a similar pattern which exists among Red Xhosa migrants in East London.

VI

The Red People

The distinctive moral code of the Red people, at variance with the codes of the people around them, is the opposition to 'white men's ways' and the insistence that old traditional Xhosa ways are best for Xhosa. It is for this reason—as I mentioned—that Red Xhosa migrants in town shun the ordinary leisure-time pursuits and recreations of the others. Where their disapproval happens to hit the same object as Bhenguist disapproval, the reasons are different. Thus Bhenguists disapprove of town-style drinking because drink is sinful, but Red people disapprove because it is town-style—they keep to the old-fashioned Xhosa beer drink. Bhenguists disapprove of pre-marital pregnancy because sex relations outside marriage are sinful, but Red people disapprove because it offends fathers and senior kin—a Red man is entitled to beget children by a mature unmarried woman who looks after herself.

In a rural community where there are both Red and school families, each section constitutes a bounded field of interactions of its own; each keeps itself to itself for associational purposes. But when Red and school people migrate into town, there appears the difference which I have documented elsewhere. The school migrants branch out into various activities, friendships, and associations; they do not only make friends with other migrants, but also with born townspeople; and they form 'open' networks of personal relations, according to their different pursuits and inclinations. The Red migrants do not branch out, but voluntarily incapsulate themselves within a closed circle. Confining themselves deliberately to the few leisure pursuits which are authorized by Red morality, the Red migrants can confine themselves also each to his little clique of Red friends, who have no different inclinations from his own.

Red migrants in town move mainly within little circles of intimates constituted by persons coming from the same home place in the country. These *amakhaya*, or home-boys, will provide the migrant with his room-mates in town, his clique of regular drinking companions who meet each evening as a set (*iseti*), his moral guardians, and his protectors in need or emergency, such as illness or trouble with the law. There is a demand for maximum participation. A Red migrant cannot just stay out of the group activities of his home people in town, if he wants to remain acceptable to them. Just as in the country Red people frown on a man who keeps to himself and never goes to beer drinks or attends the locational moot, so in town they frown on one who absents himself from the nightly drink of the 'set' or from the occasional more formal meetings of home people. The ultimate censure is to be branded as an 'I don't care' and to be 'washed off' (as the Xhosa say): 'He does not want us, so we do not want him either.'

It is one of the explicit duties of a Red migrant to watch and counsel his Red home-boys, warning them against 'unsuitable company' in town (meaning non-Red company). Of course there will be no escaping the company of non-Red people at work, and in some other contexts, but the injunction is to avoid making close friends of them. Most Red men faithfully obey.

The small circles of Red *amakhaya* in East London fit together to make up a bounded field of interactions composed by the Red migrants generally, with minimum participation outside and maximum participation inside. As between this Red 'honeycomb' and the similar 'honeycomb' pattern of the Bhenguists, one difference is that the body of Red migrants, as a whole, does not have the corporate aspect of the Bhengu congregation, as a whole. With the Red people, more of the specific corporate activities are vested in the individual cell, and none in the total body. Nevertheless, the concept 'all of us Red people in town' is important as a reference group, and as forming a kind of moral community within the community. A Red migrant knows that what his own *amakhaya* disapprove would also be disapproved by all the other Red people in town.

The exclusiveness of the Red people in a non-Red environment is sanctioned by their highest supernatural authorities, the ancestor spirits. The spirits of the ancestors, it is believed, want their descendants to remain attached to the parental home in the country; they want them therefore to remain under the supervision of the home-boys, and they deplore it if the descendant 'vanishes' or 'gets lost'. Ancestor spirits do not even like it if a descendant changes his lodging in town; they want to be able to find him easily, and so do his home-boys—it is a necessary condition for effective guardianship. The face-to-face community, as an enclosing circle, is all-important.

It is explicitly stated by Red people that the moral judgement of ancestor spirits is simply a transcendent version of the moral judgement of ordinary Red people—that is, when the people are judging morally and not as selfish individuals; 'The things the ancestors dislike are the very same things which are disliked by us ordinary people on earth.' Important among them are the anti-social kinds of behaviour which 'disturb the peace of communities'. Ancestors do not want their descendant to 'get a bad name' by crime or delinquency; anyone who does so 'is shaming his ancestors as well as himself'. But in addition, the ancestors—like the living Red people—disapprove of behaviour which is non-Red without being anti-social. They greatly dislike *Ukurumsha*, as it is called: literally this means 'speaking English', but figuratively it means adopting white-inspired customs and ways of thought, as the school people have done.

These, then, are the circular or self-reinforcing mechanisms which produce among Red migrants the tight social control which is so much admired by other residents of East London locations. The Red man has little scope for anti-social behaviour because he is always under the eye of his home people (and consequently of the guardian ancestor spirits). He remains always under their eye because he has no non-Red friends: he needs no non-Red friends because his own patterns of activity are limited to Red patterns—but on the other hand he restricts himself to these limited patterns because he has no other friends.

VII

Comparing the Bhenguist and the Red migrant, we have seen that both types remain incapsulated within a circle of like-minded people, constituting a close-knit network, in which all those who know Ego also know each other. Therefore, no moral voice from outside is able to penetrate. Any outside voices which may be heard are rejected. The distinctive moral code is not effectively challenged.

Secondly, it is obvious that both for Bhenguists and for Red migrants the moral community must speak with a *unanimous* voice. The whole totalitarian code is binding on everyone; there are no gradations; the 'message' is the joint heritage of all the members. Thus he is doubly secure against conflicting or inconsistent moral pressures—secure from outside and inside the group.

Thirdly, this unanimous voice of the moral community is one and the same with the voice of God in the Bhengu case, or the ancestors in the Red case. The *vox populi* is echoing the *vox dei*. Thus the sanctions of guilt and shame are fused. I mentioned the contrasting situation in other Churches, where a member will be left open to influences from his other associates outside the Church; and where, even in the Church itself, there may be one code for the nucleus and another for the fringe. When that is so, a person who drinks may feel a little guilty about infringing the Church's prohibition, but not ashamed, 'because everyone does it'. The coincidence of 'shame' sanctions and 'guilt' sanctions produces the strongest possible pressure to conformity.

Conclusions

These contrasts between the sectarian and non-sectarian religious bodies in East London might be said perhaps to illustrate a more fundamental dilemma. In situations of change, doubt, and insecurity, two alternative patterns seem to offer themselves. One is rigid, exclusive, total control by some group. This will effectively counter anomie in so far as the standards imposed by the group will operate effectively on all members. The price paid is that the member loses individual freedom or the power of choice. He hears the one moral voice, he is enclosed in the circle, he is constantly watched, he must conform. This totalitarian solution seems appropriate to extreme nationalist, or religious, movements on the one hand, and to certain tribal systems on the other. It is a likely producer of good moral discipline, but also of self-righteousness or a 'chosen people' mentality.

The opposite solution is to leave choice and decision to the individual—choice of associates and choice of activities. In a city the individual finds himself within a wide field of possibilities, some of which are 'good' from his own and/or the society's point of view while others are 'bad'. Instead of having a complete package thrust upon him—a total moral and behavioural system with all its complement of good and bad features—the individual in the second pattern is permitted to create his own personal syndrome. He is capable of more satisfactions and achievements, but he is also open to more disappointments and temptations.

REFERENCES

1. MAYER, PHILIP, *Townsmen or Tribesmen*, Oxford University Press, Cape Town, 1961.
2. DUBB, A. A., 'The East London Assembly of God', M.A. Thesis, Rhodes University, Grahamstown, South Africa.
3. Ibid., 187.
4. Ibid., 36.
5. MAYER, op. cit., 292.

Acknowledgement is due to the African Studies Centre, Edinburgh University, at whose Inaugural Seminar an earlier version of this chapter was delivered.

10

KOGILA ADAM

DIALECTIC OF HIGHER EDUCATION FOR THE COLONIZED: THE CASE OF NON-WHITE UNIVERSITIES IN SOUTH AFRICA

The institution of education in any society lends itself to a two-fold function: a conservative and a progressive one. On the one hand, it can be viewed as a custodian of societal values, with the main aim of transmitting traditional values. As such, education constitutes a means through which ruling political goals and objectives are induced and a generation socialized into accepting dominant societal values. On the other hand, education also constitutes a threat to the traditional social order. The mere fact of literacy itself opens new vistas and hence alternatives to the existent order. People reflect on their situation and begin to look through the natural spell of their fate and realize that this is one created by their dominators. It can have the effect of challenging and questioning generally accepted values and lead to contemplation of alternatives and the means to achieve them.

Viewed against this background, a society such as South Africa's, which is not legitimated by the majority of its population, and which relies on coercion rather than on consensus, appears all the more contradictory in extending higher education to its politically excluded majority. The past few years have indicated a definite acceleration in this programme. By the introduction of the Extension of University Education Act, 1959, the Government proposed to replace attendance of non-whites at 'open' universities with ethnic-group institutions.

o

The aim in doing this was gradually to prohibit white universities from accepting non-white students. The University College at Durban was established for Indians, the University of the Western Cape for Coloureds, the former University College of Fort Hare[1] for Xhosa-speaking Africans, the University College of Zululand at Ngoye for the Zulu- and Swazi-speaking, and the University College of the North at Turfloop for Sotho-, Venda-, and Tsonga-speaking Africans. This involved considerable expenditure, especially since the explicit aim was to provide facilities equal in all respects to white institutions.[2] In 1960, the State spent £137 per white student.[3]

Ambiguity in the function of education and the possibility of its being self-defeating for the system raises the question how the provision of such services can be reconciled with its long-term political objectives. Is this extension of African university education, for example, on the part of a system often described as repressive, purely gratuitous? In addressing itself to this central question, this chapter will focus on the following related questions: why provide non-European higher education at all? how can this be reconciled with the system's interests? to what extent is this successful? and, finally, is there a dialectic of education in so far as inherent contradictions of necessity could bring about the very opposite of the intended consequences?

It would seem necessary to look first of all at the background of higher educational facilities for non-whites, prior to Nationalist control of education. The four Afrikaans-language universities had never accepted non-white students, while the English-speaking universities, such as Cape Town, Witwatersrand, and Natal, had. Until 1959, there was a certain amount of social segregation at the so-called open universities with regard to extra-curricular activities. At the University of Cape Town no university residences were available for non-whites. Segregation with regard to sporting activities was maintained either as a matter of definite university policy or at any rate in actual practice. At the open universities, meals were served in communal restaurants, but on the other hand non-whites were not admitted to university dances or to any other social occasions.

In 1948, after the National Party came into power, Malan, the then Prime Minister, made the following statement:

An intolerable state of affairs has arisen here in the past few years in our university institutions, a state of affairs which gives rise to friction, to an unpleasant relationship between European and non-European. . . . we do not want to withhold higher education from the non-European and we will take every possible step to give both the natives and the coloured peoples university training as soon as we can, but in their own sphere, in other words in separate institutions.[4]

These indications were concretized in the Extension of University Act. If this Act was meant to be merely a way of further implementing Apartheid, then to all intents and purposes the 'open' universities were already doing this. The University of Natal, for instance, already had a non-European section with separate student organizations, and virtually all activities were, in fact, separate. Furthermore, this would be an inadequate explanation for the need to take over already segregated institutions such as Fort Hare. The existing facilities for non-whites could easily have been expanded, even under Apartheid conditions, at lesser cost than it involved to establish four new colleges.

What appeared then to be a progressive programme to extend non-white higher education and, above all, make the university colleges more accessible geographically, in fact, turned out to the contrary, if the new ethnic admission policy is taken into consideration.

As has been pointed out by the former Principal of Fort Hare, Professor Z. K. Matthews:

If a non-white university college is established in the Northern Transvaal, why should a Zulu student resident within reach of that university college be refused admission to it? Or why should a Xhosa student resident on the Reef be compelled, even with the aid of a bursary, to go to the so-called Xhosa university college rather than to the one which is nearer to him?[5]

While in terms of acquiring intellectual and academic expertise ethnic grouping is an irrelevant category, it was obviously an important aspect of the Government's tribal fragmentation scheme. However, the real reason for the reorganization of non-white higher education was stated by the Minister of Education in a parliamentary debate:

Control by the government was needed as it was necessary to prevent undesirable ideological developments such as had disturbed the non-white institutions not directly under the charge of the government and as the 'Bantu authorities' had not developed to take over this control.[6]

It becomes increasingly apparent then, that to *provide* non-white university education would seem the only way to ensure that its establishment, maintenance, management, and control lie in the right hands. Faced with already existing non-white education, the Government was in no position to abandon the extension of higher educational opportunities, nor could it allow its continuation uncontrolled under the liberal influence of the 'open' English-speaking universities. The best way out of this totalitarian dilemma was to take control of education and justify this by extending its scope, especially since African education under these conditions would hardly seem to pose the threat that it had done previously. Furthermore, the provision of lavish buildings, equipment, and sports facilities never before afforded non-whites served important propaganda functions by demonstrating the Government's apparently sincere intentions, both within South Africa and to the rest of the world. The large and constant flow of foreign visitors who are shown around the university colleges as the embodiment of the Government's sincerity indicate this, as do numerous publications on the subject by the South African information service.

In spite of the initial rejection of university Apartheid by major sections of the non-white public, the recognition of their powerlessness through the non-viability of realistic alternatives led to a tendency to resign themselves to viewing ethnic education as a force which would nevertheless lead to increased political opportunities, and, ultimately, liberation. Leo Kuper, in a perceptive satire on the then newly-initiated idea of 'tribal universities', articulates this viewpoint in a conversation between two students at such an imagined college:

But there is nowhere else Zulus can get a university education. And now we must try to get educated as well as we can. We'll be of far more use educated, than as ignorant non-co-operators on a ten-point programme.

You won't get education here, can you understand? The Herrenvolk has been sitting on our necks for three hundred years and they're not going to get off them now because Mr. 'Scuse-me' can speak a little Latin. This college is not to give education, it's to take away education.[7]

The essential argument lies in the definition of education. From the Nationalist perspective, for education to serve the purposes of domination, the institutions must of necessity follow the model of the larger society. In this sense, the university is nothing more than a microscopic representation of Nationalist aspirations, ideals, and values. Accordingly, there is a hierarchical arrangement of teaching staff, mirroring societal designations. The quality of education, especially methods of instruction, reflects as well as cements the surrounding racial structure.

After a decade of non-white colleges in existence, there are some discernible trends. In order to make non-white education compatible with Nationalist aspirations, it was inevitable that this had to be a special kind of education, the most central theme of which is adjustment. Hence education is viewed essentially as part of a process of political socialization, encouraging adjustment to one's group's given position in the society. This theme of adjustment and the attempt to narrow the gap between expectations and reality has been expressed by the then Prime Minister, Verwoerd, in the following statement:

My department's policy [that is, the Department of Native Affairs] is that education should stand with both feet in the reserves and have its roots in the spirit and being of Bantu society. . . . The basis of the provision and organization of education in the Bantu community should, where possible, be the tribal organization.

And in referring to African education in general:

There is no place for him in the European community above the level of certain forms of labour. . . . Until now, he had been subjected to a school system which drew him away from his own community and misled him by showing him the green pastures of European society, in which he was not allowed to graze.[8]

Inevitably, not all aspects of various ethnic-group heritages were acceptable and reconcilable with Nationalist ideology; in fact, considerable selection is implicitly involved. For example, in the University College for Indians the concept of caste receives particular attention, in an attempt to show the supposed affinity between Indian and Afrikaner thought. Public lectures viewing Kautilya as having preached obedience to the State above all else have been accorded high praise and held up as exemplary.

The intended goal is thus secured through institutional restrictions and isolation, rather than through crude indoctrination, while the rules are essentially aimed at preventing the student from exposure to the 'outside agitator'. At the African colleges, for example, there are rules to the effect that no student or group of students, and no person or persons not under the jurisdiction of the university college, may be upon the college ground as visitors, or visit any hostel or any other building of the institution, without permission of the Rector or his duly authorized representative and then only under such condition as may be determined. All students are accordingly prohibited from becoming members of the National Union of South African Students. Within this context, student politics and political involvement, for instance the formation of a Students' Representative Council, has become so farcical, due to restrictions and lack of autonomy, that students have decided to forgo any such opportunities for student organization. At Fort Hare, for instance, for the eighth year in succession, students decided against having an S.R.C. for fear that members of such a body would be forced to become government 'stooges' or would be labelled as such. They feared victimization and police interrogation if students spoke out freely.[9]

Yet another instance of non-participation of students for political reasons occurred with the Debating Society of the University College for Indians. The Debating Society decided to disband 'on principle' after it had been denied permission to invite Alan Paton, Ben Ngubane, and Peter Behr to address students. The comment made by the acting Rector, in support of the decision, was, 'At this stage we don't feel it is appropriate for students to be subjected to these influences.'[10] '. . . It is the policy of the College not to allow people who take an active part in politics to address students on the campus.'[11]

The notion of discipline is highly stressed. Students are under constant pressure to dress 'respectably'; that is, for men, jackets and ties must be worn at all times on the campus, regardless of the season or day's temperature. Lecturing staff have been instructed to dismiss from classes students who appear in a lecture room without either of these items of dress. Although the lecturing staff seldom enforce these rules, it is always the white administrative staff who take it upon themselves to harass students into conformity. The administration, being made up largely of ex-civil servant Afrikaners unable to clothe their prejudices as successfully as their counterparts in the academic sector, is often a source of embarrassment to those committed to making the non-white colleges workable in terms of Nationalist interests. In addition, a certain deference is required of students towards their teachers, and of non-white lecturers towards their white counterparts, and there is a high premium attached to 'knowing one's place' in the race hierarchy. Such discipline renders the student body more manageable and is functional for the system.[12] By enforcing a senseless ritual, considerable control of its objects is secured.

An important feature of the African university colleges is their geographical isolation. They are all situated away from large cities in remote peaceful settings. In Turfloop and Ngoye, their location in the middle of nowhere was chosen with great care, particularly with the Utopian aim of developing the academic location in a booming centre of the prospective homelands. The white lecturers proudly explain to the visitor the pseudo-tribal architecture of the university buildings, while the students in these places have no access even to a shop where they can buy a local newspaper. Location and intended perspectives would appear to be in harmony with each other. This implicitly embodies the commonly held Nationalist belief that the African is a noble being in the rural context and that the city is a contaminating evil influence. Hence inaccessibility constitutes a further limitation on the students' awareness through experience of what is going on in other parts of the country, and the falsely idyllic nature of non-white colleges contrasts all the more sharply with the lot of Africans in the non-university world. In fact, the filtering of certain kinds of information and exposure to limited experiences is regarded as being one of the strengths of the non-white colleges. J. A. G. Mare, the sophisticated Rector of the Zulu College, in outlining the advantages of these colleges for an international jury, among other reasons has pointed out that 'there are no expensive bioscopes and theatres in the vicinity, whilst good quality bioscope shows are provided on campus at least once a week, at a nominal entrance fee to help cover expenses'.[13] Through these means, motivated paternalism and guardianship permeate the whole process of deciding what knowledge is valuable.

Furthermore, the university colleges, in an attempt to extend control over the actions of students, exploit traditional bonds between students and their parents, especially as they occur in the African and Indian community. Selected parents from the traditional elite are frequently called upon to serve in a consultative capacity and although these are usually highly placed individuals in the community, never having had the opportunity of higher education themselves, they frequently hold antiquated notions concerning it. They by and large tend to consider the present generation of youth highly fortunate in the opportunities afforded them, and tend to be less critical of the establishment than individuals who have had some exposure to a higher education. The following statement by the acting Rector of the University College, Durban, serves to illustrate this point: 'I can tell you candidly that many parents have expressed their pleasure that we look after the academic interests of students and do not allow them to get involved in politics.'[14]

An implicit anti-intellectual trend rejects theoretical exploration and social criticism in favour of guided efforts 'to do something for the community' in the way of practical projects and social work. While one cannot underestimate the value of such work, it also tends to produce a greater number of 'do-gooders' than 'critical thinkers'. Though these are by no means mutually exclusive, by putting the focus on micro-level projects, important and immediate though they may be, more pertinent questions relating to fundamental conditions of existence are side-stepped.

The presentation of non-white colleges to the respective groups is not unlike a missionary's invitation for people to be 'true believers' not so much in the belief itself as in the sincerity of those offering it. In doing this, however, the proponents of Apartheid attempt to lend a scientific and experimental aura to the whole idea of separate development. S. P. Olivier, the Rector of the Indian College, for example, frequently repeats the following statement, especially in the presence of foreign visitors to the College: 'We are all grappling with the problem —on what basis must we proceed, being made up of a number of heterogeneous groups—we are seeking a solution.' In line with this pseudo-scientific and searching note is the highly questionable suggestion that non-whites always have the freedom to express disagreement with the attempted 'solutions' of the establishment. Several quiet dismissals of teaching staff who have been known to question rules, and who by their very bearing challenge the assumptions of Apartheid at least within the context of the non-white colleges, would seem to make these 'liberties' doubtful. Similar sentiments have been expressed regarding students: 'There is no suppression here: if a student wishes to make a hot-headed speech, he does so.'[15] On the other hand, the desire to display their qualified liberalness through separate development enhances the value of such outspoken critics of government policy as Adam Small, the Coloured poet on the staff of the University College of the Western Cape. To some extent, there is method in this madness, in that the co-operation of such critics, provided they are of no direct threat in terms of actually mobilizing student opposition, serves to authenticate the real intentions latent in governmental actions. The important effect of such seeming concessions is that in including conflict-producing elements, dissent and protest are bureaucratized. They are integrated and trivialized and so made to serve the interests of the system they are supposed to be attacking, by showing that free speech is allowed. Munger alludes to this in illustrating what he sees as the diminishing authority 'of white officials to speak for Africans over whom they have control' and points to the factor of leading whites having to ask the advice of prominent Africans, and this neither as Uncle Toms nor condescendingly:

It is sometimes thought that the African staff of the new university colleges are spinelessly subservient to their white principals. However, those white principals who are not genuinely sympathetic to some African aspirations and prepared to battle for them, and who do not rely heavily upon the advice and wisdom of their African staff, have experienced nothing but trouble.[16]

Although this viewpoint is commendable for pointing to the humanity of white college principals, which should not be denied, it tends to overlook that in order to function well in this administrative capacity, co-operation from 'subject peoples' is of considerable assistance in easing what would otherwise be an extremely difficult task. Since the stability of any social system is dependent on the degree to which the value system of the ruling class is accepted as 'truth' by the underprivileged, white principals of the non-white colleges are under strong pressure to make these institutions palatable to the various ethnic groups. Co-operation with non-white teaching staff is, therefore, strategically valuable and helps to mirror the structure of their subjected groups.

Education is a functional necessity for the continuation of the system, and its perpetuation requires trained manpower. Since a society such as South Africa cannot be wholly administered by whites, it becomes necessary to train non-whites to work on their behalf. Even though skilled non-whites then have the appearance of being independent, they have, in fact, been 'given' this position by whites. Furthermore, the South African economy cannot expand progressively unless education policies are overhauled with considerable expansion of non-white educational facilities. This applies especially to technical and vocational training. If non-whites are excluded from certain occupations or if the expansion of non-white education is allowed to lag, greater demands for skill will be made on the white population than it is capable of meeting, and one of the chief sufferers as a result will be the white. For the long-term survival of the whites as a cultural entity, nothing could be more disastrous.[17] This argument is to a large extent recognized by the South African Government, especially in so far as the needs of supposedly self-governing groups are concerned. In terms of the long-term political objectives of the ruling group, it is necessary to maintain some kind of equilibrium; that is, co-operation on the part of the ruled. Conflagratory situations involving direct humiliating contact between suppressor and suppressed must in the interests of the system and its perpetuation be avoided. This is all the more so when the distinction is clearly visible in terms of 'colour'. The training of people in each group to act in administrative capacities minimizes this direct naked contact and does not present a clear line between ruler and ruled. In this way, trained people within each group function for the rulers. Viewed from this perspective, education in its capacity as a vital lever for domination is by no means a concession but a necessity.

To the extent that the Nationalist Government established, defines, and provides non-white education, as well as manages to obtain compliance from non-whites impeded through a lack of realistic alternatives, it could be argued that a measure of success has been achieved in reconciling non-white university education with the aims of the regime. The structure of the educational institutions in themselves is an educational factor which determines to a large extent the content of education; while the provision of more financial aid in bursaries, scholarships, and the like, together with the interlocking governmental network in proving employment, ensures that political conformity is maintained. Even scholarships for study abroad granted by foreign governments require the approval of the respective government departments for each group. The powerlessness of the student within an institutional setting, in which one false move could end prospects of any higher education as well as chances of employment in the future, is an increasing source of intimidation. Consequently, education tends to be viewed as a means to an end, and the process itself is rejected as not intrinsically valuable. Fear of the consequences of critical comments, not only in terms of examination results, but also with regard to future political implications, has a castrating effect on critical thinking.

Moreover, in terms of sheer numbers the relatively small percentage of non-whites attending universities, even making allowances for a gradual increase, is highly unlikely to pose any threat to ruling interests. While the total African primary school population in 1966 was 1,270,000, in 1967 only 127 Africans received university degrees and 113 received diplomas.[18] The comparative figures for white/non-white university enrolments further reaffirm this.

Even if students acquire a developed political consciousness, the means to communicate this are limited. There are numerous restrictions affecting organization, there is no access to the media, and there is the ever-present fear of intimidation, all of

COMPARATIVE ENROLMENT IN SOUTH AFRICAN UNIVERSITIES

	1958				1969			
	Whites	Coloured	Asian	African	Whites	Coloured	Asian	African
White Universities								
O.F.S.	1,709				3,858			
Potchefstroom	1,474				3,701			
Pretoria	6,324				11,900			
Stellenbosch	3,694				7,526			
Port Elizabeth*	—				962			
Cape Town	4,408	388	127	37	7,218	282	126	2
Natal	2,530	31	373	188	5,538	44	328	175
Witwatersrand	4,756	22	158	73	8,583	20	239	5
Rhodes	1,098				1,791		44	
South Africa†	6,144	204	601	1,179	16,557	478	996	2,144
	32,137	704	1,318	1,797	68,549	1,598	3,354	3,911
Non-White Colleges								
Fort Hare		59	59	320				486
The North								671
Zululand								428
Durban							1,621	
Western Cape						774		

* A new university founded in 1967.   † Bilingual correspondence university.

Sources: M. Horrell, *A Survey of Race Relations in South Africa, 1959–1960*, South African Institute of Race Relations, Johannesburg, 1960, 227; and *1969*, 210.

which militate against any organized articulation of critical awareness.

Quite apart from this stifling influence on education and freedom of thought, it is becoming openly apparent that even the stated aims of separate development are not being met. Contrary to the initial assurance that the colleges would eventually be staffed by non-whites, trends thus far evidence that the colleges in fact provide a channel for launching, not non-whites, but Afrikaner graduates into the academic realm. A sizeable number of these appointments are regarded as promotions for Afrikaners previously employed in the civil service. At the three African colleges, compared with 202 posts occupied by white professors and lecturers, there are only 39 Africans occupying similar positions.[19] At the Indian college, teaching staff consisted of 115 whites as against 33 Indians[20] while the Coloured college indicated a staff of 66 whites and 2 Coloureds.[21] These figures become all the more astounding when one recognizes that the non-white colleges have been in existence for close to a decade now; hence this gross imbalance in no way reflects a shortage of qualified non-whites to fill the positions. Furthermore, the university colleges, despite their often repeated dedication to the service of different non-white groups and their close contact with faculty members of those groups, present only a façade of 'community'; when it comes to such issues as salaries and decision-making, they revert to official differentiation based on racial criteria. Even the few non-white professors who have been appointed are as yet not entitled to full participation in decision-making. Since no integrated bodies are allowed, there are separate 'senates' and 'councils' for whites and non-whites, the latter serving merely in an advisory capacity.

Gradually the fears of the opponents of Apartheid education are being realized. Whereas formerly, due to the supervision of the University of South Africa, it was difficult to point to a difference in terms of formal standards apart from the more obvious inequities of separate education *per se*, the recent granting of autonomy to the various colleges and their elevation to university status, although they have overtones of freedom for the colleges, are further steps in enhancing the disadvantages of racial isolation. What this means, in effect, even though such 'autonomy' is still subject to ministerial approval, is that each college will be completely at the mercy of white decision-making groups, instead of as previously under an at least academically reputable University of South Africa. Such 'autonomy' is, therefore, not in the interests of the various non-whites concerned, but renders white college administrators freer to pursue their individual 'visions' for non-white education.

In summary, therefore, there are very real areas of potential conflict inherent in the provision of separate education, based ultimately on the difference of goals on the part of the white administrators on the one hand, and those of the various ethnic communities on the other. For the most part, the administrators see these institutions as places for schooling people to accept their positions in the society, to learn orderly procedures of requesting changes through the correct channels with the right demeanour, to learn the power of 'positive thinking', and, above all, to be patient in waiting for such gradual changes as may be yielded from time to time. A further implicit assumption is that egalitarian demands arise only out of situations providing opportunities for cultural integration; and hence, from this viewpoint, separate institutions would appear to forestall such demands.

On the other hand, the various non-white groups see higher education as a source of liberation and alleviation for their situation. They view such institutions for what they consider their practical value; that is, for their potential in equipping non-whites to face the life-struggle ahead. Consequently, their expectations are high, and the better the buildings and the greater the propaganda, all the more is expected to come out of them. At present, these expectations seem destined not to be realized; and all the power in the dialectic would appear to be on the side of the white administration. Yet this is not entirely so, however, for what this reasoning overlooks is that organization of education along ethnic lines, instead of being a divisive force among non-whites as a whole, may possibly provide a basis for the unification of these groups by virtue of the confrontation with, and rejection of, white structures, as well as an increased sense of moral dignity in being non-white. This could ultimately have a more assertive influence in terms of demands for equality than the previous token integration in supposedly 'open' universities, and hence have an effect contrary to that desired by the policy-makers.

In spite of the repressive conditions described above, it is not too far-fetched to speculate that education could become a disintegrative agent for the present South African system, displaying as it does such caste-like features, and lacking any integrative principle in the community of shared societal values. Non-white students, exposed to 'universal concepts' and thought processes, regardless of the extent to which these are clothed in pro-Apartheid categories, could be expected to reiterate these universal demands; and, through education, to develop a heightened consciousness enabling them clearly to perceive the discrepancy between their own lot and that of more privileged sectors of society, and to become motivated by it. In support of this thesis, students have often expressed the feeling that their political consciousness and dissatisfaction with Apartheid have deepened during their period of study at non-white colleges. For example, one anonymous student reported in a newspaper:

When I went to Fort Hare, I wasn't politically conscious. My political awareness grew as my education at the college progressed and with it my resentment of the administration as a symbol of separate development.[22]

Student political protest becomes all the more remarkable within the context of repression described above, and indicates clearly that non-white students in no uncertain terms reject separate development and all its implications for education. They are caught between the contradictions of a system that stimulates questioning and yet renders the articulation of these questions dangerous. These tensions are reflected in the comments of the same student:

We are treated like school children by the administration. The lecturers teach you to question things, but then you find that if you start questioning some things like police presence on campus, you are immediately victimized by the administration.[23]

Hope finally arises from the prospect that despite the divergent cultural lines on which segregated education is being conducted, a newer convergence will emerge among people who have shared a common exposure to this colonial-type educational experience and, more fundamentally, share in its rejection.

REFERENCES

1. The University College of Fort Hare had been founded in 1916 with funds provided mainly by the Churches and was the only existing institution which was specifically established for the higher education of the African community. Roughly one-third of the non-white students were trained at Fort Hare. It represented a special place where many non-white leaders had been educated.

2. The Deputy Minister of Bantu Development gave the following figures relating to expenditures of the State up to March 1966 on the non-white colleges since their establishment in 1959: Fort Hare—R4,178,697; University College of the North—R4,150,381; Zululand—R3,335,012; Muriel Horrell (ed.), *A Survey of Race Relations in South Africa*, South African Institute of Race Relations, Johannesburg, 1966, 270. The Indian College involved expenditure on premises alone of R10 million: *S.A. Digest*, 20 Dec. 1968, 4.

3. *Apartheid—Its Effects on Education, Science, Culture and Information*, UNESCO, Paris, 1967, 92. For further expenditure figures see *Survey of Race Relations*, loc. cit.

4. House of Assembly Debates, *Hansard*, *64*, 1948, col. 219.

5. MATTHEWS, Z. K. 'Ethnic Universities', *Africa South*, July–Sept. 1957, 45.

6. Minister of Education, House of Assembly Debates, *Hansard*, 27–9 May 1957, as quoted in *Apartheid*, op. cit., 87.

7. KUPER, LEO, *The College Brew*, Universal Printing Works, Durban, 1960, 21–2.

8. Ibid.

9. HORRELL, MURIEL (ed.), *Survey of Race Relations*, 1968, 266.

10. 'Student Leaders Resign', *The Leader*, 13 June 1969.

11. Ibid., 9.

12. This is well reflected in a statement by the Rector of Fort Hare in relation to student strikes: 'They have a democratic right to form their own opinions but this must be done with discipline. I disagreed with the recent strike because it went beyond the bounds of discipline.' *Rand Daily Mail*, 28 Sept. 1968, 11.

13. MARE, J. A. G., 'The University Colleges', unpublished manuscript, 1966.

14. *The Leader*, 13 June 1969.

15. MARE, op. cit.

16. MUNGER, EDWIN S., in William A. Hance (ed.), *Southern Africa and the United States*, Columbia University Press, New York and London, 1968, 36.

17. *Education and the South African Economy*, 2nd report of the 1961 Education Panel, Witwatersrand University Press, Johannesburg, 1963.

18. *The Star*, Johannesburg, 21 Dec. 1968, 11. Also quoted in the article is the differential expenditure on white and non-white primary and secondary education. Whereas the State spends R11·50 per child per year on African primary education and R52 on African secondary education, the corresponding figures per white child are R250 and R300 per year.

19. HORRELL (ed.), *Survey of Race Relations*, 1969, 216.

20. Ibid., 215.

21. Ibid.

22. *Rand Daily Mail*, 28 Sept. 1968, 11.

23. Ibid.

II

H. F. DICKIE-CLARK

THE DILEMMA OF EDUCATION IN PLURAL SOCIETIES: THE SOUTH AFRICAN CASE*

It is a stock theme of sociologists[1] that all societies, by definition, have some measure of stability, adaptability, and integration. There are, however, many ways of attaining the necessary amounts of these properties, and societies differ not only in the means they use and the extent to which they use them, but also in how successfully they are used.

Some societies enlist willing support for the social order by means, among other things, of consultation, sharing in decisions, legal equality of status, and equality of opportunity for all. Other societies may rely heavily on means such as economic interdependence, material rewards, propaganda, or sheer force. Probably most societies use almost the whole range of means at their disposal at one time or another, and a major task of the social sciences is, therefore, to assess these various means and their consequences as objectively as possible so that informed and effective practical choices can be made.

There are some societies in which certain of these means are not used because they would radically change the character of the society. Among these societies are the so-called 'plural' ones which consist of two or more culturally different and socially distinct segments dominated politically by one of them. South Africa with its highly developed 'parallelism' is possibly the best

* For critical comment on earlier drafts of this paper, I am grateful to Professors Eileen Krige, W. R. G. Branford, and H. Adam, and Doctors G. C. Kinloch and A. T. Turk.

modern example.* In a society of this kind, legal equality, universal franchise, and careers open to talent are by implication precluded.

The inability of such a society to make use of these means of achieving stability, adaptability, and integration places it in the fundamental dilemma of those who try to eat their cake and have it. For a society of this kind tries to be a single society in a political and economic sense, but at the same time insists on cultural and social differentiation.

Turning to the educational institutions in such plural societies, one can readily see that these cannot be conducted in such a way as to open all careers to talent, and so make the fullest use of their human assets, without endangering the plural character of the society. Since education is one of the chief means in modern societies of directing talents to suitable careers, this will clearly have serious consequences for the education of subordinate segments in plural societies. This chapter attempts to trace some of these consequences as they have shown themselves in the education of Africans in South Africa. It may also serve to indicate, in this one case at least, how much contradiction and conflict a society can absorb and counteract without breaking up completely. The long-foretold revolution in South Africa has not yet taken place and, now that the earlier neglect by sociologists of the positive contributions of social conflict has been redressed, perhaps the most important issue is the question of disruptive conflict and how one may judge when such conflicts are about to take place. If Coser[8] is right, then the very limited area of normative agreement in plural societies must be a 'built-in' source of disruptive conflicts. Moreover, these societies often display the other danger signs noted by Coser, namely, deep cleavages on cultural and social lines and 'total' commitment and participation in sect-like political organizations which tend to be rigid and unresponsive to change. In fact, almost all such societies *do* have in the way of integrative factors are economic dependence and political force.

* The concept of a plural society used here is that based on the writings of J. S. Furnivall,[2] John Rex,[3] M. G. Smith,[4] and P. L. van den Berghe.[5] Their usage is almost the complete opposite of the term pluralism as it is used, for example, by Kornhauser,[6] Helge Pross,[6] and others, to describe societies in which a number of elites or interest groups have a share in making decisions and thus prevent the rise of a single ruling class.

In a society of this kind, the education of the subordinate segments is likely to be torn between the need to equip them with the knowledge, skills, and attitudes they must have to play their part in the common economic and political institutions, and the need to preserve and even reinforce the cultural diversity and social segmentation on which the society rests. The thesis of this chapter is that, owing to this contradiction, not only is the education of subordinate strata in plural societies seriously impaired, but also that it serves to intensify the tensions and conflict already engendered by the plural character of the society as a whole.

Evidence for this thesis is provided by the case of African education in South Africa during the years before 1954 when it was for the most part in the hands of Christian missions. After that date, the central government, acting on the Bantu Education Act of 1953, began to take over African education with clearly very different aims. To what extent this so-called 'Bantu' education, as compared to 'mission' education, also provides support for the thesis of this chapter will be discussed later. The main evidence here presented is, however, drawn from the period of 'mission' education.

'Mission' education for Africans in South Africa has a history of over a hundred years. As time passed, the Churches received more and more financial assistance from provincial and the central governments; and these bodies gradually came to control and administer the academic side of the missionary establishments, although leaving the boarding and other domestic arrangements in religious hands. But despite this increasing help from government, African education remained as a kind of charitable good work, rather than reflecting any deliberate effort on the part of a wealthy government to uplift and make the fullest use of its people. Begun by missionaries more interested in conversion than in education for its own sake, it was tolerated rather than encouraged. It was vaguely thought to be useful to the whites but, as yet, there was little demand for the services of educated Africans and the need for them was hardly recognized by whites other than those actually engaged in the education and administration of Africans. Thus their education received only half-hearted official support, and was sustained chiefly by the devotion of the missionaries and the determination of the Africans themselves to get as much education as they could.

It must first be acknowledged that despite the grievous limitations of mission education, some of which are examined below, it did nevertheless achieve some measure of success. Quantitatively, this success can be gauged by the numbers of Africans who have gained various educational standards. According to figures given by the South African Institute of Race Relations in 1953,[9] one year before the central government began to take over African education, 31 per cent of Africans over ten years of age were literate and out of a population of some 10–11 millions, 167,126 had passed Standard 6 (elementary school), 38,572 had passed Standard 8 (secondary school), 8,488 had passed Standard 10 (matriculation), 1,064 were university graduates.* The number of Africans of school age receiving more than a very elementary education, totalling only some 3 per cent by 1953, is small indeed considering the wealth and development of the country. Nevertheless, the long years of missionary endeavour have meant that in South Africa there are a fair number of educated and professionally trained Africans.

Turning from this quantitative measure of achievement to a more qualitative assessment of mission education, it becomes readily apparent that many of its fundamental characteristics were directly determined by the plural structure of South African society. The strict segregation, the problems of which language(s) to use, the inadequacy of funds, and the fact that only about one-third of the population of school-going age ever got to a school of any sort are all features which are consequences of the subordinate position of the Africans in South African society. That these features seriously reduce the efficacy of educational institutions can hardly be gainsaid.

Two other features of the education of Africans at this time can also be traced to pluralism. First, the excessively 'bookish'

* *A Survey of Race Relations in South Africa 1952–1953*, p. 68. Not all the graduates would have come from the 'mission' university of Fort Hare since at this time the Universities of Cape Town, Natal, and the Witwatersrand admitted Africans. In 1962 figures given in the Race Relations *Survey* of that year, p. 183, were as follows:

Standard 6	295,600
Standard 8	75,000
Standard 10	15,200
University graduates	c. 2,000

curricula followed in most schools, especially after the primary stage. Almost no technical nor commercial subjects were taught, and often the only relief from book-work was gardening or some such lowly skill. No doubt, the more 'academic' subjects found favour in part because they were the cheapest to provide and partly because fairly early on the Africans themselves became determined to have as nearly as possible the same bookish education as the whites received. But more important than these is the fact that careers based on technical and commercial curricula were simply not open to Africans.

Secondly, there was rigorous economic selection of pupils beyond the primary level. The costs of high school and university education were considerable and it was by no means certain that the best brains were the ones being educated. A study by the writer of matriculants at a large mission school over the years 1949-53 showed that virtually all the pupils were children of peasant farmers, teachers, clergy, and government clerks. There were almost no workers' children. Further evidence of the restricted mobility of subordinate strata in plural societies is the fact that these Africans on leaving school or university tended to follow their parents into these same callings.

A less obvious result of the Africans' position but one which also served to reduce the efficiency of African education, although in a less serious fashion, was the tendency of teachers and educational administrators 'to make allowances' for Africans in matters of standards of behaviour or scholastic achievement required. Where hardships are so obvious and the difficulties in getting an education are so great, it is a hard man, or one very confident of the worth of his own cultural values, who will not 'make allowances' but insist on the same standards for black and white! In the domestic aspects of educational establishments it is virtually impossible not to take the disadvantaged situation of the African student into consideration. In purely academic matters there is a far more concerted and conscious effort to maintain standards and there are also more objective means of doing so. Nevertheless, while it is doubtful whether anybody has ever got through an examination simply because he was an African, it is certain that many African students have not done anywhere nearly as well as they could have done simply because allowances were always being made for them and their best was never demanded.

These features of African education are, moreover, not only harmful in themselves; it could also be argued that they aggravate certain attitudes among pupils and students which further hinder their education and contribute to increased tension and potentially disruptive conflict. Certain of these attitudes would seem to be widespread among educated Africans and have been noted by other observers also.[10] The attitudes selected for discussion here have to do with power and they are part of the larger sentiment favouring African rule and opposing continued white dominance. They express one side of the major division in South African politics which threatens the kind of fundamental cleavage along a single axis which Coser[11] considers to be so disruptive.

The first, and perhaps most obvious of these attitudes is distrust of, and dislike for, whites. Under the circumstances, any other attitude would be well-nigh miraculous. While it is true that an attitude of complete trust and affection would be equally dysfunctional in some human relations, there are areas, and education is surely one of them, in which excessive suspicion and dislike are especially damaging. For it leads to such distance between African students and white teachers as to make their relationships often sterile and frustrating to both. The elaborate ritual of politeness and the fear of giving offence tend to stultify contacts which should have been emotionally stimulating and fruitful for the education of the student and the teacher. No doubt sensitivity towards some issues may be sharpened precisely by suspicion and conflict, but in general an unrelieved atmosphere of distrust must serve to blunt or even block completely the reception of other ideas and insights. Where education goes beyond the imparting of information and skills to the passing on of values and attitudes, the learner must surely have some measure of confidence in the teacher's good faith and intentions. If, due to a blanket distrust of all whites, the white teacher is seen as an agent of domination, either deluded or dishonest, then but little can come of his teaching.

Also stemming from their profound distrust of whites is the demand of many Africans for an 'all-or-nothing', total commitment on the part of whites offering friendship and support. This requirement for uncritical identification with the African cause is well illustrated in a book by Hopkinson,[12] sometime white editor of *Drum*. He reports an argument with Can Themba, an African reporter, in which Themba praises Father Huddleston for his whole-hearted identification with the Africans. Hopkinson attacks this abandonment of one's own judgement as wrong. But Themba replies:

Nothing less is any good to us. We don't want someone who supports us when he thinks we're okay, but withdraws his support when we do something un-Western or ungentlemanly. We have had too much of this patronizing liberal attitude—pat us on the head when you think we're going the right way, kick us in the pants when we take a different turning.

Such a demand for total, unreserved commitment to a cause or belief is, of course, a well-established characteristic of all sect-like organizations engaged in conflict. Its importance for the present thesis is that this kind of total commitment and participation in a movement or group is one means of bringing about a single disruptive cleavage and of finding, as Rex[13] puts it, 'that the enemy on one front is also the enemy on others'. Segmental, conditional commitment which reduces the chance of a single basic rift is precluded by this kind of overweening loyalty.

The next cluster of attitudes to be considered is made up of African students' notions about the scope and uses of political activity.

In a country like South Africa where effective consensus about fundamentals is slight and where as a result political coercion is prominent, it is not surprising that people should come to think that there is politics in everything and that everything must be dealt with in political terms. Certainly many educated Africans accept this view and act upon it. Almost every issue, even the most trivial, seems to have political implications for them. This is probably no more than the simple truth and if that were all no great harm would be done. But this attitude often seems to go even further in that not only is everything thought to have political implications, but that this political significance is invariably considered to be *the most important aspect* of the event in all situations. Consequently, the other aspects are played down or ignored. This kind of single-minded oversimplification easily leads to the 'all-or-nothing' attitude already noted.

The practical consequences of the 'politics is all' mentality can be unfortunate in many routine activities. It sometimes entails that typically political *methods* of formal negotiations and agreements, boycotts, appeals to solidarity, and even intimidation are used in and out of season and for the slightest and most unsuitable purposes. Thus complaints or difficulties which could easily be put right by a word or action in the appropriate quarter are magnified into political issues which then necessitate meetings of the student body, petitions, formal negotiations, and all the paraphernalia of politics. When this happens the day-to-day running of an institution like a school or university, a newspaper or a hospital, becomes simply impossible.

The Fort Hare Commission of Inquiry[14] contains an excellent picture and diagnosis of this particular attitude, which indeed threatened totally to disrupt the College at one time. On the topic of the relationship between the Students' Representative Council and the Senate, the commissioners say:

> The humourless correspondence between these two bodies, which we have studied, reads like negotiations conducted between two 'High Contracting Parties' of equal standing in an atmosphere of cold war. The exaggerated sense of self-importance of the students as indicated in this correspondence is perhaps due to the feeling that the College must be looked upon as being in the vanguard of the political and racial struggle; but no university can run its ordinary day-by-day business on these lines, and it is very desirable that the students should learn what a Students' Representative Council is and what it is not.

The appeal to African solidarity is possibly the most notable and most frequently misused political technique in what could be relatively 'non-political' situations. This appeal to solidarity is traditionally and understandably the weapon of the powerless, but when used indiscriminately and outside its proper sphere it can only be damaging. For example, in universities devoted to objective scholarship and independence of thought it is singularly out of place.

It is obvious how such appeals for a united front contribute to a single disruptive cleavage along the single axis of colour, but the attitude is dysfunctional in the more immediate context of education as well. Anthony Ngubo of the University of California at Los Angeles, a former student of Natal University, is quoted by Leo Kuper[15] as suggesting that it is very difficult for Africans to achieve scholarly detachment because of 'their mental energy being spent in political thinking' and because of the need to better themselves in employment and in status.*

Another component in the political attitudes of many educated Africans is the view of democracy as being simply majority rule. There is plenty of support for this attitude of both a practical and a theoretical kind. Successive white governments in South Africa have acted on this belief in respect of the enfranchised whites and so have other governments elsewhere. D. V. Cowen[16] quotes with approval Sir Carleton Allen's claim 'that on the whole, though no doubt with many exceptions, majority opinion does reach a sensible and workable solution of most practical problems of social life'. None the less, there are reasons for believing that, in a plural society, such a view of democracy as unqualified majority rule would contribute to conflict through its neglect of minority interests and rights.

The first of these reasons is that in their enthusiasm for the principle of majority rule, the qualifications and limitations set up by democratic theorists are overlooked. Thus Cowen[17] insists on a fundamental bill of rights which would seriously hamper the majority in its attempts to achieve its aims. No doubt the desperate importance in an impoverished Africa of social and economic security makes African leaders impatient of restraint, but, as Andreski[18] points out, this is why democracy has been so ineffective in Africa.

* Clearly, this line of argument that excessive concern with the political aspects of education is detrimental to some 'educational process', conceived as politically 'impartial', is open to the charge that it is a disguised defence of the *status quo* and of white dominance. One suspects that here is an example of the kind of basic value conflict which Max Weber held to be impervious to logical or scientific solution. Either one holds that education 'at its best' has, or ought to have, some measure of autonomy; or one sees it as entirely determined by social and especially political forces. Stated more generally and in the terms of the current debate in sociology over functionalism: either one tries, as objectively as possible, to set up criteria or standards on the basis of what men and societies appear from the evidence to 'need' and in this way attempts to measure existing social arrangements against them, or one becomes 'committed' to one side or the other of the prevailing political tussle and then uses this commitment as the measuring-rod.

The second reason for holding majority rule, as understood by many educated Africans, to be disruptive in a plural society, was first set out by Georg Simmel[19] in his note on the phenomenon of outvoting. There he showed that majority decisions have come to be invested by many of their supporters with a moral overtone. It is not merely *expedient* for the minority to submit, they are morally obliged to do so because in some mystical way the decision of the majority is taken to be the expression of a larger unity to which the minority is also considered to belong and which it is morally bound to obey. It would seem that this moral backing of majority decisions rests in turn on a consensual view of society as some kind of emergent unity over and above its component groups. It may be that where a large measure of consensus exists in a particular society, some such emergent unity can usefully be postulated and on this basis majority decisions may be justified. But where on the contrary no such measure of consensus exists, as is the case for instance in South Africa, then the attempt to give majority rule any moral backing is without doubt wholly unwarranted and can lead only to the repeated violation of the opinions and rights of minorities. In the process, the healthy criss-crossing temporary alliances of changing segments will be submerged in a single rift between a majority which is always morally right and minorities which never have a moral claim to prevail in any difference of opinion or clash of interests. If, then, in a plural society majority rule is thus invested with a moral claim on the minority, it can only increase the possibility of a single disruptive cleavage between whoever constitutes the majority and those making up the minority.

With the features listed earlier and with the attitudes just discussed, it is not surprising that mission education was in its later years racked by conflicts. For the most part, those teaching in the mission schools and colleges believed that they were educating Africans for a common, unified society which lay not too far off in the future. Hence they aimed to produce Africans who were culturally white and who would be able to fit into the common society which was thought to be evolving. Hence, also, the feature of social equality which was never able to get beyond the gates of the missionary establishments and, sometimes, not even that far. Looking back now, it is easy to see that this view underrated both the resilience of culture and the capacity of a pluralistic society to hold together despite deep cleavages and glaring inconsistencies.*

On the face of things, the new 'Bantu' education introduced by the Government after 1954 is quite different. In this kind of education for Africans the plural character of South African society is not only clearly recognized, but also presumed to continue indefinitely. Careers are to be open to African talents only in their own areas and there are to be no more 'black Europeans'. In the words of the Minister for Bantu Education in Parliament, 'it is the basic principle of Bantu education in general that our aim is to keep the Bantu child a Bantu child. . . . The Bantu must be so educated that they will want to remain essentially Bantu.'[21]

But is this lip-service to the plural character of South African society not perhaps just as superficial as was the social equality of the 'mission' kind of education? For the *content* of Bantu education remains 'Western' and it has to do so if the common economic and political structure of the plural society is to be served and to continue. The advocates of Bantu education may foster cultural diversity as much as they like and they may place their schools and universities as far out in the country as they please, but they must still reckon with and serve the common economy and political order of the plural society. Thus one may argue that Bantu education in *its* turn tends to underrate the *similarities* brought into being by the common institutions in South African society. It is possible to pretend not to *see* the similarities but it is impossible to stop the acculturation which produces them. As long as the plural character of South African society is maintained, the contradiction will remain, and the pressure of cultural similarity on the barriers maintaining social segregation must increase even if slowly. The effect of Bantu education, no matter how segregated and controlled, must be to heighten the Africans' desire and ability to share in the common society. Thus one could expect Bantu education to produce somewhat similar attitudes and resentments on the

* John Horton[20] seems to be suggesting that American liberals made something of the same mistake in believing that all the Negroes wanted was to become just like all the other Americans and happily compete with them for the latest model car and other outward signs of the American way of life.

part of its students to those produced by 'mission' education. For both kinds of education must serve the plural society in the same way—by fitting the Africans to serve the economic and political institutions common to the whole society.*

Therefore the conclusion suggested by these considerations is that in pluralistic societies all forms of education of subordinate groups must display features and attitudes similar to the ones discussed here. In this way the educational institutions will be reduced in efficiency and will have the latent effect of enlarging the conflicts of those societies.

However, experience shows that it is easy to overestimate the disruptive effect of such contradictions and dilemmas in a society. For it seems that they can be effectively 'contained' for long periods and perhaps even be compensated for in various ways. The case of women's inequalities and disabilities suggests that this might be so. The questions whether the effects of such gross inequalities as are found in South Africa *could* be cushioned and how this may be attempted lie outside the scope of this chapter. But perhaps two possibilities may be hinted at in conclusion. First, if the expectations of those suffering from discrimination are very low to begin with, then clearly they can be appeased by small material improvements in their lot over a considerable length of time. Secondly, the opening of even *some* careers to talent seems to be a surprisingly effective means of winning support. South African Bantustans and the whole paraphernalia of Apartheid may be far from an adequate substitute for full citizenship, but they do provide careers of a kind and, after all, the man who first effectively opened careers to talent in Europe also held that 'It is with baubles that men are led.'

In any event, it is clear that simplistic reliance on 'inherent contradictions' and incompatibilities between economic development and Apartheid or between authoritarian rule and stability will have to be revised and sharpened if future developments in Southern Africa are to be foretold with any useful degree of accuracy.

* It may be argued against this that Bantu education is designed to supply the needs of ultimately separate Bantu states. However, even if that is so, the dilemmas of a pluralistic society will only be intensified, for some Africans, Indians, and Coloureds are bound to remain in the so-called 'white' state.

REFERENCES

1. E.g., FALLDING, HAROLD, 'Functional Analysis in Sociology', *American Sociological Review*, Feb. 1963, *28*, 5–13.
2. FURNIVALL, J. S., *Colonial Policy and Practice*, Cambridge University Press, London, 1948.
3. REX, JOHN, 'The Plural Society in Sociological Theory', *British Journal of Sociology*, June 1959, *10*, 114–24, and *Key Problems of Sociological Theory*, Routledge & Kegan Paul, London, 1961.
4. SMITH, M. G., 'Social and Cultural Pluralism', *Annals of the New York Academy of Sciences*, Art. 5, Jan. 1960, *83*, 763–77, and 'The Plural Framework of Jamaican Society', *British Journal of Sociology*, Sept. 1961, *12*, 249–62.
5. VAN DEN BERGHE, P. L., *South Africa: A Study in Conflict*, Wesleyan University Press, Middletown, Conn., 1965, and *Race and Racism*, Wiley, New York, 1967.
6. KORNHAUSER, WILLIAM, *The Politics of Mass Society*, Free Press, Glencoe, Ill., 1959.
7. PROSS, HELGE, 'Zum Begriff der pluralistischen Gesellschaft', in Max Horkheimer (ed.), *Zeugnisse, Th. W. Adorno zum 60 Geburtstag*, Europäische Verlagsanstalt, Frankfurt, 1963, 439–50.
8. COSER, LEWIS, *The Functions of Social Conflict*, Routledge & Kegan Paul, London, 1956.
9. HORRELL, MURIEL, (ed.), *A Survey of Race Relations in South Africa, 1952–1953*, South African Institute of Race Relations, Johannesburg, 1953, 68.
10. DUMINY, J. P., BOTHA, M. C., and BROOKES, H. E., *Report of the Fort Hare Commission, July 1955*, Lovedale Press, Alice, South Africa, 1955; also Leo Kuper, *An African Bourgeoisie*, Yale University Press, New Haven and London, 1965.
11. COSER, op. cit., 76–7.
12. HOPKINSON, TOM, *In the Fiery Continent*, Gollancz, London, 1962.
13. REX (1961), op. cit., 118.
14. DUMINY *et. al.*, op. cit., 5–6.
15. KUPER, op. cit., 163–4.
16. COWEN, D. V., *The Foundations of Freedom*, Oxford University Press, Cape Town, London, and New York, 1961.
17. Ibid., 121.
18. ANDRESKI, S., *The African Predicament*, Michael Joseph, London, 1968.

19. SIMMEL, GEORG, *Soziologie*, 2nd edn., Duncker & Humboldt, Munich and Leipzig, 1922.
20. HORTON, JOHN, 'Commentary and Debate', *American Journal of Sociology*, May 1966, *71*, 701–21.
21. *Hansard, 20*, 17 June 1959, cols. 8318–20.

12

A. S. MATHEWS

SECURITY LAWS AND SOCIAL CHANGE IN THE REPUBLIC OF SOUTH AFRICA

The interaction between the law and the social forces of a society is in modern times a very complex process. The one thing that is certain is that the law has no fixed or predetermined role to play in the growth or stagnation of a society. It may respond by accommodating itself to importunate social pressures, thereby reducing the state of tension between the legal normative order and the currents of social life. It may equally set itself against a rising social tide by attempting the construction of an impenetrable legal fortification backed by police and military force. These are obviously two extreme and over-simplified positions between which there lies a whole range of possibilities. In some areas there may be no response at all, either favourable or hostile. Where this happens the law will be a dead letter, completely severed from the 'living law'. In a given society there may be continuous interaction between law and social pressures in some areas of life while in other areas healthy interplay may be entirely lacking. Then again a law directed against a particular social current may itself be the expression of some other social force in competition with the first.[1] This is clearly the case in South Africa where the Nationalist Government has brought in a battery of laws to prevent certain kinds of social change. These very laws are the outcome of strong forces operating in white society, particularly in white Afrikaner society. New complexities in the relationship between law and social forces come into the reckoning in a plural society in which one group has political power over the others.

There are no constitutional hindrances to the legal recognition of social change in South Africa as there are in federal systems.[2] With a unitary constitution and a sovereign parliament there is full freedom to adapt the law to the pressing demands of the society. At the same time the constitutional structure of the Republic does not in any way limit a legislative programme designed to curb or to turn back certain kinds of pressures which would be difficult or impossible to resist under an American-type bill of rights enforced by the courts. In the absence of constitutional guarantees in South Africa, the Nationalist Government has thus far successfully denied almost all the political, and many of the social and economic, demands of the non-white people of the country.[3] It is true that, as happened in the United States, constitutional guarantees may be used to hamper social progress. It is nevertheless also true that their absence in South Africa has paradoxically strengthened the legal authority in deflecting social change. The concentration of power under a constitution reserving political rights to the white group puts the ruling party in a strong position to control social change by legislative and executive action. As Friedmann observes,[4] the tension between the legal and social orders in a democracy is usually small because public opinion is more readily translated into legal action where fully representative institutions prevail. On the other hand social movements may be countered and even destroyed by a ruthless dictator or oligarchy. Government in South Africa resists easy classification along these lines because it has both representative and autocratic features. The parliamentary system resembles the Western democratic type, but Parliament is representative only of the white minority. There is a second main reason why government in South Africa, though not entirely despotic or totalitarian, can yet not be classified as democratic—it is not based on the free interchange of opinion. Barker has said that representative democracy

... involves representation of different currents of opinion, freely ventilated and freely attracting their adherents in the social area, and freely translated and freely acting (by the process of discussion and compromise) in the political area. . . .[5]

A growing body of South African legislation[6] has converted the
Q

democratic *right* to express opinion into a precarious *privilege* enjoyable at the discretion of the ruling party. The right to organize opinion hostile to the fundamental policies of the Nationalist Government has suffered almost total destruction. While a democracy institutionalizes the processes of consent, in South Africa laws have tended to institutionalize the elimination of dissent. The movement towards absolutism in the Republic has been accompanied by a growth of totalitarian rule.[7] If Sidney Hook has correctly defined totalitarianism as 'an absolute and interlocking monopoly of power—economic, juridical, military, educational and political—in the hands of a minority party which countenances no legal opposition or is not removable by the processes of freely given consent',[8] then South African rule is an ever-increasing approximation to it. Thus although an analysis of government in the Republic reveals the outward forms and some of the substance of democratic rule, its autocratic and totalitarian elements are strong and tend to predominate over the others.[9] It follows that both the political power structure and the constitutional system make possible, and even favour, an iron-handed regulation of social change.

It has been said that law is inevitably deeply imbedded in the ideologies of the society in which it operates.[10] Without accepting the Marxist proposition that ideology is simply a reflection of economic interests, it may be said that law is as much rooted in interests, both economic and social, as it is in ideology. Analysis of the South African situation discloses the phenomenon of a system of law which in a large measure reflects the interests and ideology of a minority group—the Afrikaner Nationalists.[11] Since capturing political power, the Nationalists have fortified white economic privilege by vigorous legislative action. In this programme ideology and economic privilege have gone hand-in-hand, with each giving sustenance to the other. The shaping of ideology to bolster social and economic privilege is one of the great themes of the history of South Africa. This fusion of ideology with the economic aspirations of the Afrikaner, and to a lesser extent with the economic security of all white South Africans, is in part the explanation of the strength and success of the Nationalist programme. As Professor Gwendolen M. Carter has said, 'economic security and an intense sense of racial identity underlie the Nationalist appeal.'[12]

While the mutually sustaining roles of interests and ideology in the past can hardly be denied, it is questionable that Nationalist ideology squares as closely as before with the contemporary economic interests either of the Nationalists or of white South Africans as a whole. The largely negative programme of Apartheid in operation before Dr. Verwoerd became Prime Minister preserved privilege at small cost. The development of the homelands and establishment of border industries under Verwoerdian Apartheid, however much a myth this policy may be, demands higher government expenditure and the curbing of economic development. The continued application of 'negative Apartheid' guarantees to white South Africans the right to skim off the cream; but the layer of cream is likely to thin out as the application of 'positive Apartheid' is intensified.[13] This is certainly one of the issues on which the *verligtes* and *verkramptes* divide, the *verkramptes* openly espousing a policy of 'separate and poor' rather than 'rich and mixed'. Whatever questionings of the ideology underlying Apartheid on economic grounds may now be taking place,[14] there is at present no sign of the modification of Verwoerdian Apartheid at the points where it rubs against the white-orientated economic policy.[15] The Physical Planning and Utilization of Resources Act,[16] which is designed to enforce the transfer of further industrial development dependent on African labour to the border areas, subordinates economic progress to the Apartheid programme. The Nationalists may be groping towards a formula which will once more bring about a full reconciliation between Nationalist ideology and white economic interests. This formula is not yet reflected in the law,[17] and it is likely to be a long time before it is.

What is the nature of the ideological superstructure which has served, and still continues to serve, Nationalist interests so well? It is tempting to categorize South Africa as a laager society and to attribute to it a corresponding philosophy; but to do so without qualification is to succumb to the stereotype. Many of the characteristics of the closed[18] (tribal or arrested) society are undoubtedly present. What distinguishes the Republic from the archetypal clan society is development of its economic and industrial possibilities. In this sector phenomenal changes have taken place since Union—changes which have been accompanied by fundamental alterations in the social structure. Though these alterations have yet to be fully reflected in the legal order, they are nevertheless significant enough to falsify the picture of South Africa as a static society. While encouraging economic growth,[19] the Government has concurrently introduced legislation and taken executive action to arrest concomitant social and political change. Under this legislation the non-white citizens of the country have been denied the economic, personal, and political position to which they are entitled by their ever-increasing economic contribution. On a closer analysis, South Africa does not present a straight picture of a closed society. In some sectors of her national life there has been phenomenal growth, in others almost complete petrifaction. This is a situation which will obviously produce great internal strains.

Yet in its emphasis on the destiny of the nation (tribe) one of the leading features of the closed society is exemplified in the Republic. In a plural society, it may become the doctrine by which the ruling group justifies the hierarchical arrangement under which other groups are subordinated to it.[20] The chosen race is entitled to preserve its integrity by perpetuating its own culture and institutions and by ensuring for them a dominant, if not exclusive, place in society. The emphasis on the group (tribe or race) subjects the interests of the individual to the claims of the mystical national or racial entity. As Talmon has said,[21] the concepts of racial and organic entities are alien to both individualism and rationalism. The need for preservation of the power and privilege of the dominant group leads it inexorably towards authoritarian and totalitarian methods of government. As social changes begin to threaten the established order of things the grip of totalitarian rule is tightened, resulting in further weakening of the individual's place in society. In such a situation there is bound to be what Ernest Barker called 'a passion for security rather than liberty'.[22] That passion is nourished by roots in the frontier society of not long ago where government tended towards the principle of 'blood and iron' rule. A government which does not display 'kragdadigheid' is no government at all. The desire for strong-arm rule is all the more felt in a continent convulsed by change. Of course, the crude frontier methods of rule have been replaced by the more sophisticated techniques of the modern totalitarian state; but the same authoritarian principle underlies both. It must, however, be stated that government in South Africa is not wholly despotic or fully totalitarian. There is in Afrikaner history and tradition a strong element of individualism which in its more extreme forms becomes a distrust of all organized government.[23] This element and the strain of pragmatism[24] in Nationalist rule have held in check the urge towards a more thoroughgoing totalitarian control. The South African Government has not reduced life in the country to a single political plane of existence.[25] It has, however, as will be shown below, drawn heavily on the armoury of totalitarianism to suppress all political change.

Afrikaner nationalism, fortified by a sense of divine mission, has a morality very different from the political moralities of the Western world with their emphasis on the legitimate claims and private conscience of the individual.[26] In the first place, the leaders of Afrikanerdom, being divinely appointed, are alone qualified to interpret God's will for the destiny of His peoples in South Africa. The influence of the Calvinist doctrine of God-given state authority is at work here.[27] By an act of self-levitation the rulers of the national state place themselves beyond the reach of criticism based on Western systems of political morality. But, as Barker has shown, the national state may free itself from moral obligation to its subjects without the aid of doctrines of divine authority.[28] It does this by subordinating all rules and standards to its own inner commands (as interpreted by its 'true' spokesmen). Citizens who do not respond to the 'inner laws' of the self-evolving national state may be denounced as enemies of the people and the State is free from all obligations to them.[29] National self-realization becomes the highest law, and the State, through the agency of which that law is given fulfilment, has a correspondingly inviolable status. Moreover, the fulfilment of the nationalistic aspirations of the dominant group in a plural society obviously demands social replanning on a grand scale. In securing the physical and geographical separation necessary for cultural integrity, whole races are made pawns in a vast programme of social reorganization. In such a game, individual suffering and injustice are seen as a small price to pay for the ultimate success of the scheme. Indeed, criticism based on such grounds is likely to be dismissed as both irrelevant and irreverent, all attention being focused on the ultimate realization of the grand conception and none (or very little) on the means for its achievement.[30] The preceding analysis shows that Nationalist doctrine seeks to free itself from the control of moral judgement partly by an appeal to the theory of divine sanction for State action and to the transcendent validity of the 'natural laws' of national self-realization, and partly by focusing the mind on the ultimate fulfilment of a Utopian dream. The dream (which appears to recede as it is being implemented) is the vision of the national (racial or tribal) state in the full flower of its development, to which condition it will have been brought by adherence to the higher claims of the State and the rejection of the tenets of liberal and humanitarian ethics. The denial of these tenets is inevitable when the authoritarian-minded leaders of the racial group which controls the State machinery attempt to turn back powerful social forces by totalitarian techniques of repression.[31]

The mystical and irrational elements in Nationalist ideology are obvious; but the legislation which expresses it is rationally conceived and systematic in its application. As one writer has said, 'the irrational force of prejudice is harnessed to the rational purpose of maintaining a system of discrimination to ensure the survival of the *status quo* based on colour.'[32] The maintenance of this system of discrimination is dependent upon a strong and pervasive regime of political control. The introduction of a thoroughgoing and ubiquitous regime of political control has been one of the outstanding features of twenty years of Nationalist rule in South Africa. The maintenance of white privilege is possible only through full control of the political machine—a fact which the Nationalists have grasped from the beginning. That the redress of grievances and the elimination of discrimination cannot be achieved without the backing of political power is a lesson which the non-whites have learnt more slowly and painfully.[33] Recognizing that political control is the key to economic, cultural, and social domination, the Nationalists have since their accession to power in 1948 introduced a series of laws which have crushed all challenges, especially non-white challenges, to their political ascendancy.[34] The forces of industrialization and of the African 'winds of change' have beaten in vain against the statutory barrier constructed to hold off political change.[35] The deeper consequences of this operation, and the manner of achieving it, are worthy of special analysis.

Soon after their accession to power in 1948, the Nationalists took steps to consolidate their position and to suppress opposition. It was not long before they sought to silence the small voice which non-whites still had in the political institutions of the country, although they concluded the first stage in their campaign only after a long and bitter constitutional struggle.[36] Long before these struggles had concluded, they had already turned their attention to the control and elimination of extra-parliamentary opposition. With participation in the country's governing institutions denied them, the non-white opposition was forced to operate outside these institutions. In 1948 civil liberties and the rule of law, although already weakened by legislative programmes of previous governments, were still living concepts in the political life of the country. There was in a large measure freedom to meet, to organize politically, to protest, and to express dissent. By the introduction of a series of legislative measures which are fully expressive of the Nationalist ideology already mentioned, this freedom has suffered almost total extinction.[37] While even a sketchy analysis of the laws responsible for the present situation is not possible in a chapter of this kind, a brief reference to the major changes may be helpful. A key measure is the misnamed Suppression of Communism Act,[38] passed originally in 1950, and since then amended many times so as to make it a bludgeoning instrument capable of use against any political opponent. The act empowers the executive or the Minister to suppress organizations, newspapers, and the expression of opinion, and to 'ban' or 'house arrest' individuals, without the regulation of such power by the courts. Its provisions may be (and have been) used against non-communists (or even anti-communists) as much as against communists. The Criminal Law Amendment Act[39] prescribed severe penalties for 'passive resistance', and the Unlawful Organizations Act[40] outlawed the chief African political organizations (the African National Congress and Pan-Africanist Congress). This last Act is also outside the sphere of judicial control and authorizes the executive to ban other political organizations. The 'Sabotage Act'[41] defines the offence of sabotage so widely that many comparatively innocuous political activities (such as the disruption of traffic caused by a protest march) become capital offences punishable by death. The '180 day' detention law[42] authorizes detention of any person by a police officer of defined rank for periods of 180 days and deprives the detainee of the right to approach the court on any question relating to his detention. The Terrorism Act[43] provides for unlimited detention without trial and defines the capital crime of 'terrorism' so widely that obviously non-terrorist acts are also punishable by death. The Prohibition of Political Interference Act[43a] outlaws political parties with a multi-racial composition and makes certain forms of 'interference' by members of one race group in the politics of another race group criminal offences.

The legislative measures just referred to have been fashioned for the specific purpose of putting down political opposition. Certain other laws, not originally designed for political purposes, have been used in conjunction with these to stifle opposition. To select an example, no African person has a permanent right of residence anywhere in the 'white' areas of the Republic.[44] A politically troublesome African may be 'endorsed out' of the white area in which he lives and sent to his homeland. Inevitably this means the loss of his employment and income with almost no hope of work in the homeland. A power like this need not be exercised frequently; the threat will generally be enough. In the African reserves there are laws prohibiting meetings of more than ten persons without permission.[45] Meetings called by suspect persons, or meetings for suspect purposes, can easily be prohibited by the authorities with no effective right of redress to the aggrieved persons. The use of these and other similar laws, combined with the enforcement of laws like those referred to in the preceding paragraph, explains the total capture of political power by the National Party.

In enacting and enforcing these laws the Nationalist Government has all along claimed, with limited justification only, that it was acting in the interests of order and security. This plausible but meretricious argument has taken in many well-intentioned and intelligent observers whose judgement has been weakened by politicians' assiduous exploitation of the psychological shock-value of political disorder in some of the emergent African states. The utilization, for questionable ends, of man's psychologically based respect for security is an old game understood by politicians centuries ago. In Greek times, as now in South Africa, the critics of excessive government power are represented as the enemies of order, as if the mere appeal to public order is enough to justify the assumption of any political power. The claims of those who are for ever repeating the '*salus populi suprema lex*' maxim should always be carefully scrutinized, for they very frequently conceal the quest for power in pursuit of sectional ends. A scrutiny of the legislation under discussion compels the conclusion that it is the statutory programme of a political party more interested in power and privilege than in law and order. For this admittedly serious indictment there are two main evidential foundations. The first is the preoccupation of the Nationalist Government with the symptoms of disorder and social tension and its almost consciously assumed myopia towards the deeper malaise. Now a government genuinely committed to order would dedicate itself to the achievement of social justice on which any lasting order must rest. The claims (expressed in general terms) which justice makes upon a government have been well summed up as 'the demands for equality, rightful deserts, human dignity, conscientious adjudication, confinement of government to its proper functions, and fulfilment of common expectations'.[46] While the present Government has a better record than most earlier ruling parties in meeting many of the material demands[47] of the voteless majority, this is in itself only a fractional fulfilment of what a meaningful system of social justice requires. But the observer of the South African situation is confronted with more than mere inattention to the legitimate claim of the majority. Disorder is generated also by the oppressive government of laws imposed without consent upon the majority. A government which implements a policy of repression[48] must assume a large share of the responsibility for the threat to peace and security. At this point of the argument one is brought face to face with the ambivalent attitude of the Nationalist Government towards disorder: it implements a policy which contains within it the seeds of disorder; but that very disorder, so long as it does not become cataclysmic, is a condition of, and justification for, the policy being implemented. This ambivalence lies at the heart of the repeated assurances, given when new powers are assumed, that South Africa is the most peaceful country in the world. The second pillar of the argument that the predominating interest of the Nationalists is in power and privilege, is the unquestionable fact that security legislation goes far beyond the requirements of security even on the gloomiest interpretation of the current situation. The 'security laws' have been put permanently on the statute book; in form they are ordinary laws. The impression gained from their form is fortified by an examination of content. Such an examination[49] discloses a policy of stifling all political change, not just disorderly political changes. The definition of communism in the Suppression of Communism Act is the most striking illustration that a policy of that kind underlies the security programme. According to the definition, communism includes any doctrine or scheme

which aims at bringing about any political, industrial, social or economic change within the Republic by the promotion of disturbance or disorder, by unlawful acts or omissions or by the threat of such acts or omissions or by means which include the promotion of disturbance or disorder, or such acts or omissions or threat. . . .[50]

According to judicial interpretation, a doctrine or scheme of the kind described is an independent statutory form of communism.[51] It follows that anyone working for the furtherance of such a doctrine or scheme will be guilty of furthering the aims of communism and subject to severe criminal punishment. Any political programme the implementation of which is likely to involve breaches of the most technical offence,[52] is therefore outlawed as a criminal offence. An analysis of the scope of the 'Sabotage Act' and the Terrorism Act will reveal the same policy of perpetuating Nationalist political control in South Africa. The policy is also implicit in the implementation of some of these laws against the *lawful* opponents of the Government[53] and the intimidation and persecution of people for *lawful* political activities. It is not possible in this chapter to collect and review all the evidence but sufficient has been said to show that, to put it at its lowest, there is a powerful case for the argument that in form, content, and implementation the 'security laws' are designed to perpetuate Nationalist political domination, the maintenance of security being only a necessary condition for the success of a policy of political domination.[54] This critique of the Nationalist security programme does not rest on any facile belief that a different government committed to a just policy would not be faced with threats to peace and order. The government of a country consisting of people of different race groups at different stages of development is a task fraught with difficulties and dangers. The problems are exacerbated by the international conflicts and misunderstanding between communists and non-communists, between white and non-white people, and between the rich and the poor nations. Yet these very dangers make it necessary that security should be built into the fabric of the nation's social, economic, and political arrangements, and not imposed from the top. If a threat to public order nevertheless occurs, it can be dealt with first by the use of the ordinary laws of the land[55] and, if these fail, by such temporary *emergency* powers as are demanded by the situation.[56] If instead of so acting the Government liquidates the rule of law and other institutions of good government, it imposes on society evils similar to those that it holds up as a threat.

The programme of security laws enacted during the past twenty years of Nationalist rule has been represented by its framers as a system of Western justice. Ludicrous as this claim may seem, it does not lack support in South Africa even among non-Nationalists. The reason for this support lies in the successful creation by the Nationalist Government of the image of itself as a bulwark against communism. Communism has never been a formidable threat in South Africa, but by identifying opposition to the policy of Apartheid with communism[57] the Nationalist Government has created an illusion of imminent danger and simultaneously assumed the role of the people's protector against it. In this way a system of laws undermining some of the most basic principles of Western government has been dressed up in the habit of Western justice. This habit has been made to look slightly less ill-fitting in the crisis atmosphere continuously fomented by the men who control government; after all, even Western governments abridge individual liberties in times of crisis. Of course there is a difference: the crisis in South Africa is permanent. A closed society will always be in a condition of crisis because it sets itself against change and will constantly feel threatened by the changes in and around it. As we have seen, South Africa is in some important respects a closed society—a fact which explains why its nationalistic leaders have successfully posed as the guardians of a society surrounded by a sea of unrest. In a country governed by Western traditions change does not seem to be a monstrous enemy which society must resolutely shut out. By reason of their traditions and institutions Western societies can face a changing world and make the necessary accommodation without sacrificing the liberal-democratic principles and institutions which are the distinguishing features of such societies. It is because it is inflexibly opposed to change that the South African Government has sacrificed these principles and institutions. But because the Government has acted in the name of the very principles it has destroyed, much discredit has been brought upon Western notions of law, justice, and government. To many South Africans, and especially to many non-white South Africans, the rule of law must appear indistinguishable from the rule of force, and justice no more than the right of the stronger.

A debased and distorted conception of law is implicitly expressed in the South African security programme. In an essay entitled 'Power, Law and Race Relations', Professor Julius Lewin has described the power struggle between English and Afrikaans in the Republic in the following terms:

> Both sides . . . want to have 'The Law' behind them and both sides argue as if The Law were some majestic arbiter, instead of recognizing law as essentially an instrument of policy in the hands of those exercising power.[58]

In this admirable description the writer has too readily yielded to the view that law is simply an instrument for giving effect to the will of those in power. The present rulers in South Africa have debased law by making it a tool of power, whereas, properly conceived, it is also a framework within which *both ruler and ruled* must operate.[59] A political party returned to power has a mandate which it will wish to implement in a legislative programme. To the extent that it does so the law enacted by it may be described as an instrument of policy. But the right of a political party to use the legislative machinery for this purpose falls away when it begins to dismantle the structure of rules under which all parties must operate to secure their mandate. To that extent the law must be a 'majestic arbiter' under whose general control the contestants compete for power.

At the heart of the idea of law and of the rule of law is the notion of a transcendent order to which all in society, even (perhaps especially) governments, must submit. It is the acceptance of that notion which differentiates a society ruled by law from one ruled by naked power.

In some respects South Africa has become a society ruled by law only in the most formal sense. 'The powers of Louis XIV, of Napoleon I, of Herr Hitler, and of Signor Mussolini are derived from the law, even if that law be only "The leader may do and order what he pleases".'[60] A principle of this kind is operative in the political area in the Republic by virtue of legislation now in force. The most significant thing about the Suppression of Communism Act (to take only one instance) is that it embodies the rule that the ruler (usually the Minister) may do as he pleases. Under that Act the dissolution of an organization, the suppression of a publication, and the 'banning' of an individual are in the absolute discretion of a Minister or of the State President.[61] In its least contentious sense[62] the rule of law requires that an order depriving a man of his liberty shall be made in terms of rules precisely defining the forbidden conduct and administered by an impartial tribunal. Neither requirement is satisfied by the provisions of the Suppression of Communism Act or by those of many other 'security' laws. We thus have the paradox that officials operating in terms of the law are in truth operating outside it. They are outside it in the sense that what they do need not conform to any prescribed norms and is exempt from judicial regulation or control.[63] Law has then ceased to be a body of regularly applied norms and has become instead a vehicle for personal rule with all its attendant dangers.

The misuse of a legal system by politicians will have far-reaching and incalculable consequences for society. By the sacrifice of valuable traditions and institutions like the rule of law, the gains of centuries of painstaking evolution and development are squandered overnight. The return to a society governed by law in the full (not merely formal) sense will be terribly difficult so long as the laws themselves are animated by a spirit of power rather than justice. The task of return is made all the more difficult by the attitudes engendered by such laws. Though it may in some sense be true that countries get the legal system they deserve, it cannot be denied that the law of a country may be a profoundly constructive force by its power to make public opinion more enlightened. It is a partial view which sees law as a reflection of society, for society is also a reflection of the law. The capture of power by the Nationalist rulers in South Africa and the subordination of the legal system to their political ends have severely limited, if not ended, the beneficent influence of the Roman-Dutch law. That system, enriched by English law, embodied a 'philosophy' which exercised a forming influence on the society in which it operated. It was, for example, suffused with the vital principle of fair trial with a full hearing to both sides.[64] The hold of the new 'philosophy' can be gauged by acceptance in the common mind of rules for action like the one expressed in the 'no smoke without fire' maxim. The baleful influence of Nationalist abuse of the legal system is in fact far more extensive than that. The destruction of institutions like the rule of law which have served to impersonalize government and thereby reduce tyranny and injustice makes it likely that change will take the form of a new tyranny supplanting the old. The weapons of legal oppression which have been forged by the Nationalist Government can serve a new government equally well. This will be all the more likely in a society which has ceased to comprehend the notion of law as an impersonal, objective order which may not properly be manipulated to serve sectional interests.

When law loses its transcendent quality and becomes an instrument of domination, as it does under communist rule,[65] the free and natural response between the legal order and its environment is terminated. The ready translation of social into political power, and thereafter into legal power, can no longer take place. But what is far worse is that the creative springs in society dry up under an oppressive legal order. Sidney Hook has said that

The philosophy of democracy rests not on the belief in the natural goodness of man but in his educability, not in the inevitability of social progress but in the potentialities of human nature and intelligence.[66]

A repressive government of laws turns the *possibility* of social progress into the certainty of social stagnation, if not regress.

REFERENCES

1. As W. Friedmann points out in *Law in a Changing Society*, Stevens, London, 1959, 6, the men who control the machinery of state are themselves, to a greater or lesser extent, the product of social forces.

2. FRIEDMANN, op. cit., 18.

3. Certain South African laws, for example those denying non-whites the right to own land, would be unconstitutional in the United States. A great number of the laws denying political rights and civil liberties would be struck down if enacted in the United States.

4. FRIEDMANN, op. cit., 10.

5. BARKER, ERNEST, *Reflections on Government*, Oxford University Press, Oxford, 1942, 323.

6. Some of which is discussed later in this chapter.

7. Absolutism and totalitarianism are not identical. Absolutism is conceivable without totalitarianism but the converse does not hold; see Barker, op. cit., 165.

8. HOOK, SIDNEY, *Political Power and Personal Freedom*, Criterion, New York, 1959, 145.

9. Professor G. H. L. Le May has summed up the position as follows: 'This country is a hybrid; so far as whites are concerned, it has the appearance of a Western type state with representative government, but it also has characteristics of the single party state.' *Rand Daily Mail*, 16 Dec. 1967.

10. LLOYD, DENNIS, *The Idea of Law*, Penguin, Harmondsworth, 1964, 219.

11. The law also reflects the interests, especially economic, of the English-speaking whites, but not their ideology (if they have one!).

12. CARTER, GWENDOLEN M., *The Politics of Inequality*, Thames & Hudson, London, 3rd edn., 1962, 237.

13. The cream is also likely to thin out as the gap between the demand for and supply of skilled labour widens. By preventing the non-whites from becoming skilled, the Government is stunting economic growth and at the same time increasing the strain on the 'white economy'. While the non-white population is denied the opportunity to become economically self-sufficient, white charity on a large scale will remain necessary. (The economic cost of Apartheid has all along been disguised by the great growth of wealth in South Africa.)

14. Professor Le May has suggested that the *verligtes* are 'trying to count the cost of ideology'.

15. Shortly after these words were written down, the Minister of Bantu Administration and Development made a speech which represents the first clear sign of a back-pedalling on the Verwoerd policy of separate development. The Minister shifted the emphasis away from the consolidation and development of the homelands to the 'freeing of the Bantu people from guardianship and anchoring them to their homelands traditionally, spiritually and politically'. *Sunday Times*, 24 Mar. 1968.

16. No. 88 of 1967.

17. It is possibly reflected in the non-application of some Apartheid laws, for example job reservation.

18. The concept of the 'closed society' is fully analysed by Karl Popper in *The Open Society and Its Enemies*, Routledge & Kegan Paul, London, 1963. Its leading characteristics are the taboo-like sanctity which attaches to its institutions and castes and the elimination of 'foreign influences', with a resulting intolerance towards criticism and dissent.

19. Possibly with the aim of making the country independent of outside influences, as Professor Gwendolen M. Carter suggests; op. cit., 15. With South Africa's independence now firmly established, the Nationalists can begin to limit economic growth, as they have threatened to do under the Physical Planning and Utilization of Resources Act.

20. POPPER, op. cit., 8–9. There is no doubt that the Nationalists in South Africa have bolstered their policy with the 'higher race' philosophy. It has frequently been expressed directly as a fundamental belief and underlies their policy statements, e.g. the well-known description of the Afrikaner as the trustee of the interests of the black races.

21. TALMON, J. L., *The Origins of Totalitarian Democracy*, Mercury Books, London, 1966, 6–7.

22. BARKER, op. cit., 311.

23. VAN DEN BERGHE, PIERRE L., *South Africa: A Study in Conflict*, Wesleyan University Press, Middletown, Conn., 1965, 29; Leo Marquard, *The Peoples and Policies of South Africa*, Oxford University Press, Cape Town and London, 3rd edn. 1962, 5.

24. A pragmatism which is derived partly from self-interest and partly from the English influence in politics in the Republic.

25. There has, of course, been a very considerable politicization of cultural life in the country. For example, censorship controls literature with great strictness, and organization for almost any purpose is under a tight statutory regulation.

26. J. D. Mabbott has said that ' "the good of the state" or "the

national interest" must be analysable into the interests of individual citizens; anything claimed to be a "national interest" and not so analysable is an illusion and a false goal of policy'; see *The State and the Citizen*, Hutchinson's University Library, London, 1955, 139.

27. MARQUARD, op. cit., 241. The distinction between the State and its temporary controllers is often conveniently overlooked by those who invoke the doctrine.

28. BARKER, op. cit., 391.

29. Mabbott shows that the fanatical implementation of a nationalistic policy leads inevitably to the persecution of those who are 'different'; Mabbott, op. cit., 166–8.

30. The irrelevance of means, and therefore of ordinary moral criteria, is only one of the objectionable features of Utopian social planning. The weaknesses and dangers of Utopian planning are fully exposed by Popper, op. cit., 137 *et seq.*

31. The permanent dilemma of the Nationalists is that the social changes generated by their policy of economic growth are by their very nature destructive of the society of their vision.

32. LEGUM, COLIN, 'Colour and Power in the South African Situation', *Daedalus*, Spring, 1967, 483.

33. The Africans only fully appreciated this in the fifties when the Freedom Charter marked their determination to work for political ascendancy. See Julius Lewin, *Politics and Law in South Africa*, Merlin Press, London, 1963, 52. By then the locks of the awakening black Samson had been shorn.

34. As Lewin points out, English-speaking South Africans have never effectively challenged the Nationalist rise to power because their own economic interests were advanced by a policy which limited privilege to the white groups and guaranteed a plentiful supply of cheap black labour. Op. cit., 16 and 30.

35. The Bantustan policy has so far made only a slight concession to African demands for political control. Even in the Transkei the transfer of power has been only nominal.

36. This concluded with the removal of the Coloured voters from the common voters' roll under the South Africa Act Amendment Act, No. 9 of 1956, which brought the Separate Representation of Voters Act, No. 46 of 1951, into operation as from the date of commencement of the 1956 Act. Subsequently, the separate-roll representation of the Coloured through white representatives in Parliament and the Cape Provincial Council was abolished by the Separate Representation of Voters Amendment Act, No. 50 of 1968. Africans were earlier removed from the common rolls by the Representation of Natives Act, No. 12 of 1936, and they

R

lost all voice in Parliament by the Promotion of Bantu Self-Government Act, No. 46 of 1959.

37. Though the campaign was directed against non-white opposition, the freedom of whites was inevitably lost in the political suppression of non-white political movements.

38. No. 44 of 1950.

39. No. 8 of 1953.

40. No. 34 of 1960.

41. Section 21 of the General Law Amendment Act, No. 76 of 1962.

42. Section 215 *bis* of the Criminal Procedure Act, No. 56 of 1955.

43. No. 83 of 1967.

43a. No. 51 of 1968.

44. Bantu (Urban Areas) Consolidation Act, No. 25 of 1945.

45. See for example Proclamation No. 198 of 1953 (G. G. No. 5138 of 18 Sept. 1953) discussed in *South African Law Journal*, 1965, *82*, 454.

46. HAHLO, H. R., and KAHN, E., *The South African Legal System and its Background*, Juta, Cape Town, 1968, 31, quoting Edmund N. Cahn. The writer is well aware of the difficulty inherent in claims for equality, just deserts, and so on. The difficulty does not appear to the writer to arise in the South African situation, because the present government, far from trying to satisfy the basic postulates of justice even in a limited sense, has made a frontal attack upon them. It would be inconsistent for the government to reject the postulates and simultaneously justify its policy as being an honest attempt to meet them as best it can.

47. For example, housing.

48. A government obviously cannot yield completely and immediately to all social pressures. At the same time, the construction of an impenetrable barrier against such pressures creates the conditions of disorder.

49. Of particular laws and of their total and cumulative effect.

50. Section 1 (1) of the Suppression of Communism Act, No. 44 of 1950.

51. *R.* v. *Sisulu* 1953 (3) S.A. 276 (AD).

52. For example, holding a meeting without local authority consent. In some cities and towns the local authorities, acting in consultation with the police, refuse permission for meetings or processions to disfavoured political groups.

53. A good illustration is the banning of over forty-one Liberals under the Suppression of Communism Act. A few of these banned Liberals did commit subversive acts, but they were not banned for these acts; in fact the acts were usually committed after the ban.

SECURITY LAWS AND SOCIAL CHANGE 247

54. This conclusion is one which cannot be conclusively 'proved'. To the writer the evidence is overwhelming. It may seem less so to others. The writer cannot take seriously the argument that the rationale of the Nationalist Apartheid programme is establishment of peace and security by the only method possible—the separation of the races. The Nationalists themselves have yet to take separate development seriously. Moreover, if the aim is security by separation it is hard to justify the grossly unequal treatment of the races.

55. These laws, which include the crimes of treason, sedition, public violence, incitement, and so on, are much more sweeping than is generally realized. They will be found inadequate by any government which aims to entrench itself in power rather than promote peace and order.

56. The identification in South Africa of opposition with subversion, and the artificially engendered crisis atmosphere, make a cool and realistic assessment of the situation impossible.

57. In 1962 the Minister of Justice (now the Prime Minister) said of opposition to a measure which would greatly enlarge the powers of government, 'surely then it amounts to nothing but protection of the communists and of what they stand for to attack this Bill and to rave against it'. House of Assembly Debates, *4*, col. 6069, 21 May 1962.

58. LEWIN, op. cit., 56.

59. Even law in the debased sense is technically law; this argument does not deny that it is. The argument is basically a dispute about political morality and the rule of law. It is a question of what function the law ought to have in society.

60. JENNINGS, SIR IVOR, *The Law and the Constitution*, University of London Press, London, 3rd edn. 1943, 46.

61. *S.A. Defence and Aid Fund* v. *Minister of Justice* 1967 (1) S.A. 263 (AD); *Kloppenberg* v. *Minister of Justice* 1964 (4) S.A. 31 (N).

62. In this sense the rule of law corresponds broadly to the notion of formal justice. See Lloyd, op. cit., 121.

63. Many court judgements on legislation of this kind are no more than declarations of judicial impotence. In its security programme the Nationalist Government has relegated the courts to an insultingly trivial role. The fact that the power of the court is limited has not saved it from undeserved odium due to the fact that it has had to confirm the decisions of the executive and impose the punishments prescribed by the law.

64. In the Hamlyn Lecture entitled *Protection from Power under English Law*, Stevens, London, 1957, 73, Lord MacDermott has said, 'The safeguard to which I give pride of place because of its

fundamental character and its wide applicability lies in the
practice of hearing both sides before reaching a decision which
is enshrined in the maxim *"audi alteram partem"'*.

65. LLOYD, op. cit., 221. This is one of the many striking parallels
between Nationalist and communist rule.

66. HOOK, op. cit., 26.

13

RICHARD B. FORD

THE URBAN TREK: SOME COMPARISONS OF MOBILITY IN AMERICAN AND SOUTH AFRICAN HISTORY

Interpreters of contemporary affairs in South Africa frequently cite 1948 as a year of decision. The victory of the National Party, they note, changed drastically and permanently the direction of events in South African history. That 1948 marked a crucial turn of events is clear, but that this decisive change came about solely because of the election is another matter. A demographic development deserves equal consideration. In 1947–8, the number of Afrikaans-speaking, white South Africans living in urban areas overtook for the first time the number of white, urban English-speakers.[1] For South Africa the importance of the Afrikaners' urban trek rivals and perhaps even surpasses that of the Great Trek of the previous century.

The difference in importance between the two treks lies in the degree of mobility which resulted from each. Although the Great Trek reflected the wide scope for geographic movement available to South Africans in the 1830s and before, subsequent events showed how limited were their opportunities for social and economic mobility. These scarcely existed in South African society before the discovery of diamonds and gold and the concomitant industrialization–urbanization process, and even then the Afrikaners were slow to participate; so slow, in fact, that only in the last generation or two has the full effect of urbanization and economic-social mobility become apparent. 1948 thus marks not only a political victory for the National Party, but the emergence of a new-style Afrikaner: the upwardly mobile urbanite. This new dynamic within the Afrikaans-speaking population could conceivably promote social change greater than any known thus far among South Africa's white population.

In this regard, some comparisons with developments in American history are valuable. In America, unlike South Africa, physical mobility from its earliest days produced urban concentrations which gave rise to opportunities for social and economic mobility.[2] There are several reasons for this difference. First, America's natural resources encouraged urbanization: access to the interior was possible because the Connecticut, Delaware, Hudson, and Mississippi–Ohio rivers, Chesapeake Bay, and the coastal inlets of tide-water Virginia gave inland regions easy contact with the outside world. South Africa possessed no such water routes. In addition, America's eastern mountain ranges, although severe, were less precipitous than those surrounding the Cape settlement. From the beginning, Americans migrated to the interior of the continent earlier and in greater numbers than did free burghers in South Africa, and as their numbers increased, so did their need for specialized goods and services. Moreover, Americans living in the interior depended more heavily on the outside world for trade than did their counterparts in South Africa.[3] In response to these demands, new urban centres sprang up, first along the coast and later in the interior.

Ocean ports such as Boston (15,500 in 1765),[4] New York (12,000 in 1761),[5] Philadelphia (20,000 in 1755),[6] and Charleston (11,000 in 1770—roughly one-half of these were slaves)[7] were active centres by the middle years of the eighteenth century. At the same time, further inland, Hartford, Connecticut (5,000 in 1774)[8] and Albany, New York (500 houses or roughly 2,500 people in 1769)[9] prospered. Less than a century later, inland trading centres dotted the Ohio valley and old Northwest territory. These urban areas included Pittsburgh (22,500 in 1830),[10] Cincinnati (27,000 in 1830),[11] and Chicago (30,000 in 1850).[12]

The ocean ports and inland cities served essentially similar functions. Initially they were not manufacturing centres so much as exchange points. Long before the advent of industrialization, cities such as Pittsburgh, Cincinnati, and Chicago performed three important services: they served as a collection and processing point to which farmers, hunters, and herders brought their surplus stocks; they imported machinery, furniture, and luxury goods which the new settlers desired; and they provided a population base for some of the 'finer' things of life such as schools, newspapers, legal and commercial services, and artistic activities.[13]

In South Africa, in contrast, only Cape Town qualified as a 'city' until after the discovery of diamonds and gold, and even Cape Town, as late as 1865, numbered fewer than 30,000 residents, and almost one-half of these were non-white.[14] Port Elizabeth, South Africa's second largest city in 1865, counted only 8,700 residents;[15] Kimberley and Johannesburg were not yet important; Durban, at present the nation's busiest port, had attained only 6,300 people of all races in 1872.[16] Although a few English artisans had settled in small villages and towns, the predominant flavour of South Africa, well into the nineteenth century, was rural.

Natural resources created other differences in the patterns of urbanization in the United States and South Africa. The presence of industrial raw materials in the United States coincided with the areas of earliest European settlement. Water power, coal, and iron ore were abundant in the New England and Middle Atlantic regions, precisely in the areas where the inland exchange cities first appeared. When manufacturing began to take hold in the nineteenth century, America had already established concentrated sources of labour, regionalized markets, and a rudimentary transportation system, all within easy access to industrial raw materials. These cities had also developed basic financial institutions as well as facilities for communication, education, and recreation. Thus America's inland cities provided a ready-made base upon which industrial development could flourish.

South Africa was less fortunate. Water power was largely absent; and coal and iron ore, although plentiful, were buried in remote regions of Natal and the Transvaal, areas which no white man explored until more than 150 years after the first European settlement. Thus South Africa's inland expansion was, until the 1870s, an agricultural expansion. No urban infrastructure developed to facilitate the transition from an agrarian to an industrial society.

South Africa's limited production reflected this rural character. Annual exports averaged £2,500,000 for the years 1866 to 1870.[17] This amount equalled only about £10 per year for each European resident.[18] Moreover, raw wool alone amounted to three-quarters of these exports.[19]

Internal markets were also poorly developed. Railway construction lagged woefully behind the rest of the world. As late as 1874, only sixty-three miles of track were open for general freight and passenger traffic,[20] while in 1870 the United States had already built 53,000 miles of track.[21] Without railroads, lacking waterways, and with urban centres almost non-existent, South Africa's commercial activities were minimal. Although the world market influenced to some degree the economy of South Africa, the bulk of her production was agricultural, and confined in the main to a purely local subsistence economy.[22] Thus the extensive physical movement of the South African frontier expansion did not lead automatically to opportunities for economic or social mobility—a further step, that of urbanization, was needed.

Subsistence agricultural practices and economic and social isolation in South Africa fostered a fierce emotional attachment to things agrarian. Eric Walker,[23] C. W. De Kiewiet,[24] and Sheila Patterson[25] have written at length about the religious and cultural character of this bond between the Afrikaner's soul and his soil. This bond also assumed economic and political dimensions. Following the Anglo-Boer War thousands of poverty stricken whites, largely Afrikaans-speaking, flocked to the major urban centres seeking work, and they eventually came to be known as the 'poor whites' of South Africa. In 1905 a commission spent several months investigating the causes of indigency in Pretoria and as a result made recommendations to solve the problem. It is of particular interest that the commission did not urge that indigents be trained to perform urban or industrial skills. Rather they recommended:

1. That the indigent population in and around Pretoria is mainly drawn from the old Burgher class, or original rural settlers of this country, and are on the whole best fitted, no matter what their

immediate occupations may have been before the War, to take up agricultural pursuits.

2. That the bulk of them have expressed a desire to resume the occupation of tilling the soil, if assisted by the Government to that end.

3. ... That the presence of these people in the towns is not desirable from an economic and moral standpoint, and that endeavours should be made to settle them on the land.

4. That the creation of agricultural settlements with small holdings, of which the settlers should be in a position to acquire the owner-ship, appears to us to be the best method, not only of assisting these people on to the land and making them self-supporting, but also of improving the economic conditions of the country.[26]

Afrikaners in the nineteenth and even the very early twentieth century did not look to cities as places of opportunity, nor urban occupations as a mechanism for solving economic and social problems; generally they preferred life on the veld.

America's rural involvement was different. Although the soil held a special place in the hearts of Americans, they were not averse to non-agricultural occupations. A legend of frontier-agricultural life developed in America, but simultaneously there grew up the image of Americans as versatile.[27] If farming proved unsatisfactory, Americans always had alternatives of com-merce, manufacturing, transport, or the professions. Thus for Afrikaners agriculture became an end in itself, but for Americans it was one of several possible means to a different objective: social and economic mobility and material prosperity.

The role of the indigenous populations in the United States and South Africa created further differences in patterns of urbanization. Americans seldom used Indians for labour. Their Stone Age culture made them unsuitable for all but the most elementary tasks. In addition, the American frontier expanded in a solid line and pushed the Indian ahead so that, unlike South Africa, in America the settlers and the indigenous population seldom came into close economic contact. In America, then, labour was usually a scarce commodity and therefore priced dearly. Hence there were strong incentives for Americans to develop labour-saving devices, and efficiency of production became a symbol of right action in America. Such was not the case in South Africa. Because the cost of an African's service was minimal, South Africans had little reason to conserve labour. Little specialization or division of labour was needed; and few urban centres developed to exchange specialized skills and services.

Subsistence agriculture and a cheap labour supply not only stifled urbanization and industrialization but discouraged European immigration as well.[28] From 1820 to 1870 fewer than 50,000 Europeans migrated to South Africa.[29] From 1870 to 1929, with urban-industrial opportunities becoming available, European immigration increased to approximately 800,000, most of whom were skilled and semi-skilled workers from England.[30] The total migration of Europeans to South Africa from 1820 to 1929 was less than one million. Europeans in the nineteenth century simply did not look to South Africa as a land of opportunity. Urban employment was too scarce; and competition with African labourers was too severe.

In contrast, industrial-urban America attracted masses of unskilled immigrants. Almost 6,000,000 Germans, 4,500,000 Italians, another 4,500,000 Irish, and more than 7,500,000 Eastern Europeans and Russians were among the 32,000,000 who flocked to America between 1820 and 1929.[31] Many of these, particularly the Irish, Italians, Eastern Europeans, and Russians, went directly to cities. Others, such as Germans and Scandinavians, who tended to settle on farms, could do so only because America's rapidly expanding urban centres created enormous demands for food products. American farming, in contrast to South African, was market-orientated commercial agriculture.[32] The opportunity which America came to symbolize was created not by geographic space, but by the great latitude of economic and social mobility available in or through its cities.

The migration of Irish peasants to America in the 1840s and 1850s offers an excellent illustration of urban mobility in the United States.[33] Between the years 1841 and 1860 approximately 160,000 Irish peasants landed in Boston, and of these, many stayed on to find work in Boston itself.[34] By 1850 roughly every fourth Bostonian was Irish,[35] and by 1855 the figure was approaching one in three.[36] These Irish were unaccustomed to urban living; they possessed no capital nor skills with which to enter business; they had no experience nor training as artisans;

they had never received adequate education to enter the professions. Instead they found work whenever and wherever they could, and more often than not it was heavy, manual labour. The first generation lived in poverty.

In 1850, although 25 per cent of Boston was Irish, they numbered only 2 per cent of her teachers and 5 per cent of her physicians. In business, slightly less than 2 per cent of the city's financiers and merchants were Irish. However, of a total of 14,595 gainfully employed Irish (male and female), 9,299 or nearly 65 per cent earned a living as labourers or domestic servants. Taken another way, about 70 per cent of Boston's domestic servants and 80 per cent of her labourers were Irish.[37]

These statistics are not surprising. Initially there were few agencies available to help the immigrants. The meagre resources of the then struggling Roman Catholic Church in New England were no match for the challenge, and immigrant aid societies similarly lacked adequate funds. Employers hesitated before hiring Irish for semi-skilled or skilled work, and the notice 'None need apply but Americans' became a familiar mark in mid-century Boston.[38] Yet the Irish were unwilling to accept permanently this unhappy situation.

For the first-generation immigrant Boston's construction industry offered some opportunity. In 1850, approximately 15 per cent of the carpenters, 25 per cent of the masons, 12 per cent of the painters, and 18 per cent of the plumbers were Irish.[39] The Irish also did well in service occupations which dealt directly with their own people. Butchers, fruiterers, family grocers, and peddlers earned a reasonable though frugal living; others opened restaurants and boarding houses, again catering largely to their own people. Although involvement in business and finance was minimal, its humble beginnings for the Irish came through shipping brokers, bankers, insurance companies, and real estate agencies which involved Irish customers. The few professional people among the first-generation immigrants also tended to minister to their fellow Irish. These minor inroads in construction and services, however, were inadequate to raise the level of the great bulk of Boston's newly arrived Irish. Moreover, the old Yankee elite offered little help to the hated 'Papists'. The Irish had no alternative other than to help themselves.

Religious organizations offered one obvious means of self-help. As Boston's Irish population swelled, so did the number of Roman Catholic congregations. But more important, so did the number of parochial schools. Fearful that Irish children would lose their Catholic traditions if mixed too freely with Protestant children, the Church gradually opened schools, at all grade levels, for the immigrants. Nominal tuition fees excluded the poorest families. Yet many children managed to acquire a basic education—certainly more than their parents had received. Irish newspapers, together with the Catholic schools, helped to preserve the identity of the Irish-Catholic as well as to guide immigrants to better opportunities.

The big effort at self-help, however, came through the political process. Challenged by antagonistic elements within Boston's Protestant ranks, the Irish organized groups such as the 'Irish Emigrant Aid Society', ostensibly to assist in the settlement of new arrivals, but actually to co-ordinate political energies to defeat their Protestant enemies.[40] Although the disruptions of the Civil War temporarily thwarted this effort, ultimately political activity provided the largest single avenue of upward mobility for the Irish.[41] By the early 1870s they had gained control of Boston's police and fire departments.[42] At the same time Irish aldermen and councilmen wielded enormous political power to place Irish in other government positions. In 1884 Boston elected its first Irish mayor.[43] As political power increased, so did the hold of the Irish on a multitude of related activities. Better jobs led to better educational opportunities for children and eventually to entrance into business and the professions. By the turn of the century, although there was still no real equality between Yankee and Irish, at least the Irish had achieved a position where they could challenge the social and economic power of the old Yankee elite.

The Census of 1900 revealed significant changes over the previous fifty years. In 1900 about one-third of Boston was Irish. Whereas only 2 per cent of the teachers had been Irish in 1850, by 1900 the figure had jumped to 19 per cent. Only 5 per cent of Boston's physicians were Irish in 1850; at the turn of the century the percentage had increased to 12 per cent. Irish merchants had increased from 2 to 21 per cent over the same period. Of particular interest were the police and fire depart-

ments which included more than 43 per cent Irish in their ranks
in 1900. Although the city's labourers were still heavily Irish
(down to 65 per cent in 1900 from 80 per cent in 1850), the
proportion of Irish labourers to total Irish workers was down
significantly from 50 per cent in 1850 to 14 per cent in 1900.[44]
The Irish, by the end of their second generation of urban residence in the United States, were well on their way towards
respectable economic and social status. As individual Irishmen
gained such positions they became more secure and gradually
lost their vigorous group identity which had been so important
in their years of upward mobility.

In South Africa, the Afrikaner's trek to the city, beginning in
the early twentieth century, is closely comparable with that of
the Irishman's migration to Boston. Prior to the discovery of
diamonds and gold, South Africa had virtually no cities. When
the mines opened, there were few people living in South Africa
who possessed the skills or the interest to exploit the new wealth.
Skilled workers came largely from overseas.[45] Time after time,
in the 1870s and 1880s, Afrikaners sold their land to mining
speculators and trekked off to more remote pasture land. As a
result of these continuing treks, the mining cities such as
Kimberley and Johannesburg became predominantly English-
speaking cities.[46]

For example, in 1896 only 19 per cent of Johannesburg's
European population belonged to any one of the Dutch
Churches while more than 62 per cent were members of Anglican, Presbyterian, Methodist, Lutheran, or Roman Catholic
congregations and another 12 per cent were Jews. Eight years
later the difference was even more exaggerated: only 14 per cent
of Johannesburg's Europeans were affiliated with a Dutch
Church.[47] In marked contrast, for the Transvaal as a whole in
1904 (including Johannesburg) 49 per cent of the residents
belonged to one of the Dutch Churches.[48] Although religious
affiliation is not an exact measure of home language or cultural
background, these statistics indicate clearly that early Johannesburg was an English-speaking island in the midst of an
Afrikaans-speaking sea.

Dominance in urban affairs enabled English-speakers to
acquire control of the means of production in South Africa, and
therefore of the country's economic power. The Census of 1921

revealed that 76 per cent of the directors of companies in all of South Africa were born abroad; as also were almost 70 per cent of the merchants and business managers and 62 per cent of the physicians. In contrast only 10 per cent of South Africa's unskilled labourers in 1921 were born overseas.[49] Although some of these labourers were Africans, many were Afrikaners.

In spite of English dominance in the cities, Afrikaners eventually began an urban trek. In 1911, of a total Afrikaans-speaking population of roughly 700,000, only 200,000 or 29 per cent lived in urban areas.[50] In 1926, 391,000 Afrikaans-speakers or 41 per cent of all Afrikaners lived in South Africa's cities.[51] By 1936, the figure was approaching 50 per cent as 535,000 Afrikaners lived in cities as against 585,000 who remained in rural areas. The migration resulted, by 1960, in 1,369,000 or more than three-quarters of the white, Afrikaans-speaking population living in South African cities.[52]

They came for many reasons.[53] Some had lost their land under South Africa's peculiar system of land inheritance, or had been unable to earn a decent living from the soil.[54] Landlessness created a white *bywoner* or squatter class in the rural areas, and many of these poor whites saw no hope to better themselves other than by moving to urban areas. There were other reasons for the rural poverty. The coming of railroads to the Witwatersrand, first in 1892 from the Cape and then in 1895 from Natal and Delagoa Bay, put practically all the long-distance wagon drivers, mostly Afrikaners, out of work. In addition, the railroads brought food products from America to Johannesburg at a price frequently lower than the South African farmers could meet.[55] The result was disastrous.

In 1896, rinderpest; in 1899, war; and in 1903, drought and depression further complicated the agriculturalist's woes. With tragedy behind and a hope for regular work before them, Afrikaners trekked. In a word, they sought the same thing which the Irish before them in their trek to Boston had desired: opportunity.

Just as the Irish did not immediately find better opportunities in Boston, so Afrikaners encountered untold hardships in their new and unfamiliar environment. In part, as with the Irish, the hardships were to be expected. Life on the veld did not prepare people to survive in the city.[56] Moreover, unskilled Europeans found themselves in direct competition with Coloured and African labourers, some of whom had moved to the city before the Afrikaners. But of special significance for the Afrikaners, as with the Irish in Boston, was the frosty reception which the old elite accorded to the newcomers. For the Irish, it was the Yankee; for the Afrikaner, it was the English. The following quotation, from testimony delivered to the Transvaal Indigency Commission by Major Thomas William Marshall Fuge, Deputy Commissioner of Police, Pretoria, is representative of the English attitude towards the recently arrived Afrikaners:

Amongst the Dutch indigents the chief fault appears to be a disinclination to manual labour, and I have come to the conclusion that some of their present poverty is owing to this failing. . . .

Returning to the question of sloth, it would appear that this fault is the direct cause of a proportion of the poverty amongst the Dutch. They are an agricultural race, yet in this town there are numerous Dutch squatters in a state of poverty, who make little or no attempt to improve their condition by market gardening. . . .[57]

The parallel with Boston's Irish continued. Afrikaners worked predominantly in menial jobs. For example, in 1910 the bulk of the skilled and therefore highly paid miners on the Witwatersrand were immigrants, largely from England,[58] while in contrast in a sample of unskilled, white railway labourers from Uitenhage in 1906, colonial-born, Afrikaans-speaking labourers outnumbered non-colonial-born whites by 254 to 26.[59]

By the 1920s, when the first comprehensive data on occupations and ancestry became available, Afrikaners were still very much in a disadvantaged position, holding a disproportionate number of low-pay, low-prestige positions. So low was their status that the Carnegie Commission found for the year 1931 (a depression year) that possibly one-third of the Afrikaans-speaking population were 'as a conservative estimate, very poor'.[60]

For example, in 1926, although Afrikaners comprised 27 per cent of the white population of the six largest cities, males of Dutch South African parentage in those cities accounted for only 13 per cent of the physicians, 6 per cent of the proprietors and company managers, and 12 per cent of the bankers. In the textile industry, although 40 to 50 per cent of the factory workers were of Dutch South African parentage, only 7 per cent of the employers and managers were Afrikaners. In the mining and quarrying industry, although just 13 per cent of the owners, agents, and managers were Afrikaans-speaking, 55 per cent of the miners and 46 per cent of the other workers below ground were of Dutch South African parentage.[61] Bear in mind that the urban migrations of Afrikaners had been under way for about twenty years when these statistics were compiled.

Thus by the 1920s Afrikaners had already experienced some upward mobility, but these gradual advances were insignificant when compared with the progress they achieved through the medium which Boston's Irish had also used successfully; namely, political activity.

In 1912 General J. M. B. Hertzog had formed the National Party, and it grew rapidly. Within twelve years of its founding, the party had won a general election and Hertzog himself became Prime Minister at the head of a Nationalist-dominated coalition with the Labour Party. One of Hertzog's first moves was to formalize the 'civilized labour policy' which had been practised informally in South Africa since as early as 1907.[62] Under this policy poor whites were hired in government enterprises, particularly in the Post Office and on the railways, in preference to blacks.

By 1926, among the European, male population, 49 per cent of the defence force, 56 per cent of the police force, 50 per cent of the bus and tram conductors, 38 per cent of the postmen, 71 per cent of the railway labourers, 66 per cent of the railway shunters, and 41 per cent of the railway engine-drivers and firemen were of Dutch South African parentage.[63] The direction of upward mobility continued through the thirties and forties.

The Census of 1946 revealed that government occupations had become even more heavily dominated by Afrikaans-speaking, white, male South Africans. The police force had increased to 79 per cent Afrikaans; bus and truck drivers (trucks operated by South African Railways) were 71 per cent Afrikaans; postmen had jumped to 56 per cent Afrikaans; railway labourers had soared to 90 per cent Afrikaans; and the Civil Service included 55 per cent (male and female) Afrikaans-speaking South Africans.[64] Afrikaners were also pushing on the fringes of the professional classes. In 1926, they had provided only 27 per cent of the male school-teachers; in 1946, 73 per cent of the male, white school-teachers spoke Afrikaans as their home language.[65]

Yet, in 1946, although substantial gains had been realized, the giant's share of the professional and business world still remained English. Only 8 per cent of the stockbrokers were Afrikaners; less than 10 per cent of the civil and electrical engineers, only about 20 per cent of the medical doctors, and 20 per cent of the business managers were Afrikaners. The one professional group which showed marked progress were Afrikaans-speaking bankers, who constituted roughly 30 per cent of all bankers in South Africa.[66] Of these growing numbers of professionals, most ministered primarily to fellow Afrikaners.

Their progress in these fields, however, had increased markedly by the 1960s. In 1966, 71 per cent of the Civil Service and 87 per cent of the South Africa Police spoke Afrikaans as a home language.[67] Advances in the professions were similar. Of a total of 12,600 males engaged in health services (doctors and nurses) in 1960, 5,200 or about 41 per cent were Afrikaners. In education, which included school-teachers and college professors, Afrikaans-speaking males numbered 71 per cent of the total.[68] They are still not on a par with English-speakers at the very highest levels of business.[69] For example, in the mid-1960s only 55 per cent of urban Afrikaners earned more than R2,000 per year whereas among the English the figure was 77 per cent;[70] yet the gains of Afrikaners are still formidable.

These many advances have not been achieved through co-incidence. They have resulted from a conscious group action among Afrikaners. In part, these efforts have been religious and cultural.[71] But more important for Afrikaners have been their political activities. Just as Boston's urban Irish found it possible to advance their interests through political action, so have Afrikaners. The success of these political activities is apparent in the many 'stepping-stone' urban jobs which Afrikaners have found with the government. These jobs have led the sons of the first urban generation into better educational opportunities and eventually into non-governmental positions in business and the professions. But full economic and social equality with English-speakers has not yet been achieved. The struggle continues.

S

The stepping-stone occupations which the Irish and Afrikaners entered possessed several similarities. They tended to be low-risk, high-security jobs. They involved a minimum of capital investment. Generally, salaries were reasonable but not high. The jobs tended to be positions available only in urban or semi-urban areas. With the exception of school-teaching, the jobs usually required certain formal training but not necessarily a university education, and of the school-teachers most appeared during the middle years rather than the early years of urbanization. As indicated above, the employment was largely, although not exclusively, in government or government-related service. Finally, the stepping-stone occupations of both the Irish and the Afrikaners have been such that the children of the migrants received a better education than their parents.

What emerges, then, is a significant pattern, common to both groups, through which economic and social equality have been or are being achieved. The comparison suggests four conclusions.

Physical mobility alone is an inadequate vehicle to achieve social and economic mobility. An intermediate step of urbanization is necessary. In America physical mobility led to urbanization at an early date, thus creating opportunities for economic and social mobility. Because physical mobility did not lead automatically to urbanization in South Africa, social and economic mobility was thwarted.

The most recent migrants to a city usually work at the lowest economic levels. Poverty and discrimination, such as that encountered by Afrikaners and Irish, provide common grievances which elicit group responses, and when groups share a common ethnic, linguistic, religious, or cultural bond, this group consciousness intensifies. Group solidarity is especially strong in an urban atmosphere simply because communication is easier. In Boston and in South Africa group identification bolstered the migrant's struggle for economic and social equality.

Group activity may assume many forms. In Boston and South Africa the most effective vehicle of expression proved to be the political process. A reciprocal relationship developed between urbanization and political activity. Urbanization was an essential prerequisite to political power; the political process enabled both groups to break out of their low-status urban situations.

In Boston and South Africa the subsequent arrival of additional groups of urban migrants helped the cause of the Irish and Afrikaners. For the Irish, it was the Italians, and for the Afrikaners, it was the Africans who took up the menial, low-pay positions which the upwardly mobile groups vacated. Had there been no subsequent migrations to Boston or South Africa's cities, the upwardly mobile groups would have found their struggle far more difficult.

This comparative study of social and economic mobility raises two intriguing questions about the future. First, will Afrikaners follow the pattern of Boston's Irish, and once full economic equality with the English-speakers has been achieved, lose their aggressive group identity? Will their primary self-perceptions as Afrikaners give way to other identities which fall along economic, social, political, occupational, or professional lines? Glimmers of such tendencies are beginning to appear in the Afrikaner business and political communities. One wonders what the future will hold for new political groups among Afrikaners. Secondly, will the most recent urban migrants in the United States (American blacks and Puerto Ricans) and in South Africa (Africans) find it possible to break through existing obstacles and acquire political power? The thesis of this article argues that urban political power is the prerequisite to economic and social mobility. With political power, mobility will develop; without it, stagnation and frustration will prevail. For both nations a resolution of these questions is critical.

REFERENCES

1. Bureau of Census and Statistics, Pretoria, *Union Statistics for Fifty Years: Jubilee Issue 1910–1960*, Pretoria, 1960, A–18. The actual statistics are: 1946, urban English, 833,654, and urban Afrikaans, 821,561; 1951, urban English, 949,224, and urban Afrikaans, 1,035,214.
2. In particular, see George W. Pierson, 'The M-Factor in American History', *American Quarterly*, Summer 1962 Supplement, 275–89. Pierson argues that social and economic mobility have been unique influences in American history.
3. NEUMARK, S. DANIEL, *Economic Influences on the South African Frontier, 1652–1836*, Stanford University Press, Stanford, 1957, 172–86. Neumark suggests that the South African frontier was an exchange economy, 'linked directly with either local or

foreign markets. . . .' Although there is some evidence to support
Neumark's thesis, the rise of urban concentrations on the
American frontier indicates that commercial agriculture and
division of labour was far more extensive on the American
frontier than on the South African.

4. GREENE, EVARTS B., and HARRINGTON, VIRGINIA D.,
American Population before the Federal Census of 1790, Columbia
University Press, New York, 1932, 22.

5. Ibid., 101.

6. Ibid., 118.

7. Ibid., 178.

8. Ibid., 58.

9. Ibid., 102.

10. WADE, RICHARD C., *The Urban Frontier: The Rise of Western
Cities, 1790–1830*, Harvard University Press, Cambridge, Mass.,
1959, 194.

11. Ibid., 195–6.

12. BOORSTIN, DANIEL J., *The Americans: The National Experience*,
Random House, New York, 1965, 117.

13. BILLINGTON, RAY ALLEN, *Westward Expansion: A History of
the American Frontier*, The Macmillan Company, New York, 2nd
edn., 1960, 7.

14. THEAL, GEORGE MCCALL, *History of South Africa from 1795–
1872*, George Allen & Unwin, London, 1889, IV, 42.

15. Loc. cit.

16. Ibid., IV, 174.

17. GROSSKOPF, J. F. W., *Economic Report: Rural Impoverishment and
Rural Exodus* (Part I of *The Poor White Problem in South Africa:
Report of the Carnegie Commission*, 5 parts), Pro Ecclesia-Drukkery,
Stellenbosch, 1932, 51.

18. These estimates based on Eric Walker's estimate of 260,000
whites in South Africa in 1865: Eric A. Walker, *South Africa,
Rhodesia, and the Protectorates* (Vol. VIII of A. P. Newton and E.
A. Benians (eds.), *The Cambridge History of the British Empire*,
8 vols.), Cambridge University Press, 1936, 771–2. Laurence
Salomon cites figures of 350,000 in 1865 which would make the
per capita share even less: Laurence Salomon, 'The Economic
Background to the Revival of Afrikaner Nationalism', in Jeffrey
Butler (ed.), *Boston University Papers in African History*, I, Boston
University Press, 1964, 222.

19. GROSSKOPF, op. cit., 51.

20. *Statistical Year-Book of the Union of South Africa, 4—1915–1916*,
U.G. 41—1916, Government Printing and Stationery Office,
Pretoria, 1917, 159.

21. *The Statistical History of the United States from Colonial Times to the Present*, Fairfield, Stamford, Connecticut, 1965, 427.

22. NEUMARK, op. cit., 172–86. In spite of Neumark's thesis, the evidence suggests that the frontier regions of South Africa maintained only limited contact with the outside world.

23. WALKER, ERIC A., *The Great Trek*, A. and C. Black, London, 4th edn. 1960.

24. DE KIEWIET, C. W., *A History of South Africa: Social and Economic*, Clarendon Press, Oxford, 1941.

25. PATTERSON, SHEILA, *The Last Trek: A Study of the Boer People and the Afrikaner Nation*, Routledge & Kegan Paul, London, 1957.

26. *Report of Commission In Re Pretoria Indigents, 1905*, Government Printing and Stationery Office, Pretoria, 1905, 12–13.

27. BOORSTIN, op. cit., 3–48.

28. The growth of the European population in South Africa was seriously retarded by the policy of the Dutch East India Company, which stopped all immigration in 1707. Not until the arrival of the British in the nineteenth century was immigration resumed: George McCall Theal, *History of Africa South of the Zambesi: From the Settlement of the Portuguese at Sofala in September 1505 to the Conquest of the Cape Colony by the British in September 1795*, George Allen & Unwin, London, 1907, II, 474.

29. DE KIEWIET, op. cit., 70–2; Walker, op. cit., 770.

30. The figure of 800,000 is an estimate based on Walker, op. cit., 773; Salomon, op. cit., 223; *Official Year Books of the Union*, 1–7, Government Printing and Stationery Office, Pretoria, 1917–24; and *Union Statistics for Fifty Years*, op. cit., C–7.

31. WITTKE, CARL, *We Who Built America: the Saga of the Immigrant*, Prentice-Hall, New York, 1939, xvi.

32. HOFSTADTER, RICHARD, *The Age of Reform: From Bryan to F. D. R.*, Alfred A. Knopf, New York, 1955, 38–9.

33. HANDLIN, OSCAR, *Boston's Immigrants: A Study in Acculturation*, Harvard University Press, Cambridge, Mass., rev. and enlarged edn. 1959, 54–87.

34. Ibid., 242, Table V.

35. Ibid., 243, Table VI.

36. Ibid., 244, Table VII.

37. Ibid., 250–1, Table XIII.

38. Ibid., 62.

39. Ibid., 250–1, Table XIII.

40. Ibid., 205.

41. HANDLIN, OSCAR, *The Uprooted: The Epic Story of the Great Migrations that Made the American People*, Little, Brown, Boston, 1951, 226; and Barbara Miller Solomon, *Ancestors and Immigrants:*

A Changing New England Tradition, Harvard University Press, Cambridge, Mass., 1956, 48.

42. SOLOMON, op. cit., 47.

43. Ibid., 48.

44. All statistics in this paragraph are taken from United States Bureau of the Census, *Special Reports: Occupations at the Twelfth Census: 1900*, Government Printing Office, Washington, 1904, 494–9.

45. *Report of the Transvaal Indigency Commission, 1906–8*, T. G. 13—1908, Government Printing and Stationery Office, Pretoria, 1908, 10; *Third Interim Report of the Industrial and Agricultural Requirements Commission*, U.G. 40—1941, Government Printer, Pretoria, 1941, 10; Salomon, op. cit., 225, n. 24.

46. *Results of a Census of the Transvaal Colony and Swaziland Taken on the Night of Sunday the 17th April, 1904*, Waterlow, London, 1906, vii and xiii, Plate II; *Report of the Unemployment Investigation Committee*, U.G. 30—1932, Government Printer, Pretoria, 1932, 7.

47. *Results of a Census of the Transvaal, 1904*, op. cit., xxvi.

48. Ibid., xxv.

49. SALOMON, op. cit., 226, Table I, as found in S. Pauw, *Die Beroepsarbeid van die Afrikaner in die Stad*, Pro Ecclesia-Drukkery, Stellenbosch, 1946, 122, Table VII.

50. *Census of the Union of South Africa, 1911*, U.G. 32—1912, Government Printing and Stationery Office, Pretoria, 1913, liv.

51. Office of Census and Statistics, *Fourth Census of the Population of the Union of South Africa, 4th May, 1926, Report*, U.G. 4—1931, Government Printer, Pretoria, 1931, 79.

52. *Union Statistics for Fifty Years*, op. cit., A-18.

53. *Report of the Economic and Wage Commission (1925)*, U.G. 14—1926, Cape Times, Cape Town, 1926, 106. For a good discussion of the motivations see Salomon, op. cit., 226–33.

54. *Hearings of the Transvaal Indigency Commission, 1906–8*, op. cit., 189–93 and Diagrams I, J, K which follow page 192, provide an excellent explanation of the fragmentation of landholdings under the inheritance system.

55. *Report of the Transvaal Indigency Commission, 1906–8*, op. cit., 10; Salomon, op. cit., 229.

56. *Report of Commission In Re Pretoria Indigents, 1905*, op. cit., 7; *Report of the Transvaal Indigency Commission, 1906–8*, op. cit., 12, 15; Cape of Good Hope, *Report of the Select Committee on the Poor White Question*, A-10—1906, Cape Times, Cape Town, 1906, iv; Grosskopf, op. cit., 109–10.

57. *Hearings of the Transvaal Indigency Commission*, op. cit., 107–8.

58. SALOMON, op. cit., 225, and M. H. De Kock, *Selected Subjects in the Economic History of South Africa*, Juta, Cape Town, 1924, 283.
59. Cape of Good Hope, *Minutes of Evidence, Select Committee on Poor White Question*, op. cit., 35.
60. GROSSKOPF, op. cit., vii–viii.
61. *Population of South Africa, 1926, Report*, op. cit., 79, 193–4. All statistics in this paragraph are for the six largest cities.
62. South African Railways and Harbours, *Special Bulletin No. 135: European Labour on the South African Railways and Harbours*, Office of the General Manager of Railways and Harbours, Johannesburg, 1929, 318.
63. *Population of South Africa, 1926, Report*, op. cit., 193–4.
64. Union of South Africa, *Census, 1946*, V: *Occupations and Industries*, U.G. 41—1954, Government Printer, Pretoria, 1955, 42–55.
65. Loc. cit.
66. Loc. cit.
67. Republic of South Africa, *House of Assembly Debates* (Hansard), First Session, Third Parliament, 16 Sept. 1966, 2185, 2143.
68. Republic of South Africa, *Population Census, 1960*, 6: *Industry*, Government Printer, Pretoria, 1969, 62–3.
69. 'The Expanding World of Afrikaner Business', Supplement to the *Financial Mail*, 30 July 1965, 7–24.
70. 'Afrikaners in an Economic "Backlog",' Johannesburg *Star*, 17 Nov. 1967.
71. SALOMON, op. cit., 237–42.

14

G. V. DOXEY

ENFORCED RACIAL STRATIFICATION IN THE SOUTH AFRICAN LABOUR MARKET

The South African economy today is highly developed and becoming increasingly diversified. It is ranked by the World Bank within the middle-income powers and its inhabitants enjoy the highest *per capita* incomes on the African continent.[1] Nevertheless the labour market remains rigidly defined along racial lines, giving substance to both the narrow and wider interpretations of the doctrine of Apartheid. In the narrow economic sense Apartheid preserves and reinforces the economic *status quo* which divides the labour market into racial compartments and which, while permitting interracial economic co-operation, limits as strongly as possible any permanent spill-over from one racial labour compartment to another. The role of each race group in the economy is rigidly defined. The traditional prejudice of white South Africans is against undertaking that which is regarded as 'Kaffir' work below the dignity of the white man. This is reserved for non-whites; while the latter for their part are only occasionally permitted to undertake jobs considered to be the preserve of whites. This racial compartmentalization of the labour market is accomplished through custom and an ever-widening range of laws and administrative regulations.

With the development of the Bantustan concept the arguments for a racially divided labour market have been given a new force. Africans, it is suggested, can enjoy freedom from restrictions in their 'homelands', but those who wish to work in the 'white areas' can do so only within the framework of the laws governing labour mobility and job classifications. The various influx regulations are now rigidly applied to govern the flow of African workers to or from any particular area. In their attempt to give substance to the concept of the Bantu home-lands the authorities have considerably widened the scope of restrictions under Bantu labour regulations. As the demand for labour expands with the spread of industry, Africans are still allowed to enter the advanced economy, but only with the status of temporary workers, without any guarantee of residen-tial tenure for either themselves or their families. The result is that the natural process of labour migration from the rural to the urban areas which characterizes all industrializing societies is being deliberately prevented. The complicated legal structure now governing the labour market aims to make permanent the traditional migratory system which characterized its early development. It is argued in defence of this policy that the number of African workers in the white areas could be reduced without serious effect on the economy, by a combination of influx control, more effective use of labour, increased mechani-zation, and the development of the Bantu homelands.

The South African labour market also includes people of mixed racial origin (Coloured people), East Indians, and some other non-white groups such as Chinese. Even if, therefore, the dream of a South Africa divided between white and African could be realized, the problem would still remain of finding homelands for the other non-white races. The interdependency of all groups determines the continued economic progress of the country and it will never be possible to devise a set of completely independent racially defined economies. South African industri-alization began with racial co-operation, and without it the development of the diamond and gold-mining industry in the nineteenth century would not have been possible.[2]

Before considering the efficiency of the present situation it would be, therefore, useful to review the historical forces which moulded the present South African labour market.

The diamond discoveries of the 1860s rudely disrupted the paternal agrarian economy which had characterized South Africa since the seventeenth century. Both white and black were thrust into the newly developing international economy.

No longer was the Boer able to enjoy the splendid isolation which he had sought when he trekked from the Cape of Good Hope in the 1830s to found the new Republics of the Transvaal and the Free State. The immense wealth of Kimberley and the Witwatersrand became a magnet which attracted capital and adventurers from the world over. It was the beginning of a universal industrial society in which white and black came to play significant though widely differing roles: the white as capitalist or entrepreneur and skilled artisan or overseer, and the black as basic labourer. The capitalists and financiers concentrated their activities in Kimberley and Johannesburg and they were mainly English or European immigrants (Uitlanders). Their expertise and ability to raise the considerable capital needed for the more complicated mining processes placed them in the position to exploit South Africa's mineral wealth.

The Afrikaner farmers were content either to continue as farmers or to try their luck on the diamond fields of Kimberley where the initial impact of the discoveries had attracted fortune-hunters from the world over. Some were also able to enjoy reasonable prosperity through mining royalties and retire to a 'dorp' on the proceeds of the sale of their farms to the mining companies. For many, however, the future was less rosy. Untutored in the ways of an advanced economy, they proved unable to cope with the more wily foreigners; gradually they emerged as a new class of wage-earners often without any special attributes in the labour market other than the fact that they were white. Thus there began the 'poor white' problem which was to persist until the 1940s.[3] It was made worse by the conventional wisdom which refused to permit whites to fall to the level of Africans, and the prevailing attitude of whites who saw all manual labour as fit only for non-whites.

The Africans who were drawn into the new industrial society were primitive tribesmen with little or no knowledge of a market economy. Their needs were simple and they became 'target' workers. At first they were only interested in earning the price of a rifle, and when after a few months work they had acquired this longed-for treasure, they asked for nothing more from European civilization and headed back by the quickest path to the native kraal.[4] As time went on they acquired the urge to satisfy other wants, and a challenge to manhood became the goal of the many who were to offer their labour on the mines. Thus began the migratory system under which Africans commuted to work for varying periods to the advanced economy leaving their wives and families in the traditional economy.[5]

What began by choice of the Africans later became the cornerstone of Apartheid and led to mounting inefficiencies and injustices in the labour market. The primitive simplicity of the average African from the start ensured his easy relegation to the role of basic labourer. Few remained long enough in the new environment to grow attuned to its character. They had no capital, no skills, and no leadership. They lacked cohesion, so that unlike their proletarian counterparts in other parts of the world they were unable to organize.[6] All they had was their labour and this could be easily exploited. Being cheap and in plentiful supply they formed a key factor enabling South African industrialism to begin.

In the early stages it was necessary to 'induce' Africans to forsake the tribal areas to work in the money economy by the imposition of such regressive devices as the poll tax, which is still levelled on Africans today. As time went on, rural impoverishment also contributed to African migration; they were forced to seek work in the advanced economy in order to subsidize their subsistence agriculture. With the spread of European land-occupation, the consequent contraction of the permissible area for African cultivation and pasture, and growing population pressure, the need to seek work in the advanced economy became imperative.[7] The pressure to migrate permanently from the rural areas grew, but unlike their white counterparts the Africans were to find that, as the years went by, the hurdles which they had to overcome to settle elsewhere than in the Reserves grew more and more rigorous, while conditions in their areas grew worse.

The mining industry also set a pattern for the South African labour market by recruiting male workers and housing them in compounds on mine property for periods of nine to eighteen months. There was little regard for the family or the conjugal needs of the men. While this suited the needs of mining, and later was made essential by the heavy recruitment of workers from neighbouring territories, secondary industry has found it increasingly difficult to cope with a labour force in a continual state of turnover. Under such conditions, there is little incentive

to train workers beyond a basic level, and workers feel little identity with their employers. Nevertheless, the authorities have to
this day consistently sought to enact laws closely linked with a
desire to maintain the migratory system and preserve the tribal
character of the so-called Bantu homelands.[8] When linked with
the laws governing non-whites generally, it can be described as
essentially an attempt to make primitivism the permanent
feature of African life.

With the extension of industrialism in South Africa there
developed an acute shortage of skilled artisans to work in the
mines. At first diamond mining was relatively uncomplicated,
but with the need for more advanced mining methods and
consequently greater capital the day of the individual digger
operating with one or two African helpers came to an end. With
the development of scientific methods of mining and the opening
up of underground workings in 1885, there was need to import
professionals.[9] A new element was thus introduced into the
labour market which through its scarcity value played a vital
part in enlarging the disparity between white and non-white
wages. The fact that these newcomers were white made it
convenient for them to take over the existing prejudices towards
non-whites. Using the initial advantage of scarcity, the new
artisan class rapidly entrenched themselves and concentrated
not only on maintaining a high level of wages for themselves,
but on resorting to rigid 'closed shop' principles to maintain
their supremacy and prevent non-white inroads into their
sphere of the labour market. At first they could easily hold their
position because of the relative unsophistication of the bulk of
the non-white workers. What began by custom, reinforced by
the universal belief that Africans were largely uncivilized or
uncivilizable, was gradually to be backed by legislation. By
whites trade unionism was seen as the means by which white
supremacy could be maintained.

What began in industry as essentially a move by skilled trade
unionists to protect themselves from being ousted by less skilled
workers, gradually spread to all occupational planes; whereas
race was initially coincidental, with the non-white not being
regarded as worth consideration, the advance of industrialism and
non-white emergence made the purely 'colour' factor of far greater
importance in determining rigidity in the labour market.[10]

The later attempts of trade unionists to organize non-white workers were met with new legislation limiting the scope of such unions, and in many cases the organizers were silenced through the operation of such laws as the Suppression of Communism Act, which through its broad definition of communism made it relatively easy to limit the activities of non-white labour leaders.[11]

The poor white problem was to dominate thinking for many years, and its shadow still casts itself over the labour market today. Many of the whites who chose to try their luck in Kimberley or Johannesburg were largely backward subsistence farmers who had no acquaintance with a money economy and who had had little or no formal education. Essentially they were equipped for little else than the 'Kaffir' work which they despised as beneath the dignity of the white man. Following the South African War at the turn of the century the problem grew worse, and by 1932 it was estimated that about 10 per cent of the white population, or about 220,000 people, were poor whites.[12] It was not simply a problem of poverty but of the state of mind which accompanied it. How could one be expected to compete with people whom the dictates of tradition designated inferior? There was no attempt to look at the problem of poverty on a national basis. Action was nearly always influenced by the notion that non-whites should not be entitled to employment while any whites were unemployed. This concept persists to this day in spite of changes in the economy and increasing labour shortages. What began as a notion of protecting whites from falling to the level of non-whites gave way to the notion of preventing non-whites from reaching the occupational levels of whites, even if this led to a shortage of workers to fill white jobs or if jobs were filled by whites less efficient than non-whites.[13] Thus it is thought desirable to mechanize or automate rather than suffer the humiliation of having non-whites work in white jobs. Throughout the inter-war period policy was concerned with the creation of artificial bolsters to poor whites in order to maintain them at an economic level above that of 'uncivilized' living.*

* In the interim what most whites failed to appreciate was that the non-whites were growing in sophistication and that by the 1950s South Africa probably had within its borders the most sophisticated non-white population in Africa.

The economy and the organization of society as a whole became geared to the creation and subsidization of a privileged inner white group, able to maintain living standards comparable with the highest in the world largely through the enforced acceptance of lower wages by the non-whites who crowded the lower levels of the labour markets.

The legalization of colour stratification in the South African industrial labour market began in the gold-mining industry with the enactment in 1926 of the Mines and Works Act, which effectively barred non-whites from advancing in mining activities. Since then all attempts in the face of problems arising from the fixed price of gold (even on the part of the authorities) to allow a wider use of African labour on the mines have been successfully resisted by the all-white mineworkers' union. Gradually, through new legislation and amendments to earlier legislation, a framework of legal controls has been created which dictate the occupational patterns of all the inhabitants of South Africa.

These regulations have become increasingly difficult to circumvent. The movement of Africans to the urban areas is now rigidly controlled in keeping with the concept of 'Separate Bantu Nations'. Speaking in the South African Parliament the Minister of Bantu Administration and Development said that his object was to give shape to every Bantu nation in accordance with its own national character:

the white nation is superior to all other nations in South Africa . . . it demonstrates our duty as guardians. . . . It also demonstrates the utter folly of saying that a minority government is ruling South Africa. Our policy is based on the facts . . . [of] separateness and the diversity of the various Bantu nations in South Africa as separate national entities set on separate courses to separate destinies. The Bantu in the White Areas are here for the work we have to offer them and which they also need. . . . They are not here to anchor themselves. . . . We must help the Bantu to maintain their national ties . . . with their homelands and their families, even if they are born here in the white areas. In the 'white areas' the Bantu has always been subject to restrictions . . . not because we regard him as an inferior being . . . [but because] we regard him as being present in another man's country.[14]

This statement is all the more remarkable when one considers that there are now entire generations of Africans who have had no links whatsoever with the so-called Bantu homelands and whose only home is in the so-called white areas. There is thus not only a valiant attempt to give substance to the illusion that South Africa is a white society, but a belief that it is possible to create some form of political separateness while continuing economic co-operation in the country as a whole. The immense social problems and the resulting frustrations and resentments of the system can only be contained by a zealous enforcement of security and denial of political activity on the part of non-whites. For over three centuries South Africans have pursued the illusion that somehow their non-whites will disappear from the scene. They have always found it impossible to visualize a society in which colour might cease to determine a man's stake in the labour market. Instead they have nurtured a racial ego-centricism which refuses to judge a man by his qualities rather than by his colour, and which clings in a variety of ways to the notion that there exist 'civilized' and 'uncivilized' labour. Thus ultimately no white man can permit himself to do menial tasks.[15]

There is every reason why the Bantu areas should be developed. They are at present the depressed areas of South Africa, and government policies to encourage the diversification of these and the modernization of agriculture are to be commended, but not for the official reasons. It is difficult to visualize how an advanced economy can operate indefinitely with dependence upon labour from 'foreign' areas. In cases where there is an overall shortage of labour it might sometimes be sensible to recruit temporary workers from abroad, as has been the case in the German economy. But the South African situation is different. The so-called foreign workers are in fact South Africans, many of whom under Apartheid are expected to spend the greater part of their lives in the so-called white areas. The costs in human and economic terms are immense.

In order to prove his right to be in any area the African must be a collector of documents from the day of his birth to the day of his death. ... For thousands of Africans these laws result in broken families, in unemployment, in poverty, malnutrition, insecurity and instability, and in a state of hopelessness. ... Millions of rands are spent in administering these laws, and millions of man-hours are wasted in the attempt to enforce these unenforceable laws.[16]

The complications which result from these procedures are immense. It has, for instance, become official government policy severely to curtail the number of Africans in the Western Cape, ostensibly to protect the Coloured people, even though industrialists complain that there are insufficient Coloured workers willing to undertake heavy labour jobs.[17] They are therefore forced to make do with inadequate workers, while they and African work-seekers must undergo endless bureaucratic procedures to obtain satisfaction. An African must, for instance, register with a labour bureau in his home area, and if he accepts a job in the Western Cape he may only work there for one year and it is illegal for him to break the contract or to change jobs. An employer on the other hand has to register first with the Department of Labour to find out whether there are any suitable Coloured workers available for the job he has, and only after that may he apply to the Department of Bantu Administration for the Africans he needs. If there are no suitable Africans already in the area and available for employment he must then pay 15 rand to import 'contract' workers. The frustrations endured by both employer and worker under such a system are self-evident.

The economy as a whole does not escape the effects of the attempts to stratify the labour market legally. In the past some at least of the impact of rigidity was overcome by subterfuge. During the war, for instance, non-whites were used in many areas of work which had been regarded as white spheres, and it is often the custom to utilize the services of non-whites in jobs normally requiring skilled workmen, though at labourers' wage-rates. Before the enforcement of racial classification, it was not uncommon in the Cape for instance for persons of different races to attempt 'occupational passing'.[18] In many cases Coloured people worked in positions normally considered as reserved for whites only. Employers are often unwilling to question the race of job applicants where there is a shortage of personnel in the particular sphere. In most cases the people concerned would in all appearances seem to be white, but might live as Coloured people or belong to families who were predominantly darker in complexion. Since 1 August 1966, however, it has become compulsory for all citizens of the Republic over the age of 16 to possess identity cards and be able to produce these to any authorized person.[19] In each case the race identity of the person concerned is shown on the card. The complications are numerous and there have been numbers of cases where members of the same family have been classified differently. This is not surprising when one considers that the main definition of a white person in South Africa is a person who is generally accepted as white. It was estimated in 1966, for instance, that some 148,000 people on the racial borderline had not applied for identity cards for fear, among other things, that they would lose their employment.[20] In the interest of racial purity it was deemed necessary to deprive individuals of their livelihood and in many cases to accentuate the already serious shortage of workers in the white sphere of the labour market.

A case can no longer be effectively argued for the retention of the industrial colour bar. Certainly in the past one of the enabling factors for the beginnings of South African industrialization was the existence of a supply of cheap basic labour. Without this the high-cost gold-mining industry would have been unable to continue operations. It was the exploitation of low-wage African labourers that subsidized the industry which generated the wider industrialization of South Africa. Low productivity, excessively high 'white' wages, combined with a relatively small protected market, have prevented South Africa from repeating in secondary industry the pattern of the mining generally. It has not been able to repeat the performance of a Japan or a Hong Kong for these reasons, in spite of the availability of low-wage basic labourers. The migratory system furthermore acts as a major stumbling-block to increased productivity. Even where they are permitted to do so, few employers are willing to invest in any sensible training of workers who remain with them for short periods. Furthermore workers, during lengthy sojourns in their 'homelands', often forget what they were taught in the advanced economy.

The problem is made worse by the fact that with the rapidly expanding economy the demand for skilled workers of all types has now expanded beyond the resources of the white group. Immigration of artisans from Britain and elsewhere has been one sought-after solution, but industrialists and other employers continue to complain that they are not able to meet their labour needs. In an attempt to meet these problems the South African

T

Government created in 1964 an Advisory Council for Manpower Research and Planning. It became clear that there was
an urgent need to increase productivity in order to combat a
growing problem of inflation. Experts in various fields warn that
the country's economic growth cannot be maintained unless
there is a more intelligent use of labour resources including the
development of non-white skills. The arguments are backed by
the suggestion that a proper utilization of non-white labour and
a concerted effort to increase its efficiency will be the key to
granting higher wages to non-whites.

The paradox of the South African situation is that while it
can no longer be convincingly argued that non-whites are a
threat in the labour market to whites, the restrictions on their
economic advance are now more severe than ever before. In its
November 1966 report the Education Panel appointed by the
Witwatersrand Council of Education pointed out that 'practically all economically active whites are now engaged in skilled
work, so that if the proportion of the total population which is
engaged in such work is to rise (as it must do) all recruits to the
skilled ranks needed to bring about this increase must be non-
whites'. They went on to claim that 'further economic growth
in South Africa is quite impossible without the constant shifting
of the boundaries between work done by whites and non-whites
. . . a good deal more rapidly than in the past.'

Meanwhile, in spite of these pressures, the Government
continues to think largely in terms of permitting non-whites
advance only in those areas designated for their particular race
group. In June 1966, for instance, the Prime Minister pointed
out that the authorities concerned with non-white education
were giving particular attention to technical training in order
to relieve the pressure on skilled manpower, but only within the
framework of the Government's policy.[21]

In 1956 the Government amended the Industrial Concilia-
tion Act which permitted the Minister of Labour, among other
things, to authorize investigations into the need for the reservation of defined types of work for specified racial groups whenever it appeared to the Minister that such measures should be
taken to safeguard the economic welfare of any of the groups.
In introducing the measure the then Minister pointed out that
it was 'a precautionary measure to safeguard the standards of

any other race'.[22] In the circumstances which have prevailed then and since, the measure can only be viewed as stemming from purely irrational racial prejudice rather than being based upon valid economic assumptions. Nevertheless, ten years later some 17 job reservations have been made in various sectors of industry employing 20 per cent of the labour force. While some flexibility has been shown in meeting changing conditions, the attitude of the authorities, as in all matters concerning race, has been largely to ignore the protests and complaints of those who must contend with the consequences of the measures.

In 1956, for instance, the jobs of waiters, wine stewards, pages, 'barboys', and others in the liquor and catering trades in the Western Cape and certain Natal towns were reserved for Coloured or Asian people, and Africans already employed had to leave. In spite of pressures from the hoteliers and numerous applications for exemptions on the grounds that the hotel tourist trade was suffering, the Minister of Labour simply replied that he regarded 'the hotel attendants' trade here in the Cape as a trade which is pre-eminently suited for the Coloured'.[23]

In the footwear industry, for instance, white workers may now not be replaced by Coloured people and Coloured people may not be replaced by Africans.

The absurdity of such measures is self-evident. Employers are forced to give up the services of workers who may be pre-eminently suitable, and utilize workers of a different race who may be totally unsuitable in contrast to those they are replacing. Employers and employees are placed in an economic straitjacket which has profound effects on the sound working of the economy. Advanced planning is made difficult, expensive training schemes may be shelved for fear of a sudden change in government attitudes, and above all the morale of the work force is undermined and worker productivity remains low. The freedom of the individual to choose an occupation to his own bent is denied, while the rigidities make impossible the workings of a free market for labour and prevent the best use of the country's manpower resources. There is thus the paradox of a market system where the sphere of employment is being subjected to a degree of control only equalled in a totalitarian command economy, the only difference being that in South

Africa controls upon labour have no economic basis nor can they be justified upon an economic theory.

The disparities between white and non-white incomes which were set in the early days of South African industrialism have also persisted. Although African and other non-white wages have been increasing, the average wage ratio between skilled and unskilled labour changed little in the decade from 1954, being 4·6 to 1 in 1955 and 4·5 to 1 in 1964.[24]

There now seems little likelihood of fundamental change through peaceful evolution. White South Africans continue to chase comforting illusions and remain unwilling to concede to non-whites full opportunities to develop their potentials within the framework of the economy as a whole. Their thoughts and policies are guided by a combination of feelings of racial superiority, fear of non-white reprisals, and blind spots which prevent them from seeing South African society in terms of an integrated whole. They are unable to concede freedom, either political or economic, to the majority of South Africans, on the mistaken assumption that to do so will destroy their society. They cannot conceive that non-whites are capable of becoming part of a new dynamic society, and that given greater freedom and if treated more justly non-whites would contribute a great deal to the creation of an enriched country, not only materially but also in mind and spirit.

There is no reason why more flexibility could not be allowed within the labour market even within a rigid political framework. Without this the economy will suffer and economic growth will become increasingly difficult to maintain. Even if the present population of 18 million were regarded, for economic purposes, as a single entity, there would still be problems resulting from the high proportion of untrained or inadequately trained workers. This would, nevertheless, be preferable to the white entrenchment guaranteed by the several nations concept. It is also unlikely that the Bantustans will ever be capable of becoming completely viable—the interdependency upon the wider economy will remain, particularly for markets for their 'new' industries.

The key to greater efficiency and productivity in the South African labour market is to permit a free movement of labour of all races. At present the controls upon the horizontal and vertical mobility of labour do little else than create bottlenecks in all sectors of the labour market and seriously impair the efficient use of labour potential. A free market for labour would encourage employers to make greater efforts to train and improve the productivity of the labour force.

It seems unlikely that whites will be persuaded that, while the economy continues to expand, there can be no threat to their position as workers through the vertical mobility of qualified non-whites into areas of labour shortages. But to permit this would be to open a 'Pandora's box' with all the many challenges to the myths of Apartheid. Meanwhile whites prefer to cling to the belief that the old racial order can be maintained through vigilant emphasis upon the building up of a security network capable of withstanding any aggressive onslaught.

REFERENCES

1. REID, ESCOTT, *The Future of the World Bank*, 1965 60 *et seq.*
2. DOXEY, G. V. *The Industrial Colour Bar in South Africa*, Oxford University Press, Cape Town, 1961.
3. DOXEY, op. cit., 13.
4. VON WEBER, ERNST, *Vier Jahre in Afrika*, Brockhaus, Leipzig, 1878, *2*, 443, *et seq.*
5. See S. T. van der Horst, *Native Labour in South Africa*, Oxford University Press, Cape Town, 1942.
6. DOXEY, op. cit., 19.
7. There have been various detailed studies of the problems of the 'Reserves'; see particularly the Tomlinson Commission (V.G. 61/55) and the Native Economic Commission (V.G. 22/32).
8. HUTT, W. H., *The Economics of the Colour Bar*, André Deutsch, for the Institute of Economic Affairs, London, 1964, 92.
9. WILLIAMS, GARDNER, *The Diamond Mines of South Africa*, Macmillan, London, 1902, and Sir Theodore Gregory, *Ernest Oppenheimer and the Economic Development of Southern Africa*, Oxford University Press, Cape Town, 1962.
10. DOXEY, op. cit., 24.
11. ROUX, EDWARD, *Time Longer Than Rope*, University of Wisconsin Press, Madison, 1968.
12. *The Poor White Problem in South Africa: Report of the Carnegie Commission*, Pro Ecclesia-Drukkery, Stellenbosch, 1932.
13. HUTT, op. cit.
14. *Hansard*, 11, 13 Oct. 1966, 4131–7.

15. HUTT, op. cit.
16. *Memorandum on the Application of the Pass Laws and Influx Control*, Black Sash, Johannesburg, quoted in *A Survey of Race Relations in South Africa, 1966*, South African Institute of Race Relations, Johannesburg, 1967.
17. *Survey of Race Relations, 1966*, op. cit., 202.
18. DOXEY, G. V., 'Racial Stratification in the Labour Market in Relation to Labour Turnover among Non-Europeans in the Cape Peninsula', in Proceedings of the Social Science conference relating to problems arising from the structure and functioning of a multiracial society, University of Natal, Durban, 1956.
19. The Population Register Act.
20. TAYLOR, MRS. C. D., M.P., *Hansard*, 7, 15 Sept. 1966, 2155–6.
21. *Survey of Race Relations, 1966*, op. cit., 204.
22. *Hansard*, 23 June 1956, 276.
23. *Hansard*, 11, 11 Oct. 1966, 3978.
24. HORWOOD, O. P. F., quoted in *Survey of Race Relations, 1966*, op. cit., 211.

KURT DANZIGER

MODERNIZATION AND THE LEGITIMATION OF SOCIAL POWER

The technological changes of industrialization are still sometimes seen as 'automatically' producing a type of social structure in which power conflicts can be fought out in relatively democratic forms. In view of the very long historical periods during which high levels of industrialization have been maintained in societies with profoundly undemocratic power structures, faith in such an outcome cannot be said to have a very firm basis in reality. If technological change does produce major changes in the power structure, it is only likely to do so in so far as it undermines the effectiveness of existing techniques of legitimation. Only when modernization affects the realm of 'ideas' does it become potentially subversive for the old forms of domination.

In order to trace such a development in a particular case, as for instance South Africa, it is inadequate to treat the realm of legitimating ideas in the abstract. Ideas can function to legitimate forms of social domination only in so far as they are able to appeal to real individuals with real social personalities. What is more, different forms of legitimation appeal to different kinds of people. A semi-literate farmer may be impressed by appeals founded on the Bible, but remain confused in the face of elaborate sophistries based on the notion of cultural relativism. For his son at the university, however, the situation may well be reversed. Changes in acceptable and effective techniques and symbols of legitimation must therefore involve important psychological changes. It is these psychological changes which mediate between changes on the level of technology and

284 SOUTH AFRICA: SOCIOLOGICAL PERSPECTIVES

changes in the way in which people think about the power
structure of their society. If modernization produces new kinds
of people, it is likely at least to lead to new forms of legitimation
and perhaps to new forms of domination.

Forms of Legitimation

A more systematic treatment of forms of legitimation is possible
in terms of two criteria: (a) the form of rationality on which the
appeal of the system of legitimating ideas is based; (b) the
salient focus of attachment for these ideas.[1] The first criterion
simply represents Weber's distinction between *wertrational* and
zweckrational: whether the institutions are legitimated in terms
of their intrinsic or their instrumental value. Thus, we must
distinguish between an appeal to group charisma which implies
the sacredness of *blankedom* as such, its divine mission, etc., and
a justification of white rule in terms of its greater efficiency in
satisfying the needs of both black and white. The second criterion
for distinguishing between systems of legitimating ideas refers
to the institutional or cultural sphere which is of special salience
for these ideas. Thus intrinsic or instrumental value may be
preferentially assigned either to a national–ethnic–cultural
entity or to the state as such—an important distinction where
the two do not coincide, as in South Africa. Thus supreme value
may be seen either in the Afrikaner nation and its culture or in
the State and its organs—not necessarily in both. But there is a
third institutional sphere to which legitimating ideas can become attached, the system of social and economic roles which
support those institutions that are neither political nor cultural.
The institutions of the capitalist economic system would be an
appropriate example here.

It is obvious that our two criteria always operate together, so
that attachment to cultural, political, or economic institutions
may be justified either in terms of their intrinsic or their instrumental value. Thus, the State may be regarded as the absolute
good, or it may be defended because it is the guarantee of the
stability of other institutions. Similarly, there is a difference
between an 'ideological' defence of capitalism in terms of 'freedom', let us say, and an instrumental justification of it because
it delivers the goods.

The historical changes which the dominant ideas of dominant groups undergo can be conveniently charted in terms of the criteria outlined above. Thus, it is possible to raise questions about the trend of development of legitimating ideas in terms of a shift (*a*) in the primary focus of reference of these ideas, and (*b*) in the predominant form of rationality which gives these ideas coherence as a system. Most systems of legitimation in fact undergo changes on both these dimensions, though they differ greatly in the speed with which these changes take place and the ease with which they can be detected. Such ideological changes are important in facilitating or obstructing actual changes in the pattern of domination in a society.

Modernization and Domination

Over the last two centuries, that is, since the beginning of massive industrialization in western Europe, it is possible to detect a close reciprocal relationship between the forms of domination and their legitimating ideas on the one hand, and the process of modernization on the other. Economic development is crucially affected by existing forms of domination; first, because such forms always imply a certain pattern of distribution of goods and services, and secondly, because they set limits to the productive human energy that can be mobilized in the service of modernization and industrialization. In fact, most forms of domination known to man are an obstacle rather than a help to economic development, as history, both recent and ancient, so convincingly shows. It is also clear, however, that men have more recently discovered several forms of domination that help rather than hinder the process of modernization.

If we examine the history of legitimating ideas in those societies which have demonstrated a relatively continuous pattern of economic growth, we find that changes in these ideas are not random but follow a very distinct pattern. In particular, we can detect a clear shift from a justification of existing institutions in terms of intrinsic value to their justification in terms of their instrumental utility or effectiveness. Secondly, we observe a shift from cultural to political and finally to economic institutions as the main focus for legitimating ideas. This process of ideological change is one which has occurred over and over again as new groups have been drawn into the modernization process.

The change in legitimating ideologies is closely related to actual changes in patterns of domination. Rigid systems of power and privilege based on the ascribed criterion of descent become replaced by more flexible institutional forms which allow for a sensitive balancing of the conflict of interests between dominators and dominated. At the same time, the influence of universalistic media of social exchange, like money and achievement-based status, extends over ever larger segments of social life, replacing the old particularistic exclusiveness of culturally or geographically defined groups. Such changes assist the process of economic development by preventing disrupting social upheavals, by making the more efficient employment of resources more likely, and by extending an adequate system of incentives to ever wider strata.

But this is certainly not an automatic and inevitable process.[2] For every society which shows a steady curve of economic progress one can point to another where early promises of progress have been utterly disappointed, and yet another whose path has been difficult, slow, and full of ups and downs. In all these cases, however, the forms of domination and the ideas that legitimate them will be seen to have stagnated or retrogressed along with the stagnation or retrogression of economic development, at least over the longer term. Perhaps the most striking examples of this alternative are to be found in Latin America, and one way of expressing the problem of African development is to ask whether it is to follow the Latin American path.

Even in South Africa the alternative of economic stagnation and periodic social disruption is not completely beyond the limits of possibility. Although it is true that the immense value of the country's mineral resources to the Western powers provides its ruling elite with an almost foolproof insurance against failure, a sufficient degree of inflexibility and stupidity just might ruin even this patient and powerful source of protection. It therefore becomes meaningful to ask whether the ruling ideas of the present ruling group are likely to present a significant obstacle to economic development in the foreseeable future. If they do, the resulting economic stagnation is likely to lead to social unrest of a kind that might conceivably pose a threat to the existing pattern of domination. On the other hand, if a reasonable rate of economic progress can be maintained the future of the present social system seems assured, at least in its essentials.

Afrikaner Nationalism as a Modernizing Elite

Before addressing ourselves to the problems of the future it is necessary to survey the achievements which the present ruling group already has to its credit. For the past two decades the group of Afrikaner Nationalists organized in a distinctive political party has successfully challenged the previously dominant position of the English-speaking elite. The two groups constituting white leadership have in fact changed places, those who were once a secondary elite are now predominant, and those who once had almost a monopoly of power and privilege now occupy a secondary place.

It is not necessary to emphasize here how much the two groups have in common. Obviously they both seek to preserve white privileges, but equally clearly they are both committed to goals of modernization and economic development. Certain differences in the relative emphasis placed on these two sets of goals should not be allowed to obscure the modernizing function of the Afrikaner elite. In fact, the most significant historical event which marked the reconstruction of the Afrikaner elite in its present form was the Eerste Ekonomiese Volkskongres of 1939. From that time on, the group that counted among Afrikaner Nationalists was the group that had unambiguously committed itself to the goals of economic self-aggrandizement, goals which in South Africa could not be pursued without a positive attitude to economic development in general. Indeed, while in power, this elite has proved itself to be truly a modernizing elite, and under its rule the processes of industrialization and urbanization have proceeded apace.[3] At no point have colour policies been allowed actually to halt overall economic development, although it is also true that they have probably slowed down the pace of that development. It is in fact arguable that the Afrikaner leadership has been much more effective as a modernizing elite than its predecessors; its greater emphasis on the economic role of the state, its less subservient position *vis-à-*

vis foreign economic influence, and its more ruthless maintenance of surface social stability have all worked in this direction.
These features of its policies can ultimately be traced to its
greater isolation from the rest of the world, both morally and
institutionally. Moral isolation promotes ruthlessness, for moral
condemnation by out-groups is ineffective; institutional isolation leads to greater reliance on one's own political and economic forms.

While the Afrikaner Nationalist elite was peculiarly isolated
from the rest of the world it was exceptionally close to those
broader strata on which its political success depended. From
this point of view the legitimating ideas of Apartheid in its
different versions have been remarkably successful. It is to this
factor, more than to any other, that this elite group owes its
victory, not only against the old elite, but also against the far
more dangerous African-Indian elite which began to make
meaningful demands after the end of World War II. Whereas the
ideals of Afrikaner Nationalism were most effective in mobilizing a very high proportion of its potential followers, the rival
claims to legitimacy by non-white nationalists succeeded in
mobilizing only a minority of the potentially much larger strata
to whom they might be expected to have some appeal.

Limits to Modernization

The fact that its present position of undisputed dominance was
won in sharp struggles against rival elites has left the present
Afrikaner elite with an ideological legacy that must exert a
negative effect on economic development in the long run. At an
abstract level these negative effects can be summarized under
two headings: (*a*) the prevalence of an ideology of coercion, and
(*b*) the failure to provide adequate economic incentives for the
majority of the population.[4] The ideology of coercion has not
only been heavily reinforced in the recent period of successful
struggle against rival claimants to power, it also has exceptionally deep roots in the history, both real and mythical, of the
Afrikaner elite. As long as it holds sway, the country will not be
permitted to develop those institutions for balancing conflicting
interests that are characteristic of advanced industrial societies.
This means that the institutions of this society are deprived of

that capacity for non-violent self-change without which the inevitable conflicts generated by continuous modernization become a permanent threat to the system. For the ideology of coercion the police remains the primary agent of conflict-resolution in perpetuity, but no known society has been able to maintain the more advanced levels of modernization in this manner. Unless non-coercive forms of handling the threat of social change can be found, a state of economic stagnation and sporadic violence will eventually come about.

The second major condition for the maintenance of a society at an advanced level of modernization is the provision of universal media of exchange which make possible not only the effective linking of all the units of a highly differentiated organism but also provide the only permanently effective technique for motivating individuals to make the goals of vast economic organizations their own. The most important of these media of exchange are money and achieved status.[5] The latter, like the former, is exchanged among individuals on a universalistic basis. Just as money designates the worth of scarce resources, so status designates the individual's worth on some valued achievement which is in relatively short supply. As money is the enemy of subsistence economy and payment in kind, so achievement status is incompatible with particularistic claims to prestige based on descent. The allocation of money and status on the basis of race rather than of achievement simply robs South African society of the best energies and potential talents of most of its members.[6] As long as this state of affairs exists, strict limits are set to economic progress and modernization.

Shifts in Patterns of Legitimation

What then are the chances that the governing elite will be able to rid itself of the twin evils of ideologically demanded coerciveness and racial particularism? Certainly, on the surface of social life nothing at present indicates any significant changes in regard to these matters. But before we dismiss the case as hopeless it is desirable to look below the surface at the evolution of the relevant ideological and psychological patterns.

On the ideological level certain trends have become clearly defined in the course of the past quarter-century. Whereas before 1948 even the most sophisticated legitimation of Afrikaner domination was entirely in terms of group charisma, generally based on religious parables, this type of literature had already become an embarrassment to the new rulers by 1960. Thus in 1947 the authoritative Professor Cronje could find no better justication for the then new principle of Apartheid than this:

Throughout the Scriptures there is evidence of the submission of one nation to another. In such cases the one holds the sceptre and the other bears the yoke. . . . Israel, the nation of God, will subdue the others, but the nations of the world will benefit from Israel because she is the bearer of God's revelation.[7]

By contrast, the apologetics of Apartheid current in the 1950s became secularized and appealed to group norms and cultural relativism.[8] More recently a distinctly instrumental line of defence has come into vogue. The existing pattern of domination is held to be justifiable, not because it is intrinsically good, but because it ensures continued economic progress. It is probably no accident that the first clear statements along these lines originate from some of the key architects of the present system; thus it is none other than Dr. Eiselen, long in charge of 'Bantu Affairs', who declares, 'The maintenance of White political supremacy over the country as a whole is a *sine qua non* for racial peace and economic prosperity in South Africa.'[9]

It would be a relatively straightforward research task to apply modern techniques of content-analysis to justifications of government policies that have appeared in the Afrikaans-language press since 1948. If this were done I suspect that it would be possible to demonstrate a clear historical tendency along the lines sketched above. If this trend were to continue it could be expected to have certain practical consequences. In particular, the instrumentalistic justification of a policy implies that there are other values than those intrinsic to the policy, values which this policy merely serves. No longer is one caught in a system of absolute values and sacred taboos, and so one's outlook gains considerably in flexibility. If racial domination is no longer justified because it is in the nature of God or of man, but because it leads to 'economic prosperity', then indeed it becomes possible to modify its forms in the interests of a presumably greater good. This means that rational criteria of efficiency replace divine sanctions. If it is politic to do so, one will, to take a trivial but well-known example, shake hands with a black man, though one's father might have considered such an act the betrayal of a divine mission. But then what is to stop one from sharing one's table and one's house on the same rational basis?

The shift to policies that are explicitly *zweckrational* and not *wertrational* robs one of the peculiar strength of one's previous ideological appeal. No compromises were to be tolerated in the field of racial discrimination, because the constant pressure of the oppressed would inevitably widen any breach, no matter how thin the end of the wedge. To entertain the possibility of compromise is to open the door to balancing and conflict-resolving mechanisms other than pure coercion. Slowly but surely the ideology of coercion becomes undermined. Similarly, one is tempted to adjust the effects of the economic colour bar so that universalistic achievement criteria begin to enter to a greater extent into the assignment of status. That the faint beginnings of such processes can be detected in South Africa is beyond question; what remains in doubt is whether these changes will keep pace with the demands of economic development. Apart from this there is also the question whether the rest of the world will always remain sufficiently preoccupied with its own problems to leave the South African elite to its own snail's pace of ideological development.

The Role of Self-Rationalization

At the beginning of this discussion it was indicated that various patterns of legitimating ideas had a differential appeal to various individuals. Ideologies do not arise, flourish, and decay in a vacuum, they arouse the passions of real men engaged in real social relationships. At least since the studies on *Autorität und Familie*, social psychologists have been sensitive to the intimate connection between ideology and personality.[10] Most of the empirical studies in this area, however, have been concerned with 'authoritarianism' as an ideology and as a personality pattern. In the present context we are pursuing a different line of investigation. Our concern is with the shift to legitimating ideas that are *zweckrational* or instrumentalist in nature; that is to say, a system of ideas that justifies existing institutions on grounds of effectiveness in satisfying human needs and aspirations. It is, of course, possible to defend authoritarian as well as democratic institutions on these grounds—the crucial feature lies in the *form* of justification, not in its objective referent.

At this stage we may advance the hypothesis that legitimating ideas with an instrumentalist orientation are likely to have a preferential appeal for individuals who display a particular personality pattern that has been referred to as *self-rationalization*, its original description going back to Karl Mannheim.[11] One speaks of self-rationalization when the individual treats his own life as an enterprise in which each step is controlled by reference to its calculated contribution to the success of the whole. The individual systematically evaluates his own actions in terms of their potential contribution to his career success. The subordination of other goals to that of success in a career involves a personality pattern based on the calculating control of impulse in the interests of a deliberately formulated life-plan.

In an empirical investigation by the present writer it was suggested that a convenient and valid index of the degree of self-rationalization might be derived from the 'future autobiography' which an individual produces in response to the request to write freely about his hopes, plans, and aspirations for the future.[12] High self-rationalization is revealed mainly by a very realistic level of planning, a relative absence of unrealistic fantasy and of non-career goals, a concentration on personal rather than community goals, a preoccupation with economic incentives, and the use of a well-articulated temporal structure shown by precise time references and orderly succession of life-stages. These characteristics are statistically interrelated and can be reliably assessed by means of a content-analysis of the future autobiographies.

In 1950 Professor Gordon Allport collected a number of future autobiographies from various groups of South African students at a number of universities and teacher training colleges.[13] The present writer subsequently analysed this material in terms of the index of self-rationalization described above, and in 1962 collected a further batch of future autobiographies from students in the same institution, faculty, and year of study as those in the original sample. A previously un-published comparative analysis of the average index of self-rationalization among English-speaking and Afrikaans-speaking white students revealed some interesting relationships. In 1950 the mean index of self-rationalization of the Afrikaans students was significantly below that of the English-speaking students (1 per cent level of significance), while in 1962 the difference between the two groups was no longer statistically significant, though the mean index for the Afrikaans group was still below that of the English group. On the other hand, there was a statistically significant (1 per cent level) rise in the index of self-rationalization from the Afrikaans sample tested in 1950 to the Afrikaans sample tested in 1962.

While these results are based on only 67 Afrikaans auto-biographies in 1950 and 86 in 1962 the force of the suggestion they imply is somewhat strengthened by certain additional data.* Thus the relative ranking of various groups of South African students on the index of self-rationalization is in line with sociological expectations: English-speaking whites, Afrikaans-speaking whites, Indians, and finally Africans a long way behind the others. Again, differences in the production of achievement fantasy among English-speaking and Afrikaans-speaking students parallel the findings with regard to self-rationalization, the former group being significantly higher also on this measure which has been frequently shown to be associated with modernizing attitudes to social life.[14] A final indication of this kind of difference comes from the analysis of the performance of English-speaking and Afrikaans-speaking children on certain tests of intelligence. The fact that the latter consistently perform more poorly than the former, even when differences in urbanization are taken into account, has been correctly interpreted as evidence for the better adaptation of the English-speaking children to the demands of a modernizing society.[15] It may be assumed that the kind of rationality required in certain intellectual tasks is not dissimilar to the kind of rationality demonstrated on the personal level by the pattern of self-rationalization.[16]

Both the lower starting-point of the Afrikaans group and the apparent narrowing of the gap between it and the English

* The number of English autobiographies was greater in each case.

U

group can readily be traced to differences in their degree of involvement in the modernizing sectors of the economy. The English-speaking section, which had settled in the country in the course of the nineteenth century, came from a society in which industrialization was already far advanced. For the most part they already possessed the skills and attitudes of people thoroughly adapted to the institutions of industrial capitalism, and it is not surprising that most of them preferred the towns to life on the veld. For a long period they practically monopolized trade and commerce, and in the mining industry they supplied all the managerial and entrepreneurial talent as well as the skilled work-force. In the development of secondary industry they again played a leading role, and in earlier days they laid the foundations of a rationalized civil administration, army, police force, and legal system. At all times they were aligned with modernization and technological progress on a capitalistic basis, and one may expect this pattern to find its precipitate in the common characteristics of this group.

Matters were far different for the Afrikaans-speaking section of the white group.[17] Until the beginning of the twentieth century this group had consisted almost entirely of farmers, and even today about 85 per cent of white farmers belong to this group. A large proportion of these farmers had long ago cut both spiritual and material ties with the outside world. The nineteenth century with its rationalization of production and of thought passed them by. Difficulties of transport, lack of markets and of capital resources, and the temptation of living at the expense of the native inhabitants produced an economic and cultural stagnation, not to say deterioration, which made it very difficult for the individuals affected by it to adapt to the demands of modernization. Not only were they without skills that might be useful in the new context but they had developed the outlook of landowners who despised productive work, which they usually left to their African tenants. Thus the process of urbanization which affected large sections of this group during the first half of the present century was a difficult and bitter experience for many of them.[18] But in the end they found it possible to utilize their political power to restore to themselves the privileged position which they felt was theirs by right of skin colour.

Moreover, as the process of industrialization and rationalization continued, the Afrikaans-speaking group became increasingly adapted to it. They drifted to the towns in their hundreds of thousands, they entered trade and commerce, founded insurance companies and banks, acquired some technical skills, and in a few cases even appeared as industrial entrepreneurs. Many of those that remained on the land were gradually transformed into capitalist farmers and land speculators. Thus in 1946 there were some 112,000 white farms in the country; but only 44,000 farmers or farmers' sons were actually working on their farms, the majority of those styled farmers acting purely as financiers, entrepreneurs, or supervisors.[19] Whereas in 1911 only one-fifth of the Afrikaners were domiciled in towns, that figure has now risen to over 70 per cent. During this period the number of Afrikaners engaged in industrial employment quadrupled. In the crucial period of industrialization, between 1939 and 1949, the Afrikaner share in commerce rose from 8 to 25 per cent and in industry from 3 to 6 per cent.[20] Further relative gains have been registered since then. The last thirty-year period has also been marked by the rise to prominence of powerful Afrikaner-controlled financial institutions like banks and insurance companies, and in the countryside many of the farms were being transformed into mechanized capitalist enterprises. After the accession to power in 1948 of an Afrikaner Nationalist Government, the resources of the State were used in various ways further to accelerate the engagement of this group in the modernization process. The result is that whereas until recently only a small minority of the group had been fully assimilated to modern conditions, this no longer applies, especially for the younger generation which has grown up under very different conditions from those that had become traditional for the group.

It is now possible to generalize the social-psychological relationships that have been suggested in the preceding paragraphs. From the point of view of the individual involved in them the institutions of modern societies, and especially the economic institutions, involve a radical process of *rationalization*, the systematic arrangement of means in the service of some fixed goal without respect for person or traditions. This means the precise structuring of social actions in terms of the fulfilment of functionally specific social roles determined by the needs of rationally organized social institutions, such as industrial or commercial enterprises, police forces, political parties, etc. The process of modernization involves the establishment of new sets of social norms, new control-mechanisms for regulating the investment of human energy and for organizing the social relationships between people. In other words the process of modernization demands that the individual mobilize his energies in the service of the organizations that characterize the industrial system. It demands individuals who will ensure the continued functioning of rationalized institutions by acting in a dependably rational manner. The most successful individuals in meeting these demands, and hence those most rewarded by the process of modernization, are the individuals who have developed the pattern of self-rationalization.

It is suggested therefore that the process of modernization not only depends on the initiative of certain groups of persons, but in turn selects and reinforces certain personality patterns among those that are drawn into its ambit. Extended reproduction of the economic system depends on the extended reproduction, through appropriate socialization, of individuals who can make the expanded system function. Thus men are transformed in the course of their efforts to reap economic advantages.

In the context of the present discussion the crucial element in this process is seen to lie in the generation of a generalized 'cognitive style' or type of rationality which expresses itself not only in effective functioning within modern organizations, but also in the planning of one's own life, in the solution of certain intellectual tasks, and last but not least in the preference for instrumentally orientated legitimating ideas on the political level. The circle of reciprocal influence between economy and polis can only be closed by reference to the psychology of the individual.

The Focus of Legitimating Ideas

It has been mentioned that modernization not only brings with it a shift to instrumentalist notions about the existing social structure, it also leads to a change in the primary focus of systems of legitimation. Whereas modernizing elites that have not yet captured control of the State are likely to legitimate their claims to power in terms of an appeal to cultural values, they are much more likely to base their appeal on loyalty to the State as such, once they are in control of its machinery. It is only at a relatively late stage in the process of modernization that it becomes possible to appeal to people's loyalty to non-political institutions on a large scale. The Afrikaner elite has clearly made the first transition, but is probably a generation or more away from the second. At least since 1961 the primary focus of official attempts at legitimating the existing system has been in terms of loyalty to the State rather than in terms of loyalty to the ideals of Afrikaner cultural exclusiveness—a theme which retained considerable prominence in National Party propaganda right through the 1950s. On the other hand, there are few signs of any further change of focus among the ruling elite.

In this connection the following empirical observation is of some interest. In the late 1950s and early 1960s this writer collected essays on the 'History of South Africa over the next fifty years' from both English-speaking and Afrikaans-speaking students. One of the themes in terms of which the content-analysis of these essays was conducted was concern with military strength and national power. No other theme yielded as marked a difference between the groups as this one. Whereas almost two-thirds of the Afrikaans subjects mentioned it in a positive sense, hardly one-fifth of the English subjects did so. Moreover most of the references were of a somewhat extreme kind. A few sample excerpts will communicate their flavour:

In the field of war equipment South Africa also made great progress. South Africa is now equipped with the latest war equipment and we have almost drawn level with America and Germany.

In 2000 the Third World War broke out. . . . Russia and America were economically annihilated. . . . South Africa is the only one able to eliminate the traces of the war within three years. In 2010 Europe began to refer to South Africa as the 'Fourth Reich'.

In 1978 a new type of radiation weapon was produced with which South Africa could destroy the whole planet if it wanted. Then all the various countries tried to win South Africa's favour and tried to make economic and political treaties. But South Africa refuses to reveal the secret of its weapon.

In about 2015 South Africa will be producing its own atomic bombs and rockets. South Africa will then be the greatest and most attractive country to which many foreigners will flee.

In the Third World War South Africa took a leading part by defeating Egypt on its own and then conquering the whole of Africa with the help of the Portuguese and the British. In this war South Africa gained much territory and continued its policy of separate development with great success.

Statements of this kind appear to reflect a strong positive evaluation of state power as such, and they are probably representative of large sections of those on whom the present leadership of the country relies for political support. The shift from a relatively isolationist to a more threatening foreign policy is not unconnected with the ideological shift from the cultural entity to the State as the main focus of legitimating ideas. While the ever-increasing power of the South African State remains the final criterion in terms of which the value of day-to-day policies is determined, the risk of serious external involvements must be a salient factor in the assessment of the success chances of the present ruling elite.

But even if this genuinely totalitarian attachment to state power as such is gradually replaced by more instrumentalist legitimation patterns, as the spread of the modernization process seems to indicate, the practical results would be a strengthening rather than a weakening of the present system of domination. The instrumentalist defence of institutions of political power does not derive any emotional satisfaction from the exercise of power as such, but instrumental violence is violence nevertheless. In fact, the pattern of instrumental violence, demanded by a more or less rational calculation of group interests, is quite characteristic of societies at relatively advanced levels of modernization, and there is absolutely no reason to suppose that South Africa would be an exception. It is precisely in these societies that rationality has on occasion taken on the quality of a nightmare, threatening its victims with 'rational deceit, rational cruelty, endless and implacable rational hostility, rational despair and rational terror'.[22] With every passing year this description becomes more true of the South African system of social domination.

The industrialization of the South African economy and the

process of general modernization under conditions of extreme coercion and inequality have not removed the opposition of social interests but sharpened them. Under these circumstances the process of rationalization will probably continue to have its main influence on the power conflict by rendering the apparatus of domination more efficient. All that can be expected is that irrational components will gradually come to play a lesser role in the conflict situation. This does not change the nature of the fundamental conflict, but merely increases the likelihood that the goals of the ruling elite will be pursued by means of more flexible strategies.

REFERENCES

1. For a similar distinction see H. C. Kelman, 'Patterns of Personal Involvement in the National System: A Social Psychological Analysis of Political Legitimacy', paper presented at the XI Interamerican Congress of Psychology, Mexico City, Dec. 1967.
2. EISENSTADT, S. N., *Modernization: Protest and Change*, Prentice-Hall, New York, 1966, and other recent publications by the same author.
3. For a discussion of different kinds of industrializing elites, see C. Kerr, *Industrialism and Industrial Man*, Harvard University Press, Cambridge, Mass., 1960.
4. DANZIGER, K., 'Some Social Psychological Aspects of Economic Growth', *South African Journal of Science*, 1963, *59*, 394–8.
5. For a more extended treatment of the similarity between money and status in social exchange, see P. M. Blau, *Exchange and Power in Social Life*, Wiley, New York, 1964, ch. 10.
6. DANZIGER, K., 'The Psychological Future of an Oppressed Group', *Social Forces*, 1963, *42*, 31–40.
7. CRONJE, G., *Regverdige Rasse-Apartheid*, Citadel Press, Cape Town, 1947, 62.
8. RHOODIE, N. J., and VENTER, H. J., *Apartheid*, National Commercial Printers, Cape Town, 1960.
9. EISELEN, W. W. M., 'Harmonious Multi-Community Development', *Optima*, 1959, *9*, 8.
10. HORKHEIMER, M., (ed.), *Stüdien über Autorität und Familie*, Alcan, Paris, 1936.
11. MANNHEIM, K., *Man and Society*, Routledge & Kegan Paul, London, 1940.
12. DANZIGER, K., 'Validation of a Measure of Self-rationalization', *Journal of Social Psychology*, 1963, *59*, 17–28.

13. ALLPORT, G. W., and GILLESPIE, J. M., *Youth's Outlook on the Future*, Doubleday, New York, 1955.

14. MORSBACH, H., 'The Measurement of the Achievement Syndrome', unpublished Ph.D. thesis, University of Cape Town.

15. BIESHEUVEL, S., and LIDDICOAT, R., 'The Effects of Cultural Factors on Intelligence Test Performance', *Journal of the National Institute for Personnel Research*, 1959, *8*, 3–24 and 153–5.

16. DANZIGER, K., and MORSBACH, H., 'Personal Style in Planning', *Journal of General Psychology*, 1967, *76*, 167–77.

17. MARQUARD, L., *The Peoples and Policies of South Africa*, Oxford University Press, London, 4th edn. 1969, chs. 1 and 3.

18. For interesting information on this process see R. W. Wilcocks, *The Poor White*, Report of the Carnegie Commission, II, Pro Ecclesia, Stellenbosch, 1932.

19. DE SWARDT, S. J. J., 'Die Behoefte aan en die Beskikbaarheid van Arbeid in die landboubedryf', South African Bureau of Racial Affairs, Stellenbosch, 1954.

20. SADIE, T. L., *Die Afrikaner in die Landsekonomie*, South African Broadcasting Corporation, Johannesburg, 1958.

21. DANZIGER, K., 'Ideology and Utopia in South Africa', *British Journal of Sociology*, 1963, *14*, 59–76.

22. BOULDING, K. E., review of J. C. Schelling's 'The Strategy of Conflict', *Contemporary Psychology*, 1961, *6*, 426.

COMPREHENSIVE BIBLIOGRAPHY ON SOUTH AFRICA SINCE 1960

This bibliography comprises all kinds of books, articles, and pamphlets on South Africa which have been published since 1960. Important contributions by social scientists are marked with an asterisk.

Books on South Africa published before 1960 have been included only in exceptional cases or when a later edition has come out. The date 1960 has been chosen because of significant events at this stage for future developments. The withdrawal of the country from the Commonwealth and the establishment of a Republic, but above all the final prohibition of all non-white political activity outside the Apartheid framework and the accelerated economic boom after Sharpeville, led to an almost new situation at the beginning of the decade. In the light of these developments, earlier studies retain their value as historical documents, which are, however, less important for the analysis of the contemporary scene in South Africa.

Indispensable additional data can be found in the various publications by the South African Institute of Race Relations, especially in its annual *Survey of Race Relations* compiled by Muriel Horrell. Its Afrikaner counterpart, the South African Bureau of Racial Affairs (SABRA), presents the Government point of view and publishes the bilingual *Journal of Racial Affairs*. Further material not mentioned in this bibliography is regularly published by international organizations such as the United Nations, or the Organization of African Unity, and many private associations concerned with South Africa.

ADAM, HERIBERT (1969) *Südafrika: Soziologie einer Rassengesellschaft*, Suhrkamp, Frankfurt.

(1971) *Modernizing Racial Domination: South Africa's Political Dynamics*, University of California Press, Berkeley.

ADENDORFF, J. (1967)'Ekonomiese Ontwikkeling in die Tuislande', *Journal of Racial Affairs*, Pretoria, April, *18*, 65–71.

ALLIER, JACQUES (1968) 'Visite au pays de l'apartheid', *Revue de Défense Nationale*, Paris, March, *24*, 403–27.

ALLIGHAN, GARRY (1960) *Curtain-Up on South Africa: presenting a national drama*, Boardman, London.
(1961) *Verwoerd—the End: A look-back from the Future*, Boardman, London.

*ANDRESKI, STANISLAV (1964) 'Aspects of South African Society', in *The Elements [Uses] of Comparative Sociology*, Weidenfeld & Nicolson, London, and University of California Press, Berkeley, 263–81.

ARCHIBALD, DREW (1969) 'The Afrikaners as an Emergent Minority', *British Journal of Sociology*, December, *20*, 416–25.

ARRIGHI, G. (1967) *The Political Economy of Rhodesia*, Mouton for the Institute of Social Studies, The Hague.

ARRIGHI, G., and SAUL, J. S. (1969) 'Nationalism and Revolution in Sub-Saharan Africa', *Socialist Register*, 137–88.

ASHERON, A. (1969) 'Race and Politics in South Africa', *New Left Review*, London, January–February, 55–68.

AUERBACH, G. (1965) *The Power of Prejudice in South African Education: an enquiry into history textbooks and syllabuses in the Transvaal high schools*, Balkema, Cape Town.

AUSTIN, DENNIS (1966) *Britain and South Africa*, Oxford University Press, London.
(1968) 'White Power?', *Journal of Commonwealth Political Studies*, July, *6*, 95–106.

BADERTSCHER, JEAN (1962) *La Ségrégation Raciale en Afrique du Sud,* Horizons, Lausanne.

BALLINGER, MARGARET (1969) *From Union to Apartheid*, Juta, Cape Town.

BALLINGER, R. B. (1961*a*) *South-West Africa—The Case Against the Union*, South African Institute of Race Relations, Johannesburg.
(1961*b*) 'South Africa; a problem in race relations', *Australian Outlook*, Melbourne, April, *15*, 5–28.

BAMFORD, B. R. (1967) 'Race Reclassification', *South African Law Journal*, Cape Town, February, *84*, 37–42.

*BANTON, MICHAEL (1967) 'White Supremacy in South Africa', in *Race Relations*, Tavistock Publications, London, 164–92.

BARATA, OSCAR SOARES (1964) *A Questão Racial: introdução*, Instituto Superior de Ciências Sociais e Política Ultramarina, Lisbon.

BARROS, ROMEO JULIUS (1967) *African States and the United Nations Versus Apartheid*, Carlton Press, New York.

BARTLETT, VERNON (1969) *The Colour of Their Skin*, Chatto & Windus, London.

BELLWOOD, W. A. (1964) *Whither the Transkei?* Howard Timmins, Cape Town.

BENSON, MARY (1963) *Chief Albert Lutuli of South Africa*, Oxford University Press, London.
(1964) 'South Africa and World Opinion', *Current History*, Philadelphia, March, *46*, 129–35.
(1963) *The African Patriots: the story of the African National Congress of South Africa*, Faber & Faber, revised as
(1966) *South Africa: the struggle for a birthright*, Penguin, Harmondsworth.

BERNSTEIN, HILDA (1967) *The World That Was Ours*, Heinemann, London.

BIERMANN, E. R. (1965) 'Die maatskaplike Ontwikkeling van die Bantoe', *Journal of Racial Affairs*, Pretoria, April, *16*, 78–84.

BIERMANN, H. H. H. (ed.) (1963) *The Case for South Africa as Put Forth in the Public Statements of Eric H. Louw, Foreign Minister of South Africa*, Macfadden, New York.

BLACK, MARGARET (1965) *No Room for Tourists*, Secker & Warburg, London.

BLAXALL, ARTHUR (1965) *Suspended Sentence*, Hodder & Stoughton, London.

*BLEY, HELMUT (1968) *Kolonialherrschaft und Sozialstruktur in Deutsch-Südwestafrika 1894–1914*, Leibniz, Hamburg.

BLOOM, LEONARD (1960) 'Self Concepts and Social Status in South Africa: A Preliminary Cross-cultural Analysis', *Journal of Social Psychology*, *51*, 103–12.
(1964) 'Some Problems of Urbanization in South Africa', *Phylon*, *25*, Winter, 347–61.

BLOOM, LEONARD, DE CRESPIGNY, A. R. C., and SPENCE, J. E. (1961) 'An Interdisciplinary Study of Social, Moral, and Political Attitudes of White and Non-White South African University Students', *Journal of Social Psychology*, *54*, 3–12.

BLUMBERG, MYRNA (1962) *White Madam*, Gollancz, London.

BOARD, CHRISTOPHER (1964) 'The Rehabilitation Programme in the Bantu Areas and its Effect on the Agricultural Practices and Rural Life of the Bantu in the Eastern Cape', *South African Journal of Economics*, Johannesburg, March, *32*, 36–52.

BOSHOFF, C. W. H. (1965) 'Die Bantoejeug in die Stad', *Journal of Racial Affairs*, Pretoria, April, *16*, 85–94.

BOSMAN, W. (1966) 'Die Besit, Okkupasie, en Gebruik van Grond deur Bantoes in Suid-Afrika', *Journal of Racial Affairs*, Pretoria, October, *17*, 12–19.

BOTHA, M. C. (1964) 'Ons stedelike Bantoebeleid teen die Agtergrond van ons Landsbeleid', *Journal of Racial Affairs*, Stellenbosch, January, *15*, 12–21.

BOWMAN, LARRY W. (1968) 'The Subordinate State Systems of Southern Africa', *International Studies Quarterly*, XII September, *3*.

BOYCE, ARNOLD NAPIER (1961) *Europe and South Africa: A History of the Period 1815–1939*, Juta, Cape Town.

BRETT, E. A. (1963) *African Attitudes: A Study of the Social, Racial and Political Attitudes of Some Middle-Class Africans*, South African Institute of Race Relations, Johannesburg.

(1964) 'African Attitudes to South African Society: the reactions of some middle-class Africans to their position in South Africa', *Race*, London, July, *6*, 52–62.

BRITISH COUNCIL OF CHURCHES, LONDON: INTERNATIONAL DEPT. (1965) *The Future of South Africa: a study by British Christians*, edited by T. A. Beetham and N. Salter, S.C.M. Press, London.

BROOKES, EDGAR H. (1960a) *The City of God and the Politics of Crisis*, Oxford University Press, London.

(1960b) 'South Africa and the Wider Africa, 1910–1960', *Race Relations Journal*, Johannesburg, January–March, *27*, 3–15.

(1961) 'While There is Time', *Optima*, Johannesburg, June, *23*, 1–11.

(1967) 'Native Administration in South Africa', in I. Schapera (ed.), *Western Civilization and the Natives of South Africa: studies in culture contact*, Routledge & Kegan Paul, London.

(1968a) *Apartheid*, Barnes & Noble, New York.

(1968b) *Apartheid: A Documentary Study of Modern South Africa*, Routledge & Kegan Paul, London.

BROOKES, EDGAR H., and VANDENBOSCH, AMRY (1964) *The City of God and the City of Man in Africa*, University of Kentucky Press, Lexington.

BROWN, DOUGLAS (1966) *Against the World: A Study of White South African Attitudes*, Collins, London.

BROWN, WILLIAM E. (1960) *The Catholic Church in South Africa*, Kennedy, New York.

BULL, THEODORE (1968) *Rhodesia: Crisis of Colour*, Quadrangle Books, Chicago.

BUNTING, BRIAN (1964) *The Rise of the South African Reich*, Penguin, London.

BUTLER, JEFFREY (1968) *The Liberal Party and the Jameson Raid*, Oxford University Press, London.

CALLAN, EDWARD (1962) *Albert John Luthuli and the South African Race Conflict*, Western Michigan University Press, Kalamazoo. (1968) *Alan Paton*, Twayne, New York.

CALVOCORESSI, PETER (1961) *South Africa and World Opinion*, Oxford University Press, London.

CAPLIN, GEORGE H. (1969) *At Last We Have Got Our Country Back*, Buren, Cape Town.

CARROLL, FAYE (1967) *South-West Africa and the United Nations*, University of Kentucky Press, Lexington.

*CARSTENS, PETER (1966) *The Social Structure of a Cape Coloured Reserve: A Study of Racial Integration and Segregation in South Africa*, Oxford University Press, New York.

*CARTER, GWENDOLEN M. (1958, 1962) *The Politics of Inequality: South Africa since 1948*, Thames & Hudson, London, and Praeger, New York. (1966) *Separate Development: The Challenge of the Transkei*, South African Institute of Race Relations, Johannesburg.

*CARTER, GWENDOLEN M., KARIS, THOMAS, and STULTZ, NEWELL M. (1967) *South Africa's Transkei: The Politics of Domestic Colonialism*, Northwestern University Press, Evanston.

CAWOOD, LESLEY (1964) *The Churches and Race Relations in South Africa*, South African Institute of Race Relations, Johannesburg.

CHAULER, P. (1960) 'Tragédie en Afrique du Sud', *Études*, Paris, June, *305*, 348–53.

CHILCOTE, RONALD H. (1969) *Emerging Nationalism in Portuguese Africa: A Bibliography*, Hoover Institution Press, Stanford.

CHKHIKVADZE, V. (1965) 'Racism: an abominable international crime', *International Affairs*, Moscow, February, *2*, 49–53.

CHURCHILL, RHONA (1962) *White Man's God*, Hodder & Stoughton, London.

CILLIERS, S. P. (1968) *Productivity and Human Relations*, South African Institute of Race Relations, Johannesburg.

CLEMENS, FRANK (1969) *Rhodesia: The Course to Collision*, Pall Mall Press, London.

COLE, ERNEST (1967) *House of Bondage*, Random House, New York.

COLE, MONICA M. (1961) *South Africa*, E. P. Dutton, New York.

COPE, JOHN (1965) *South Africa*, Ernest Benn, London.

CORA, GIULIANO (1965) 'Sud Africa 1965', *Rivista di studi politici internazionali*, Florence, July–September, *32*, 409–34.

CORREA VILLALOBOS, F. (1965) 'El "apartheid"', *Foro internacional*, Mexico, January–March, *5*, 427–52.

*COWEN, DENIS VICTOR (1961) *The Foundations of Freedom with Special Reference to Southern Africa*, Oxford University Press, Cape Town.

CRIJNS, ARTHUR GERARDUS JOANNES (1960) *Race Relations and Race Attitudes in South Africa: A Socio-Psychological Study of Human Relationships in a Multi-Racial Society*, Janssen, Nijmegen.

CRONJE, SUZANNE (1966) *Witness in the Dark: police torture and brutality in South Africa*, Christian Action Pamphlet, London.

DADOO, Y. M. (1961) 'Racial Crisis in South Africa', *Pakistan Horizon*, Karachi, *14*, 10–17.

DALE, RICHARD (1966) 'South Africa and the International Community', *World Politics*, XVIII, January, 283–96.
(1969) 'Ovamboland: Bantustan Without Tears?' *Africa Report*, Washington.

D'AMATO, ANTHONY A. (1966) 'The Bantustan Proposals for South-West Africa', *Journal of Modern African Studies*, Cambridge, October, *4*, 177–92.

*DANZIGER, KURT (1963a) 'Ideology and Utopia in South Africa: A Methodological Contribution to the Sociology of Knowledge', *British Journal of Sociology*, *14*, 59–76.
(1963b) 'The Psychological Future of an Oppressed Group', *Social Forces*, *42*, 31–40.

DATTA, A. K. (1963) 'Urbanization and Apartheid in the Republic of South Africa', *Africa Quarterly*, New Delhi, July–September, *3*, 82–91.

DAVENPORT, T. R. H. (1960) 'Civil Rights in South Africa, 1910–1960', *Acta juridica*, Cape Town, 11–28.
(1966) *The Afrikaner Bond: the History of a South African Political Party, 1880–1911*, Oxford University Press, Cape Town.

(1968) 'African Townsmen? South African Natives (Urban Areas) Legislation through the Years', *African Affairs*, 95–109.

DAVIS, J. A., and BAKER, J. K. (eds.) (1966) *Southern Africa in Transition*, Praeger, New York, and Pall Mall Press, London.

DE BEER, Z. J. (1961) *Multi-Racial South Africa: The Reconciliation of Forces*, Oxford University Press, London.

DE BLIJ, HARM J. (1962) *Africa South*, Northwestern University Press, Evanston.

DE CRESPIGNY, A. (1965) 'Political Equality in South Africa and Methods of Reform', *Australian Journal of Politics and History*, December, 350–63.

DE KIEWIET, C. W. (1964) 'Loneliness in the Beloved Country', *Foreign Affairs*, New York, April, *42*, 413–27.
(1965) 'South Africa's Gamble with History', *Virginia Quarterly Review*, Winter, *40*, 1–17.
(1941, 1966) *A History of South Africa: Social and Economic*, Oxford University Press, London.
(1969) 'The World and Pretoria', *Africa Report*, Washington, February, 46–52.

*DE RIDDER, J. C. (1961) *The Personality of the Urban African in South Africa*, Routledge & Kegan Paul, London.

DE VILLIERS, RENÉ (1967) *The Role and Challenge of the Student in Southern Africa*, South African Institute of Race Relations, Johannesburg.

DE WET, CAREL (1966) 'Apartheid, the Political Philosophy of South Africa', *Commonwealth Journal*, London, February, *9*, 19–22.

DE WET NEL, M. D. C. (1961) 'Bantu Policy in South Africa', in James Duffy and Robert A. Manners (eds.), *Africa Speaks*, Van Nostrand, Princeton.

DEL BOCA, ANGELO (1962) *Apartheid: affano e dolore*, Valentino Bompiani, Milan.

DEPARTMENT OF INFORMATION, SOUTH AFRICA (1966) *Ethiopia and Liberia versus South Africa: An Official Account of the Contentious Proceedings on South West Africa before The International Court of Justice at The Hague, 1960–1966*, Pretoria.

DHANAGARE, D. N. (1967) 'Apartheid—Its Theory and Practice in South Africa', *India Quarterly*, October–December, 338–61.

*DICKIE-CLARK, H. F. (1966) *The Marginal Situation: a Sociological Study of a Coloured Group*, Routledge & Kegan Paul, London.

DJERDJA, J. (1964) 'Racial Policy of the Republic of South Africa', *United Asia*, Bombay, July–August, *16*, 261–4.

*DOXEY, G. V. (1961) *The Industrial Colour Bar in South Africa*, Oxford University Press, Cape Town.
(1963*a*) *The High Commission Territories and the Republic of South Africa*, Oxford University Press, London.
(1963*b*) 'The South African Problem; a conflict of nationalism', *International Journal*, Toronto, Autumn, *18*, 501–12.

DOXEY, G. V. and M. P. (1965) 'The Prospects for Change in South Africa', in *The Year Book of World Affairs 1965*, Stevens, London, 69–88.

DRASCHER, W. (1964) 'Die Rassenpolitik in Südafrika 1652–1910', *Saeculum*, 15, 2, 177–206.

DREYFUS, FRANCINE (1967) 'Nationalisme Noir et Séparatisme Religieux en Afrique du Sud', *Mois en Afrique*, July, *19*, 12–32.

DRURY, ALLEN (1967) *A Very Strange Society: a journey to the heart of South Africa*, Trident Press, New York.

DU TOIT, BRIAN M. (1966*a*) 'Politics and Change in South Africa', *International Journal of Comparative Sociology*, VII, March, 96–118.
(1966*b*) 'Color, Class and Caste in South Africa', *Journal of Asian and African Studies*, I, July, 197–212.

DUGARD, C. J. R. (1966) 'The Legal Effect of United Nations Resolutions on Apartheid', *South African Law Journal*, Cape Town, February, *83*, 44–59.

DUNCAN, PATRICK (1963) 'Toward a World Policy for South Africa', *Foreign Affairs*, October, 38–48.
(1964) *South Africa's Rule of Violence*, Methuen, London.

DUVE, FREIMUT (1965) *Kap Ohne Hoffnung*, Rowohlt, Hamburg.

EGELAND, L. (1968) 'South Africa's Role in Africa', *Rivista di studi politici internazionali*, April–June, 276–89.

EISELEN, W. W. M. (1964) 'Die Aandeel van die Blanke ten opsigte van die praktiese Uitvoering van die beleid van afsonderlike Ontwikkeling', *Journal of Racial Affairs*, Pretoria, January, *16*, 6–23.

ERASMUS, B. P. (1961) 'The Policy of Apartheid', *African Affairs*, London, January, *59*, 56–65.

EVANS, G. (1964) 'Partition and South Africa's Future', *Journal of International Affairs*, New York, *18*, 241–52.

FAGAN, H. A. (1960) *Our responsibility: a discussion of South Africa's Racial Problems*, Universiteits-Uitgewers en Boekhandelaars, Stellenbosch.
(1963) *Co-existence in South Africa*, Juta, Cape Town.

FAIR, T. J. D., and SHAFFER, N. MANFRED (1964) 'Population Patterns and Policies in South Africa', *Economic Geography*, July, 261–74.

*FEIT, EDWARD (1962) *South Africa: the Dynamics of the African National Congress*, Oxford University Press, for the Institute of Race Relations, London.
(1966) 'Conflict and Cohesion in South Africa: A Theoretical Analysis of "Separate Development" and its Implications', *Economic Development and Cultural Change*, July, 484–96.
(1967a) *African Opposition in South Africa: the Failure of Passive Resistance*, Hoover Institute, Stanford.
(1967b) 'Community in a Quandary: the South African Jewish Community and "Apartheid"', *Race*, April, 395–408.
(1970) 'Urban Revolt in South Africa: A Case Study', *Journal of Modern African Studies*, April, *8*, 55–72.

FERRER, D. (1963) 'L'apartheid en Afrique du Sud', *Revue de défense nationale*, Paris, November, *19*, 1699–1721.

FIRST, RUTH (1963) *South West Africa*, Penguin, Harmondsworth and Baltimore.
(1965) *117 Days: An Account of Confinement and Interrogation under the South African Ninety-Day Detention Law*, Penguin, Harmondsworth and Baltimore.

FLEMING, IAN G. (1962) 'The Secondary and Tertiary Economic Development of the Transkei', *Journal of Racial Affairs*, Stellenbosch, December, *14*, 43–56.

FLOHR, ERNST FRIEDRICH (1965) 'Bevölkerungsprobleme und die Politik der eigenständigen Entwicklung der Bevölkerungsgruppen in Südafrika', *Mitteilungen der Geographischen Gesellschaft in Lübeck*, Lübeck, 51.

FÖLSCHER, G. C. K. (1967) 'The Economic and Fiscal Relationships of the Transkei *vis-à-vis* the Rest of the Republic as Determinants of Its Economic Development', *South African Journal of Economics*, Johannesburg, September, *35*, 203–18.

FRANCIS, EMERICH (1965) *Ethnos und Demos*, Duncker & Humboldt, Berlin, 216–27.

FRANKEL, SALLY HERBERT (1960) *The Tyranny of Economic Paternalism in Africa: A Study of Frontier Mentality, 1860–1960*, supplement to *Optima*, Anglo-American Corporation of South Africa, Johannesburg.

FRASER, G. (1964) 'L'ONU et l'apartheid', *Année politique et économique*, Paris, June, *37*, 207–12.

FREED, L. F. (1963) *Crime in South Africa*, Cape Town.

FRIEDMAN, BERNARD, SUTHERLAND, J., and BALLINGER, R. B. (1961) *Looking Outwards: Three South African Viewpoints*, South African Institute of Race Relations, Johannesburg.

FRIEDMANN, MARION VALERIE (ed.) (1963) *I Will Still Be Moved: Reports from South Africa*, A. Baker, London.

FRYE, WILLIAM (1968) *In Whitest Africa: the Dynamics of Apartheid*, Prentice Hall, Englewood Cliffs.

FRYER, A. K. (1965) 'National Self-Determination and the Multi-Racial State: the Problem of South Africa', *Australian Outlook*, Melbourne, August, *19*, 180–91.

GALBRAITH, JOHN S. (1963) *Reluctant Empire: British Policy on the South African Frontier, 1834–1854*, University of California Press, Berkeley.

GALTUNG, JOHN (1967) 'On the Effects of International Sanctions: with Examples from the Case of Rhodesia', *World Politics*, April, 378–416.

GEISS, IMANUEL (1968) *Panafrikanismus: Zur Geschichte der Dekolonisation*, Europäische Verlagsanstalt, Frankfurt.

GINIEWSKI, PAUL (1961) ' "Bantustan" und das Dilemma Südafrikas', *Europa-Archiv*, Frankfurt, April, *16*, 163–74.
(1965a) 'La décolonisation sud-africaine: la signification politique du "développement séparé" ', *Revue de défense nationale*, Paris, December, *21*, 1945–54.
(1965b, 1961) *The Two Faces of Apartheid*, Henry Regnery, Chicago. Issued originally as *Bantustans: A Trek Towards the Future*, Human & Rousseau, Cape Town.

GOLDBERG, ARTHUR J. (1967) 'The United States, the United Nations and Southern Africa', *Department of State Bulletin*, Washington, D.C., 20 February, *56*, 289–94.

GOLDBERG, H. (1965) *Work Opportunities, Labour Utilization: A Function of Management*, Bantu Wage and Productivity Association, Johannesburg.

GOLDING, G. (1962) 'Race and Opportunity in South Africa Today', *African Affairs*, London, October, *61*, 308–13.

GONZE, COLLIN, et al. (1962) *South African Crisis and United States Policy*, American Committee on Africa, New York.

GRAAF, DE VILLIERS (1961) 'South African Prospect: Thoughts on an Alternative Race Policy', *Foreign Affairs*, New York, July, *39*, 670–82.

GREYLING, H. L. (1964) 'Enkele Beskouings oor die moontlike sosio-ekonomiese Posisie van die Kleurlinggroep in die toekomstige Bevolkingspatroon', *Journal of Racial Affairs*, Pretoria, October, *15*, 155–63.

GROSS, ERNEST A. (1968) 'The Coalescing Problem of Southern Africa', *Foreign Affairs*, July, *46*, 743–57.

GRUNDY, KENNETH W. (1970) 'Host Countries and the Southern African Liberation Struggle', *Africa Quarterly*, April–June, X.

HAHLO, H. G. (1969), 'A European–African Worker Relationship in South Africa', *Race*, July, 13–34.

HAHLO, H. R., and KAHN, E. (1968) *The South African Legal System and its Background*, Juta, Cape Town, and Carswell, Toronto.

HAIGH, A. (1963) *South African Tragedy*, World Distributors, London.

HAILEY, WILLIAM MALCOLM (1963) *The Republic of South Africa and the High Commission Territories*, Oxford University Press, London.

HALPERN, JACK (1965) *South Africa's Hostages: Basutoland, Bechuanaland, and Swaziland*, Penguin, Harmondsworth and Baltimore.

HAMER, E. (1964) *Die Industrialisierung Südafrikas seit dem zweiter Weltkrieg*, Stuttgart.

HAMMOND-TOOKE, W. D. (1962) *Bhaca Society: A People in the Transkeian Uplands, South Africa*, Oxford University Press, Cape Town.

(1964) 'Chieftainship in Transkeian Political Development', *Journal of Modern African Studies*, December, *2*, 513–29.

HAMPTON, J. D. (1962) 'The Role of the Coloured and Bantu in the Economic Pattern of the Cape Province', *South African Journal of Economics*, Johannesburg, December, *30*, 253–68.

HANCE, WILLIAM A. (ed.) (1968) *Southern Africa and the United States*, Columbia University Press, New York and London.

HANCOCK, WILLIAM KEITH (1962) *Smuts: The Sanguine Years*, Cambridge University Press, New York and Cambridge.

(1966) *Are There South Africans?*, South African Institute of Race Relations, Johannesburg.

HARRIGAN, ANTHONY (1966) *The New Republic*, van Schaik, Pretoria.

HARTMANN, HANS WALTER (1968) *Südafrika: Geschichte-Wirtschaft-Politik*, Kohlhammer, Stuttgart.

*HARTMANN, HEINZ (1962) *Enterprise and Politics in South Africa*, Princeton University Press, Princeton.

HAWARDEN, ELEANOR (1966) *Prejudice in the Classroom*, South African Institute of Race Relations, Johannesburg.

HEARD, K. A. (1962) *Political Systems in Multi-Racial Societies*, South African Institute of Race Relations, Johannesburg.

HELLING, G. (1960) 'Die Unterdrückung der süd-afrikanischen Bevölkerung durch die Nationalisten', *Deutsche Aussenpolitik*, Berlin, September, *5*, 1023–34.

*HELLMANN, ELLEN (1968a) *Soweto: Johannesburg's African City*, South African Institute of Race Relations, Johannesburg.
(1968b) 'The Effects of Industrialization on Social Structure and Family Life', in *Council Papers on Industrialization and Human Relations*, South African Institute of Race Relations, Johannesburg.
(1969) 'Urban Bantu Legislation', *New Nation*, Pretoria, September, 9–11.

HEPPLE, ALEXANDER (1966) *South Africa: A Political and Economic History*, Pall Mall Press, London.
(1967) *Verwoerd*, Penguin, London.

HEY, P. D. (1961) *The Rise of the Natal Indian Elite*, Natal Witness, Pietermaritzburg.

HILL, CHRISTOPHER R. (1964) *Bantustans: the Fragmentation of South Africa*, Oxford University Press, for the Institute of Race Relations, London.

HOPKINSON, HENRY THOMAS (1964) *South Africa*, Times, New York.

HORRELL, MURIEL (1960) 'Jours de crise en Afrique du Sud', *Civilisations*, Brussels, 3, *10*, 365–72.
(1961a) 'Quelques prises de position du gouvernement sudafricain', *Civilisations*, Brussels, 1, *11*, 101–7.
(1961b) *South African Trade Unionism: A Study of a Divided Working Class*, South African Institute of Race Relations, Johannesburg.
(1963) *Action, Reaction and Counteraction: A Review of Non-White Opposition to the Apartheid Policy, Counter-Measures by the Government and*

the Eruption of New Waves of Unrest, South African Institute of Race Relations, Johannesburg.

(1964) *A Decade of Bantu Education*, South African Institute of Race Relations, Johannesburg.

(1965) *Reserves and Reservations: A Comparison of Plans for the Advancement of Under-Developed Areas in South Africa and the United States, including Information about the Development of the African Reserves in South Africa as at June, 1965*, South African Institute of Race Relations, Johannesburg.

(1966a) *Group Areas: the Emerging Pattern with Illustrative Examples from the Transvaal*, South African Institute of Race Relations, Johannesburg.

(1966b) *Legislation and Race Relations: a Summary of the Main South African Laws which Affect Race Relationships*, South African Institute of Race Relations, Johannesburg.

(1967) *South West Africa*, South African Institute of Race Relations, Johannesburg.

(1968a) *Bantu Education to 1968*, South African Institute of Race Relations, Johannesburg.

(1968b) *Terrorism in South Africa*, South African Institute of Race Relations, Johannesburg.

(1968c) *The Rights of African Women: Some Suggested Reforms*, South African Institute of Race Relations, Johannesburg.

(1969) *South Africa's Workers: Their Organization and the Patterns of Employment*, South African Institute of Race Relations, Johannesburg.

*HOROWITZ, RALPH (1967) *The Political Economy of South Africa*, Weidenfeld & Nicolson, London.

HOUGHTON, DESMOND HOBART (1960a) *Economic Development in a Plural Society: Studies in the Border Region of the Cape Province*, Oxford University Press, Cape Town.

(1960b) ' "Men of Two Worlds" in Some Aspects of Migratory Labour', *South African Journal of Economics*, September, *28*, 3.

(1961) 'Land Reform in the Bantu Areas and Its Effects upon the Urban Labour Market', *South African Journal of Economics*, Johannesburg, September, *29*, 165–84.

(1964) *The South African Economy*, Oxford University Press, Cape Town.

HUDSON, W., JACOBS, G. F., and BIESHEUVEL, S. (1966) *Anatomy of South Africa*, Purnell, Cape Town.

HUNTER, ARCHIBALD P. (1963) 'The Reorientation of Educational Policy in South Africa since 1948', Ed.D. thesis, University of California, Los Angeles.

HURLEY, D. E. (1964) *Apartheid: A Crisis of the Christian Conscience*, South African Institute of Race Relations, Johannesburg.

HURWITZ, NATHAN (1964) *The Economics of Bantu Education*, South African Institute of Race Relations, Johannesburg.

HURWITZ, NATHAN, and WILLIAMS, OWEN (1962) *The Economic Framework of South Africa*, Shuter and Shooter, Pietermaritzburg.

HUTT, W. H. (1964) *The Economics of the Colour Bar* André Deutsch, for the Institute of Economic Affairs, London.

IMISHUE, R. W. (1966) *South West Africa*, Pall Mall Press, for the Institute of Race Relations, London.

INTERNATIONAL COMMISSION OF JURISTS (1967) *South Africa and the Rule of Law*, Geneva.

(1968) *Erosion of the Rule of Law in South Africa*, Geneva.

INTERNATIONAL LABOUR ORGANIZATION (1965) *Special Report on the Application of the Declaration Concerning the Policy of 'Apartheid' of the Republic of South Africa*, Geneva.

(1966) *Second Special Report on the Application of the Declaration Concerning the Policy of 'Apartheid' of the Republic of South Africa*, Geneva.

(1967a) *Third Special Report on the Application of the Declaration Concerning the Policy of 'Apartheid' of the Republic of South Africa*, Geneva.

(1967b) *Discrimination in Employment and Occupation: Standards and Policy Statements Adopted under the Auspices of the I.L.O.*, Geneva.

JABAVU, NONI (1960) *Drawn in Colour*, Murray, London.

(1963) *The Ochre People: Scenes from a South African Life*, Murray, London.

JAFF, FAY (1963) *They Came to South Africa*, Bailey & Swinfen, London.

JAMESON, H. (1960) 'Apartheid et Racisme', *Présence Africaine*, Paris, 32–3, June–September, 103–20.

JASPAN, M. A. (1961) 'South Africa 1960–1961: the Transition from Passive Resistance to Rebellion', *Science and Society*, 25 (2), 97–106.

JENNY, HANS (1961) *Afrika Ist Nicht Nur Schwarz*, Econ, Düsseldorf.

JOHNS, SHERIDAN W., III (1967) 'The Birth of Non-White Trade Unionism in South Africa', *Race*, London, October, 9, 173–92.

JOHNSTONE, FREDERICK A. (1970) 'White Prosperity and White Supremacy in South Africa Today', *African Affairs*, April, 69, 124–40.

JONES, ROBERT CARLESS (1966) 'The Development of Attitudes Leading to the Nationalist Apartheid Philosophy of Bantu Education in the Republic of South Africa', University Microfilm, Ann Arbor.

*JOOSTE, C. J. (1965) 'Community Development in the Lower Orange River Area with Special Reference to the Coloured Population', *Journal of Racial Affairs*, Pretoria, 16, July, 112–23.

(1966) 'Local Government for Coloureds and Indians', *Journal of Racial Affairs*, Pretoria, January, *17*, 23–41.

(1967) 'Ontwikkeling in Grensgebiete', *Journal of Racial Affairs*, Pretoria, April, *18*, 71–83.

JOSEPH, HELEN (1963) *If This Be Treason*, André Deutsch, London.

(1967) *Tomorrow's Sun: A Smuggled Journal from South Africa*, John Day, New York.

JUTA, C. J. (1966) 'Nationalism in South Africa', Ph.D. thesis University of Natal, Durban.

KADALIE, CLEMENTS (1970) *My Life and the I.C.U.: The Autobiography of a Black Trade Unionist in South Africa*, Humanities Press, New York.

KAHN, ELY JACQUES (1968) *The Separated People: A Look at Contemporary South Africa*, W. W. Norton, New York.

KAPPELER, F. (1965) 'Südafrika ist anders als die Welt glaubt', *Schweizer Monatshefte*, Zürich, 44, March, 1089–1109.

KARIS, THOMAS GEORGE (1961) 'The South African Treason Trial', *Political Science Quarterly*, 56, 217–41.

(1963) 'South Africa', in Gwendolen M. Carter (ed.), *Five African States*, Cornell University Press, Ithaca, 471–616.

(1965) *The Treason Trial in South Africa: A Guide to the Microfilm Record of the Trial*, Hoover Institution, Stanford University, Stanford.

(1966) 'The Republic of South Africa', *Jahrbuch des Öffentlichen Rechts der Gegenwart*, *15*, 589–629.

KATZEN, LEO (1961) 'The Case for Minimum Wage Legislation in South Africa', *South African Journal of Economics*, Johannesburg, September, *29*, 195–212.

(1964) *Gold and the South African Economy: the Influence of the Goldmining Industry on Business Cycles and Economic Growth in South Africa, 1886–1961*, A. A. Balkema, Cape Town.

KATZEW, HENRY (1965) *Apartheid and Survival*, Simondium, Cape Town.

KAUNDA, KENNETH D. (1967) 'The Problem of Racialism', *Africa Quarterly*, New Delhi, July–September, 7, 132–6.

KEPPLE-JONES, A. (1949, 1966) *South Africa: A Short History*, Hutchinson, London.

KEYTER, CARL (1962) *Industrial Feeding of African Workers*, South African Institute of Race Relations, Johannesburg.

KISTNER, HANS (1967) 'Die Verschwörung im Süden Afrikas', *Deutsche Aussenpolitik*, Berlin, May, *12*, 562–77.

KLEIST, P. (1963) *Südafrika: Land für Weiß und Schwarz*, Göttingen.

KNIGHT, J. B. (1964) 'A Theory of Income Distribution in South Africa', *Bulletin of the Oxford University Institute of Economics and Statistics*, Oxford, November, *27*, 289–310.

KOMAMBO, KATITI (1964) 'Le Développement du Nationalisme Africain en Afrique du Sud-Ouest', *Présence Africaine*, *49*, 80–103.

KOTZE, D. A. (1966) 'Bantoe-owerhede in die Transkei: Werksaamhede en Probleme', *Journal of Racial Affairs*, Pretoria, July, *17*, 19–28.

(1967) 'Stam- en streekowerhede in die Transkei', *Journal of Racial Affairs*, Pretoria, April, *18*, 85–8.

KRUGER, D. W. (1960) (ed.) *South African Parties and Policies, 1910–1960*, Human & Rousseau, Cape Town.

(1970) *The Making of a Nation: A History of the Union of South Africa 1910–1961*, Humanities Press, New York.

KRUGER, T. M. D. (1968) 'Afrikaner Intellectuals and Apartheid', *New Nation*, Pretoria, October.

KUPER, HILDA (1960) *Indian People in Natal*, University of Natal Press, Durban.

(1963) *The Swazi: A South African Kingdom*, Holt, Rinehart and Winston, New York.

(1964) 'The Colonial Situation in South Africa', *Journal of Modern African Studies*, *2*, July.

KUPER, LEO (1957, 1960a) *Passive Resistance in South Africa*, Yale University Press, New Haven.

(1960b) 'The Heightening of Racial Tensions', *Race*, *2*, 24–32.

(1960c) *The College Brew*, privately published, Durban.

(1963) 'Racialism and Integration in South African Society', *Race*, *4*.

(1964) 'The Problem of Violence in South Africa', *Inquiry*, 7, 295–303.

(1965) *An African Bourgeoisie: Race, Class, and Politics in South Africa*, Yale University Press, New Haven and London.

(1967) 'Structural Discontinuities in African Towns: Some Aspects of Racial Pluralism', in H. Miner (ed.), *The City in Modern Africa*, Praeger, New York.

(1968) 'The Political Situation of Non-Whites in South Africa', in W. A. Hance (ed.), *Southern Africa and the United States*, Columbia University Press, 85–104.

(1969a) 'Political Change in White Settler Societies: the Possibility of Peaceful Democratisation', in Leo Kuper and M. G. Smith (eds.), *Pluralism in Africa*, University of California Press, Berkeley.

(1969b) 'Conflict and the Plural Society: Ideologies of Violence among Subordinate Groups', in L. Kuper and M. G. Smith (eds.), *Pluralism in Africa*, University of California Press, Berkeley.

(1970a) 'Continuities and Discontinuities in Race Relations: Evolutionary or Revolutionary Change', *Cahiers d'Études Africaines*, X, 361–83.

(1970b) 'Nonviolence Revisited', in Robert I. Rotberg and Ali A. Mazrui (eds.), *Protest and Power in Black Africa*, Oxford University Press, New York, 788–804.

(1970c) 'Stratification in Plural Societies: Focus on White Settler Societies in Africa', in Leonard Plotnicov and Arthur Tuden (eds.), *Essays in Social Stratification*, University of Pittsburgh Press, Pittsburgh, 77–93.

LACOUR-GAYET, ROBERT (1968) 'Impressions d'Afrique du Sud', *Revue Politique et Parlementaire*, Paris, February, *786*, 13–28.

LANDIS, ELIZABETH S. (1962) 'South African Apartheid Legislation', *Yale Law Journal*, *71*, January.

LASS, HANS DETLEF (1969) *Nationale Integration in Südafrika: Die Rolle der Parteien zwischen den Jahren 1922 und 1934*, Hamburger Gesellschaft für Völkerrecht und Auswärtiger Politik, Hamburg.

LAURENCE, JOHN (1968) *The Seeds of Disaster*, Taplinger, New York.

LAWRIE, G. C. (1964) 'South Africa's World Position', *Journal of Modern African Studies*, 2, 41–54.

(1968) 'What Will Change South Africa? Seeds That Await a New Political Climate', *Round Table*, January, *229*, 41–55.

LAZARUS, A. D. (1962) 'The Aspirations of the Indian People in South Africa', *Optima*, *12*, 53–8.

LEE, F. J. T. (1964) 'The Socio-Economic Situation in South Africa', *Review of International Affairs*, Belgrade, January, *15*, 12–15.

LEGASSICK, MARTIN (1967) *The National Union of South African Students: Ethnic Cleavage and Ethnic Integration in the Universities*, University of California African Studies Center, Los Angeles, Occasional Papers, 4.

LEGUM, COLIN (1960) 'Crisis in South Africa', *World Today*, London, June, *16*, 233–42.

(1963) 'South Africa: the West at Bay', *Nation*, New York, August, *197*, 70–73.

(1967) 'Colour and Power in the South African Situation', *Daedalus*, Spring, 483–95.

(1968) 'British Policy Towards Africa', *Venture*, October, *20*, 6–11.

(1970) 'Independent Africa and the Liberation of the South', *Africa Quarterly*, April–June, X, 9–14.

LEGUM, COLIN and MARGARET (1964) *South Africa: Crisis for the West*, Pall Mall Press, London, and Praeger, New York.

(1968) *The Bitter Choice: Eight South Africans' Resistance to Tyranny*, World Publishing, Cleveland, Ohio.

LEISS, AMELIA CATHERINE (ed.) (1965) *Apartheid and United Nations Collective Measures: An Analysis*, Carnegie Foundation, New York.

LEISTNER, G. M. E. (1964) 'Patterns of Urban Bantu Labour: Some Findings of a Sample Survey in the Metropolitan Area of Pretoria', *South African Journal of Economics*, XXXII, 275.

(1967) 'Foreign Bantu Workers in South Africa: Their Present Position in the Economy', *South African Journal of Economics*, Johannesburg, March, *35*, 30–56.

LE MAY, G. H. L. (1965) *British Supremacy in South Africa 1899–1907*, Clarendon Press, Oxford.

*LEVER, H. (1967) 'Reducing Social Distances in South Africa', *Sociology and Social Research*, 51, *4*, July.

*LEVER, H., and WAGNER, O. J. M. (1967) 'Ethnic Preferences of Jewish Youth in Johannesburg', *Jewish Journal of Sociology*, IX, *1*, June, 34–47.

*LEWIN, JULIUS (1963) *Politics and Law in South Africa*, Merlin Press, London.

(1967) *The Struggle for Racial Equality*, Longmans, Green, London.

*LOUBSER, JAN J. (1968) 'Calvinism, Equality and Inclusion: the Case of Afrikaner Nationalism', in S. N. Eisenstadt (ed.), *The Protestant Ethic and Modernization: A Comparative View*, Basic Books, New York, 367–83.

LOCKHART, JOHN GILBERT, and WOODHOUSE, C. M. (1962) *Rhodes*, Hodder & Stoughton, London (*Cecil Rhodes: the Colossus of Southern Africa*, Macmillan, New York).

LOMBARD, J. A. (1964) 'Die ekonomiese Beskouingswyse t.o.v. die Beleid van afsonderlike Ontwikkeling en die Aandeel van die Blanke daarin', *Journal of Racial Affairs*, Pretoria, October, *15*, 167–85.

(1967) 'The I.L.O. Programme for the Elimination of "Apartheid" in Labour Matters in the Republic of South Africa: A Review Article', *Journal of Racial Affairs*, Pretoria, January, *18*, 5–13.

LOTHE, H. (1963) *Die Christliche Mission in Südwest Afrika*, Akademie Verlag, Berlin.

LOUW, ERIC H. (1963) *The Case for South Africa as Put Forth in the Public Statements of E. H. Louw, Foreign Minister of South Africa*. Macfadden, New York.

LOWENSTEIN, ALLARD (1962) *Brutal Mandate*, Random House, New York.

LUTHULI, A. (1962a) 'Africa and Freedom', *Présence Africaine*, Paris, *16*, 9–22.

(1962b) *Let My People Go: An Autobiography*, Collins, London.

MABHIDA, MOSES (1962) *For International United Action to End Apartheid: the Curse of South Africa*, W.F.T.U., London.

MCCLELLAN, GRANT S. (ed.) (1962) *South Africa*, Wilson, New York.

MACMILLAN, WILLIAM MILLER (1928, 1963) *Bantu, Boer, and Briton: the Making of the South African Native Problem*, Clarendon Press, Oxford.

MACRAE, NORMAN (1968) 'The Green Bay Tree', *Economist*, 29 June 1968.

(1970) 'What Will Destroy Apartheid?', *Harper's*, March, 30–42.

MALHERBE, E. G. (1964) 'Die Geskiedenis en Ontwikkeling van die Nie-Blanke Afdeling van die Universiteit van Natal', *Journal of Racial Affairs*, Stellenbosch, March–June, *15*, 111–30.

(1967) *Need for Dialogue*, South African Institute of Race Relations, Johannesburg.

(1968) *The Nemesis of Docility*, South African Institute of Race Relations, Johannesburg.

(1970) *Bantu Manpower and Education*, South African Institute of Race Relations, Johannesburg.

MALHOTRA, R. C. (1964) 'Apartheid and the United Nations', *Annals of the American Academy of Political and Social Science*, Philadelphia, July, *354*, 135–44.

MANDELA, NELSON (1965) *No Easy Walk to Freedom*, Heinemann, London.

MANN, J. W. (1962) 'Race-linked Values in South Africa', *Journal of Social Psychology*, *58*, 31–41.

(1963) 'Rivals in Different Rank', *Journal of Social Psychology*, *61*, 11–27.

MANNING, CHARLES A. W. (1964) 'In Defense of Apartheid', *Foreign Affairs*, October, 135–64.

MANSERGH, NICHOLAS (1962) *South Africa 1906–1961: The Price of Magnanimity*, Allen & Unwin, London, and Praeger, New York.

MARAIS, J. S. (1961) *The Fall of Kruger's Republic*, Clarendon Press, Oxford.

MARQUARD, LEO (1955, 1960) *The Story of South Africa*, Faber & Faber, London.

(1965) *Liberalism in South Africa*, South African Institute of Race Relations, Johannesburg.

(1952, 1969) *The Peoples and Policies of South Africa*, Oxford University Press, London.

MASON, P. (1964) 'South Africa and the World: Some Maxims and Axioms', *Foreign Affairs*, New York, October, *43*, 150–64.

MATHEWS, A. S., and ALBINO, R. C. (1966) 'The Permanence of the Temporary: An Examination of the 90 and 180 Day Detention Laws', *South African Law Journal*, February, 16–43.

MAYER, PHILIP (1961) *Townsmen or Tribesmen*, Oxford University Press, Cape Town.

(1962) 'Migrancy and the Study of Africans in Towns', *American Anthropologist*, *64*, 576–92.

MBEKI, GOVAN A. M. (1964) *South Africa: the Peasants' Revolt*, Penguin, Harmondsworth and Baltimore.

MEER, FATIMA (1960) 'African and Indian in Durban', *Africa South*, *4*, 30–41.

(1969) *Portrait of Indian South Africans*, Avon House, Durban.

MENON, K. N. (1962) *Passive Resistance in South Africa*, New Delhi.

MEZERIK, A. G. (1960) 'Apartheid in the Union of South Africa', *International Review Service*, New York, *6*, 1–51.

(1964) 'Apartheid in the Republic of South Africa', *International Review Service*, New York, *10*.

MINTY, ABDUL S. (1969) *South Africa's Defence Strategy*, Anti-Apartheid Movement, London.

MODISANE, BLOKE (1963) *Blame Me On History*, Thames & Hudson, London, and Dutton, New York.

MOOLMAN, J. H. (1964) 'The Resettlement of Urban Bantu in the Bantu Homelands', *Journal of Racial Affairs*, Stellenbosch, January, *15*, 52–63.

MORLAN, GAIL (1970) 'The Student Revolt against Racism in South Africa', *Africa Today*, May–June, *17*, 12–20.

MPHAHLELE, EZEKIEL (1962) *The African Image*, Faber & Faber, London.

MULLER, A. L. (1965*a*) 'The Economic Position of the Asians in Africa', *South African Journal of Economics*, Johannesburg, June, *33*, 114–30.

(1965*b*) 'Some Non-Economic Determinants of the Economic Status of Asians in Africa', *South African Journal of Economics*, Johannesburg, March, *33*, 72–9.

(1968) *Minority Interests: the Political Economy of the Coloured and Indian Communities in South Africa*, South African Institute of Race Relations, Johannesburg.

MULLER, C. F. J., VAN JAARSFELD, F. A., and VAN WIJK, THEO (eds.) (1966) *A Select Bibliography on South African History*, University of South Africa, Pretoria.

MULLER, HELGARD (1965) *The Role of the Coloured People in the Economic Pattern of the Republic of South Africa*, University Publishers and Booksellers, Grahamstown.

MUNGER, EDWIN S. (1961*a*) 'Christians and Race Relations in South Africa: Pt. 2: The Dutch Reformed Church', American Universities Field Staff Reports, Central and Southern Africa Series, New York, *9, 3*.

(1961*b*) 'South Africa's Coloured Population Gropes for an Identity', American Universities Field Staff Reports, Central and Southern Africa Series, New York, *9, 2*.

(1963) 'Race and National Identification: the Republic of South Africa', in K. H. Silvert (ed.), *Expectant Peoples: Nationalism and Development*, Random House, New York.

(1965*a*) *Bechuanaland: Pan-African Outpost or Bantu Homeland?*, Oxford University Press, for the Institute of Race Relations, London.

(1965*b*) *Notes on the Formation of South African Foreign Policy*, Castle Press, Pasadena.

(1967) *Afrikaner and African Nationalism: South African Parallels and Parameters*, Oxford University Press, for the Institute of Race Relations, London.

(1968) 'New White Politics', in W. A. Hance (ed.), *Southern Africa and the United States*, Columbia University Press, New York and London.

(1969) 'South Africa: Are There Silver Linings?', *Foreign Affairs*, January, 375–86.

NATION EUROPA (1963) *Sudafrika-Sonderheft*, XIII, 7.

NARAIN, I. (1961) 'Disfranchisement of the Natal Indians', *India Quarterly*, New Delhi, October–December, *17*, 396–402.

(1962) *The Politics of Racialism: A Study of the Indian Minority in South Africa down to the Gandhi–Smuts Agreement*, Shivalal Aggarwal, Delhi.

NAUDÉ, BEYERS (1968) *The Afrikaner and Race Relations*, South African Institute of Race Relations, Johannesburg.

NEAME, LAWRENCE ELWIN (1962) *The History of Apartheid: the Story of the Colour War in South Africa*, Pall Mall, London.

NGUBANE, JORDAN K. (1963) *An African Explains Apartheid*, Pall Mall, London, and Praeger, New York.

NICHOLS, GEORGE HEATON (1961) *South Africa in My Time*, Allen & Unwin, London.

NIDDRE, DAVID L. (1968) *South Africa: Nation or Nations?* von Nostrand, Princeton.

NIELSEN, WALDEMAR A. (1965) *African Battleline: American Policy Choices in Southern Africa*, Harper & Row, New York.

NIEUWENHUYSEN, J. P. (1964a) 'Economic Policy in the Reserves since the Tomlinson Report', *South African Journal of Economics*, Johannesburg, March, *32*, 3–25.
(1964b) 'Prospects and Issues in the Development of the Reserves', *South African Journal of Economics*, Johannesburg, June, *32*, 128–47.
(1965) 'African Attitudes to South Africa', *Australian Quarterly*, Sydney, June, *37*, 56–66.
(1966) 'Economic Development in the African Reserves of South Africa', *Land Economics*, Madison ,Wis., May, *42*, 195–202.

NIXON, CHARLES R. (1959) 'Nationalisms in South Africa', *World Politics*, XI, 44–67.

O'MEARA, PATRICK 'Tensions in the Nationalist Party', *Africa Report*, Washington, February, 24–44.

ORLIK, PETER B. (1970) 'Divided against Itself: South Africa's White Policy', *Journal of Modern African Studies*, July, *8*, 199–212.

PATON, ALAN (1965) *Hofmeyr*, Oxford University Press, Cape Town (*South African Tragedy: The Life and Times of Jan Hofmeyr*, Scribner's, New York).
(1968) *The Long View*, Pall Mall, London, and Praeger, New York.
(1969) *Portrait of South Africa*, Lutterworth, London.

PATTEN, J. W. (1963) 'Separate Development: A Look at the Facts', *Optima*, Johannesburg, March, *13*, 17–23.

PATTERSON, SHEILA (1957) *The Last Trek: A Study of the Boer People and the Afrikaner Nation*, Routledge & Kegan Paul, London.

*PAUW, B. A. (1963) *The Second Generation: A Study of the Family among Urbanized Bantu in East London*, Oxford University Press, Cape Town.

*PETTIGREW, THOMAS F. (1960) 'Social Distance Attitudes of South African Students', *Social Forces*, *38*, 246–53.

PHILLIPS, NORMAN CHARLES (1960) *The Tragedy of Apartheid: A Journalist's Experiences in the South African Riots*, D. McCay, New York.

PIENAAR, S., and SAMPSON, A. (1960) *South Africa: Two Views of Separate Development*, Oxford University Press, for the Institute of Race Relations, London.

PIERCY, MARY V. (1961) 'The Promise of "Separate Development"', *South African Journal of Economics*, Johannesburg, December, *29*, 294–8.

PIERSON-MATHY, PAULETTE (1964) *La Politique Raciale de la République d'Afrique du Sud*, Institut Royal des Relations Internationales, Brussels.

(1965) 'Apartheid in Zuid-Afrika', *International Spectator*, The Hague, July, *19*, 1004–1120.

PILLAY, V. (1960) 'Apartheid and African Poverty', *Economic Weekly*, Bombay, June, *12*, 973–7.

PINCUS, ROBERT (1966) 'Apartheid Legislation: the Suppression of Communism Act', *Columbia Journal of Transnational Law*, New York, *5*, 281–97.

*POLLAK, H. (1960) *Social Development since Union*, South African Institute of Race Relations, Johannesburg.

POSNER, ROBERT (1961) 'The Economic Costs of Apartheid in the Union of South Africa', M.A. thesis, Berkeley.

QUIGG, PHILIP W. (1965) *South Africa: Problems and Prospects*, The Council on Religion and International Affairs, New York.

RAINERO, ROMAIN (1965) *La segregazione razziale nel Sud Africa*, Edizioni di Comunità, Milan.

RAMBIRITCH, B., and VAN DEN BERGHE, PIERRE L. (1961) 'Caste in a Natal Hindu Community', *African Studies*, *20*, 217–25.

RANDALL, PETER (1967*a*) *Migratory Labour in South Africa*, South African Institute of Race Relations, Johannesburg.

(1967*b*) *The South African 'English' and Race Relations*, South African Institute of Race Relations, Johannesburg.

RANDALL, PETER, and DESAI, YUNUS (1967) *From 'Coolie Location' to Group Area*, South African Institute of Race Relations, Johannesburg.

RANSFORD, OLIVER (1969) *The Rulers of Rhodesia*, Murray, London.

RAUTENBACH, P. S. (1965*a*) 'The Economics of Border Areas', *Journal of Racial Affairs*, Pretoria, *16*, July.

(1965*b*) 'Geskeie universitêre Ontwikkeling: Imperatief van die Geskiedenis in wording', *Journal of Racial Affairs*, Pretoria, January, *16*, 24–49.

READER, D. H. (1961) *The Black Man's Portion*, Oxford University Press, Cape Town.

REEVES, RICHARD AMBROSE (1960) *Shooting at Sharpeville*, Gollancz, London.

(1962) *South Africa—Yesterday and Tomorrow: A Challenge to Christians*, Gollancz, London.

REGALA, ROBERTO (1967) 'Rallying Forces Against Apartheid', in R. Regala, *New Dimensions in International Affairs*, Central Law Book Publishing, Manila, 103–11.

REIJIC, LJUBO (1968) 'The Structure and Action of Apartheid', *Review of International Affairs*, Belgrade, April, *19*, 14–20.

REINDERS, R. C. (1968) 'Racialism on the Left', *International Review of Social History*, *1*, 1–28.

REINTANZ, G. (1969) *Apartheid in Südafrika*, Staatsverlag der DDR, Berlin.

RENSBURG, P. F. S. J. VAN (1964) 'Die Uitskakeling van Bantoe-arbeid in Stadsgebiede', *Journal of Racial Affairs*, Stellenbosch, January, *15*, 40–51.

RHOODIE, E. (1968) *The Third Africa*, Nasionale Boekhandel, Pretoria.

*RHOODIE, N. J. (1965) 'Sosiologiese Probleme wat gepaard gaan met die Gebruik van Bantoe-arbeid in blanke Gebiede', *Journal of Racial Affairs*, Pretoria, July, *16*, 124–45.

(1966) *Apartheid en Partnership*, Pretoria.

*RHOODIE, N. J., and VENTER, H. J. (1960) *Apartheid: A Socio-Historical Exposition of the Origin and Development of the Apartheid Idea*, De Bussy, Amsterdam.

RISSIK, GERARD (1967) 'The Growth of South Africa's Economy', *Optima*, June, 52–60.

ROBERTAZZI, C. (1963) 'Apartheid realtá sudafricana', *Communitá*, Milan, May, *17*, 18–22.

ROBERTS, M. (1963) 'South Africa: Behind the Boom', *World Today*, London, October, *19*, 415–22.

ROBSON, PETER (1967) 'Economic Integration in Southern Africa', *Journal of Modern African Studies*, December, *5*, 469–90.

ROGERS, CYRIE A., and FRANTZ, C. (1962) *Racial Themes in Southern Rhodesia*, Yale University Press, New Haven and London.

ROSE, BRIAN (ed.) (1970) *Education in Southern Africa*, Collier-Macmillan, London.

ROSEAM, KARL LODEWIJK (1960) *Apartheid and Discrimination: Some Remarks with regard to the Relationships between the White and Respective Non-White Ethnic Groups in the Union of South Africa*, A. W. Sytholt, Leyden.

ROUX, EDWARD (1948, 1968) *Time Longer Than Rope: A History of the Black Man's Struggle for Freedom in South Africa*, University of Wisconsin Press, Madison.

SABBAGH, M. ERNEST (1968) 'Some Geographical Characteristics of a Plural Society: Apartheid in South Africa', *Geographical Review*, January, *58*, 1–28.

SABIKHI, VANITA (1966) 'The South African Scene', *Africa Quarterly*, New Delhi, October–December, *6*, 206–17.
(1967) 'United Nations Seminar Highlights Danger Point in Southern Africa', *Afro-Asian World Affairs*, New Delhi, Winter, *4*, 345–54.

SACHS, BERNHARD (1961) *The Road from Sharpeville*, Marzani & Munsell, New York.

SACHS, E. S. (1965) *The Anatomy of Apartheid*, Collet's, London.

SACKS, BENJAMIN (1967) *South Africa: an Imperial Dilemma; Non-Europeans and the British National, 1902–1914*, University of New Mexico Press, Albuquerque.

SALOMON, LAURENCE (1964) 'The Economic Background to the Revival of Afrikaner Nationalism', in Jeffrey Butler (ed.), *Boston University Papers in African History*, Boston University Press, I.

SCHLEMMER, LAWRENCE (1970) *Political Policy and Social Change in South Africa: An Assessment of the Future of Separate Development and of Possible Alternatives to the Policy*, South African Institute of Race Relations, Johannesburg.

SAMPSON, H. F. (1966) *The Principle of Apartheid*, Voortrekkerpers, Johannesburg.

SCHOLTZ, G. D. (1960) 'Die Indier-vraagstuk in Suid-Afrika', *Journal of Racial Affairs*, Stellenbosch, April, *11*, 145–58.

SCHREINER, O. D. (1964) *The Nettle—Political Power and Race Relations in South Africa*, (Three Presidential Addresses) South African Institute of Race Relations, Johannesburg.

Y

SCHULER, WOLFGANG (1961) *'Apartheid' regiert Südafrika*, Dietz, Berlin.

SCHÜTTE, H. G. (1963) *Weisse Issmen—Schwarze Fakten: Vom Sinn und Notwendigkeit des gegliederten Volksorganismus, insbesondere in Südafrika*, Arndt, Vaterstetten.

(1967) 'Apartheid in die Moraal', *Journal of Racial Affairs*, Pretoria, January, *18*, 24–7.

SCOTT, M. (1960) 'L'essentielle mauvaise foi de l'"apartheid"', *Présence Africaine*, Paris, February–March, *30*, 62–71.

(1965) 'Whither South Africa?', *Présence Africaine*, Paris, *22*, 67–89.

SEGAL, RONALD MICHAEL (1963) *Into Exile*, Cape, London, and McGraw-Hill, New York.

(1964) (ed.) *'Sanctions Against South Africa': International Conference on Economic Sanctions Against South Africa*, Penguin, Harmondsworth.

(1966) *The Race War*, Cape, London, and Viking Press, New York.

SEGAL, RONALD, and FIRST, RUTH (eds.) (1967) *International Conference on South West Africa*, André Deutsch, London.

SHINGLER, JOHN, and LEGASSICK, MARTIN (1968) 'Students in South Africa', in D. K. Emmerson (ed.), *Student and Politics in Developing Nations*, Praeger, New York, 103–45.

SICHEL, FRIEDA H. (1966) *From Refugee to Citizen: A Sociological Study of the Immigrants from Hitler-Europe Who Settled in Southern Africa*, Balkema, Cape Town, C. Hurst, London, and Tri-Ocean, San Francisco.

SIMONS, H. J. and R. E. (1969) *Class and Colour in South Africa 1850–1950*, Penguin, Harmondsworth.

SNELLEN, I. T. M. (1967) 'Apartheid: Checks and Changes', *International Affairs*, London, April, *43*, 293–306.

SNETHLAGE, J. L. (1964) *Meer begrip voor Zuid-Afrika*, Buitjen & Schipperheiju, Amsterdam.

SNYMAN, H. W. (1966) 'Die Lewering van Gesondheidsdienste in die Bantoetuislande', *Journal of Racial Affairs*, Pretoria, January, *17*, 10–22.

SOUBEYROL, J. (1965) 'L'action internationale contre l'apartheid', *Revue générale de droit international public*, Paris, *69*, 326–69.

SOUTH AFRICA FOUNDATION, WINDHOEK (1965) *South Africa in the Sixties: A Socio-Economic Survey*, Cape Town.

SOUTH AFRICAN DEPARTMENT OF FOREIGN AFFAIRS (1966) *Questions Affecting South Africa at the United Nations during 1965*, Pretoria.

SPENCE, J. E. (1962) 'The Political Implications of the South African Bantustan Policy', *Race*, May, *3*, 20–30.

(1964) 'Prospects for Change in South Africa', *World Today*, London, September, *20*, 365–72.

(1965*a*) *Republic under Pressure: A Study of South African Foreign Policy*, Oxford University Press, for the Royal Institute of International Affairs, London.

(1965*b*) 'The Origins of Extra-Parliamentary Opposition in South Africa', *Government and Opposition*, October, *1*, 55–84.

(1968*a*) *Lesotho: the Politics of Dependence*, Oxford University Press, for the Institute of Race Relations, London.

(1968*b*) 'South Africa's "New Look" Foreign Policy', *World Today*, April, 137–45.

SPOONER, F. (1960) *South African Predicament*, Cape, London.

SPOTTISWOODE, HILDEGARDE (ed.) (1960) *South Africa: the Road Ahead*, Bailey Bros. & Swinfen, London.

STACEY, R. D. (1966) 'Some Observations on the Economic Implications of Territorial Segregation in South Africa', *South African Journal of Economics*, Johannesburg, March, *34*, 50–67.

STANTON, HANNAH (1961) *Go Well, Stay Well: South Africa, August, 1956 to May, 1960*, Hodder & Stoughton, London.

STEENKAMP, W. F. J. (1962) 'Bantu Wages in South Africa', *South African Journal of Economics*, Johannesburg, June, *30*, 93–118.

STEVENS, RICHARD P. (1970) 'South Africa and Independent Black Africa', *Africa Today*, University of Denver, May–June, *17*, 25–32.

STEWARD, ALEXANDER (1962) *The Challenge of Change*, Howard Timmins, Cape Town.

STEYN, ANNA F., and RIP, COLIN M. (1968) 'The Changing Urban Bantu Family', *Journal of Marriage and the Family*, 30, *3*, 499–517.

STONE, JULIUS (1967) 'Reflections on Apartheid after the South-West Africa Cases', *Washington Law Review*, June, *42*, 1069–82.

STRAUSS, JOHANN (1966) 'Die Selfstandigwording van die Transkei: Geboorte van 'n selfregerende Staat', *Journal of Racial Affairs*, Pretoria, October, *17*, 20–31.

(1967) ''n Prinsipieel-sosiologiese Analise van Apartheid as deel van die Volksetos', *Journal of Racial Affairs*, Pretoria, July, *18*, 144–60.

STULTZ, NEWELL M. (1964) 'Creative Self-Withdrawal in the Transkei', *Africa Report*, April, *9*, 18–23.

(1969) 'The Politics of Security: South Africa under Verwoerd, 1961–6', *Journal of Modern African Studies*, 7, *1*, 3–20.

STULTZ, NEWELL M., and BUTLER, JEFFREY (1963) 'The South African General Election of 1961', *Political Science Quarterly*, March, *78*, 86–110.

SUELLAN, I. T. M. (1967) 'Apartheid: Checks and Changes', *International Affairs*, April, 293–306.

SUNDKLER, B. G. M. (1961) *Bantu Prophets in South Africa*, Oxford University Press, London.

SUTTNER, SHEILA (1966) *Cost of Living in Soweto*, South African Institute of Race Relations, Johannesburg.

(1968) 'Toward Judicial and Legal Integration in South Africa', *South African Law Journal*, *85*, 435–52.

SWANSON, MAYNARD W. (1968) 'Urban Origins of Separate Development', *Race*, July, *10*, 31–40.

SWART, MARIUS J. (1966) 'Die Indiers in ons Middle: 'n historiese Oorsig', *Journal of Racial Affairs*, Pretoria, July, *17*, 4–11.

TABATA, I. B. (1960) *Education for Barbarism in South Africa*, Pall Mall, London.

TACCONE-GALLUCCI, N. (1963) *La politica dell'apartheid nel Sud Africa*, Grafiche Ciccolella, Bari.

TARDON, RAPHAEL (1961) *Noirs et Blancs*, Denoël, Paris.

TATZ, C. M. (1961) 'Apartheid: Battle for the Mind', *Australian Quarterly*, Sydney, June, *23*, 18–29.

(1962) *Shadow and Substance in Africa: A Study in Land and Franchise Policies Affecting Africans, 1910–1960*, University of Natal Press, Pietermaritzburg.

TAUBENFELD, H. J. and R. F., and CAREY, JOHN (eds.) (1968) *Race, Peace, Law and Southern Africa: Background Paper and Proceedings of the Tenth Hammarskjold Forum*, Ocean, Dobbs Ferry.

*THOMPSON, LEONARD M. (1960) *The Unification of South Africa 1902–1910*, Clarendon Press, Oxford.

(1962) 'Africaner Nationalist Historiography and the Policy of Apartheid', *Journal of African History*, III, *1*, 125–41.

(1964) 'The South African Dilemma', in Louis Hartz (ed.), *The Founding of New Societies*, Harcourt, Brace & World, New York, 178–218.

(1966) *Politics in the Republic of South Africa*, Little, Brown, Boston.

THOMPSON, RICHARD (1964) *Race and Sport*, Oxford University Press, for the Institute of Race Relations, London.

THORMEYER, H. G. (1960) 'Südafrika: Partnerschaft oder Apartheid?', *Aussenpolitik*, Stuttgart, November, *11*, 743–9.

TIMES, THE (1960) *Anatomy of Apartheid, 1960: Articles from* The Times, The Times Publishing Co., London.
(1968) *The Black Man in Search of Power*, Nelson, London.

*TIRYAKIAN, EDWARD A. (1960) 'Apartheid and Politics in South Africa', *Journal of Politics*, *22*, 682–97.
(1967) 'Sociological Realism: Partition for South Africa?', *Social Forces*, 46, 2, December, 208–21.

TOERIEN, P. S. (1963) 'Primary Economic Development of the Transkeian Territories', *Journal of Racial Affairs*, Stellenbosch, March, *14*, 103–14.

UNESCO (1967) *Apartheid—Its Effects on Education, Science, Culture and Information*, UNESCO, Paris.

UNITED NATIONS (1964) *A New Course in South Africa: Report of the Group of Experts Established in Pursuance of the Security Council Resolution of December 4, 1963*, United Nations, New York.

UNITED NATIONS DEPARTMENT OF POLITICAL AND SECURITY COUNCIL AFFAIRS (1967a) *Unit on Apartheid: Military and Police Force in the Republic of South Africa*, United Nations, New York.
(1967b) *Unit on Apartheid: Review of United Nations Consideration of Apartheid*, United Nations, New York.
(1967c) *Unit on Apartheid: Foreign Investment in the Republic of South Africa*, United Nations, New York.

UNITED NATIONS ECONOMIC COMMISSION FOR AFRICA (1963) *Economic and Social Consequences of Racial Discriminatory Practices*, United Nations, New York.

*VAN DEN BERGHE, PIERRE L. (1960a) 'Apartheid: Une Interpretation Sociologique de la Ségrégation Raciale', *Cahiers Internationaux de Sociologie*, *28*, 47–56.
(1960b) 'Miscegenation in South Africa', *Cahiers d'Études Africaines*, *4*, 68–84.
(1962a) 'Some Trends in Unpublished Social Science Research in South Africa', *International Social Science Journal*, 4.
(1962b) 'Apartheid, Fascism and the Golden Age', *Cahiers d'Études Africaines*, *8*, 598–608.
(1962c) 'Race Attitudes in Durban, South Africa', *Journal of Social Psychology*, *57*, 55–72.
(1964) *Caneville: the Social Structure of a South African Town*, Wesleyan University Press, Middletown, Conn.

(1965) *South Africa: A Study in Conflict*, Wesleyan University Press, Middletown, Conn.

(1967a) *Race and Racism: A Comparative Perspective*, John Wiley, New York.

(1967b) 'Language and Nationalism in South Africa', *Race*, July.

VANDENBOSCH, A. (1963) 'Reappraisal in South Africa', *International Spectator*, The Hague, December, *17*, 560–75.

(1970) *South Africa and the World*, University of Kentucky Press, Lexington.

*VAN DER HORST, SHEILA T. (1960) 'The Economic Implications of Political Democracy', *Optima*, June.

(1965a) *African Workers in Town: A Study of Labour in Cape Town*, Oxford University Press, Cape Town.

(1965b) 'The Effects of Industrialisation on Race Relations in South Africa', in G. Hunter (ed.), *Industrialisation and Race Relations*, Oxford University Press, for the Institute of Race Relations, London.

VAN DER MERWE, W. (1962) 'Stratification in a Cape Colored Community', *Sociology and Social Research*, *46*, 302–11.

(1969) 'The Economic Influence of the Bantu Labour Bureau on the Bantu Labour Market', *South African Journal of Economics*, March, 4–54.

VAN DER SCHREIDER, D. M. 'History on the Veld: Toward a New Dawn?', *African Affairs*, April, *68*, 149–59.

VAN DER WALT, A. J. H. (1962) 'Konstitusionele Ontwikkeling in die Transkei', *Journal of Racial Affairs*, Stellenbosch, December, *14*, 29–42.

VAN DYK, J. H. (1966) 'Whither Bantu Education?', *Journal of Racial Affairs*, Stellenbosch, January, *17*, 4–9.

VAN JAARSFELD, F. A. (1961) *The Afrikaner's Interpretation of South African History*, Simondium, Cape Town.

VAN RENSBURG, PATRICK (1962) *Guilty Land*, Cape, London.

VAN ROOYEN, T. S. (1963) 'Die Stryd om die Siel van die Bantoe', *Journal of Racial Affairs*, Stellenbosch, June, *14*, 163–72.

VATCHER, WILLIAM HENRY (1965) *White Laager: The Rise of Afrikaner Nationalism*, Pall Mall, London.

VIGNE, RANDOLPH (1969) *The Transkei: A South African Tragedy*, Africa Bureau, London.

VILAKAZI, ABSOLOM (1962) *Zulu Transformations: A Study of the Dynamics of Social Change*, University of Natal Press, Pietermaritzburg.

VILJOEN, S. (1961) 'Higher Productivity and Higher Wages of Native Labour in South Africa', *South African Journal of Economics*, Johannesburg, March, *29*, 35–44.

VISSER, A. J. (1966) 'Die Ontwikkeling van Grensnywerhede met spesiale Verwysing na die Wes-Transvaalse en Noord-Kaaplandse Gebiede', *Journal of Racial Affairs*, Pretoria, October, *17*, 4–11.

WALKER, ERIC ANDERSON (ed.) (1963) *South Africa, Rhodesia, and the High Commission Territories*, Cambridge University Press, Cambridge.

(1928, 1964) *A History of Southern Africa*, Longmans, London.

WALKER, OLIVER (1964) *Kaffirs Are Livelier*, Muller, London.

WALLERSTEIN, IMMANUEL (1969) 'Penetrating the Continent', *Africa Report*, Washington, February, 14–15.

WALSHE, A. P. (1963) 'The Changing Content of Apartheid', *Review of Politics*, Notre Dame, Indiana, July, *25*, 343–61.

(1969) 'The Origins of African Political Consciousness in South Africa', *Journal of Modern African Studies*, 7, 583–610.

(1970a) 'Black American Thought and African Political Attitudes in Southern Africa', *Review of Politics*, January, 51–77.

(1970b) *The Rise of African Nationalism in South Africa*, C. Hurst, London.

WÄSTBERG, PER (1963) *Auf der schwarzen Liste: Tatsachen aus Afrika klagen an*, Hans Deutsch, Vienna.

WATSON, R. G. T. (1960) *Tongaati: An African Experiment*, Hutchinson, London.

WEISBORD, ROBERT G. (1967) 'The Dilemma of South African Jewry', *Journal of Modern African Studies*, 5, *2*, 233–41.

WELLINGTON, JOHN H. (1967) *South West Africa and its Human Issues*, Clarendon Press, Oxford.

WELSH, DAVID (1969a) 'Urbanization and the Solidarity of Afrikaner Nationalism', *Journal of Modern African Studies*, 7, *2*, 265–76.

(1969b) 'Capital Punishment in South Africa', in A. Milner (ed.), *African Penal Systems*, Praeger, New York.

WERTHEIMER, R. (1963a) 'Die Bantu und ihr Anspruch auf Südafrika', *Aussenpolitik*, Stuttgart, February, *14*, 133–9.

(1963b) 'Die Bantu in der Südafrikanischen Union', *Aussenpolitik*, Stuttgart, October, *14*, 710–19.

(1963*c*) 'Lager-Mentalität der Afrikaaner in Südafrika', *Aussenpolitik*, Stuttgart, March, *14*, 203–10.

(1963*d*) ' "Poor Whites" und Apartheid in Südafrika', *Aussenpolitik*, Stuttgart, January, *14*, 59–66.

(1964) 'Die Zukunft des weissen Mannes in Südafrika', *Aussenpolitik*, Stuttgart, February, *15*, 128–35, and March, 205–13.

WHITE, J. H. (1966) 'Some Attitudes of South African Nurses—A Cross Cultural Study', *Journal of Social Psychology*, *69*, 13–26.

WHYTE, QUINTIN (1967*a*) *Present Realities and New Directions*, South African Institute of Race Relations, Johannesburg.

(1967*b*) *Peaceful Co-Existence and South Africa*, South African Institute of Race Relations, Johannesburg.

WILLIAMS, BASIL (1946, 1962) *Botha, Smuts and South Africa*, Colliers, New York.

WILLSON, F. M. G. (1966) 'Prospects for Southern Africa', *Current History*, Philadelphia, March, *50*, 165–71.

WILSON, MONICA (1961) 'South Africa', *International Social Science Journal*, XIII, *2*, 225–44.

*WILSON, MONICA, and MAFEJE, A. (1965) *Langa: A Study of Social Groups in an African Township*, Oxford University Press, Cape Town.

WILSON, MONICA, and THOMPSON, LEONARD (eds.) (1969) *The Oxford History of South Africa, I: South Africa to 1870*, Clarendon Press, Oxford.

WODDIS, J. (1960) 'Après les massacres de Sharpeville', *Cahiers du communisme*, Paris, May, *36*, 838–48.

WOODHOUSE, C. M. (1961) 'Apartheid, das Problem Südafrikas', *Europa-Archiv*, Frankfurt, January, *16*, 1–30.

WOOLHEIM, O. D. (1963) 'The Coloured People of South Africa', *Race*, October, *5*, 25–41.

(1966) *The New Townsmen: The Legal Position of the African in the White Areas Today*, Civil Rights League, Cape Town.

WORLD FEDERATION OF TRADE UNIONS (1965) *A Fighting Record: the World Federation of Trade Unions against Apartheid*, Prague.

WORRALL, DENIS (1967) 'Partition: An English-Speaking Point of View', *Journal of Racial Affairs*, Pretoria, January, *18*, 14–23.

YELD, R. W. A. (1963) 'Housing', *Journal of Racial Affairs*, Stellenbosch, June, *14*, 173–86.

ZIVS, S. (1956) 'Racial Discrimination in the Union of South Africa', *International Affairs*, Moscow, March, *3*, 51–60.

INDEX

Papists, 255
Paraguay, 30
Paraguayans, 27
Parliamentary Legislation Act, 106
passive resistance, 143, 145
  Resistance Campaign, 110, 134, 147
Paton, Alan, 202
Patterson, Sheila, 252, 265n
Pauw, B. A., 163, 167, 175n, 176n
personality, 54; authoritarian, 54, 55;
  Calvinistic-puritanical, 54, 55
Pettigrew, Thomas, 53–8, 60, 71n, 83, 102n
Philadelphia, 250
Physical Planning and Utilization of
  Resources Act, 231
Pierson, G. W., 263n
Pim, Howard, 106
Pittsburgh, 250, 251
plural society, 214, 215, 232
police, 39, 47, 156–7n; stations, 40
political prisoners, 26
Popper, Karl, 244n
population registration, 47
Poqo, 12, 16, 148
Port Elizabeth, 135, 147, 251
Portuguese, 31, 38
Potchefstroom, 135
Poto, Victor, 44, 119
predestination, 2
Presbyterians, 182, 257
Pretoria, 19, 20, 43, 161, 252, 259
Programme of Action, A.N.C., 110, 111, 115
Progressive Party, 93
Progressives, 105
Prohibition of Improper Interference
  Bill, 236
Promotion of Bantu Self-Government
  Act, 246n
Pross, Helge, 215n, 225n
Protestants, 256; puritanism, 34
Protestantism, 33
Puerto Ricans, 263

race awareness, 58
  preferences, 58
racial ghettos, 39
  pollution, 39
Rand, 147
Reader, D. W., 71n, 175n
Rectors, of non-white universities, 202, 204, 212n
Red: amakhaya, 193; creed, 184; families,
  192; home-boys, 193; man, 192,
  194; migrants, 189, 193–4; patterns, 194; world, 185
reference books, 47
Reid, E., 281n
relative deprivation, 25

religion, 177, 179–84, 186–91, 193–5
Representation of Natives Act, 245n
Republic of South Africa, 41
retribalization, 19, 20
Rex, John, 215n, 220, 226n
Rhodesia, 33, 38
Rhoodie, N. J., 299n
Richard, Dirk, 100
Roman Catholics, 110; Church, 255, 256–7
Roman-Dutch law, 242
Roosevelt, President F. D., 109
Roux, E., 281n
Rush, G. B., 73n
Russell, Margo, 71n
Russia, 26, 152
Russians, 254
Rwanda, 26

Sabotage Act, 235, 238
Sadie, T. L., 300n
Salomon, L., 264n, 266n, 267n
Santo Domingo, 25
Scandinavians, 254
school families, 192
  people, 192
Scottish, 107
sects, 182
security laws, 228
Senate, University College of Fort Hare, 221
segregation, 37, 38
self-rationalization, 291, 292, 296
Senegal, 27
separate development, 118, 175, 209, 274
Separate Representation of Voters Bill, 112
Separatist Movement, 15
Seventh Day Adventists, 182
Shaka, 10, 110, 131, 143
shanty communities, 5, 11, 14, 16
Sharpeville, 12, 18, 25, 115, 147
Sherwood, R., 71n
'shilling marriages', 168
Simmel, Georg, 223, 227n
Sisulu, Walter, 109, 246n
Small, Adam, 205
Smith, M. G., 215n, 226n
Smuts, General J. C., 108, 135, 142, 147
Sobukwe, Robert, 109, 115, 116, 120n
social change, 228, 229
  control, 177
  Darwinism, 79
  distance, 54, 57; scale, 52, 53
Somalis, 26
Sotho, 3, 6, 7, 10, 43, 198
South African Coloured Peoples' Organ-
  ization, 132
  Congress of Trade Unions, 114

$760170951

DT763
A6247
197
C2

$760170951

CIRCULATION BOOK CARD

$760170951

T/P

CONTROL NO.

LOC.

CALL NO.

PITT-I205 (II-57)
1 2 3 4 5 6 7 8 9 10 11 12 13 14 15 16 17 18 19 20 21 22 23 24 25 26 27 28 29 30 31 32 33 34 35 36 37 38 39 40
IBM 084044

UNIV
OF PI

LI

DATE DUE

	MAR 1 1 2009		

GAYLORD   PRINTED IN U.S.A.